BLUELIGHT TO PUCKER HUDDLE

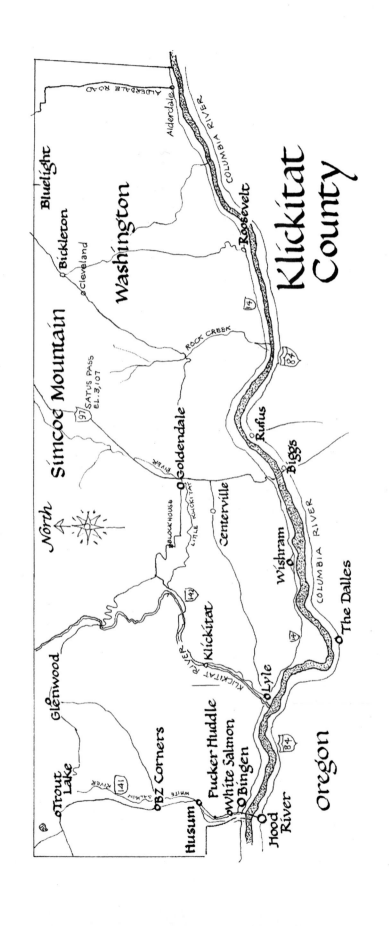

Bluelight to Pucker Huddle

Discovering Klickitat County

Edited by Ruth Miles Bruns and Nancy Barron

This book is dedicated to Wilma Segraves Olsen
April 10, 1913 - August 25, 1997

She was born Wilma Segraves and grew up in Wishram.
In 1934 she married Ortis Olsen and moved to Goldendale,
where Ort and his brother, Vern, owned Olsen's Pontiac.

Her love, generosity, and concern for her adopted community
have benefited all who live here.

The photograph was provided courtesy of sons, Joel and Marc.

Outside the economy of money and the modern, there lives an economy of stories. Families with abundant stories, neighborhoods with known characters and quirky events, communities with legends, and special ways of seeing and saying all make us rich.

A drive on the interstate is a matter of miles. A drive on a known local road, by contrast, may be abundantly peppered with 'There's where ... and one time ... maybe you never heard about ... would you believe ... they say and it's true ...' Stories and particular references deepen ordinary days into resonant wealth. As my father used to say, "The greatest ownership of all is to look around and understand."

With this book, you begin to be lucky like that. Bravo to the writers. But, this book is not the last word. It is an invitation to you: Be a friend to the future by knowing local stories, savoring local characters, creating local ways of understanding so we may each contribute to a broad economy of stories. Again, as my father said, "Your job is to find what the world is trying to be."

Kim Stafford, Director of the Northwest Writing Institute, Lewis & Clark College

A camel, they say, is a horse put together by a committee. This book was put together by a committee, and it may resemble a camel: lumpy in places, knobby in others, and exasperating at times. Like a camel, it will take you to amazing places that you can see from a new point of view. At the same time, we hope it will tickle your fancy and your funny bone, and make you want to know more.

In creating this book, we followed the pattern described by Jim Heynen in his manual, *Writing About Home: A Handbook for Writing a Community Encyclopedia* (Northwest Writing Institute of Lewis & Clark College, 1991). Jim developed the manual out of his experience with three communities in the Northwest Writing Institute's program, "Writing About Home in Oregon Libraries," conducted in 1989-90. We drew on the experience of the groups in Enterprise and Hood River, Oregon. Where our circumstances diverged, we blazed our own trail.

We started with a steering committee who declared our aim was to preserve and promote the culture of Klickitat County, its character, lore, and diversity, through our book. Each member brought an array of special skills to the task. Members formed the necessary sub-committees: fiscal, editorial, publicity, writing, illustration, publication, and distribution. Each member performed multiple tasks and cooperated magnificently. We contracted for the work we could not do: Wendy Warren provided instructional workshops and consultation, Kathleen McKinney provided desktop publishing, and Cheryl Cosner provided her unique way of seeing Klickitat County for our cover illustration. Volunteers provided all the rest — writing, illustrations, and design. Our committee met once or twice a month for over two years. We reached consensus where we could, voting when necessary.

Because many people with stories didn't think of themselves as "writers," we scheduled a series of monthly Saturday morning workshops to help develop confidence and skills. Some people, to their surprise, discovered they *could* write. Some were surprised at how rewarding writing could be.

We sought the widest possible participation. Eighty-five people have sent us their accounts of the Klickitat County experience. Each had a unique contribution; each is part of the whole. Some were historical; some were present-day.

Many had stories about coming to Klickitat County and, although the stories might include common elements, each was distinctive. It might include a mysterious encounter, getting stuck in the mud, a stop on the way to some place else, or the need for a job. For many more, the "coming to Klickitat County" story includes 19th century settlers who laid down foundations for the communities to come. Complementing the stories of arriving are the experiences of living here.

This book holds only a sampling of the stories to be told. For each one published here, a hundred more are waiting to be told. I implore you to write your stories, however lacking in skill you may think you are, however unimportant your stories may seem. You will create an immeasurable legacy. Besides, if we don't each tell our own story, someone else may — and they might get it all wrong!

As you browse through this book, notice the wide margins. They are for you to use. You may find yourself saying, "But they don't have anything about_____!" (Fill in the blank). Or, "They got that wrong." Or, possibly, "They left out the best part!" Use those margins. Make notes for the Revised Edition, which will surely be forthcoming whenever an enthusiastic, curious, energetic group gets together and says, "We should write a book about Klickitat County!" Then you can come forward with this tattered tome in your hand and say, "Yes, and I know what you need to put in it!"

Teddy Cole, Coordinator, Klickitat County A to Z

Individuals:

Naomi Fisher, Goldendale Community Librarian, for her invaluable expertise, for organizing the writing workshops and writers' colony meetings held at the library, and for smoothing our way on innumerable occasions.

Wendy Warren, our instructor and consultant, for her enthusiasm and high standards, and for her encouragement to all of us, especially to new writers.

Kathleen McKinney for her skillful professionalism in the design and layout of the book you are holding. Her graciousness and cooperative spirit were a welcome gift.

Cheryl Cosner, for expressing her love of her native county in the images on our cover and for sharing her art with us so generously.

Members of our Steering Committee: Nancy Barron, Ruth Bruns, Teddy Cole, Mary Anne Enyeart, Kathleen Goode, Mary Jean Lord, Barbara Patterson, Joan Stone, Judy Thomas, Sara Wu. While each one had specific assignments, all pitched in for the greater good where needed. We couldn't have had a finer group.

Jan Nelson, for sharing her extensive knowledge of the Trout Lake community.

Sidne Steindorf, for transcribing numerous manuscripts and audio taped conversations.

Organizations, Institutions:

Fort Vancouver Regional Library Foundation, for support, encouragement and advice.

Fort Vancouver Regional Library Graphics Department, for designing and creating flyers.

Goldendale Library Advisory Board, for its excellent management and wisdom.

Friends of the Goldendale Community Library — always encouraging, helpful and supportive.

The Klickitat County Historical Society, especially Bonnie Beeks, Terry Durgen and Leah Huntingdon.

The West Klickitat Historical Society, especially Ruth Winner.

Maryhill Museum archives.

Public Utility District #1 of Klickitat County, for the use of the collection of *Ruralite* magazines.

The Goldendale Sentinel for information and publicity.

KLCK radio for on-air interviews, publicity.

Others:

All of our writers, whose names appear with their contributions.

Our many illustrators and photographers, whose names appear in the back pages of the book.

Oral sources, acknowledged with other sources at the end of each article.

The many residents who stopped us on the street, in the store or at the post office to ask about our progress and contribute tidbits of local wisdom. We thank you all, individually and collectively, for your interest.

The universe is made of stories,
not of atoms.

"The Speed of Darkness (1968)," Part V, Stanza IX,
from The Collected Poems of Muriel Rukeyser,
McGraw-Hill, 1978.

Since those days when Ben Snipes and the early settlers had that winter disaster and the cattle died, farmers have cut grass, wheat, or other forage, cured (dried) it, and stored it to feed during the winter.

Great-grandfather heard how good alfalfa was for cattle, so he planted it. It grew, and he turned the cows in to the field. Unfortunately, the cattle bloated and died. Thinking the alfalfa must have been poison, great-grandfather started pulling out the plants.

With time, the farmers got to know the advantages of alfalfa. With proper curing and storage, it became good feed for many animals. Using care when turning cattle into even dry-looking stands, farmers now take precautions against bloating.

During the 1940s and 1950s, alfalfa became a very big crop for the valley. Goldendale alfalfa was well known and sought after as top quality feed. Cows gave lots of milk with Goldendale dryland alfalfa. Then dry areas in the Columbia Basin and eastern Oregon went under irrigation, and the market became much more competitive. Irrigated hay, which is usually greener and finer-stemmed than dryland, though not necessarily more palatable, became available.

Alfalfa grown in our area works well in our crop rotations. With our relatively short growing season and rainfall averages (12"-18" per year), alfalfa hay can be a good cash crop. We often hear that our low protein hay (13%-15%) is just not as good as the irrigated alfalfa (17%-22%).

A local trucker told of taking hay to a dairy in southwestern Washington. This herd was one of the top producing herds in the state, and the dairyman had fed Goldendale dryland hay continuously. He sent his kid off to college, and when the kid came home after four years he said, "Dad, we must use irrigated hay from the Tri-Cities and Hermiston area." Dad wanted to be fair, felt he had paid to get his son a college education, and thought the new ideas must be good, so they doubled their herd and tried the irrigated hay for three years. The herd's milk production average dropped. At the end of the study, the dad said they needed Goldendale hay. The son said, "I quit," took his half of the herd and moved to Tillamook. Dad got Goldendale dryland alfalfa, and his herd's milk average came back up.

Another trucker brought a load of hay, and the

landowner said to the dairyman leasing his property, "What did you do? Buy a load of straw? Your Jerseys aren't going to eat that coarse, bleached-out alfalfa!" A week later the dairyman ordered another load of hay. When the trucker arrived, the landowner said, "Come see the test we're trying." The dairyman's Jersey heifers were fed Goldendale dryland alfalfa in one feeder, while in a nearby feeder the landowner's Holsteins were fed irrigated hay. The Holsteins just stood there and watched the Jerseys eating that sweet-smelling Goldendale dryland hay. The landowner apologized.

Some folks at WSU told me they had never done a test with dryland hay, since there wasn't much available. They said they would gladly do a study for $10,000 and a whole lot of hay. Maybe it would be best to let the animals decide.

Recently, Goldendale dryland alfalfa has had its challenges. An alfalfa weevil has attacked the plants, causing considerable loss of tonnage and extra cost to the farmers. Hopefully we will soon find a solution to this problem.

Conversations with Stub Magnuson, Richard Lefever

Stories Told By Cecil V. Allyn (1914-2003)

Submitted by his children Marjorie and James

Carp Lake (now North Shores)

A long time ago, a settler found a nice little valley north of Goldendale and proceeded to build himself a cabin. One day a spring appeared which kept spouting water until he had to move. The spring became a small lake and covered the cabin. It was named Carp Lake.

The Brass Cannon

A regiment of soldiers started out from Fort Blockhouse back in the Indian fighting days. They were on their way to Fort Simcoe, taking a brass cannon over the Simcoe Mountains by way of the old road that is now Monument Road north of Goldendale. They thought they would be overtaken by a band of Indians and knew that they could not outrun them, so they decided to ditch the cannon to lighten their load. They pulled it off the trail and covered it with brush. The cannon was never found.

Goldendale's First Swimming Pool

Cecil V. Allyn bought the old Golden ranch in 1944. It is the property located along Mill Street, which turns into Fairgrounds Road on the east line, with the Little Klickitat River to the south, Highway 142 to the west, and the Fairgrounds on the north. When we bought the property, there were the remains of an earth dam just to the west of the Bloodgood Creek bridge on Fairgrounds Road. There had been wooden gates to shut off the flow of Bloodgood Creek, with mounds of dirt on the sides to make the water deep. We understood that it was built by the CCCs, but the water was too cold, so it was let go back to nature. Jim and I enjoyed floating on some of the old 2" x 12" lumber in the creek during the summers.

ANCIENT HISTORY

Kathleen Goode

A friend of mine, Elsie David, declared with some exasperation that she could not understand why they call it the Lewis and Clark Trail. The trail was here long before they arrived — over 10,000 years ago in fact. The human history of our area began then at the end of the last ice age when the Columbia River was formed by massive flooding. The pathways that Lewis and Clark followed were long-established trade routes. The river was lined with Indian villages whose inhabitants continued ancient traditions.

The earliest human history in our area has been defined as part of the Plateau culture. Researchers have a variety of definitions for the area belonging to this culture, but all of them include Klickitat County. The people of the Plateau culture share fairly uniform mythology, artistic styles, and religious beliefs based upon vision quests, life-cycle observances, and seasonal celebrations of the fishing-gathering-hunting cycle.

Artifacts from the Post-Clovis culture (11,000 years ago to 5000/4400 BC) were found in Goldendale. Archeologists believe these were the remains of a short-term camp, located in an area where camas was gathered. Items found included many milling stones, making it one of the best examples of a plant-processing site for this period. Another site from this period is at Fivemile Rapids (which begins at Horsethief Lake); it showed evidence of intensive salmon fishing dated to 9,800 years ago.

One of the best known sites was the Wakemap Mound, about 8 miles west of present day Wishram. The site, flooded after the construction of The Dalles Dam, was 350 feet long, 270 feet wide, and about 20 feet deep. There is controversy over the age of the mound, but many agree it must be at least 2000 years old. The excavations at Wakemap yielded chipping points, harpoons, mauls, dice used for gaming, stone sculpture, and fine carvings in bone and antler.

Everywhere that ancient artifacts were found, they were removed — occasionally for scientific study, but often for personal collections or to sell to a collector. Grave sites, often on islands in the Columbia River, were plundered for collections or profit. When tribes protested, the government announced that the burial grounds were not to be disturbed. This was not enforced, and the "curio hunting" did not stop until an area was stripped of everything but the bones of the dead. Even these were not safe; on one occasion a man attempted to take a box full of human bones off Memaloose Island. He was fined and forced to return the remains. When the dams were built, the final remains were removed from the islands and reburied on higher ground.

Today, attitudes have changed somewhat. The removal or defacing of artifacts carries serious fines and even prison time. The tribes and various agencies now work together to protect the few things that remain to tell the story of the ancestors. A good example of this is the effort to preserve the petroglyphs at Columbia Hills State Park. Yet, if there are many who are still angry, who can blame them? How would people feel if new immigrants arrived and dug up Lewis and Clark, just to steal their coat buttons?

Museums, including Maryhill, preserve some small part of the ancestors' story; the cultural centers at Yakama, Umatilla and Warm Springs tell more. Yet, one has to wonder what a wealth of wisdom has been lost in the zeal to collect a "few curios."

Ballou, Robert. *Early Klickitat Valley Days*. 1938, Goldendale, WA: *The Goldendale Sentinel*.
Handbook of North American Indians Volume 12: Plateau. Deward E. Walker, Jr., ed. 1998, Washington: Smithsonian Institution.

Robert Ballou's, *Early Klickitat Valley Days* contains our earliest "juicy bits:" the priceless anecdotes that bring history to life. Like many of us who came to Klickitat County as adults, he found this windswept valley and its people fascinating, and he brought an outsider's keen sensibility to the accounts he wrote. Ballou knew good stories when he heard them, and he collected and wrote them with a zest that makes them real even today.

However, Ballou was close with his personal history. He wrote little about his life and nothing about his parents, birthplace, war service or education — except for a note about "a former fellow law student, who became a circuit court judge in The Dalles."

Ballou came to the Klickitat valley as a land examiner for a London syndicate interested in the Northern Pacific land grants. He was a veteran of the Spanish American War and at various times served as a hand on the river steamer "Nellie," a fireman, a weigher and seller of wheat, and a deputy sheriff. He became a wheat buyer for Portland exporters. His obituary says that he held a full membership in the Yakama Indian tribe.

Ballou married Cora Van Hoy, daughter of Klickitat County pioneers. They had at least two sons, Robin J. and Paul Edward. Paul was born July 4, 1903. The birth record tells us that Robert was then 25 years old and Cora was 23, and that Paul was their second child. Ballou's obituary names what appears to be a third, Van Hoy, as Ballou's only surviving son.

Robert and Cora Ballou moved to Oregon City, Oregon, where he died in 1939 at the age of 61. For the last nine years of his life he was blind and bedridden.

Early Klickitat Valley Days became Robert Ballou's monument in Klickitat County. Published the year before his death, it was compiled during his invalidism from previously published newspaper articles (the *Sentinel* referred to him as "our feature writer") and new material dictated from memory to his wife. Cora, Van Hoy and Mrs. Paul Ballou helped with collecting fresh material through interviews with surviving pioneers, verifying and fleshing out the details of the old, and proofreading the manuscript before it went to the printer.

ROBERT BALLOU (C1878-1939), TELLER OF TALES

Teddy Cole

In the preface to the book, Ballou wrote, "My work started nearly a half century ago, making notes in conversations with pioneers when plenty were alive and active...."

Thanks to his writings, we can come to know personally those pioneers of "early Klickitat Valley days."

Ballou, Robert, *Early Klickitat Valley Days*,
    The Goldendale Sentinel, 1938
Obituary, "Death Writes Thirty to Life of Robert Ballou,
    Pioneer Author," *The Goldendale Sentinel*, June 15, 1939.

BALSAMROOT

Kathleen Goode

One of the brightest flowers of spring is the balsamroot. It looks like a small sunflower with bright yellow petals and large leaves on an upright stem. This is one of the important food plants to the Native people. It is gathered with the kapin and wapas (digging stick and food collecting basket). Balsamroot is one of the plants known as Indian celery (hahan): it is gathered in the late spring for its stalks. The plant also has edible roots that can be eaten raw or roasted and rich oily seeds that can be eaten raw or cooked with deer fat.

There are two varieties common in Klickitat County, Deltoid balsamroot and Carey's balsamroot. Both plants have many leaves and flowers and are about 3 feet tall. Deltoid balsamroot, *Balsamorhiza deltoidea*, has a greater density of petals and a larger seed section.

This plant usually has one flower at the top of a stem and one below it. Carey's balsamroot, *Balsamorhiza careyana*, usually has 2 or 3 flowers at the top of each stem. Both plants have leaves that are the same color on both sides, but Carey's balsamroot has very shiny leaves, and they keep their color well into the summer. Look for hillsides of balsamroot in May.

Personal experience
Hunn, Eugene S. with James Selam and family. *Nch'i-Wana "The Big River": Mid-Columbia Indians and Their Land.* 1990. Seattle: University of Washington Press.
Lyons, C.P. *Wildflowers of Washington: a Lone Pine Field Guide,* 2nd Edition Revised. 1999. Renton, WA: Lone Pine Publishing.

Klickitat County is a wonderful place to ride bikes. Not only is the countryside beautiful, but the volume of automobile traffic is very low in comparison to many other places we have ridden.

Each year for the past four years, we leave our home in the greater Goldendale area for a week-long bike ride that leads us from Klickitat County to Government Camp and back. The route we have settled on takes us through Glenwood, where we stop at the Shade Tree Inn for lunch with Jennifer and Elizabeth. From there we finish the day's ride at a bed and breakfast in Trout Lake called The Farm, operated by Dean and Rosie.

The next day we ride from there to Stevenson, Washington. Riding west on Hwy 14 presents some challenges, mostly related to the windy conditions, as we ride west through the five tunnels that dot the route. Stevenson is home to the Walking Man Brew Pub. Over the years, employees of the pub have come to recognize us and always greet us, "We were wondering if you were coming again this year!" Following that brief stop, we pedal up to the Skamania Lodge, drop off our gear, then pedal back down to Stevenson for some fine dining at the Big River Grill. The food as well as the atmosphere there is wonderful. The owner always makes his way to our table for a few minutes of conversation.

Our ride the next day takes us across the Bridge of the Gods and onto I-84 for the journey to Hood River, where we stay with our life-long friends Bill and Mel, before heading out to Parkdale, where we stop in at the Eliot Glacier Brew Pub. That stretch of the trip is a serious climb that takes up the better part of the day, but the ride is rewarded by good friends and food.

Following an overnight stay with friends, we set out next morning for Government Camp. We always stop at the Mt. Hood store to visit as well as to buy a couple of their wonderful homemade power bars. We also stop at the local cafe there for breakfast. This year, the Mt. Hood store owner told us she recognized us riding up the hill and started telling her husband she had seen her friends from Goldendale.

The ride up to Government Camp is a serious climb. This year we rode the last half of that day in a cold stinging rain, but we arrived safely at the Huckleberry Inn where we stopped for the night. After dropping off our gear, we rode down to the Mt. Hood Brew Pub for

Michael W. Steinbock and
Alanna L. Powell

dinner, then back to the Huckleberry Inn in the pouring rain.

The following morning after a large breakfast at the Huckleberry Inn, we set out once again for Hood River, where we had a scheduled rest day. The weather was a bit wet, but as we climbed up to Bennett Pass again, the weather began to clear, and we had an excellent ride down to Hood River.

Following our rest day, we set out for Goldendale and home. Our friend Sinclair ferried us across the Hood River bridge, because it is illegal to ride a bike across it. We stopped in Bingen to load our gear back onto our bikes, and just as we were bidding farewell to Sinclair, we saw Dean and Rosie from the B&B in Trout Lake.

The ride along the Klickitat River, where we turn onto Hwy 142 from Hwy 14 at Lyle, is a wonderful leg of the trip. Not only is the scenery lovely, but at that point we generally start seeing people who recognize us as we ride along on our red recumbent bicycles. Sometimes they honk and wave. Other times they actually stop to talk with us.

The final climbs of the day bring us up the Klickitat Grade, into the Klickitat Valley with its expansive views, and home. We are both thankful to live in a place such as Klickitat County that offers us such spectacular cycling opportunities. We are eager to promote bicycling here.

BIGHORN SHEEP

Kathleen Goode

History came to life in February 2005 as four bighorn sheep were released in the snow covered reaches of the Yakama Reservation. The four new residents had been transplanted from the nearby Oak Creek Wildlife Area as part of an effort to reintroduce the breed to one of their traditional homelands. Efforts at reintroduction in Klickitat County's Dead Canyon area failed a few years ago, but efforts on the Warm Springs Reservation have been very successful. The return of the bighorn sheep is part of an effort by the Yakama Nation to restore the ecosystem of the area.

Klickitat County is known for ancient petroglyphs along the Columbia River. Many of them were taken by collectors, and many were submerged under the rising waters of the Columbia after the building of The Dalles Dam. The most common image among the petroglyphs is that of the bighorn sheep, appearing singly and in groups. One researcher noted that salmon, plentiful and relatively easy to catch, were seldom preserved as stone art. Bighorn sheep, difficult to catch, were frequently depicted.

The picturesque breed survives on rocky cliffs and bluffs. They are well suited to the foothills of eastern Washington because we have less winter snow cover. The bighorn sheep are well known for the head-butting tactics of males during mating season. The animals do not fight for territory but for a particular mate. The bighorn gather in herds of 8 to 100. Their hearing is excellent, and they are sure-footed among the rocky outcrops of their habitat. This gives them an edge in evading attacks by natural predators such as coyotes and wolves. With the ability to leap up to 30 feet in rocky areas, they must have been very difficult to hunt with a bow.

Columbia River tribes created beautiful and useful art from the horns of the sheep. A horn was first softened with steam, then gradually formed into the shape desired. Items made with sheep horn included bowls, ladles and spoons. The bowls are often round on the bottom with flanges on each side. Intricate designs carved on their outside feature both geometric shapes and anthropomorphic designs. Ladles and spoons often had simpler carving designs, though the handle on many ended in a bird or animal. All the examples seen in museums are a rich deep brown in color, and most have a glossy patina, perhaps from the touch of many hands and from being used to serve oily foods such as salmon.

Early explorers agreed with the local tribes that bighorn sheep were the best tasting game in the area. With the arrival of well-armed pioneers, that desirability helped lead to their demise. Hunting was only one part of the problem. Ranchers brought in cattle and other livestock that increased the competition for available forage. Sheep ranching brought diseases that finished off existing herds. The species once plentiful throughout the west was eliminated from Washington by the end of the 1920s. Reintroduction began in the 1950s with animals from healthy herds in Canada. Perhaps one day soon, we will see bighorn sheep on Mt. Adams and in the Simcoes.

Ballenger, Liz. Animal Diversity Web "*Ovis Canadensis*"
   http://animaldiversity.ummz.umich.edu/site/
   accounts/information/Ovis_canadensis.html

King, Gordon. *Yakima Herald* "Past Photos of the Week."
   February 22, 2005. http://www.yakima-herald.com/
   photo/pastpow/o22205.php

Mercer, Bill. *People of the River; Native Arts of the Oregon
   Territory.* 2005, Seattle: Portland Art Museum in
   association with University of Washington Press.

Stream, Lee. Washington Department of Fish and Wildlife:
   Game Trails "Bighorn Sheep re-introduced in south-
   central Washington." http://wdfw.wa.gov/wlm/
   game/hunter/trail/gt-17.htm

BIRTH OF A SON

Douglas L. Taylor

Winters on High Prairie could find the roads closed for days, due to deep snow and drifting. In the winter of 1933-34, Ben and Letitia Taylor needed a secure residence in Goldendale for Letitia to give birth to their first child, while Ben stayed on the farm to do the chores and care for the animals. They found that place with the Mike Laymans, old friends. There on January 16, 1934, Douglas was born, weighing in at an even 12 pounds.

Returning home to the Prairie with mother and newborn son, Ben needed to pay his debt to the doctor. Ben butchered four fat hogs, hauled them to Wahkiacus and loaded them on the train for Goldendale. He received the sum of $5.00 apiece for his efforts, and the freight cost him almost as much as the value of the hogs.

Family story

BITTERROOT

Sara Wu

Bitterroot — what an off-putting name for such a splendid flower! Many wildflower enthusiasts, my family included, make it an annual pilgrimage to enjoy this showy member of the Purslane Family. The joy of seeing bitterroot is partly due to its stark contrast with its surroundings. Found on barren, gravelly, thin soils, its cream-to-deep-pink loveliness invariably brings a "WOW" from onlookers.

The flower is similar in appearance to the cactus flower but grows close to the ground and is only one to two inches long. It has many petals, stamens and pistils that give it a delicate, feathery appearance. The leaves are succulent blades that come out as 1 to 3 inch rosettes before the plant flowers. The moisture in the leaves is depleted as the plant blossoms, so the leaves are not evident at flowering. This water reserve allows it to bloom after the spring rains have passed.

Bitterroot

Bitterroot is a relatively rare flower but is found easily in Klickitat County on the rocks beside the paved path at Catherine Creek in late April or early May. On top of Grayback, which requires a strenuous climb, it is so numerous that in late May or early June it is impossible to walk without stepping on plants.

Many tribes of Native Americans have names for the roots, such as spatlum, ax six sixie, kanigda, pe ah ke and gunga. The local Native Americans collected the roots before the flowers bloomed. Peeled and boiled, they became gelatinous and were an important food source. Lewis and Clark reportedly disliked the root's bitter aftertaste. Dried, the roots could be stored and traded. A sack full would buy a good horse!

The plant was named *Lewisia rediviva* after Captain Meriwether Lewis and the plant's ability to revive in desert conditions. Bitterroot is the State Flower of Montana and is used in many of that state's geographical place names. Although rock rose may be the more suitable name, bitterroot remains the most common moniker. Since it is no longer a food, perhaps the bitter now applies to the feeling of missing its wonderful display.

Haskin, Leslie (1970) *Wild flowers of the Pacific Coast*, Binfords & Mort, Portland OR

Jolly, Russ (1988) *Wildflowers of the Columbia Gorge*, Oregon Historical Society Press

Lyons, C. P. and Bill Merilees (1995) *Trees, Shrubs & Flowers to Know in Washington & British Columbia*, Lone Pine Publishing, Redmond, WA, Vancouver BC and Edmonton AB

Murphey, Edith Van Allen, (1957) *Indian Uses of Native Plants*, Mendocino County Historical Society, CA

Taylor, Ronald J. (1992) *Sagebrush Country, A Wildflower Sanctuary*, Press Publishing Co., Missoula MT

BLOCKHOUSE MURDERS AND FIRE

Teddy Cole

Ken and Elaine Sipe arrived to live in Goldendale in the spring of 1961. There Ken opened his dental practice. According to his March 2004 letter, about two weeks after his arrival, the sheriff called to ask him to go out to Blockhouse to identify a burn victim. He discovered that the victim was the man who had set fire to the buildings of the Blockhouse Hot Springs Resort. It seemed that he had murdered his wife and his lover, then committed suicide, after setting the fire that burned the place down on himself and the two women.

It took Dr. Sipe an hour and a half to get the man's mouth open and the teeth charted. The victim was unrecognizable, almost completely consumed by the fire. The physician from Yakima who was there spent about eight hours trying to find the bullets on the two women. It took so long because they were heavy, in the 280-320 pound range, he said. When Dr. Sipe got home, Elaine made him take off all his clothes, because, she said, "Everything smells of smoke and dead bodies." They hung the clothes outside, and Elaine served dinner. She had prepared stuffed pork chops for dinner, but he couldn't eat a bite of it.

Letter, Dr. Kenneth Sipe to Mary Anne Enyeart;
The Goldendale Sentinel, Thursday May 11 and 18, 1961

BLOCKHOUSE POOL

Darla Carratt-Hoff

Despite the fact I had taken swimming lessons at the Goldendale pool, I had failed to learn how to swim. So, in the green mineral water of the Blockhouse pool, along with an occasional frog, I practiced in the very shallow end. When I felt like I was going to sink, I had only to place my hands on the bottom and my head would still be above water. Splashing my legs vigorously, my hands on the cement bottom, I would think of my father, Ted Carratt's, words: "wheel barrow by wheel barrow, I hauled and poured every bit of cement in this pool". His brother, Tom Carratt had mixed it all. They had dug and built, by hand, the first swimming pool of the area. No fanfare was given to them. It was just their way of helping their family business. Their mother died in 1926, and their father, Harry Carratt, and Uncle Thomas A. Hooker and Aunt Ella Hooker bought the Blockhouse Hotel. Ted and Tom took the 1927-1928 school year off and built the pool.

Mary Jaekel said that it was "quite the thing to do" in the summer time, go to church then on to Blockhouse for a swim and picnic. Many people came to the hotel to take mineral baths, believing in the healing power of the water — the same water that was in the pool. Tom said he or Ted would have to swim to the bottom of the deep end after the day's swim to make sure there wasn't anyone on the bottom, as the minerals made the water a murky green. After the Goldendale Pool was built, the Health Department tried to condemn the Blockhouse pool, but the mineral in the water made it pass.

The main hotel burned down July 7, 1932. Thomas A. Hooker rebuilt a smaller hotel as well as a large dance hall. Harry Carratt returned to Goldendale and started a photography studio. In 1935 Thomas A. and Ella Hooker sold the hotel and moved to Vancouver, Washington. In the dance hall during the big band era, Ted Carratt played drums with the band the "Blue Jackets". And, in the 1950s I learned to swim at the old Blockhouse pool.

Personal experience
Family stories

Blockhouse Pool

THE BLUE DEER

Rita J. Liska

After my years of horseback riding, hiking, and driving through the Simcoes, the blue deer remain a legend to me, for I was never able to find one myself. However, during the summer of 1977, my uncle saw a blue doe several times while he was on range patrol. When my mother went out with him one morning, she also got to see the doe go down for water along Bowman Creek. She described the doe as the same color as my uncle's Australian Shepherd dogs — a definite blue roan.

I have had the privilege of seeing albino deer and paint deer (usually sorrel and white), and they are beautiful though rare. There is a story — perhaps legend — that, when Sam Hill was building the home that is now the Maryhill Museum of Art, he was also importing exotic deer from various parts of the world into the area of the Simcoes. Maybe that is the reason for some of the odd variations of colors of deer in this area.

As to the blue roans — although I have never seen one, I would hate to think that they are extinct.

BLUEBIRDS ON THE PRAIRIE

Bev Edwards

"Bickleton, Bluebird Capital of the World" is the message we have received through various publications during our six years of residing on High Prairie. That Sunday, Leap Day, was a beautiful day filled with sunshine, so we decided to make the trip to Bickleton where bluebirds are known to flock during the middle of February.

We packed a lunch, got in the van, and headed east along the Gorge. We turned north at Roosevelt, anticipating the first glimpse of bluebirds and springtime. As we arrived at the top of the mountain range, we saw our first bluebird. We watched the bird fly to a nearby post and land to check us out as we checked him out through our binoculars. He was an eastern bluebird, brilliant blue from head to tail.

We then proceeded toward Bickleton, passing a lot more birdhouses, but, alas, no more bluebirds. We arrived in town, then headed west toward Goldendale and didn't see another bluebird; in fact, there were hardly any birds at all to be seen.

So this morning, Monday, March 1, we are looking out our living room window, and lo and behold, many bluebirds are checking out our birdhouses. We hope they all find good homes in our little part of the world. And best of all, their arrival does mean springtime is coming.

Now we're wondering if the bluebirds have found that High Prairie is the place to live, just as all of us who live here have found it to be.

BLUELIGHT

Mary Jean Lord

I first heard of Bluelight in the early 1980s, soon after I moved to Goldendale to work for Klickitat County PUD Electrical outages were more common then, as the distribution system was still being developed and improved, and the winters seemed colder and longer.

The east end of the county, in particular, was prone to severe "freezing fog" that sometimes lasted for weeks. Thick layers of ice built up on everything, and after several days, the extra weight sometimes snapped power lines and brought down crossarms.

During widespread outages, the line crews would repair the lines by sections, contacting customers as they went to make sure they had electricity. On the east end, the last place called was always the Clarence McBride ranch at Bluelight. If the electricity was on at Bluelight, everyone knew that the whole east county had power.

I had felt the relief in the PUD office when someone called out that Bluelight was "on". I imagined a big blue light way out at the edge of the county that let the linemen know all was well.

Once, when I was riding with one of the engineers outside Bickleton, he nodded in the direction of a side road, and said, "That's Bluelight up there." All I could see was a farmhouse half-hidden by shade trees.

"What is Bluelight," I asked, "and why is it called Bluelight?"

The story he had heard was that an early sheepherder claimed to have seen a strange blue light in the sky above the place. Nobody knew if he really saw anything, but if he did, some people thought it might have been a flare from a pocket of natural gas, a kind of will-o'-the-wisp. Bluelight was simply a place at the northeastern corner of Klickitat County.

According to the 1982 *The History of Klickitat County*, in slower-moving, horse-and-buggy days, Bluelight was a bustling community center. Though never a real town, for a few years at the beginning of the 20th century Bluelight served homesteaders for miles around. It boasted "a general store and post office combination, a blacksmith shop, a community hall, church, a couple of homes…." The road through the village was the boundary line between Yakima and Klickitat Counties. The post office opened in Yakima County in 1901, moved across the street to Klickitat County in 1904, and combined with Bickleton in 1906.

For me, Bluelight will always be associated with those dedicated linemen from the PUD, who, regardless of the weather, always responded when the call came in that someone was out of electricity. When they went out to restore electricity to the east end, they never quit until they had Bluelight back on.

Personal memories
May, Pete, ed. *History of Klickitat County*. Klickitat County
    Historical Society, 1982.

BOLON'S LAST RIDE

Jo N. Miles

Along Monument Road in Klickitat County northwest of Goldendale there are two roadside markers commemorating Indian Agent A.J. Bolon, killed in September of 1855. Bolon's death sparked the beginning of a tumultuous three-year Indian war in Washington Territory ending in 1858.

Bolon set out on horseback from The Dalles along a popular path leading to Yakama country that led across the Simcoe Mountains, winding down the Eel Trail into the Toppenish Creek Valley. The trail served as gateway to the Ahtanum and other lower Yakima Valley destinations. The Indian agent traveled alone to investigate reports of attacks by hostile Yakamas suspected of killing miners on their way to the Colville gold fields. Bolon attempted to locate Chief Owhi to talk about his son Qualchan, the alleged instigator of the attacks. Unable to find the chief, on September 23rd Bolon stopped at the St. Joseph Mission next to Ahtanum Creek, where he left word with the priests to contact the agent at The Dalles as soon as Owhi returned.

Bolon then turned back toward The Dalles, making it as far as Wahk-shum Springs in present-day Klickitat County, where he was set upon by Kamiakin's nephew, Mocheel, and three companions. The men stabbed Bolon to death and disposed of his body. Soldiers responding to the deaths of Bolon and the miners were attacked by a large alliance of approximately 1,000 warriors under the direction of Chief Kamiakin at Toppenish Creek in October of 1855.

Andrew J. Bolon was a 20-year-old pioneer when he arrived at Vancouver by wagon train in 1846. He married Jerusha Short in 1849, was elected sheriff of Clark County in 1850, and fathered a daughter, Josephine, in 1852. The following year, Bolon worked as chief packer for the McClellan Expedition, exploring present-day Klickitat and Yakima counties searching for a possible military road route across the Cascade Mountains. While a member of the expedition, Bolon became familiar with a number of native tribes and chiefs. In 1854, he was elected to the Washington Territorial House of Representatives, serving the citizens of Clark County. During legislative sessions held at Olympia, Governor Isaac I. Stevens met the tall, red-bearded 28-year-old — and appointed him Indian Agent for the region east of the Cascade Mountains. Bolon attended the treaty council at Walla Walla where participants signed documents later ratified by Congress after the war. Two weeks after he died at Wahk-shum, Bolon's wife gave birth to their second daughter, Anna Elizabeth.

Bolon, A.J, Affidavit signed 29th day of November, 1853, "Settlers of Unsurveyed lands Claiming under the 4th section of Act of 27th September, 1850" Clark County, Washington Territory.

Bolon "Family Group Record", prepared by Anita Keller, 23 June 2002

Burnham, Howard J. "Government Grants and Patents in Vancouver, Washington" interview of Cymatha Morse, daughter of Amos Short, Oregon Historical Quarterly, vol. XLVIII June, 1947, p 9

Cain to Manypenny, Oct. 6, 1855, Records of Bureau of Indian Affairs, Letters Received, Indian Wars in Washington and Oregon 1855-58, Relander Collection, 40-2, Yakima Regional Library

Clark County Genealogical Society, *Trail Breakers*, vol. 1-6, September, 1975 Fort Vancouver Regional Library

Durieu to Ricard, Sept. 30, 1855, Archives of the Diocese of Seattle (French)

Journal of the House of Representatives of Washington Territory, Olympia, February 27, 1854, State Department Territorial Papers Washington Series copy 26, Roll 1 part 1, Relander Collection 42-10, Yakima Regional Library

Kowrach, Edward J. *Mie. Charles Pandosy, O.M.J., Missionary of the Northwest*, Ye Galleon Press, Fairfield, WA 192, pp 91-2 (English translation)

McClellan, George B., Diaries, August 22, 1853, reel 67, Library of Congress, Washington D.C.

McWhorter, Lucullus Virgil, *Tragedy of the Wahk-shum: Death of Andrew J. Bolon Yakima Indian Agent*, Donald M. Hines, ed., Great Eagle Publishing, Inc. Issaquah, WA 1994

Pioneer and Democrat, Olympia, W.T. Feb. 11, Mar 25, 1854, vol. II no. 23, 29

Seattle Genealogical Society, "Washington Territory Donation Land Claims", 1980, pp 227-8

Thompson to Palmer, Sept. 28, 1855, National Archives, Bureau of Indian Affairs, Oregon Superintendency 1848-73, M-2, Roll 5

Bull Elk Takes Offense

Rita J. Liska

My neighbor drove a big 4x4 truck to work each morning. This particular day, she topped a ridge near where I had encountered the attack geese, and came upon a huge bull elk escorting four cows down Cedar Valley Road.

She stopped, and so did he. Then he attacked, chasing her down the pavement — driving backwards — for quite some distance before returning to his herd, and leaving the road to go into an open field.

Fortunately, she was fast enough to stay out of his way, so she didn't have a head full of antlers pushing through her windshield.

[See also Goose Attack]

The William Burgen House

Kathleen Goode

The Burgen House

Ten years ago I could have told you that our family would never live anywhere but out in the country — at least not for long. That was before the Burgen house went up for sale. William Burgen was one of the early lawmen in the county, serving first as a Sheriff and later as Chief of Police in Goldendale. He was one of the earliest pioneers in the county, arriving here as a young man with his wife Susan, his brother Thomas, and his parents.

We had property in the country and were planning to build a house on it, but things were more complicated than we expected. We rented a place in town and enjoyed being able to walk to the grocery, the drugstore, and the bank. There was a house on our block that we thought rather charming, mainly due to the fact that it had two front porches and a magnificent hawthorn tree. The tree arched out over the sidewalk and was filled all summer long with tiny birds who were delighted to find a place where they were safe from cats. One day there was a For Sale sign in the window, and we thought it would be fun to look at it; just to see what the inside was like.

We barely set foot on the front walk before our youngest daughter informed us that we had to buy this house. My husband and I knew she had never been in the house so we asked her why she was so certain. The reply was emphatic, "Because it has the best climbing tree in Goldendale!" Ten-year-olds are pretty smart after all. We bought the house in spite of some major reservations, the perfect climbing tree notwithstanding. The house needed a new foundation, the paint was crumbling, the electrical wiring was ancient, and we would soon find out the plumbing was in dire straits as well. There was a rabbit (thank goodness it was not a skunk) living under the kitchen floor. Oh, and it had spiders — lots of them!

The last five years have been spent scraping off layers of wallpaper, even off the ceiling. The ceilings in this house are almost ten feet high, and my husband removed thousands of tacks from them so that we could leave the original bead board revealed. The entire electric and plumbing systems have been replaced and the foundation renewed. The outside walls were scraped, primed, and painted. Caulking was added everywhere. Exterminators were called in to deal with the hobo spiders. We put up crown molding and put down a solid tile floor. We saved the old linoleum floors in several rooms, added drywall here and there, and painted just about everything. We kept the old windows with their wavy glass; one of them has "G. B. 1924 Xmas" cut into it. This could be the handiwork of George Burgen, son of the original owners. There were a few finds: a thimble, some old bottles, and marbles lost under the porch.

The house is still standing because of the way it was built, not that it was superior carpentry, but certainly good enough. The wood was from a local mill, Douglas Fir throughout; the two-by-fours are full dimension, and there are lengths over twenty feet without a single knot. The outside of the house is clad in lapped siding that is a full inch thick. Most of the inside is clad in the same thing except the boards are simply fitted together with no overlap. There are no closets, which is just about my only complaint about the place.

There is always more to do, but after five years we are getting a feel for the old house. It is rather plain but loaded with character, and I find it a wonderful refuge from the world at large. The hawthorn is still there, just outside my office window; it was damaged in an ice storm a few years ago, but is making a grand recovery. The neighbors are all terrific, the wildlife is surprisingly abundant, and overall, I find that life in town is not so bad after all, even right on Main Street.

B.Z. CORNERS

Mary Jean Lord

William A. Biesanz and his wife, Lydia, built a service station on their property at the corner where the Glenwood Road branches off from the road between White Salmon and Trout Lake (WA 141). His friends thought he had lost his marbles and predicted he would lose everything. Whenever Billy went to town, they teased him, "How's the mayor of B. Z. Corners?"

Billy hated it and vowed to "show those guys." He built houses and sold or rented them. One man built a grocery store, another followed with a pool hall, and a third man added a beer parlor and dance hall. It became a community big enough to need a water system, and they named the water source B. Z. Creek.

Maybe because they knew he hated it so, his friends kept on ribbing him as "the mayor of B. Z. Corners." One day he stayed longer in town than usual, and when he came home, he called to Lydia, "Well, I've done it."

"Done what?"

"They called me mayor of B. Z. Corners once too often. I went to Goldendale and had it made official. This place now really is B. Z. Corners."

Billy was 80 years old when death caught up with him. He had the honor of bestowing two memorable place names on Klickitat County: Pucker Huddle and B. Z. Corners.

Bartholomew, Florence, "Pucker Huddle and why,"
Ruralite, Dec. 1964

CAMAS LAKES

Naomi Fisher

The first time I saw a camas lake, I didn't know it — Not for a few minutes, anyway.

A friend had packed me and a picnic lunch in his car on the promise of an amazing sight. He didn't tell me what it was, other than to say we'd see some wildflowers that day.

After 20 minutes or so of driving, we came out of the trees, topped a small rise in the road, and looked out onto a small valley. I looked for the wildflowers along the banks of the small stream and pond I saw, but I could see nothing of particular interest.

"Well?" he said.

"I don't see any flowers," I replied.

He laughed. "Look closer."

I gasped. The "water" — what I *thought* was water,

was in fact a dense field of beautiful blue camas, swaying gently in the breeze. It was an intense blue, I realized, almost too intense to really be water, even under the gorgeous blue sky of a Klickitat spring.

The blue camas flower grows in dry washes and seasonal watercourses where the ground is damp. It grows so dense in places, in "streams" and "ponds" of flowers, that it looks like water. It really can fool the eye.

Camas is plentiful in Klickitat County. Its bulbous root provided a staple food for the native peoples of the area in years past, and is still harvested by some folk today. I've tasted the blue camas, starchy with a slight tang, in the company of a professional naturalist. I wouldn't recommend trying it on your own, though, as it is nearly identical (when not in flower) to the white Death Camas, which is appropriately named.

The blue camas is both useful and beautiful and an important part of Klickitat county culture and history. While development and logging have made these sights a little harder to find than in the past, seeing a camas lake is an experience every newcomer or visitor to the county should have.

Camas

On March 31, 1933, the United States Congress created the Emergency Conservation Work program, later named the Civilian Conservation Corps. The stated purpose of the CCC was to relieve stress of joblessness, to build men, and to promote the conservation of our natural resources.

During the nine years of the Corps' existence, the young men planted 2-1/2 billion tree seedlings, built 6-1/2 erosion control dams, cleared 21 million acres of tree diseases and pests, and constructed 126,000 miles of roads and 38,000 bridges throughout the United States. They spent nearly 6.5 million man-days fighting forest fires.

Three million young men were employed from 1933 to 1942. The enrollees had to be unemployed, American citizens, single, between the ages of 17 and 23, and to have not received a high school diploma. Each person enrolled for six months and could re-enlist

CAMP GOLDENDALE
THE CCC BOYS

Joan Wilkins Stone

for six-month periods up to a maximum of two years. After the issuing of clothing and other equipment, the new corps member was assigned to one of 4500 camps. The camps were located in national forests, national parks, public lands, farm lands, and wildlife refuges. The members were paid $30 a month, $15 of which was sent to dependents.

In the summer of 1935, Camp Goldendale was established. There were about 200 corps members. The camp was located on the Klickitat County Fairgrounds. Small buildings were erected for living quarters. A large mess hall was built on the premises; it was later destroyed by fire.

The new camp was for Soil Conservation Service projects. "Major work accomplished in erosion control included: the construction of 200 permanent rock dams, more than 400 temporary dams, and 20,000 feet of ditches and channels; the development of more than thirty springs on rangeland; and the construction of almost 1,000,000 square yards of bank sloping. Their primary work area was 25,000 acres of crop land and natural pasture in the Swale Creek drainage," stated Edwin G. Hill. Rock walls built by CCC boys can still be seen alongside U. S. Route 97 north of Goldendale.

The CCC boys joined with young Goldendale residents in social, sports, and educational activities. Jean Van Hoy Granum met her future husband at a grange hall dance in 1936. Clifford (Poot) Granum loved to dance, and so did Jean. " My friends and I went to all the dances, and those CCC Boys were always there," said Jean. The one who returned again and again to ask her to dance was Poot. He came from Tacoma, Washington, and planned to do his two-year stint. Instead, he stayed, and in 1940 they were married. They spent their life together in Goldendale.

Camp Goldendale produced winning teams in many sporting events. Their football team was unbeaten in 1937 and 1938. Many of the CCC boys went to night school and earned their high school diplomas. Others used the skills learned on the job to gain lifelong occupations. Fond memories have stayed, and so have friendships.

Hill, Edwin G. 1990. *In the Shadow of the Mountain*. Pullman WA: Washington State University Press.

Sinclair, Donna and Richard McClure. August 2003. *No Goldbricking Here: Oral Histories of the CCC in the Columbia National Forest, 1933-1942.* Portland State University Heritage Program and History Department.

The Goldendale Sentinel. 1939. January 19, March 2, March 30.

CAMP MYSTERIOUS

Sara Wu

1905 was a time of great canal building, with the Suez completed and the Panama being planned. Klickitat County had its own grand scheme: take the water off Mt. Adams to irrigate the tableland below the Horse Heaven Hills all the way to Pasco, WA. One plan was to have a viaduct bring water from the Big Muddy Creek, across the Klickitat River Canyon, through a tunnel in Grayback Mountain into irrigation canals — some 150 miles of construction. Reservoirs would insure a year-round supply of water.

The Klickitat Irrigation and Power Company (KIPC) — Ralph Swales, President, and E.E. Kelso, Director and Vice-President — filed articles of incorporation in Seattle with an initial capitalization of $100,000. Eventually, $25,300,000 was raised from investors from Canada, England and the eastern United States. Landowners of 56,000 acres signed on. Their agreements stipulated that they were not required to pay the company until a year after the water was to be delivered.

This was also a time of controversy over water. The issues included water use for irrigation vs. electrical power and government vs. private control. Projects were carried on in secrecy because of land speculation. The Glenwood area had two Camps Mysterious where workers lived. The Northwestern Electric Company (NEC) had a camp that was southeast of town, and started to build a power plant for electricity for their railroad. These workers would come into town to play baseball with the local teams, and join the band in parades and in developing a dance hall. In 1913, NEC gave up their water rights on the Klickitat River to KIPC and moved their operation to the White Salmon River.

Little is known about the KIPC camp northeast of Glenwood. Although the *Klickitat County Agriculturist* and the *The Goldendale Sentinel* newspapers reported on the work in Cedar Valley near Goldendale, the KIPC Glenwood camp got very little press. Today, it is still referred to as Camp Mysterious.

No one knows if the KIPC was a legitimate

enterprise that failed or just a scam. Today, it seems unlikely that the promoters could have believed in its feasibility, although they had reassurances from irrigation engineers led by F.M. Rice and including Prof. O.I. Waller of the State College of Washington. There are, however, many reasons for the failure of a legitimate plan. The court battle with the NEC took time. The federal government had to approve the project through the Yakama Indian Reservation. The bureaucracy worked slowly even though the Indian Nation was probably not consulted. Finally, World War I halted further construction. The KIPC sold their interests. After the war, other groups tried to revive the plan, but none succeeded.

There are quite a few remnants of the project that make it seem legitimate. North of Glenwood there are large cuts through the side of the hill just below the lip of the Klickitat Canyon. This very impressive base for a viaduct, with its beautiful mortarless masonry, predates the similar work found on the Old Columbia River Highway. In Cedar Valley there are signs of the 1300-foot canal built on what was the Layman property. It is hard to believe that this much work was put into a scam.

Mike Layman and his brother helped to dig the canal. The boys dug a ditch from Cedar Creek into the canal, which brought the only water that ever flowed in this project. The boys had a swimming pool in the summer. In the winter, they harvested ice and stored it in the sawdust at the sawmill. The ice cream from this ice may have been the only tangible benefit from the Klickitat Irrigation and Power Company's grand scheme.

The Goldendale Sentinel. August 10, 1911; October 7, 1920.

Klickitat County Agriculturist. July 10, 1909; July 30, 1910; September 24, 1910; October 28, 1911.

The Independent, Supplement. June 5, 1913.

Klickitat Heritage. Spring 1977.

Kuhnhausen, Herman. 1990. *The Valley Below that Mountain.*

Personal communication with Ken Marvel, 2004.

Personal communication with Keith McCoy, 2003.

McCoy, Keith. 2003. *Mid-Columbia North Shore: "odds 'n ends".* Trafford Publishing.

Last Valentine's Day a smiling teenager came up my walkway carrying a bunch of balloons attached to a sack of Hershey's kisses. "This is for you, from my grandma," she said. I didn't connect right away, but then it came back: Candygrams!

Years ago — at least twenty-five — the Goldendale High School Drama club was trying to think of ways to earn money so they could afford to put on plays. They met almost daily in the back room of the high school library, where I was librarian and their club advisor, and I overheard their conversational ups and downs. They had held bake sales, they had done car washes, they had exhausted the usual ways teenagers raise money.

"How about a 'Thon,'" I suggested. 'Thons were popular fundraisers — get a list of subscribers to promise to pay so much a mile or a pound or a page for something, then do it, and try to get the subscribers to pay up.

"What kind of 'Thon?" someone said. "They've all been done."

"How about picking up trash for so much a pound?" I offered.

"Oh, great!" Tom said, heavy on the sarcasm. "The track team has a Run-a-thon. Drama Club has a Trash-a-thon!"

Kathy said, "Hey, I heard the FFA has a lot of leftover candy they haven't sold. I heard they want someone to take that over."

Sure enough, the FFA was glad to pass on their unsold candy along with the sales contract. Soon the backroom had a stack of cartons in the corner. However, Drama Club didn't have much more luck selling candy than the Future Farmers had.

After the Thanksgiving break, I said, "You'll have to do something about selling this candy. Drama Club has to pay the balance and you don't have enough money."

Daphne said, "I know! Let's do singing candygrams."

It was an electric moment. Daphne's idea energized everyone, and talented, lively teens don't need much energizing to get rolling. It was a plan even Tom couldn't disparage because they actually would be creating little performances.

The Club got permission to deliver the candy the last week of school before the holiday break, but only during the last ten minutes of class periods. They made little gift cards to tie to the boxes with red yarn, and they made a list of songs they were prepared to sing, mostly songs about Christmas or winter: Rudolph, Frosty, Jingle Bells, but a few carols and fun songs as well.

As soon as the announcement was posted, the kids found themselves swamped with orders, mainly because of the promise that the candygrams would be sent anonymously. Of all the songs on the list, "Chu-Chi Face," from Chitty Chitty Bang Bang, was the hands-down favorite, because it heightened the embarrassment factor.

Besides the classroom deliveries, many wanted them delivered during the lunch break when crowds were around to witness the recipient's discomfort. Orders for off-campus delivery came in, which meant recruiting students with cars. Soon the stock of candy was gone, but with outstanding orders to fill, they had to go shopping for more.

The last day of school before Christmas the back room was a welter of stray yarn, scraps of paper, discarded gift cards, and a few boxes of candy for which the orders had been lost. The singers were hoarse, the drivers were exhausted, but the treasury was full.

Candygrams were a hit that the Drama Club repeated every year as long as I was at the High School. Though the practices have changed through the years, they had started a tradition that still brings sweet and funny memories to people— possibly none as sweet as mine.

CANOEING THE ROCK CREEK ESTUARY

Nancy Barron

At the end of a lively creek in the hollow of a striking canyon, a long, lazy estuary opens up between the hills. Rock Creek Estuary is a pleasing place for a relaxed paddle in an open canoe. Somewhat protected from the wind by the hills around it, the slow waters meander from the creek's mouth near the Rock Creek Longhouse to join the Columbia River at the junction of SR14 and Rock Creek Road. If the day is calm, it is easy to paddle under the railroad bridge and journey up the Columbia a bit before floating back to reenter the estuary and enjoy its other shore.

A parking area, boat ramp, and toilet are available to visitors at the north end of the estuary. The drives to and from offer varied countryside. You can travel up SR14 along the Columbia or up SR142 through Goldendale and out the Bickleton Highway to Rock Creek Road along the creek, through the canyon. Either offers fascinating vistas.

I was told years ago by people who used to own that entire area, that Carp Lake was produced exactly the same way that Crater Lake in Oregon was: the top of the crater collapsed, leaving a large hole within the mound. Supposedly it is the only lake in the Cascade system that evolved in this way.

The story I was told is that someone moved into the crater, built a house, barn and corrals, and decided to develop an existing spring nearby. But the spring blew out and the lake flooded the entire bottom, forcing the people to move out.

I don't know if this story is true, but years ago while hiking around the lake in late summer, I could make out a series of old posts that may well have once been corrals along the southeast edge of what remained of the lake.

Then, according to the storytellers, the city of Goldendale began tapping springs and re-routing the water in the upper Simcoes. Although all this happened miles away, Carp Lake springs began to slow and now seem to have completely stopped feeding the crater.

Now the lake is dead, the spring is gone, and only winter runoff fills the extinct crater that we are told was once a small sister of the spectacular Crater Lake in Oregon.

CARP LAKE / CRATER LAKE

Rita J. Liska

Carp Lake Fires

Rita J. Liska

I rarely go into the Carp Lake area anymore, but I used to ride and hike it frequently. I still marvel at the sight of a nice home resting on the west side of that old cone because I remember at least two fires where it sits — both caused by lightning strikes.

As we fought fire beside old-timers who had lived in the area for years, we were often told that there is "something" in the Simcoes that attracts lightning along a two-mile by 14-mile line. If there's going to be a lightning strike, chances are very good it will be within this area.

I have saddled a horse and while riding within a short distance from my home, counted as many as five strikes near Black Butte and Carp Lake. Our local volunteer fire fighters and D.N.R. (Department of Natural Resources) have often had to fight "sleeper" fires as long as a week after a storm was over. The lightning flows down a tree, settles in the roots and "sleeps" until heat builds up and explodes among dry needles and brush — and someone finally spots the fire.

Carp Lake Science

Judy Thomas

Strange, but true: Information buried in a lake near Goldendale may keep radioactive waste buried at the Hanford Nuclear Reservation from leaking into the ground water.

To get this information, scientists drilled deep into the bottom of Carp Lake, a tiny lake seven miles northwest of Goldendale. The lake formed in a volcanic crater about 500,000 years ago, and since then has been filling up with layers of sediment and volcanic ash. Trapped in these layers are pollen grains, each identifiable by species. By knowing what plants grew there at a particular time, researchers can infer climate, including temperature ranges and rainfall, over many thousands of years. Charcoal layers produced by fires are also used in making the estimates.

Carp Lake is well known to paleoclimatologists around the world for its exceptionally long and continuous record of past climate variations. The most recent cores taken from Carp Lake span the last 130,000 years, and given the age of the volcano, it is likely that further drilling could produce a record reaching back even further. Known so far is that the region has shifted back and forth between cold periods with few trees, warm wet periods with extensive forest, and warm dry periods with few trees.

Why do scientists working at Hanford care about this? Because large amounts of high-level radioactive waste are stored at the facility, and there is a danger that radioactive particles may leak into the ground water. So, barriers must be designed to protect the waste from rainfall. Though the length of time needed for the waste to decay is well known, future climate cannot be predicted in detail. How much rain will fall and soak into the ground, and, therefore, how strong must the barriers be? By using results from the Carp Lake study, scientists can determine the range of possible climates to come, and Hanford engineers can install adequate barriers.

The Goldendale Sentinel. 1994. Scientists seek clues to historic climate in sediments of Carp Lake. April 14.
Email exchanges with Dr. Cathy Whitlock, scientist at Montana State University
Phone interview with Eric Olds, media specialist, U.S. Dept. of Energy, Office of River Protection.

CATTLE INDUSTRY IN KLICKITAT COUNTY

Bruce Cameron

In the year 1854, a young man named Ben Snipes, newly arrived by immigrant train, crossed the Columbia River from The Dalles and rode to the top of the Columbia Hills. From that vantage point, his view encompassed what would be any cattleman's dream: grass shoulder-high, stretching across the valley to the Simcoe Mountains on the north, with several streams and springs for ample water. At that moment, Snipes decided to be a cattleman. After exploring the area, including most of central Washington, he returned to The Dalles and Willamette Valley to secure a loan, and he purchased as many cattle as he could. In 1855 he moved his herd to the Klickitat valley and established his headquarters west of what is now Goldendale. His parents are buried on top of "Snipes Butte," about two miles west of Goldendale. Their monument can still be seen on the skyline on the south side of Horseshoe Bend road.

Thus began one of the largest cattle empires in the west, stretching from The Dalles to the Okanogan. At one time it included about 144,000 head of cattle and 60,000 horses.

Around 1877, settlers began to arrive in growing numbers. These settlers began to plow up the prairie grass, plant crops, and build fences to protect their property. Nearly every family had a milk cow and a few beef cattle for their own consumption. Some of these families continued to farm, and others established ranching enterprises. They developed their own herds of cattle, acquiring more land by homesteading and leasing land in the Simcoe Mountains and Mt. Adams areas for summer pasture, where, due to the higher elevation and greater rainfall, the land provided lush green pasture into late summer. Thus began one of the most important segments of an industry, deeply rooted in the customs and culture of Klickitat County, that contributes a large part to its economy and stability. Today there are approximately 30,000 head of cattle in Klickitat County.

In the 1950s for 30 years or so, many of these ranchers began raising purebred cattle, mostly Angus and Hereford, and they produced some of the finest quality and most sought-after seed stock in the U.S. Producers throughout the Northwest purchased these cattle to improve their herds. Many of the descendants of those early pioneers have stayed in the cattle business and grown into larger operations. Some of these ranchers operate in much the same way as their forefathers did: by driving or trailing their herds from their home ranches in the valley to summer grazing in the Simcoe Mountain or Mt. Adams areas, then, after roundup in October, back from the mountains to the home ranches to spend the winter. Since cattle have a legal right to travel the roads of Klickitat County as long as they are accompanied by drovers or cowboys, it is not uncommon to come up on one of these herds of 100 to perhaps 500 head traveling from one grazing area to another. Coming up to one of these trail herds, it may look like a daunting task to get through. However, usually if you just pull up close behind the herd, at the first opportunity one of the cowboys will motion you to follow his horse and will quickly split the herd and have you on your way. Upon meeting one of these herds coming your way, just slowly pull up to the first cattle and stop, and they will quickly and quietly split around your vehicle and travel on their way up the road.

Lands in Klickitat County and across the state of Washington are classified under two laws enacted by the State Legislature that leave the classification designation to the discretion of the County Commissioners under a strict set of rules. The two classifications are the range law areas and herd law areas. Both farm and grazing lands are included. Range law area is primarily made up of grazing land with adjacent farmland included. To graze livestock in range areas, the operator must own, lease, or have other agreements with land owners included in the grazing area. It is illegal for anyone else to turn animals out to graze in these areas. If land owners in range areas don't want animals on their land, they are responsible for fencing their property with a legal fence, also covered by state statute, and maintaining the fence. In herd law areas, it is the responsibility of people grazing there to keep their livestock on their own property with fencing. Usually the adjacent land owners will cooperate by building and maintaining half the fence between the two properties. The time-honored method used to determine which part of the fence is yours is to stand on your property facing the fence and the half to your right is yours. The old saying "Good fences make good neighbors" is very true.

Early in the 1900s as the legislature began enacting laws and agencies began writing rules, it became apparent that an organization of ranchers needed to be formed as a unified voice to protect their interests. Originally, it was called the Cattleman's Association; now it is called the Klickitat County Livestock Growers Association. Early on, they joined the state-wide Washington Cattleman's Association, and ranchers from Klickitat County have always shown strong leadership in both county and state organizations. Six Klickitat County men have served as President of the State Association: A.M. Matson, Larry Frazier, Art Schuster, Jack Davenport, Bruce Cameron, and Neil Kayser. Four county women have been selected to be President of the Washington Cattle Women: Marie Kreps, Sarah McBride, Marguerite Kayser, and Jane Lee. It is quite a distinction to have this many leaders from our county.

Every year, several county cattlemen and women travel to Olympia during session to meet with legislators to testify at senate hearings and to help in drafting legislation pertaining to our industry. Probably the two most important aspects that these associations diligently try to protect are private property rights and water rights. These two issues are the life blood of agriculture and affect every property owner in our county, regardless of size.

Early in the 1900s, the legislature enacted the Brand Law. Most ranchers brand their livestock with their own brand, registered with the state as their trademark showing their ownership. No two brands may be alike, and it is illegal for anyone to use a brand that is not registered and in good standing with the state. Some of the oldest registered brands belong to ranchers in Klickitat County.

Farmers and ranchers have proven to be good stewards of the land from which they derive their livelihood for over 150 years. Together they provide one of the largest segments of the economy of Klickitat County and will continue to do so for many years.

CENTERVILLE CEMETERY

Mary Anne Enyeart

The Centerville Cemetery is located on the Dalles Mountain Road two miles south of town. Originally on school ground, it had become a cluster of family plots, many within fenced enclosures. Each family took care of its own plot, and the Centerville Grange helped with the care. When Henry Miller was Home Ec Chairman of the Centerville Grange, the money from hot dogs sold at the fair was spent for a new pump and care for the cemetery. Henry was instrumental in the cemetery becoming a designated cemetery district and being placed on the tax rolls for assistance in upkeep.

A Methodist church along Harms Road once had a cemetery beside it. Sometime during the late 1940s or 1950s, the land of the church and cemetery was deeded to the Centerville cemetery district. With the help of neighbors, the graves and stones were moved to Centerville. Care was taken to line up graves and plots. The graves are placed east to west so that the heads face the rising sun.

Interviews with Alvin Randall and Henry Garner

In 1877, a small group of Finnish immigrants who had first settled in northern Michigan with jobs in the copper mines decided to move further west. The group included the families of the Crockers (Kaarakka), the Mattsons (Seppanen), the Jacobsons (Hyttinen) and John Hagen. Finnish settlers in Greasewood, north of Pendleton, Oregon, one being Elias Peltopera, had encouraged them to come there and take up homesteads in the rich grassland soils.

They came west by train to San Francisco and took a boat to Astoria and Portland. In Portland, they discovered that the directions to Greasewood had been left in Astoria with Peter Karkiainen, whose family had decided to stay there. Because only some of their children could speak English, they had trouble expressing their needs, so they were told to continue by boat to The Dalles and ask for help there.

They arrived at The Dalles on July 4, 1877, joining the celebrations of the national holiday. At The Dalles, the directions to Greasewood were still not good enough for them to continue. However, they met Al Brown, a farmer from the Klickitat Valley, who encouraged them to settle near Centerville. They agreed to check out the valley by sending a few men and boys to hike over the Columbia Hills to explore for possible new homes.

They were impressed with the grass-covered valley cut by clear streams below snow-covered mountains. In the valley, they met the Browns, Childers, Jaeckels, and Garners, who instructed them on how to stake land claims, which they did before returning to their waiting families.

In the next few days, they purchased equipment and supplies and returned to the Klickitat Valley to build cabins for the coming winter. While building the cabins and tending to their homesteads, they stayed in the Childers barn, about a half mile east of Centerville. They had a dairy cow to supply some of their food, and they trapped wild prairie chickens and rabbits through the winter.

In the fall of 1877, seven more Finnish families joined the first pioneers, and by November, seven more. By the spring of 1878, more than 20 Finnish families were established in Klickitat Valley. As many as 50 Finnish families lived in and around Centerville through the years.

CENTERVILLE FINNS

D. Herman Hill

The Centerville Finns came from the northern parts of Finland and Norway, such as Pudasjarvi, Kuusamo, Tervola, Oulu, and the region of Finnmark in Norway. My grandfather, S. Herman Lehto, came to the U. S. in 1883 from Kuusamo, staking land claims in the Klickitat Valley and then obtaining citizenship in 1891. My father John E. Hill came from Vaasa, Finland in 1905.

Mattson, Louise (Hoikka). 1977. *Centerville Finns*. Portland OR: Finnish-American Historical Society of the West. Stanley Crocker, Centerville, WA

CENTERVILLE GRANGE #81

Mary Ann Miller

Centerville Grange #81, on Centerville Highway near the only four-way intersection in Centerville, was organized August 8, 1889, by S.B. Phillips. It was officially reorganized July 5, 1902 by James Wheelhouse. The current grange hall was constructed in the early 1980s after a fire destroyed the original building.

Like many granges, the Centerville Grange serves as a community focal point. The member activities include a harvest dinner for the general public, a family Christmas party, pinochle game nights, monthly meetings, Men's Night (the men cook the dinner), and a family waffle supper. The grange members are actively involved in the Adopt-a-Highway cleanup program, the county fair, state fairs, and the county Pomona Grange. Other organizations such as the 4-H Club and Neighbors of Woodcraft use the grange hall for their meetings. The hall is rented out for organizational meetings, weddings and wedding receptions, family holidays and many other special gatherings.

CENTERVILLE SCHOOL CONSOLIDATION

Wayne Eshelman as told to Teddy Cole

"It happened in 1942 or 1944 that the State passed a law to consolidate all the smaller schools with larger districts — the law said that all the people involved would have to vote on it. Well, there were a lot more people in Goldendale than there were in Centerville, so it seemed certain that Centerville and Goldendale would merge.

"I wrote to the newspaper saying it was unconstitutional — that was the first time I ever wrote an article for the *Sentinel* — and they published it on the front page. One of the directors of the Centerville School District, Mrs. Ino Kayser, read the article and called me. We agreed that she would canvass the Centerville people and I'd canvass Goldendale people to get votes against it, and it didn't pass. A few years later the consolidation law was declared unconstitutional.

"A lot of people think these small schools are at a disadvantage, but at the same time as the consolidation effort, the manager of the New York Life Insurance Company in Portland, the assistant manager of John Hancock in Portland, and the chief accountant of the Metropolitan Life in New York were all Centerville people."

Queen Marie of Romania had promised to dedicate her good friend Sam Hill's new museum at Maryhill, Washington, November 3, 1926, and she was on her way. The red carpet was waiting to be unrolled the instant she stepped off her railroad train at The Dalles. School was to be let out so crowds of school children could see her. Cages of doves of peace had been prepared for release by the Queen at the moment of dedication.

The only problem was, Hill's castle was unfinished. It was a disgrace, people said, that the queen's eyes would rest on ugly concrete walls.

"Why not cover the walls with flowers," someone suggested. An excellent idea, though few flowers were in bloom the first of November.

Sam Hill himself appeared at the door of Mrs. Daniel (Rosa) Gunkel, known as "the flower lady" of Maryhill, and asked to purchase all of her beautiful chrysanthemums. When Queen Marie arrived, the great room that one day would hold the queen's cloth-of-gold gown, gilt furniture and other royal gifts from the Queen, was festive with colorful blossoms.

Wanda Larson, *Ruralite*, Oct. 1967, p. 12-13

CHRYSANTHEMUMS FOR THE QUEEN

Mary Jean Lord

Queen Marie and Sam Hill

CINDER CONES AND RED ROCK

Sara Wu

Klickitat County is studded with volcanic cinder cones, remnants of onetime explosive events from thousands of years ago. They pose no threat now, or else we could not be mining them. They were formed when lava was released from high pressure, rather like taking the top off of a well-shaken soda. Instead of the bubbles bursting, the lava hardens around the bubbles, forming air-filled vesicles. Technically, the rock is scoria, containing less air than pumice. Scoria can be light enough to float, although it quickly absorbs water and sinks.

During an eruption, the scoria falls around the vent, building up a symmetrical cone. This cone shape is maintained over many millennia. The rock is so porous that the water readily drains through it rather than causing erosion.

Scoria is often red, since it explodes through layers of rock that are high in iron. Green, brown, black, and white cinder cones come through different types of rock. Less explosive eruptions form rocks which are less vesicular (fewer air-filled vesicles).

Not all symmetrical hills are cinder cones. Other volcanic extrusions often become cones after the outer layers erode. These cone-shaped plugs do not have the characteristic crater and rock of a cinder cone.

The rock from cinder cones does not make good highways. In the 1960s, highways made from this rock were beautiful red ribbons, but they did not stand the test of time. The vesicles broke down, compacting too much to make a good bed. The fine gravel of the broken rock is not the right kind to make a good road surface.

The red rock is beautiful on less-traveled driveways and for landscaping. Scoria is good as gravel that is put on icy roads. The sharp edges of the broken vesicles dig into the ice, increasing traction. The rocks are so lightweight that they are not apt to damage windshields when thrown up by a passing vehicle.

Cinder cones are important land–marks. Lorena Butte with its white "G" designates Goldendale, while Blockhouse Butte and Jackknife Butte add contrast to the flat valley floor. The image of these cinder cones spouting lava belies the present peaceful valley.

Bjorn Hedges, Klickitat County Roads Dept.

"Soon after we started our little settlement at Alder Creek I circulated a petition for a U.S. mail route, from The Dalles along the Columbia River to Chapman Creek and over the Columbia Hills to Alder Creek. Of course, we thought settlers in the Goodnoe Hills, just west of Rock Creek, would be in favor of this, as they were just as much isolated from civilization as we were. I regarded Griffin Chamberlin, one of the first settlers in the Goodnoe Hills, as a friend. I thought he would sign my petition and render all the assistance he could. When I called at his home, he ridiculed the matter and said there was no demand for such mail service. When I tried to argue with him he found so many faults with my plan that I perhaps made a somewhat sarcastic retort.

"When he said I was in a small business to be circulating such a petition, I expressed surprise at such views. He got very angry and wanted to fight. When he said he could whip a whole regiment like me, I did not dispute him, but told him to start the battle. He accepted my challenge and hit me a sock over the eye. After a few passes he attempted to land another haymaker, but this time I warded off his blow with my left arm and planted my right fist just below his left eye.

"This sock knocked him down. After his head hit the ground he got up and swore he wasn't licked yet. I hit him again and knocked him down with a right upper cut that landed over the other eye. I had just kicked him in the ribs a couple of times when his brother, Timothy, who was standing by, said we must stop fighting and I must leave. My opponent got up and objected to my leaving. He said I must accept hospitality of his roof for the night, which I did. I had a cut over my right eye which bled freely. His face was swollen and both his eyes were black, but we parted much better friends than we had ever been. I did not have his name on my petition, however, and we never got my proposed mail route."

Ballou, Robert. c1938. *Early Klickitat Valley Days.*
   The Goldendale Sentinel.

CIRCULATING A PETITION: ROBERT M. GRAHAM'S STORY

Robert M. Graham, submitted by Teddy Cole

EMMET CLOUSE: A GUIDING LIGHT

Mary Jean Lord

It was Klickitat County's good fortune that Emmet Clouse fell in love with the county at first sight. He came to White Salmon in the fall of 1940 to be interviewed for the job of superintendent of the fledgling Public Utility District. The Rural Electrification Administration (REA) had required a reluctant board of commissioners to hire a manager as a condition of an REA loan to build a power line between Trout Lake and Glenwood.

In 1940 PP&L served electricity to only 2,500 customers, all inside the city limits of Goldendale, Wishram, Bingen and White Salmon. The company refused to serve farm customers because it believed rural people wouldn't use enough electricity to pay for the line. Service in the towns was unreliable and expensive.

To make sure customers would use electricity when the Trout Lake-Glenwood line was finished, Emmet arranged with Mansfield Appliance in Bingen to bring in a carload of electric ranges, water heaters, refrigerators and washing machines. Then he ensured that loans were available so people could buy them.

The rest of the county was clamoring for electricity. While REA had granted a loan for the Trout Lake-Glenwood line, it had refused the PUD's application for a larger loan to electrify all of Klickitat County. While Emmet went to work gathering the detail that would make the loan palatable to REA, his wife Mildred, who had had experience with REA accounting methods, trained the bookkeeper. (In hiring Emmet, the Board had hired Mildred as well, though she was never paid a salary.) When the loan was resubmitted, it was approved for $450,000.

Construction ground to a halt during World War II as every available man was called to serve. The number of PUD employees dropped from 42 to 2. The supplies and equipment Emmet had ordered also went to the war effort. Even so, one lineman and Emmet, acting as helper, managed to build 27 miles of line extension by hand.

Emmet and Mildred ran the PUD almost alone during the war. When their son Gary was born, he, too, came to work, sleeping in a desk drawer while his mother ran the office.

Outage reports all came into the Clouse home. To help with repairs, Emmet called on Ernie Samson, the only electrician left in the area, who had been exempted from the service to work at war plants in The Dalles.

When the war ended, materials were still scarce, but people were impatient to get on with the electrification of the county. Poles couldn't be bought, so Emmet negotiated with Casey Langfield, the national forest ranger at Trout Lake, for the purchase of trees. The poles, of exceptionally fine cedar, were floated across the Columbia River and treated at a plant that had made army tent poles during the war.

Klickitat PUD needed a new transmission line from Bonneville Power Administration to serve central and eastern Klickitat County. Emmet informed BPA that they could have the longest poles for a river crossing at The Dalles. The PUD brought five 110-foot poles from Trout Lake to Dallesport, "knocking down every sign post along the way," according to Mildred. The transmission line BPA built to serve Klickitat County is still used.

Emmet was instrumental in shaping the utility organizations that served the new PUDs and cooperatives. One of the most important was *Ruralite*, started by rural electric cooperatives and Klickitat PUD to show customers ways that electricity could help them. *Ruralite* began publishing a magazine and soon added a safety education branch for utility employees.

The needs of his customers always came first with Emmet Clouse. He also earned the respect and admiration of others: the PUD Commissioners and employees, BPA administrators, and his peers in other utilities. He received many accolades in the public power community, including life membership in the American Public Power Association.

Emmet was known for his love of local history. The PUD's popular annual reports commemorated Klickitat County's schools, cemeteries, farms, and businesses. Following his retirement as General Manager, he and Mildred devoted untold hours to the Klickitat County Historical Society and to the publication in 1982 of *The History of Klickitat County*, Washington, edited by Pete May.

For nearly forty years, Emmet Clouse *was* Klickitat PUD. He established a remarkable record of accomplishment and set an exemplary standard of integrity and commitment to public service.

This article has been modified from one that appeared in "Fifty Years of Service," Klickitat PUD's annual report for 1987. (I wrote the original article)

THEODORA COLE

Kathleen Goode

Theodora Cole is a writer, historian, genealogy researcher, community activist, and retired librarian. By local standards, she's a newcomer, even though this has been her home for over a quarter of a century. Her arrival here was in some ways similar to that of other pioneers: she came looking for a new life, new opportunities, and a place to call home.

Teddy, as her friends call her, got a very early start in her career. Her parents encouraged her interests in books and writing. Her hometown, Stockton NJ, had a tiny library that was housed in the fire department, along with the police department and city hall. A young girl had to be somewhat daring to visit the library, since it required a walk past the jail cells, which were sometimes occupied! Teddy had plenty of courage, especially when it meant access to books about science, a subject not taught at the local school. When the woman who ran the library fell ill, Teddy was asked to fill in, since she was the most fervent patron of the library. The biggest challenge she faced was dealing with the reek of cigarette smoke after the air raid warden spent time in the same room. Teddy persevered for the sake of her beloved books.

The young librarian grew up, moved away, got married, and had children. She was a stay-at-home mom because "that's what we did in those days." In 1975, Teddy's life changed; she earned her degree in Library Science from the University of Washington, and she suddenly became a single parent via divorce. The mother of five, she still had four children at home and needed to find a good job that would take advantage of her training. She had mixed feelings about moving to Goldendale to become the new high school librarian. Driving here from Seattle she told herself, "I don't have to stay here forever." Now she can't imagine living anywhere else.

In 1988, Teddy changed jobs again, becoming the

librarian for the Goldendale Public Library. Her only complaint there was the problem of people trying to ban books. Once she was attending Sunday services at a local church when the pastor announced, "The only thing a library is good for is providing a job for the librarian." He must not have known who he was messing with! If Teddy could brave the challenges of distance, smoke-filled rooms, and live criminals, she was certainly not going to be put off by a small mind or loud rhetoric. Thanks in large part to her tireless efforts, our library continues to grow and thrive.

She retired in 1997 but remains active in many different aspects of the library and the community. Retirement has given her the free time to travel with friends and hone her skills as a wordsmith. When she isn't writing, she is encouraging others. The creation of the book you are holding was one of her long time goals.

One of Teddy's dreams is to have a local center for the performing arts, especially theatre. She envisions an auditorium with elevated seating for at least 100. There would be a large stage with wings and room backstage for sets and dressing rooms. It would be a wonderful way to bring different segments of the community together and encourage local talent, and it could even serve as the nucleus for a true community center. She just might accomplish this. Goldendale women have a habit of taking on ridiculously large tasks and getting them done; after all, most of them were pioneers. Whether she sees this come to life or not, Theodora Cole has certainly lived up to the meaning behind her name; in this community she is indeed a treasured gift.

Interview with Teddy Cole and personal experience.

When Sam Hill came to Klickitat County in 1907, Columbus had been a busy little town for nearly 50 years. Upon seeing the beautiful and productive farms in the Columbus area, Hill became determined to buy property. He purchased almost 7000 acres on the bluffs above the Columbia River. He also tried to buy land on the river level, including the orchards and vineyards owned by the Reverend W. T. Jordan, but he never succeeded.

COLUMBUS: A CASE OF IDENTITY THEFT

Rachel Gunkel

Hill's plans for his vast estate included the establishment of a Quaker community, to be named Maryhill after his daughter and wife. The town was begun on the plateau above Columbus, where Stonehenge is located today.

Hill tried to have the name of the Columbus post office changed to Maryhill. The residents protested vehemently, and postal authorities denied Hill's request. Hill countered by establishing his own post office of Maryhill on top of the bluff in 1909, but it closed in 1913 due to lack of use.

When the SP&S railroad was built through Columbus, Hill used his influence to have the name of the train station changed to that of Maryhill. The SP&S was conveniently owned by Sam Hill's father-in-law, railroad tycoon James Jerome Hill.

The town of Columbus had become surrounded by acreage owned by Sam Hill. By 1910, the entire area, and sometimes the town of Columbus itself, was referred to as Maryhill in the local newspaper. The general public began to refer to Columbus as Maryhill. Sam Hill's influence —the power of his money, fame and personality, as well as his shrewd use of the press — was stronger than the resistance of Columbus' few residents. The name of the post office was changed to Maryhill on March 23, 1922, and the town of Columbus officially ceased to exist.

While many towns in Klickitat County have changed their names over the years, it was a far different matter to have it forced upon a community by an outsider. The early residents of Columbus never lost their anger over what they regarded as Sam Hill's theft of their town's identity. The old-timers are gone now, but their stories were told many times. We who are their descendants still cannot think of Sam Hill and his legacy except with a peculiar mixture of pride and resentment, admiration and scorn.

"Columbus" by Pete May, *Klickitat Heritage,*
     Summer, 1979;
Maryhill, Sam Hill and Me, by Lois Davis Plotts, Post
     Publications, 1978;
Postmarked Washington, by Guy Reed Ramsey, Klickitat
     County Historical Society, 1977.

Grover Riley told me this story about his coming to Klickitat County as a young man in 1934.

When Grover arrived, he almost immediately met three old men. He introduced himself to the first man as a newcomer to the county, and the old man replied, "When you come to Klickitat County, you never leave."

Grover thought that was an unusual comment, but went on to meet and shake hands with the second old man, who also said to him, "When you come to Klickitat County, you never leave."

Truly puzzled, Grover introduced himself to the third old man, and sure enough, the man said, "When you come to Klickitat County, you never leave." So Grover asked the three old men, "Why do you all say that when I come to Klickitat County, I'll never leave?"

The reply was simple: "When you come to Klickitat County, you'll never get enough money together to leave!"

COMING TO KLICKITAT COUNTY

Ruth Miles Bruns

A rustic cabin in a grassy meadow bursting with colorful blooms, the distinctive trumpeting of sandhill cranes, the spicy scent of ruddy-barked ponderosa pines — this is a sampler from the Conboy Lake National Wildlife Refuge. Nestled at the base of Mt. Adams near Glenwood, Conboy Lake is a large seasonal marsh surrounded by dense pine and fir forests. For centuries, swans, geese, ducks, and sandhill cranes have used this mountain oasis for nesting and for resting and feeding during spring and fall migrations. It is the year-round home to many hundreds of species of plants and animals, some quite rare.

Among the animals most likely to be seen by visitors are coyotes, deer, elk, and some of the 165 species of birds that inhabit the reserve. Less noticeable, but integral to the complex network of life, are the small mammals, reptiles, amphibians, and invertebrates.

People have been coming to the area for millennia; archeological evidence shows encampments dating back 7,000-11,000 years. Native Americans regularly visited the lake to gather berries and camas roots and to hunt waterfowl and deer. Settlers were attracted

CONBOY LAKE NATIONAL WILDLIFE REFUGE

Judy Thomas

by explorers' tales of the broad valley and abundant resources. Peter Conboy, Sr., and his family became the first permanent residents in 1872.

As settlement increased, ranchers began altering the lake environment to increase native pasture and hay production. They constructed a ditch to drain the lake and improve lake bed conditions for farming, but the drainage efforts were only partially successful. Though Conboy Lake is now only a remnant of what it was before settlement, it still retains water from mid-December through April each year.

The increase of agricultural activities brought a decrease in waterfowl and other species. By 1900, swans and sandhill cranes were no longer nesting there. The Refuge was established in 1964 to preserve the remaining wildlife habitat and to restore the lake as a migration and nesting area for waterfowl. Sandhill cranes began returning in 1979. Some land in the area remains in private ownership. About 6,500 acres of the 10,000 acres authorized by Congress have been purchased, so the map of the refuge resembles an irregular patchwork quilt.

Visitors to the refuge can walk through the Whitcomb-Cole log house, listed on the National Registry of Historic Places. A two-mile trail follows the lakeshore and passes through upland pine forests for a variety of wildlife viewing opportunities. Good viewing is also available from the roads around the refuge. Some hunting and fishing is allowed.

Refuge brochures;
Phone interview with Harold Cole, manager;
    Fish and Wildlife Service website

THE CONVICT ROAD

Teddy Cole

Sam Hill wanted to build a shorter route to the Klickitat Valley, but a rocky barrier stood in his way. A massive basaltic flow reaching to the river's edge blocked anyone who wished to continue the Columbia River Road east beyond Lyle. The Lyle-Centerville road followed the Klickitat Canyon northward and eventually arrived in the Valley, but Hill wanted a more direct route. He proposed carving a road up the face of the precipice.

Hill had pioneered the use of convicts in building on

the North Cascades Highway, and now he brought them to Lyle, "to perform the heaviest kind of rock excavation along the bluffs on the Columbia River" using hand tools — picks, shovels, and wheelbarrows. About a hundred convicts were sheltered in wooden buildings surrounded by a portable stockade constructed of heavy wooden timbers. Armed guards were on hand, but Hill also believed that inmates nearing the end of their term would be reluctant to risk an escape.

The use of convict labor to build roads in Washington State received national attention. In May 1910, Hill and Henry Bowlby, the Washington State Highway Commissioner, took a party of Portland and Seattle residents to inspect the work being done near Lyle. A prisoner who had been in jail for dynamiting was in charge of the explosives. Hill told the group that on one occasion a trusty, put in charge of some concrete construction, was missing at dinnertime. When they went out to search for him, they found him so interested in his work that he had forgotten to knock off for dinner. Three convicts would do as much work as any four men Bowlby could hire because of the convicts' fear that if they were not industrious they would be returned to the penitentiary. The state saved about two dollars a day using convicts for road labor.

Tuhy quoted Hill in a New York Times article, "One of society's by-products is the convict. Our utilization of him in the construction of our roads is strictly along efficiency lines.... The convicts are treated like men in these well-ordered, beautiful camps and many of them are rehabilitated."

After 1910, the County Commissioners refused to pay for the convicts to work on the Lyle road. Hill campaigned for a one-mill levy, telling the farmers that the road would save them two cents per bushel when taking their grain to the ferry landing at Lyle. The measure passed.

In the end, however, only about a mile of the road was completed. Tuhy wrote, "In 1911, Governor Hay withdrew the convicts from the road building camp at Lyle and put them in the Walla Walla penitentiary." Hay was soon to regret it, because Hill campaigned against his re-election in 1912, and he was defeated.

Washington State discontinued the use of convict labor after 1913, and Hill turned to creating the famous Columbia River Road in Oregon. In 1933, tunnels were blasted through the rock blocking passage along the river, and the North Bank Road — now Highway 14 — proceeded eastward. The remains of the Convict Road are visible midway up the rock face just east of the Lyle tunnels.

Dorpat, Paul, and Genevieve McCoy. *Building Washington: A History of Washington State Public Works.* c1998. Washington Chapter of the American Public Works Assn.

Tuhy, John E. c1991. *Sam Hill: Prince of Castle Nowhere.* Maryhill Museum of Art.

COOKING CAMAS

Patricia Smith

In early spring, newcomers to the area are often fooled into thinking they are seeing a deep blue lake, when in reality they are gazing at a meadow of blue camas. Lewis and Clark wrote in their journals that they were mistaken when they first saw a meadow of camas, thinking they were seeing a clear blue lake.

Two species of blue camas grow in Klickitat County. *Camassia leichtlinii*, whose common name is Great Camas, blooms in mid May. *Camassia quamash*, known as Common Camas, blooms in mid April. Both species thrive in moist meadows and other wet areas, like the swales of drainage from the fields. Camas belongs to the lily family. The edible bulbs of both the blue species were a staple food of the Native Americans, still used today, though not as extensively as in the past.

The bulbs are dug after they go to seed. Care must be used to avoid digging *Zigadenus paniculatus*, commonly called Panicled Death Camas, or *Zigademus Venenosus*, called Meadow Death camas, found on dry open slope. Both bloom in early April, their white blossoms often found growing among the blue camas. The bulb and leaves of these species are difficult to tell from the edible bulbs of blue camas, and they can cause death to anyone who ingests them. Browsing cattle and horses have been known to die from eating the leaves.

Camas can be prepared in many ways. Dried, it can be ground and used in cakes and bread. If boiled, it can be used in soups or as a steamed vegetable. It can also be cooked in a pit — a favorite method of preparing this vegetable. A large pit is dug and a fire built in the bottom. After many hours of keeping the fire burning, the coals and some of the ashes are scraped out, leaving a layer of hot ash. Green branches are laid down and the washed bulbs are placed over this, then a layer of ashes, followed by a layer of hot coals. This layering is repeated until all the bulbs are in the pit. Hot coals are kept on top for twenty-four to thirty-six hours until the bulbs are well done. It takes long hours of cooking until the starch in the bulbs is turned into sugar. At the end of the cooking period, the bulbs are raked out and left to cool. After cooling, the black outer shell is removed, and the remainder is mashed and made into small flat cakes, which are dried and stored for future use.

It is now possible to have the pleasure of blue camas in a home garden. Camas bulbs and seeds are sold at various seed companies. Currently, two on-line sellers are Paghat's Gardens and Dave's Garden.

Jolley, Russ. 1988. *Wildflowers of the Columbia Gorge.*
    Portland, OR: Oregon Historical Society Press.
Lewis & Clark as Naturalists. www.mnh.si.edu/
    lewisandclark
Cooking Camas. www.edheritage.org/1910/folkways/
    salish.htm

COUNTRY DOGS

Kathleen Goode

Living in the country is usually depicted as being in the company of dogs. Native Americans in our county raised dogs as pets; they were also a valuable trade commodity. Imagine their surprise and disgust when Lewis and Clark traded for dogs and then ate them. Many in the Corps of Discovery were sick with dysentery when they arrived here; meat was easier on their digestive tracts than high fiber roots and vegetables.

Early pioneers may have seen dogs as excellent companions for children who were basically living in the wilderness. A faithful dog would guard a child against wild animals, bark to ward off a snake, and in general be a great pal. A farmer today may depend on a dog as a valuable worker, protecting farm animals and helping with roundups. They are also great companions, and it is not uncommon to see a dog riding up front in the farm truck. They lie around in the street in Bickleton.

Problems arise when people buy their five acres

in the country and decide they need a dog or three to complete the picture. Perhaps it was growing up watching Lassie on television. A tiny dog from the city won't last long this way; they become coyote snacks. Living in the country, many people think dogs should be free to run. Dogs think this is a great deal. They are free to chase cats, squirrels, skunks, and porcupines, often with extremely painful results. Even bigger problems arrive when dogs invade the roads or neighboring farms. Farmers cannot endure the losses from dogs that run wild and kill chickens, piglets, and rabbits or harass sheep and cattle. The most likely scenario is that the farmer will have to shoot the dog, which is legal.

Dogs in or near roadways cause a different range of problems. Runners and walkers often have to deal with them, and many carry pepper spray. They don't know what the dog will do, but want to be able to protect themselves. Country dogs seem to love to chase cars, often with deadly results. A young friend of ours was driving to the high school one morning when a dog suddenly jumped out in front of his car. He swerved to avoid it and ended up rolling his car. Luckily, he escaped serious injury, but his car was totaled. The dog was right back out on the road a few days later. City or country, if you have a dog it should be trained and kept out of the road. The best trained dogs seem to belong to the kids in the 4-H program; if you have a kid and a dog, think about signing them up.

Personal experience and conversations with teens, walkers, and landowners.

ARTIST E. I. COUSE

Bonnie Beeks

Irving Couse House

Western Artist Eanger Irving Couse (1886 - 1936) and Klickitat County

E.I. Couse, a founding member of the Taos Society of Artists, was considered one of America's leading western artists early in the twentieth century.

Couse was born in Saginaw, Michigan, in 1866. He became quite interested in the Ojibwa and Chippewa tribes early in his life. He studied at the Chicago Institute of Art and at the National Academy of Design in New York City before the age of 20. In 1886, Couse enrolled at the Academie Julian in Paris. Hoping to make art a career, he studied academic figure painting. In 1887

Mr. Couse became interested in a fellow art student, Virginia Walker.

Virginia, too, had studied in the art centers of American culture, in Philadelphia and in New York; however, her home was in Klickitat County, Washington, deep in the American West.

Virginia was one of five children of W.B. Walker and Catherine Purvine who had come to Klickitat County in 1867 to ranch on Chapman Creek in eastern Klickitat County.

In 1889 Eanger Irving and Virginia were married and began putting their energies into his promising career. In 1891, they returned to Virginia's roots, and her family constructed a studio and home for them on Chapman Creek in the French country style, using stone from a nearby quarry. Here Couse worked on his technique—depicting local landscape and individuals. However, it was difficult to get the local Indians to pose for the artist, and in the sparsely populated area, patrons were few.

E.I. and Virginia returned to France to paint the more salable European subjects from 1892 until 1895. He exhibited some of his "historical narratives of the West" at Paris Salon. In 1896 the family returned to the Walker ranch, and Couse produced numerous paintings. His newly learned technique of tonalism was evident in many moonlight and firelight scenes, one of which was on display at the Maryhill Museum of Art near Goldendale in a 1993 exhibit.

In 1902, they learned of the Taos art colony from a fellow artist, Ernest Blumenschein. E.I. Couse became a founding member of the Taos Society of Artists. The desert light and the accommodating native peoples inspired the artist. His paintings received much national exposure and had a great deal of influence on the public's perception of the West. In 1909 the Couses were able to purchase an old adobe house on Kit Carson Road in Taos, which became a cultural center and is now a museum and home of The Couse Foundation. They helped establish Taos as an important Southwest art destination.

Couse was elected to full membership in the National Academy of Design in 1911. His paintings are seen in the Detroit Institute of Art, the Metropolitan Museum and the National Gallery of the Smithsonian Institution.

Descendants of Nelson Purvine, Virginia's brother, still farm the Walker Ranch. They can point to the few remaining foundation stones of the studio built for Couse on Chapman Creek. It may be depicted in the background of some of his Klickitat period paintings. A nearby road, Old Highway 8, is called the Walker Grade. It rises steeply out of Rock Creek Canyon, where Couse's favorite models, the Native Americans, meet occasionally at their longhouse for important ceremonial occasions.

Levitt, Virginia Couse. 1991. *Eanger Irving Couse, Image Maker for America*. Albuquerque.
Couse Foundation brochure, undated, Taos NM
The Legacy, Newsletter of the Couse Foundation, November 2003. Taos NM
May, Pete. 1982. *History of Klickitat County*. Klickitat County Historical Society.

COW BINGO

Kathleen Goode

My family moved to the small town of Goldendale back in the good old days when the students still grew a crop of alfalfa on the front of the school property. This was about a decade ago, which just goes to show that things do change around here.

The first year after we moved to town, a young man came to our door trying to raise money for the Future Farmers of America (FFA) program. He explained that the fund raiser that year was Cow Bingo and would we like to buy a chance to win. I grew up in the ranch country of Arizona but had never heard of this form of bingo.

We asked for an explanation.

The young man could hardly believe there was anyone who had not heard of it, but he patiently explained. The FFA members marked a small field like a set of giant bingo grids and numbered all the squares. The squares matched a chart with the names of all the contributors. The students let the cows into the field and watched them closely. The bingo numbers were not drawn out of a machine, they were chosen by which square a cow decided to leave a deposit on. When the cow dung hit the ground in the bingo square, the person who had contributed for that square was a winner. It was only $5.00 a square.

I thought about this for a moment, then told the young man he was missing a great money making opportunity. He looked confused until I told him I'd pay $20 if he would guarantee to keep my name off the squares!

Coyotes

Naomi Fisher

If you bring up the subject of coyotes in Klickitat County, you'd better watch out.

There are strong feeling about coyotes here — "love 'em", hate 'em", "don't like 'em, but —"

With our long history of ranching and agriculture, there are naturally a lot of folk who see coyotes as vermin — useless pests that kill our poultry, livestock, or cats. Others living in the rural area see coyotes as useful creatures, a vital part of the cycle of life. They feed off rodents and rabbits, keeping the balance and occasionally granting us a peek into their private lives. Then, too, there's the Native American view of playful, trickster Coyote, teaching us lessons we all need in order to get along better in this world and with each other.

Me, I love coyotes. I listen to them calling to each other on the hillsides, and I've heard the yipping of the young pups in the woods nearby. I love to catch a glimpse of them in the fields hunting.

One day last summer, I sat looking out our front window towards the copse of trees where the deer often sleep in the shade away from the cruel midday heat. As I watched, four deer suddenly burst from the brush and bounded off down the valley. A few seconds later, a coyote came trotting out of the copse, with a mischievous and happy grin on its face. The deer were all far too large for this lone coyote to take down, but you couldn't help but imagine you could hear him laughing to himself for having stirred up a little trouble on an otherwise lazy, hot afternoon. The Trickster strikes again.

Coyotes

Kathleen Goode

Coyotes are an important part of the Klickitat County story. Coyote is the most important figure in Plateau Indian mythology. He was here before mankind, leading them, assigning them a place, fixing the places where they would fish and gather other foods. Coyote was both teacher and trickster, sharing lessons by example, often at his own expense. Within the coyote tales are the lessons of cultural values such as obedience, mutual respect, honesty, generosity, and courage.

White settlers had a very different view. Mention coyotes in a public meeting today, and you will get a firestorm of different opinions. Ranchers often see coyote as a danger to their livestock and therefore their livelihood. Environmentalists see the coyote as a natural and necessary part of the ecosystem, a part whose ecological niche is being destroyed, forcing it to adapt. Newcomers have different opinions about the sound of coyote howls at night. Some find it a charming reminder of the Wild West—others find it very unnerving. Animal rights activists find it appalling that anyone would want to shoot any coyote they saw on their property. Ranchers who have lost stock find it strange that anyone would want to protect the coyotes. Some county residents see coyotes as a free animal control service.

One resident in Bickleton was asked about coyotes in the area. She replied that they were common, even seen right on the main street of town in the winter. Was this a problem? "No, they keep the cat population down." Didn't cat owners get upset about this? "Not really; if a cat is dumb enough to be outside when the coyotes are around then maybe they are not a big loss!" This explains why only smart cats live in Bickleton.

Hunn, Eugene S. *Nch'i—Wana "The Big River"; Mid-Columbia Indians and Their Land.* Seattle: University of Washington Press, 1990.
Personal experience

DALLES MOUNTAIN BUTTERCUP

Mark Gibson

A handful of biologists and volunteers kneel around a white frame of pipe, brushing away a late dusting of March snow as wind-driven snow and sunshine battle for dominance high above the Columbia River. They are surveying the Dalles Mountain buttercup in Washington's Columbia Hills Natural Area Preserve.

The buttercup is a perennial flower that grows in only a handful of sites in Washington between the Klickitat River and Goldendale, in one location at the headwaters of Mill Creek in Oregon, and nowhere else. It grows primarily on the crest of the hills above the Columbia.

"The buttercup is of the highest priority on the preserve," notes David Wilderman of the Washington Department of Natural Resources, who is leading the survey team. "We monitor the population each year, see if it is decreasing or increasing. So far, it has been pretty stable."

The survey involves counting the buttercups in a random but organized way, using a white frame of pipe moved along a series of transcribed lines. Only those buttercups that occur inside the frame are counted. Most of the buttercups are in bloom and are easily spotted. The small yellow flowers dot the hillside of the preserve, a 3,593 acre site located above Dalles Mountain Ranch State Park. The preserve contains the largest remnant of one of Washington's rarest types of grassland ecosystems as well as the state's largest populations of three rare plant species: the Dalles Mountain buttercup, also called the obscure buttercup; *Douglas' draba*, and hot-rock penstemon. The site includes oak-pine woodlands, basalt cliffs, and a number of natural springs. A primitive road that climbs from a parking area above Dalles Mountain Ranch about 2 1/2 miles to the ridge-crest provides pedestrian access to the crest.

Dalles Chronicle, March 29, 2004, "Hunting for The Dalles Mountain Buttercup"

Dalles Mountain Buttercup

THE DAM ABOVE THE CLIFF

Rita J. Liska

High above the cliff that borders Devil's Canyon sits the remains of an old dam. Silted in and surrounded by brush and grass, it was very difficult to make out but possible to identify nearly thirty years ago, along the northwest canyon rim high above Devil's Creek.

Gated off several years ago, the dam and its canals can only be reached by foot or saddle horse. Heavy logging may have destroyed the dam completely, but the canal should still exist, and that is part of the story I have to tell.

Old time neighbors first told me the story of the dam on the cliff, and I visited it many times over the years. According to the neighbors, the dam supplied water over into a dry canyon some distance away, for a couple of brothers who operated a sawmill. When I asked where the water came from, the neighbors merely shrugged and said they guessed it came from high above on Devil's Creek because that's where the dam was.

For years I rode along the canal that fed into and back out of that dam, and eventually realized that the water involved came from Mill Creek to the west instead of Devil's Creek far below.

The sawmill site no longer exists, and I never followed the canal to its mouth or its source. But Mill Creek is the only logical answer to the water supply for that particular dam above Devil's Creek.

DAY WITH THE DOLLS

Roberta Hoctor

It must have been in 1952 or 1953 when four of us high school girls were asked if we might come down to Maryhill Museum and help. Mr. Dolph, the caretaker whose son was in our class, needed helpers to dress some dolls*. In the basement apartment where the Dolphs lived, hidden behind the walls at the museum, was a large, round oak dining room table loaded with giant boxes. Each box was labeled shoes, dresses, etc., and within each box were 200 or so items, each labeled with a number, and each as different as the next. Yes, there were black metal stands with numbers (these were the dolls, so to speak: metal frames with body features), shoes, dresses, hats, and accessories. We spent at least two days sorting through these piles, matching numbers, outfits, and dressing frames and thinking what rich fabrics and what strange designs.

* These were the Theatre de la Mode French Fashion Mannequins, in the permanent collection and still on display at the Museum.

DAYS OF THE DEAD

Kathleen Goode

One of the most popular annual events at the Maryhill Museum is the celebration of Los Dias De Los Muertos — the Days of the Dead. The throne room is host to mariachi bands and colorful folk dancers. Last year a young artist shared the beautiful shrine she had created in honor of her father, which allowed her to share what a special person he had been and how he touched her life. Upstairs, an artist demonstrated painting techniques to decorate a skull with folk designs. Everyone was invited to try it for themselves.

The designation of November 1st and 2nd as the Days of the Dead can be a bit of a shock to the uninitiated. It is not macabre or sad; it is instead a celebration of life. The first day is set aside to remember infants and children. The second is dedicated to the remembrance of adults. Like most holidays, there are special foods and decorations. One of the most common features is the inclusion of marigolds and cockscomb, which are thought to welcome the souls of the departed with their bright colors and sweet fragrance. The marketplace offers many versions of sugar skeletons and skulls as well as special breads or rolls called pan de muerto. These are decorated with designs that look like crossed bones. Candlelight plays a major role; sometimes thousands of votive candles decorate the paths of a cemetery.

My favorite part of this holiday is the connection with Monarch butterflies. The Monarchs are seen only a few at a time in our county. They feed on milkweed, which is a native plant. These butterflies take part in a great migration, traveling from Mexico and southern California to areas as far north as Canada. When they return south, they gather in great numbers, sometimes covering the fir trees where they winter over. Many people in Mexico believe that the butterflies carry the souls of the departed. What a beautiful way to travel to a family reunion!

Personal experience
Los Dias De Los Muertos http://www.holidays.net/
    halloween/muertos.htm
Palfrey, Dale. 1995. *The Day of the Dead: Mexico honors those gone but not forgotten.* http://www.mexconnect.com/
    mex_/muertos.html

Wade Hampton Dean
Wade Dean, pioneer and visionary, came to White Salmon as a laborer and assistant cook for the Utah Construction Company in 1902. The company won a contract to lay rails for Western Pacific's railroad tracks

WADE AND EARL DEAN

Bob Van Alstine

through the Columbia River Gorge. Wade decided to come north with their crew.

The rest of his life he spent in Klickitat County, and it is sprinkled with projects, some important and successful, some that failed. Nevertheless, he always pursued his dreams and moved forward. Projects that have endured through the years include founding the local telephone company, now called Sprint; and introducing D'Anjou pears to the Mt. Adams Orchard. Other experiments were curing cheese in the large family-owned lava cave (often called the Cheese Cave to this day) in the Trout Lake Valley and keeping sulphur claims alive for the Glacier Mining Company for a number of years.

Earl R. Dean

"Well I guess you might say I began in the phone business at the top — at the top of the ground, that is, digging post holes."

That's the way Earl Dean of White Salmon laughingly described the beginning of his service in the Oregon-Washington Telephone Company (later called United Telephone Company of the Northwest, and later yet Sprint.)

Earl R. Dean, son of telephone company founders Wade and Effie Dean, celebrated 75 years of telephony in 1980. Earl literally grew up in the business. He was President when the company was sold to United Utilities in 1957 until his retirement in 1967. He also served on the United board of directors during his presidency. He was then appointed Chairman of the Board and served in that capacity until he turned 75.

A United Telephone history, found in the *"Earl Dean Memorial Book"* can be found at the White Salmon Library.

McCoy, Keith. c1987. *Mount Adams Country: forgotten corner of the Columbia River Gorge*. Pahto Publications.

McCoy, Keith. c2003. *Mid-Columbia North Shore*. Trafford Publications.

May, Pete. 1982. *History of Klickitat County*. Klickitat County Historical Society.
Ruralite. April 1976.

Many newspaper articles from the *White Salmon Enterprise* and the *Bingen Mt. Adams Sun*

Dickey Farms in Bingen is the oldest family-run business in Washington State. Five succeeding generations have run the farm, and the sixth is working on it, preparing to take over. Operating since 1867 means that there are many connections with the community, reaching out as far as Japan.

The names connected with the farm have changed from Warner to Henderson to Dickey, but it is all one family line. Originally, the business was logging and then livestock. Eventually they settled into fruit and vegetable farming on the rich river bottomland.

During World War II, when Japanese-Americans were interned, they had to leave their Dallesport farms. The Toda, Makino, Magaki and Akita farmers asked John Dickey to manage their properties. During the war, he worked and upgraded these farms and then returned them to their owners, rather than keeping them as some unscrupulous farmers did.

This connection with Japanese was further enriched in the 1970s, when young men from Japan came for work/study on Dickey Farms. They were taken into the home of Grandma Ruth Dickey and Bob and Loretta Dickey. Besides learning farming techniques, they formed warm connections. These men still return with their families to reminisce, getting teary-eyed, especially when they think of Loretta's kindness. They arrange their holiday to coincide with the August sweet corn and tomato harvest!

With these Japanese associations, Dickey Farms has developed small plot farming, which suits their land. They carefully plot out their plantings, rotate crops, and use cover crops to maximize the use of the land.

The work force at Dickey Farms has changed with the times. Originally the family and local residents predominated, and they still remain an important part of the farm. In the 1930s, people from Oklahoma and Missouri came looking for work. With their experience in farming, they were particularly good help, but they moved on to the better paying jobs in logging. Mexicans were brought to the farm on the Bracero Program, initiated during World War II with its labor shortage. Bob Dickey says that these contract workers often were real assets. At the end of the season, they would return to Mexico. Because of abuses of the program, especially in California, it was discontinued in 1964. After World

Dickey Farms — Keeping Connections

Sara Wu

War II, winos and hobos were a significant portion of the farm laborers. Now Hispanic workers are again the majority of the workers on the farms.

Dickey Farms produces and sells cherries, apricots, peaches, green onions, cabbage, spinach, zucchini, summer squash, cucumbers, eggplant and a variety of sweet and hot peppers. They promote other farmers by selling their produce, including berries. Seasonally, huckleberries from the wild are available.

Besides selling to outside markets, they run a store for their own and for others' local products. Responding to requests, they now have pies and other baked goods as well as knickknacks crafted by local artists. For those inspired by the produce, garden supplies are available.

Before the Bonneville Dam was built, yearly floods deposited rich loam on the farm. When the backwaters of Bonneville Dam threatened the farmland, Dickey Farms used rock out of its quarry from across Highway 14 to build a dike. The D6 CAT with carryall ran 24 hours a day, seven days a week, until it was completely worn out. But the dike has stood the test of time with little maintenance. This bulwark is a visible sign of the long-standing connections and support that Dickey Farm has given the community.

DeBolt, Merna. 2000. *Museum Musings. Skamania County Pioneer*. January 12.

Personal communication with Sherry Bryan, Bob Dickey, Stanley Dickey.

Walker, Brianna. 2004. *Dickey Farms, a study in success.* Agri-Times. Vol. 21, No.11.

www.farmworkers.org/bracerop.html (2005)

JUSTICE WILLIAM O. DOUGLAS AND MOUNT ADAMS

Keith McCoy

Young Douglas's life had an unhappy start in Klickitat County. His father, a minister, accepted a call to a church in Cleveland in 1901. At age four, young Douglas suffered crippling polio; at age six, his father died.

The bereaved family moved to Yakima, where Douglas and his sisters grew up in near poverty. Forced to work, they developed a strong work ethic. Douglas was determined; hiking and mountain climbing became his lifelong program for strengthening his impaired legs.

Douglas' strong work ethic and exceptional intelligence made him valedictorian of his Yakima class and led to a scholarship at Whitman College. Next, he was determined to study law at Columbia University in New York. Determination and hard work saw him through. These same strengths brought him attention both at Columbia and Yale.

After graduation, he drew the attention of Franklin D. Roosevelt as the New Deal was being forged. He was tapped for a series of prestigious administrative assignments in the New Deal, and appointment to the Supreme Court followed in 1930. William Douglas was the second youngest appointee to the Court and on his retirement in 1975, had the longest tenure to date — thirty six and a half years. Douglas was a member of the court during one of the stormiest periods in American history, and he became a controversial figure because of his liberal positions and his prominence in the environmental movement.

William O. Douglas

Despite his worldly successes, Justice Douglas regularly returned to his roots. For years his favorite retreat was in the Naches foothills, later in the Glenwood Valley at the very foot of his favorite mountain. It was Mount Adams that had dominated his horizon for so many years.

The living room of the rustic Douglas home was possibly the most spectacular room in Klickitat County, decorated as it was with primitive art from many parts of the world.

Justice Douglas was credited with writing a book a year for many years. While most dealt with his profession, many chronicled his extensive travels. But clearly his favorite places were Oregon's Wallowa Mountains and Washington's Cascades. His special affinity for Mount Adams is told in *Of Men And Mountains*. On the first climb in 1945, he went ill-equipped to withstand the chill winds that sweep the summit. However, he spent considerable time looking down across the glaciers to view the forests that encircle most of the peak and the tawny Columbia Plateau lands that stretch off to the east. Here are some of his thoughts:

"That spiritual experience is difficult to describe. It has to do with man's relationship to the universe and his Creator. The world on top of Mount Adams is in a real sense a strange and different world from what one ordinarily knows. It is the world as it was millions of years ago.

"There is nothing on the mountain that extends a welcome....not even a blade of grass to vibrate in the wind."

Douglas, William O. 1950. Of Men and Mountains. Harpers.

Down the Klickitat

Nancy Barron

The Klickitat River lives up to its federal designation as "wild and scenic." It arises in the Goat Rocks Wilderness, and the waters from Mt. Adams feed it. Broad, shallow, and fast, it hurries through the Yakama Indian Reservation and the towns of Klickitat, Pitt, and Lyle over 95 miles to the Columbia River. I've had many pleasures traveling down that river.

Rafting the Klickitat in the spring flow was sheer delight. From a couple of miles south of the Yakama Reservation to Leidl Park flows a section of river filled with some exciting water but no death-defying dangers. My thermal wet suit was most welcome as waves of glacier melt splashed aboard. Waterfalls cascaded from side creeks into the River. The canyon's andesite columns, pine-covered slopes, and riverside penstemon inspired our contemplation and snatches of odes. My tired back was relieved to reach the take-out at Leidl Park on the Glenwood Highway, but I was regretful that the journey was over.

I spent an entertaining afternoon at Leidl Park one fourth of July. After our picnic, my partner and I jumped into the swift current there, put our feet up, and floated whooping around the bend for several hundred yards. As it became shallow again, we hauled ourselves out, cut across the bend, and got back in again for another ride. Refreshing! I'm told that one can float the river by inner tube from the fish hatchery to Leidl Park.

From Leidl Park, a path leads to the old road, now closed to cars. The road goes north to the old Champion Lumber Company staging area at the junction of Glenwood Highway and Champion Road. The road also goes south, leaving the newer transportation corridors and wending with the river through the countryside for 12 miles to SR142 where the Little Klickitat joins the Klickitat. This old paved road is perfect for biking, except for the few washouts where dirt paths present some challenge.

The Klickitat grade, a sinuous, single-lane four-mile portion of SR142, connects Goldendale to the lower Klickitat River through the Little Klickitat River Canyon. Some travelers, myself included, consider the grade the highlight of the trip for the magnificent scenery of the canyon. Others will drive many extra miles to avoid it.

Even from my automobile, I have enjoyed the wildlife on the river. Golden or bald eagles soar over the river or survey from a snag. Cormorants perch on water-bound rocks, spreading their wings to dry in the sun. Herons stalk the shallows. Gulls who have followed the Columbia up from the sea rest in the lower river reaches. Kingfishers dart, and ouzels bob from water-side rocks. Mallards and mergansers paddle by. Some pull-outs along the road allow time to ponder.

Deer abound on the roadside shoreline and hillsides. Particularly at dusk or dawn, they can be in the middle of the road as well, necessitating vigilant driving. One woman told of her boyfriend accidentally running down a cougar early one morning. She went to the location of his collision, where no carcass was evident, but she discovered the big cat had dragged himself off to a tree in the vicinity and was dying there. Since it was cougar season, they skinned it and kept the hide.

People are often seen fishing, in waders casting, in drift boats, or at water's edge. I have seen several small parties of kayakers playing in the currents and eddies. Just north of the town of Klickitat, I once saw one pontoon boat *with* occupant and another *without* coming around a bend of the river. The second person followed through the waves, hoping to reunite with his boat.

The lower 16 miles of the 31-mile Klickitat Trail, a Rails-to-Trails accomplishment, follows the river's banks to the Columbia. This old railroad route offers hours of on-foot exploration of the river and its valley. Its upper 15-mile portion begins at the junction of Horseshoe Bend Road and SR142 and proceeds up Swale Canyon to Harms Road and on to Warwick.

Beauty, recreation, sustenance: we are fortunate to be able to experience the many faces of the Klickitat

River in its journey, and it deserves our continuing care. This wild and scenic river is open for us all to enjoy by many modes of travel.

[See also LEIDL PARK]

Personal experience
http://englishriverwebsite.com/
    LewisClarkColumbiaRiver/Regions/Places/klickitat_
    river.html
www.klickitat-trail.org

EARLY SCHOOL DAYS

Eleanor Dooley,
as told to Judy Thomas

In 1918, a 2-1/2 mile trip to school over unpaved roads could be quite a chore. So, although that was the year I was ready to start school, my parents kept me home until my younger brother was old enough to start too. I was eight years old when I began the first grade, but since I was able to skip to the fourth grade at the beginning of the next year, my late start didn't hold me up. A neighbor girl, a seventh grader, boarded with my family so that she could drive us to school in our horse and buggy — though when the horse was needed for farm work in the spring, we walked. When I first started school, we just tied the horse to the fence during the day, but soon after that the fathers got together to build a barn with numbered stalls for about 25 horses. After our first two years, the neighbor girl quit school, and my brother and I rode together on our draft horse.

Our Pleasant Valley community had had a school since about 1877, but, the school I attended was a two-room building built in 1917 by my father under contract with the County. Grades 1-5 and a teacher were on one side, separated by folding doors from grades 6-10 and their teacher on the other. The individual desks — double desks for the higher grades — were arranged in rows in front of the teacher's desk. A pot-bellied stove at each end of the building warmed us in winter, and windows on the south side let in light. Each grade had its own assignments, and each came by turns to a bench in the front of their room to recite and to write on the blackboard. Kerosene lamps attached to the walls were used for social events in the evening. The school year started just after Labor Day and let out June 1 so that the children could help with the summer farm work. The school day was from nine in the morning until four in the afternoon.

Of course, the school had no running water. Each day two of the older boys carried water from their farm about a third of a mile away. They were paid a little by the school district to do this work. In my first years, we drank from the bucket using a communal dipper; later we got individual collapsible metal cups. We didn't waste a drop of that water — water that had to be carried was precious.

Baseball and jump rope were favorite recess activities. Another popular game was Anti-over. We divided into two teams, one on each side of the schoolhouse, and took turns calling "Anti-over" and throwing a ball to the team on the other side. The object was to make it as hard as possible for the other team to catch the ball. Sometimes we played hide and seek, but with no trees and only a few buildings, there weren't many places to hide.

We loved the holidays. On Halloween we drew pictures of ghosts and witches and hung them on the windows while we listened to the teacher read a ghost story. We had a community dinner at Thanksgiving time. At Christmas we would open the doors between the two rooms and put on a program for our parents — sometimes a play, sometimes recitations and singing. We decorated a tree with paper chains and strings of popcorn. The programs were held during the day, since traveling at night on back roads, especially in winter, was not practical in those days.

We had a May pole on May Day. We attached crepe paper strips to the top of a pole and wrapped the pole with the paper by weaving the strips over and under as we walked around the pole in opposite directions. On the Fourth of July, families met at the school for a potluck dinner and a baseball game. The part I remember best is watching the men turn the hand-cranked ice cream makers and then the long wait as the ice cream was repacked in ice and salt and left to solidify while we ate our dinner.

When I was a child there was more snow than now — often over three feet — and winter temperatures were lower. But in spite of that we went to school most days. We took flat irons wrapped in gunnysacks to keep our feet warm in the buggy. Boys wore knickerbockers, pants that came just to the knee. Girls wore dresses, even in the coldest weather, just adding long stockings and hi-top shoes to keep us warm. In those days women never wore pants, even to do farm chores. A few might have worn bib overalls now and then, but it was considered very odd and unladylike.

I went to Goldendale for high school, boarding in town from Sunday evening until Saturday morning. I hated staying in town over the weekend, but my dad didn't think it was necessary for me to come home and wouldn't come to pick me up. He only made trips to town when it was really necessary, one reason being that driving our Model T Ford on hilly, rough or muddy roads was hard work.

A Model T did not have the clutch and gearshift mechanism that we know today. There were three pedals on the floor: a brake, a reverse pedal, and a gear pedal. The accelerator was a lever attached to the steering column. To run the car in high gear the driver let the gear pedal all the way out, but the pedal had to be held to the floor for the low gear. A road like ours, that needed low gear most of the time, was a tiring road to drive!

If I wanted to go home on the weekend I had to find my own way, and on Saturday morning I would go over to the post office where I knew that Bruce Spaulding, the mailman, would be loading up his car with the mail. Every week our routine was the same. He'd tell me that he couldn't take me, that he wasn't allowed to take passengers. I would just stand there and not say anything. When he was finally ready to go he'd always tell me to get in. My dad brought me back to town Sunday night. By the time my sister was in high school, ten years later, there was bus service.

ECLIPSE CITY

Mary Jean Lord

Twice during the 20th Century, Goldendale lay smack dab in the center of a complete eclipse of the sun. The first eclipse took place June 8, 1918, and the second on February 26, 1979. Both events drew visitors from far and near to the town dubbed "Eclipse City."

Muriel Books, Goldendale, who remembered the "diamond ring" from the 1918 eclipse, was thrilled to see it again during the second eclipse. Gerald Fenton, Klickitat County PUD Commissioner from 1960 to 1978, was a schoolboy in 1918. He recalled watching scientists from the Lick Observatory set up two and a half tons of scientific equipment, including a 40-foot-long telescope, on the lawn of the I. R. Morgan home west of town. (The house is still there across from the PUD substation on West Railroad.) As the eclipse became total, the scientists jotted down an official notice, which was rushed by motorcycle to the telegraph station, where an operator tapped it out to the waiting world. Out-of-town visitors arrived by train.

Thousands of people converged on Goldendale for the second eclipse in 1979. Bumper-to-bumper cars and campers lined the roads into town from north and south. With no place to go, they met at the flashing red light at the intersection of Broadway and Columbus. Every motel room within fifty miles was full, families camped out in church basements, and townspeople opened their homes to scientific observers.

The invited visitors allowed on Observatory Hill alone numbered 1,650, not counting unofficial hundreds who clambered up the back of the hill. Many took up posts on Lutheran hill or nearby buttes. The Chamber of Commerce estimated more than 5,000 visitors in Goldendale with a normal population of 3,500.

Another 1,500 watchers gathered at Stonehenge, including a group of costumed "neo-pagan Druids," who performed celebratory rites. Dorothy Brokaw, director of Maryhill Museum of Art, reported more than 3,000 visitors to the museum during the three-day weekend of the eclipse.

NBC donated $5,000 to the Goldendale Observatory for the privilege of setting up an office inside. A newsman hung a turkey wishbone over the door to scare away clouds.

NBC thought they had an agreement with Observatory director Bill Yantis for exclusive rights to be on the hill. When ABC appeared and set up shop outside, NBC demanded the removal of its rival, but Yantis couldn't see kicking them off the hill when they had come all that way. A week later NBC hadn't asked for their money back, and Yantis didn't think they would.

More than 300 local volunteers worked on the big event. They sold postmarked cachets, patches, and t-shirts for the benefit of the Observatory. Private entrepreneurs outside sold bumper stickers, "canned dark," sun peeps, and mylar sheets.

Yantis himself almost missed the moment of totality because he had to take care of a lady who had collapsed. He was also working the telescope inside.

Yantis had thought everyone would go home when it was over, but to his amazement, thousands climbed the hill and scoured the grounds and the garbage cans looking for souvenirs. They took away every scrap of mylar sheet and sun peep.

Local merchant Hoagie Nielsen and NBC correspondent Jack Perkins had a five dollar wager on the weather, Perkins betting on cloudy and Nielsen on sunny. The day began partly sunny and partly cloudy. A stray cloud covering the start of the eclipse scurried out of the way just in time, for which the Druids claimed credit. Afterwards, Nielsen and Perkins had onlookers in stitches laughing at their mock confrontation over who had won the bet.

The eclipse was about the most exciting thing that had ever happened to Goldendale, but it was exhausting. By the time it was over, everyone was happy to see the visitors leave and for peace and quiet to return.

Letha Smith, *The Goldendale Sentinel* correspondent from Maryhill, complained in the paper the next week, "It was reported that the people at Stonehenge were scaring Mr. Dooley's cattle." After discussing the massive traffic jam on Highway 14, during which cars, trucks and campers moved at 15-20 miles an hour, she summed up the opinion of many.

"I noticed the wavy lines of the eclipse shadow on my windows, the trees and the front door. During the totality I stepped out and took a look at this fantastic sight. I truly enjoyed the eclipse, but I wouldn't travel a great distance to see it."

Ruralite Magazine, April 1979, by Mary Morgan;
The Goldendale Sentinel, 1 Mar 79.

In the late 1970s or early 1980s (he can't remember the exact year), Al Sanders saw an illustration of a high voltage electric demonstration board. As a journeyman lineman and foreman of Klickitat County Public Utility District's White Salmon crew, Al had become increasingly concerned about the public's ignorance of electric safety. He realized that this board was the perfect tool to teach safety, and Al determined to make one.

The board used toy people, houses, cars, kites, trees, and ladders, but the high voltage electricity in the miniature power lines was real. When the tiny antenna a toy man was installing on one of the houses touched a power line, the flash of blue fire surging through the doll's feet made a lasting impression on the audience.

The first board Al built was a community effort. When the utility wouldn't agree to pay for the materials he needed, Al solicited help from friends in the business community. Electrician Ernie Sampson contributed a neon lighting transformer to convert ordinary household electricity to high voltage.

Chuck Oliver, who owned Chuck's ProMart, and his son Ron enthusiastically entered into the spirit of the enterprise. They donated hinges, sawed boards, and helped Al build little houses and poles for the power lines.

When the board was finished, Al took it first to volunteer fire departments. Al knew that every time they were called to a fire, they faced potentially deadly hazards they knew little or nothing about. Al showed them how to recognize electrical hazards and handle them safely.

Farmers were exposed to accidents or near-accidents when they moved large equipment or irrigation pipes. It was easy to forget about the lines overhead. In Al's hands, the demonstration board proved adaptable for teaching electrical safety for agricultural workers.

Al really hit his stride with school children, however. His passion for safety was contagious, and students and teachers responded with enthusiasm. He went to every school in Klickitat County. After Al's visits, the PUD offices were wall-papered with thank you notes and crayon pictures of Mr. Electric Safety.

By this time, of course, Al had given up his job as line foreman and moved into the new position of safety coordinator that Klickitat PUD created for him.

In addition to his safety programs for children and adults, he planned employee safety programs and oversaw tree trimming, proper storage and handling of hazardous materials, and other health and safety work at the PUD.

Al was a born teacher, and when word got around, the Northern Wasco People's Utility District and Wasco Rural Electric Cooperative arranged for Al to bring his demonstration board to Oregon school children.

Al loved working with the children. Even after he retired from Klickitat PUD, he continued to take his board to the schools. He was constantly revising and improving his programs. More than twenty years after he began, Al was on his third demonstration board.

By 2005 Al found himself teaching electricity to his second generation of students. "My own were in classes I taught in White Salmon, and now I've had my grandchildren in class. One fellow told me his kid came home from school all excited to tell him what a neat electricity program he had seen, and he said, 'I know. Mr. Sanders came to my school with that same electric show when I was a boy.'"

In an interview in April 2005, Al considered what his electric safety demonstrations had accomplished. "It's hard to measure the full effect we have had, but we can definitely see the difference. We don't have the problems and near-accidents we used to have. Both children and adults notice and report safety hazards like worn weatherheads. They know what to do if they see a downed power line. We have watched children grow up and remember what they learned from the safety programs."

Interview with Al Sanders

Electrifying Klickitat County

Mary Jean Lord

Klickitat County was one of the last places in the nation to be electrified. Pacific Power and Light Company (PP&L), who provided service to a few towns, refused to hook up farmers, who, they felt sure, would never use enough electricity to make it profitable to serve them.

Where electricity was available, it was expensive and unreliable. Eva Flock, an early mayor of Bingen, complained that voltage dropped so low at her

Evergreen Hotel in the evenings that 110-volt bulbs merely glowed. Goldendale customers paid 17 cents a kilowatt hour in 1919, lowered to only 8.5 cents when the city began considering its own power plant.

Gerald Fenton, who later served as a PUD commissioner, remembered that all of Goldendale was served by one overworked wire from Wishram. In 1945, shortly before Klickitat PUD took over from PP&L, he was sitting in the dentist's chair when the mill shut down for lunch. The power went wild, the light bulb broke, and the dentist's drill took off.

In 1928, noting the success of city-owned plants, such as Tacoma, Seattle, and Ellensburg, which already boasted the lowest electric rates in the nation, the state Grange asked Homer T. Bone to draft Initiative #1 to the state legislature to allow counties to form public utility districts. When the legislature refused to pass the measure, it went on the ballot in November 1930 as an initiative to the people. The initiative passed, with Klickitat County voting in favor 1,152 to 724.

A second vote was needed to form a PUD in the county, and in 1936 the West Klickitat County Pomona Grange asked the county commissioners to put it on the ballot. Shortly after, PP&L announced a rate cut, and the PUD measure mysteriously was missing from the ballot.

Angry Grangers formed a county-wide committee to get the measure on the ballot and passed. The campaign was headed by Gerald Fenton, Goldendale, and J. S. Degman, White Salmon. It was a hard-fought campaign and feelings ran high. When the votes were counted, November 8, 1938, the PUD had been created by a vote of 2,219 to 1,920. At the same time, the people elected the original Board of Commissioners: Degman; M. A. Collins of Bickleton; and Martin Lumijarvi of Centerville.

The board hired Emmet E. Clouse as the first manager in the fall of 1940, and the first PUD line, 60 miles serving Trout Lake and Glenwood, was energized August 24, 1941. The federal Rural Electrification Administration (REA), advanced $450,000 for a second project to serve the rest of the county, and the PUD began condemnation proceedings to acquire property PP&L refused to sell. Klickitat PUD was on the move.

By mid-1942 everything had ground to a halt for World War II. The number of PUD employees dropped from 42 to 2, as men went off to war. Materials that Clouse had ordered for construction were commandeered for the war effort. It was a hard time for the PUD. It had a big debt to REA, it was losing money, and no one could do anything about it until after the war. Clouse, with his wife Mildred as unpaid bookkeeper, ran the PUD alone. Somehow, with the help of an electrician who was 4-F as unfit for the military, he even managed to build 27 more miles of line by hand.

In 1948 the PUD took possession of the PP&L system, adding 130 miles of line. Later, Clouse told an interviewer that he was never more afraid in his 36 years as manager. The lines were in such bad repair he didn't know if they could hold the system together long enough to replace it.

Klickitat County PUD had drawn up plans during the war, and now it launched the biggest construction program ever seen in a single county in the Pacific Northwest. Farmers anxiously watched the approach of the crews installing power poles and stringing lines. When the hookups finally came, houses and barns were already wired, and radios, pumps, washing machines, refrigerators, ranges, hot water heaters, and other appliances were plugged in ready to go. By 1952 the PUD had brought service to every customer who had applied, and Klickitat County farmers moved into the age of electricity at long last.

"Fifty Years of Service," Klickitat PUD annual report, 1987
(research and writing by Mary Jean Lord)

Everyday on Ice

Rachel Gunkel

Biggs Ferry

On a stormy January afternoon in 1929, the Maryhill ferry Everyday Highway took the Richfield oil truck across the river to Biggs. The oil truck could not make it up the icy bank, so ferry pilot Ralph L. "Mac" McDonald and his two deckhands got off the boat to help push the truck. A large cake of ice broke away from shore and shoved the ferry out into the river. The ferry floated off with no one aboard, engine still running. The ferry grounded on ice that had built up on a gravel bar in the middle of the river.

The ferry's predicament had not gone unnoticed by the residents of Maryhill. The families and neighbors of the ferrymen assumed that the men were stranded aboard the trapped ferry.

"Much anxiety prevailed last night when darkness came," wrote Rosa Gunkel on January 27, 1929. "We could hear the thud of the engine but the ferry came no nearer to shore. Folks became alarmed lest the men should have to spend the night on the ferry. A fierce wind was blowing from the west and heavy rain mixed with snow was pouring down. You can imagine the consternation."

From the Oregon side of the river, the ferrymen made a dangerous rescue attempt. Mac and the deckhands tried to reach the Everyday in a rowboat, but they were defeated by the choppy water and howling wind. The men's clothes got soaked through, and they were soon freezing. Their coats were on board the ferry.

Mac telephoned his wife from Biggs to let her know that he and the deckhands were safe on shore and would return home as soon as they could. Mac told his wife to ask their neighbors to use the ferry company's launch to rescue the stranded ferry. Removing the Everyday from the middle of the river was of utmost urgency. The ice piling up on its decks could sink the ferry or tear it to pieces.

At that time, the closest bridge across the Columbia River was the railroad bridge at Celilo. The ferrymen walked to Celilo and crossed the river on the railroad bridge. It was a perilous undertaking, for the night was dark, the wind savage, and the open trestles slippery with snow. One misstep could send them hurtling into the river below. They made it across the river safely, and after reaching Wishram, Edgar Babcock drove them back to Maryhill.

The ferrymen arrived at Maryhill about 2:00 a.m. and found their friends and neighbors still working to free the ice-bound launch.

Finally they chopped enough ice away, and Mac and the deckhands took the boat out. But they were not able to free the Everyday that night. For the next four days, they blasted, chopped, and dug ice away from the ferry, without success. Late one night, long after the men had quit work for the day, the ice broke. An observer told Mac that the ferry was being carried off downriver by the current, but the ferry pilot soon had the Everyday towed safely to the winter harbor.

"The men sure had a hard, disagreeable task," concluded Rosa Gunkel in a subsequent letter, "but came out victorious."

Gunkel family letters

FAILED DREAMS: THE PLANNED COMMUNITY OF MARYHILL

Rachel Gunkel

Looking at the trees struggling for survival and the dry grasses bending double in a fierce west wind, one has difficulty imagining that the plateau and rolling hills behind Stonehenge would have been anybody's chosen location for an intentional community.

But so it was. This was the site of Sam Hill's planned Quaker community of Maryhill.

Hill platted a town of 34 blocks, with eight streets running north to south named after fruit trees, and seven east-west streets named after shade trees. The only exception was the main street, Jusserand, which was named to honor the French ambassador for coining the name "Maryhill." Jusserand Street ran east and west in front of the stone store/ post office. Peach Street led south to the edge of the bluff. Hill planned to pave all of the streets, but only Peach and Jusserand were completed.

On the edge of the bluff, where Stonehenge is today, Hill constructed the St. James Hotel. Across Walnut Street to the north, Hill built the Maryhill Land Co. office, an "annex" in which he occasionally stayed, and a couple of other cottages used as housing for laborers. West of the store, Hill constructed a carriage house, a blacksmith shop and a garage on Jusserand Street. Hill also built a bungalow for his daughter, called "Mary's Cottage," and a Quaker meetinghouse.

Hill had water piped to Maryhill from his reservoir up in the canyon. He installed hydrants at intersections for fire protection. The houses had indoor plumbing and were on a sewer system. Even though the water supply system had major problems, the town of Maryhill was, as Pete May wrote, "probably more modern than anything in its class."

But Hill's vision of Maryhill never materialized. No Quakers came to buy property. The Quaker meetinghouse was used only once by a small party of

Friends, and Hill had to pay their travel expenses to get them there. Even after Hill gave up on the idea of a Quaker community, he failed to entice other potential buyers. He eventually gave up on the idea entirely, turning his thousands of acres into a cattle ranch.

The stone store, reconstructed garage, and a concrete fountain that never held any water except after a good rain are the only surviving reminders of Sam Hill's intended utopia. He finally got his Maryhill in 1922, however, when the town of Columbus was renamed.

Sam Hill, the Prince of Castle Nowhere, John E. Tuhy, Timber Press, 1983;

Maryhill, Sam Hill and Me, Lois Davis Plotts, Post Publications, 1978;

Postmarked Washington, Guy Reed Ramsey, Klickitat County Historical Society, 1977;

"Columbus" by Pete May, *Klickitat Heritage,* Summer, 1979;

"Maryhill: Columbus Transformed," by Edgar Babcock as told to Pete May, *Klickitat Heritage,* Summer, 1979.

FALLBRIDGE-WISHRAM

Mary Jean Lord

The town next to the railroad bridge near Celilo Falls was first named Fallbridge. In 1926, railroad officials decided to erect a marker commemorating Lewis and Clark's campsite, and they thought an Indian name would be more appropriate for the town. They drew up a petition to change its name to Wishram and instructed W. C. Johnston, the local agent, to get people to sign it.

People were used to "Fallbridge", and no one, including Johnston, wanted to change it. Johnston nearly lost his job when officials came to pick up the petition and no one had signed it.

The railroad officially changed the name to Wishram anyway. For awhile people continued to call their town "Fallbridge," but gradually they were forced to accept the new name.

Local Indians laughed at the white man's distortion of Wisham. Their language has no "r" sound.

Florence Bartholomew, "The Early Days of Wishram," *Ruralite,* April 1963

THE FARMING GAME

George Rohrbacher

Christmas 2004 marked the 25th Anniversary of The Farming Game. It really was Invented on the Seat of a Tractor — I was baling hay at the time. In 1979 my wife, Ann, and I, like hundreds of thousands of other American farmers, were teetering on the edge of insolvency. We borrowed the money and bet our ranch that this crazy idea of mine was going to work.

In its first twenty-five years, The Farming Game has sold well over 500,000 copies. I think our biggest accomplishment so far is that we still live on The Breaks Ranch out on Horseshoe Bend Road. And, we are still farming! I've often been asked, after a quarter of a century on this great adventure, "Does one story jump out above the rest?"

My very best Farming Game story has this family life theme: In February of 1998, I was an exhibitor at the Montana Agricultural Trade Exposition. The last day of the show, I noticed a great big fellow (about 6'6" and 300+ lbs.) eyeballing the new game box from across the aisle. He wore well-used insulated coveralls, size 20 mud-caked boots, and a dirty CAT ball cap. His huge gray-flecked beard grew down to his chest and a shock of wild hair shot out in all directions from underneath his cap. I asked, "Are you familiar with The Farming Game?"

He looked at me and replied, "Familiar with it? Hell, I've bought three of them and we wore two of them out!" Looking at my name tag, he said, "You're the guy that invented the damn thing!" I raised my arms in mock surrender, "I guess I'm caught."

"I want to shake your hand," said the big man, as he stuck out his paw, the size of a catcher's mitt. After three or four shakes, he nearly pulled me over to his side of the display table (and I'm no dainty little thing myself). Our faces were now about a foot-and-a-half apart.

Then, he said to me with all seriousness, "You saved my boys!" A big tear welled up in his eye, rolled down his cheek and disappeared into his beard. He kind of melted, and let me go.

He told me how twelve years earlier, when his marriage was in the last round of a 15 round battle, he was given a copy of The Farming Game for Christmas. Before the New Year, his wife was gone for good, and he was left with three sons. The oldest, 13 at the time, had already been picked up twice by the cops.

Over that Christmas vacation, he and his boys really got into The Farming Game. After the vacation ended, they set up the game every Friday night and played the game all weekend long, an hour here and an hour there. Then late Sunday evenings they would audit, to see who had won. They had been doing this for 12 straight years. Having worn out two Farming Games, they were working on their third.

He said it again. "You saved my boys. You gave us something to laugh about at a time when we weren't doing nothing but yelling at each other. You kept my boys out of jail and you kept me out of the bars. You saved my boys."

I just stood there stunned. I'm not really sure what I said to him in reply. Soon he walked on, and I never even got his name.

My younger brother has been an emergency room R.N. for the last 20 years, and he helps save people all the time. This was the first time for me.

THE FARMING GAME TOO

Kathleen Goode

My husband and I discovered The Farming Game at KC Pharmacy as we were doing our Christmas shopping one year. We thought it would be fun for the family to play during the holidays. It was the best board game we ever bought. The point of the game is to succeed well enough at your farm operation to quit your town job and farm full time. As in real life, it isn't easy to succeed. Farms cost money; cattle get sick and need treatments from the vet; equipment breaks down; and just when you think you've survived the worst, bad weather hits. The ups and downs are hilarious; it's much more fun in a board game than in real life!

The game was invented by local farmer George Rohrbacher, who came up with the idea while sitting on his tractor one day. He wrote about the experience in *Zen Ranching and The Farming Game*. The book covers the early farming efforts of Rohrbacher and his wife Ann, their experience in creating and marketing the game, and the amazing things that happened afterward.

One of the people who loved the Farming Game was Dave Zimmerman. He created an adaptation called

The Construction Game, which was brought to market in collaboration with the Rohrbachers. I haven't played this one yet, but it looks like just as much fun. Since the phenomenal success of the game business, George Rohrbacher has gone on to serve as executive director of a non-profit organization promoting rural economic development, and has served in the Washington State Senate and as a Gorge Commissioner. Now if he could just help us make sense of politics.

The Farming Game website http://www.farmgame.com
Personal experience

Farming Through the Years

Don Ritzchke

Pigs have been raised in the Klickitat Valley since the early settlers came. The Ritzchke brothers, Will and Lou from south of Centerville, drove and sometimes hauled their feeders to Grayback each year, where the boys stayed herding them all summer. Hogs were often pastured in the mountains. Hunters have noticed hogwire fences high up on the Simcoes.

Pigs have been known to keep rattlesnakes away from farms. Pigs supposedly can eat rattlesnakes and not be harmed. I have heard that some folks think Centerville didn't have any rattlesnakes because of the pigs, but I haven't found out who. I did talk with someone who said his neighbor had pigs *and* snakes.

Sheep were a big crop around the area. Bands of sheep were pastured on Mt. Adams in the 1920s and 1930s, sometimes herded from as far away as Roosevelt. Then the government said "no" to pasturing, and the sheep were gone.

Little sawmills were not uncommon in the wooded areas on the Simcoes during the 1920s and 1930s. You could get all the wood you wanted for $2.50 to $5.00 a cord.

Centerville had two groups of folks. The Dutch lived in Dutch Flat, south of town, and the Finns lived on Finn Ridge, west of town, although often the folks in Goldendale just referred to those living in Centerville as "Finns". Tee Yeakel said you didn't have to cross any ditches to get to Goldendale. A two-hour buggy ride could get you to town, with any luck.

After the depression and in the 1940s, farms were acquired in a variety of ways. After poor crops, the Land

Bank would often get a place back. They might sell it to another for what was owed, or just have someone farm it and make a deal later if they couldn't find a buyer. I've heard stories of places that were paid for with just one year's crop. Paying the back taxes sometimes got folks a place.

Percherons, Shires, and other work horses had long been the horsepower for farms, then in the mid 1930s, tractors became a new "toy" for the farmers. The Fordsom tractor was introduced, but folks said a good team of horses could outdo it. The early John Deeres were better, the Internationals "weren't worth a hoot," and the "track layer" by Caterpillar was" the one to get."

Cattle have been in the valley for years, but 50 or so cows was a big herd in the 1930s and 1940s. Today, 300 to 500 head is not uncommon. Ranchers took their cattle by rail or truck to Portland. One year Frank Graham took 100 head of grain-fed steers and got $25 per head. Today those animals would bring nearly $1000.

The gulls weren't so prevalent until after the dams were built.

FERRYMAN RALPH MCDONALD

Rachel Gunkel

Sam Hill Ferry

Ferrymen had exciting lives in the days before the Columbia River was tamed by dams and bridges made crossing the river effortless. Ralph L. Mac McDonald experienced more than his fair share of adventure during his years as a ferry pilot at Maryhill.

On a hot day in August, a group of friends from Goldendale held a swimming party at Maryhill. Three boys dragged an old boat into the water, and the current pulled it into the middle of the river. Without oars, the boys couldn't get back to shore. Mac took the ferryboat out and rescued them. With the tragic drownings of Glenn Robison and Eva Strange at Alderdale the previous week undoubtedly still fresh in his mind, Mac sent the old skiff to the bottom so it could not happen again.

Tragedy was to strike again the following summer, however. Several high-spirited teenagers jumped off the Maryhill ferry as it approached the Oregon shore, intending to swim the last several hundred yards. One boy, James Willis, never made it to shore.

Mechanical breakdowns endangered the ferryboat

as well as its crew and passengers. "On Sunday morning the ferry broke down while in the middle of the river", wrote Rosa Gunkel in October 1928. "Alba Morford was manning it. He drifted over to this side below our house, then was caught by the current. Mac made a raft and got to him. They had the ferry running again before it reached the rapids."

Since all traffic had to stop and wait to board the ferry, the river was a natural point at which to apprehend criminals. When Bobby Conwell was kidnapped from the Goldendale Primary School in April 1925, the sheriff phoned Mac and told him to watch for the suspects and hold traffic until help could arrive. This he did, and when the officers arrived, the parties were taken into custody and brought back to Goldendale. Lawbreakers soon grew more cautious. Before robbing the J.C. Penney store in Goldendale, burglars took the precaution of cutting the telephone lines to Maryhill. They escaped with $500 in merchandise across the river to Oregon.

The weather contributed its own excitement to the job. The west wind, often fierce in the gorge, made operating a ferry difficult. Winter ice made crossing the river dangerous if not impossible. "The ferry boat went across the river today but there was no place to land the cars; the ice is like a mountain", wrote Rosa Gunkel on February 12, 1930. "Mr. and Mrs. Johnson could not cross the river to get home. We never saw the river so blocked with ice for such a long time."

The ferries and the men and women who operated them are gone from the Columbia River. Ferry service at Maryhill ended when the Samuel Hill Memorial Bridge was completed in 1962. Crossing the river today is both safe and convenient, although far less colorful.

Letters of Rosa S. Gunkel, 1928-1930
News items are all from *The Goldendale Sentinel*:
    Mother Kidnaps Son, Is Captured, April 23, 1925, p. 1;
    Maryhill News Items, March 10, 1927, p. 8;
    Maryhill column, September 27, 1928, p.1;
    Two Drowned at Alderdale Ferry on
        Sunday, August 8, 1929, p. 1;
    Maryhill column, August 15, 1929, p. 1;
    James Willis Looses (sic) Life in Columbia,
        July 10, 1930, p. 1;
    Maryhill column, July 19, 1930, p. 1;
    Local Gleanings column, January 22, 1931, p.3.

Klickitat County is filled with natural wonders, but there are a few things we don't have.

We don't have hurricanes, tornados, active volcanoes, tsunamis, or big earthquakes. Floods are rare, and although we do get snow, we don't get blizzards. We don't have months-on-end of rainy days and fog.

We don't have shopping malls, but then there isn't much need for fancy designer clothes either. There is no giant discount store, no traffic jams or road rage, and no need to pay for parking.

We don't have a movie theatre, but there is a rumor that the library will be able to show movies before long. There are no theme parks, miniature golf courses, or video arcades.

We don't have gang warfare, riots, or drive-by shootings.

If you want any of these things, most of them are only a few hours away in just about any direction.

THE FIRE

Clay Schuster

My grandpa and I were out harvesting wheat at the time of the catastrophe; he was driving combine and I was baling straw. As I was turning a corner at the end of the field, I noticed a small plume of smoke on the horizon west of us. I stopped the tractor and began attempting to get my grandpa's attention. He finally noticed me doing what appeared to him to be really uncoordinated jumping jacks. When I yelled, "Fire!" he began running around the combine in a frenzy, looking for flames shooting from some worn-out bearing. When he asked me where the fire was, I pointed to smoke and explained that the combine wasn't on fire.

We moved our equipment to the edge of the field and went back to the ranch to get our Cat. We got the Cat and took off toward the front of the fire. My grandpa usually stops to open gates, but when we came to the first gate he just put the blade down and plowed on through, tearing out the gate posts. Once ahead of the fire, we tried to get several fire lines started but the fire was moving too fast. We finally got a line in across a wheat field. We didn't have time to angle the blade, so cutting a smooth trail was virtually impossible.

We watched the line until some fire trucks arrived

Clay and Art Schuster

at the scene. We moved on to the north fork of the fire, plowing trails as the terrain permitted. We were plowing a trail around the north fork when a guy in a D8 came up behind us and took over our trail. We watched in amazement as he did in a matter of minutes what would have taken us over half an hour with our little D4.

On the north side of the north fork we met up with my mom on our fire truck and my dad spotting for a Cat as I was. By this time it was getting dark, and we began to wonder if our lights would work. Before we started off into the brush again, we stopped and fixed our lights. By this time we were getting pretty hungry; we had been out there for ten hours without food or water. There was a couple of guys from Bishop's Sanitary Service by the side of the road handling refueling for the equipment fighting the fire; they asked us if we needed any diesel, not noticing that they were eating ham sandwiches in front of a couple of very hungry people.

We got back on our Cat and headed for home. We had been out there from noon until midnight and were very tired. I believe now that if we hadn't come in we would have fallen asleep at the wheel. We found out later that the fire had been started by a pickup backfiring in a patch of dry grass. Several miles of our fence and about 60 acres of our range land was destroyed. In all, the fire destroyed 2,000 acres of forest and grassland.

[Clay Schuster, grandson of Art and Charl Schuster, wrote this as an 8th grader, the same year as the fire occurred, in the Pleasant Valley area.]

FIRE, WATER, BRICKS: THE REBUILDING OF GOLDENDALE

Teddy Cole

The Ancients thought the world was made of four elements: water, air, earth, and fire. We know better now, but these four may be the elements for building a city that lasts. The story of the 1888 fire that destroyed Goldendale, and the curse that was said to have caused it, is local lore. The story of how the city rose from the ashes is not so well known.

On the occasion of Goldendale's centennial in 1972, Pete May wrote, "Scarcely had the smoke ceased to rise from the ruins when plans were underway to rebuild in a safer and more substantial manner." According to *The*

Goldendale Sentinel, within six weeks the first brick was laid. By August, a dozen or more buildings were well underway. Residents relied on local materials to rebuild. Town mills turned out lumber from trees cut near home. N.B. Brooks, a local attorney, set up a brickyard along the Little Klickitat east of the Columbus Avenue bridge. Many homes and stores built of the characteristic deep red brick still stand on downtown streets.

May reported that the city widened Main Street before the rebuilding began, setting back every storefront by ten feet. "The result was a street wide enough that a four-horse team and wagon could be easily turned around at any point — at least within a three-block length of street." That decision made possible the angle parking available today in our commercial district.

The fire also demonstrated that Goldendale needed a water system, because the traditional bucket brigade from the nearest well wasn't enough when fires spread. Citizens petitioned the city council, and two years after the fire a bond issue for that purpose passed, 125 to 7. For the first two years of construction, water was pumped from the Little Klickitat. About thirteen miles north of town, the builders located three springs that would serve as the source. Straight pine trees were bored out lengthwise to create the pipes, and the pipeline was constructed by placing the tapered end of the tree into the wider base of the next log. Similarly constructed mains were laid around the city.

While the work was in progress, fire remained a danger. May wrote, "On the evening of September 4, 1890, fire broke out in a stable near the west end of Main Street. Wind was blowing from the southwest and the flames spread to the northeast." Once again, as in 1888, a bucket brigade formed, but this time the fire was caught quickly and subdued. May continued, "A suspicion gained foothold that the city was harboring an arsonist and extra guards were hired. The suspicion was borne out by the capture, a short time later, of the son of the man whose barn had been the source of the previous fire. No more fires occurred after his trial and conviction."

Eshelman, Wayne. Personal recollection.
The Goldendale Sentinel, July 1, 1888
May, Pete. 1972. *100 Golden Years, 1872-1972*. Goldendale
    Centennial Corporation.

First County Roads

Teddy Cole

Hanging Rock 1892

We take our roads and highways for granted, but that wasn't always the case. The Army built the first road to cross Klickitat County. Private subscribers built the second, from the Simcoes to Columbus (Maryhill), in order to supply Columbia River steamboats with fuel wood. No official county roads existed until after 1870. Early settlers resented government interference. When the Territorial officials attempted to impose county government, the settlers ignored it. In time, the residents of the county began to recognize that perhaps a little government might be a good thing, and in 1867 they elected officials whose first task was to lay out roads.

One route ran east from the county seat in Rockport (now Dallesport) along the Columbia River to the Umatilla ferry, the County's farthest eastern point. Another linked with the road west to Skamania. The third, marked out in 1873, ran northeast from the Military Road to Klickitat Creek, the site of present day Goldendale. It continued eastward through Pleasant Valley, on through Alder Creek (Bickleton), and over the Simcoes to Cock's (or Allen's) ferry on the Yakima River, then the county's northeastern boundary. Old Mountain Road may be all that remains of this route.

Eventually Klickitat Valley residents wanted a more direct route so they could take their produce to the developing Yakima Valley. An ancient trail crossing Satus Pass was broadened into a county road around 1890, and sections of that route were incorporated into present-day State Route 97.

One of the problems with the Satus route was the landmark "Hanging Rock," a formation above the roadway two miles north of Goldendale. Crowded on the east by the Little Klickitat and on the west by a solid wall of rock, the road had to pass under this ominous pile. Ray Gosney told that they tried to secure it with cables, but finally blasted it off. "It took a half-case of dynamite to bring it down," he said. The overhang remaining only hints at the amount of the rock demolished.

To call these early routes "roads" is an exaggeration. The road viewers appointed by the commissioners to mark out routes only indicated with notches on trees or a dab of paint on rocks where the road should go. When people got around to actually improving the way, they simply graded by dragging a split log behind a team of horses or oxen.

Robert Ballou wrote, "This beginning of a county road system was just an arm wave of approval. There was very little tax money to maintain county roads or build bridges," and he quoted Howard J. Marshall, an 1870s stage driver: 'The only work done on the roads was what people had to do, so they could travel themselves."

Traveling these roads required endurance for riders; muddy ruts in the fall froze into obstacle courses in the winter and thawed into bogs in the spring. Trips to The Dalles required an overnight stay. In bad weather, even a trip to Columbus or Blockhouse might take two days. Ballou published many colorful travelers' stories in the *Early Klickitat Valley Days* chapter, "County Stage Lines."

The coming of the automobile created the impetus for better roads. Sam Hill, the founder of Maryhill, called the county roads "mere cow trails." At Maryhill he experimented with a variety of paving materials; his famous Loops Road, built in the 1930s, was the first paved road in the state.

Perhaps remembering the effort that went into creating our present county road system will make us more tolerant of the occasional pothole.

Ballou, Robert. 1933. *Early Klickitat Valley Days.*
Personal reminiscence from Ray Gosney, local resident.
Illustrated History of Klickitat Yakima and Kittitas Counties.
    1904. Interstate Publ.
Klickitat County Road Department file #011.
Tesner, Linda Brady. c2000. *Maryhill Museum of Art.*
    Portland OR: Arcus Publ.
Post Route Map, United States Post Office Dept., 1897.
    www.secstate.wa.gov/history/maps.
Washington Good Roads Association, David Wilma,
    February 16, 2003;
Online Encyclopedia of Washington State History, www.
    HistoryLink.org, File 5219

FISH STORY

Sam Lowry

A reporter's world can occasionally be one of strange coincidence, leading to widening circles of story and new understandings about the world. A recent example led from fish to more fish to complexity of competing interests on landscape around Goldendale.

A friend from Portland has been threatening for

years to show me how to fly-fish. One weekend he arrived, maps in hand and a few tidbits of information in his head. He bought a license at McCredy's, and off we went to Spring Creek, below the Goldendale hatchery. There, after his skillful and occasionally successful casts into the cold artesian water — me on shore watching stealthily from behind bulrushes so as not to startle the fish — we had a chance encounter and the first of several fish conversations that day.

The hatchery, I learned from the encounter, is a unique gem, delivering fish — my friend was awed by their size and health — to streams throughout the state. But Spring Creek, I learned, is choked with weeds — non-native canary grass — once introduced to stabilize soils. It is the scourge of soil conservationists. (The hatchery stock, I learned, ironically come from the Andes in South America. Playing games with ecology can go well or poorly.)

Then I learned that the Little Klickitat River might be home to native steelhead and might be up for special restrictions on stocking. Some adjoining landowners, meanwhile, may be doing their own fish stocking.

Not long after my arrival home that same afternoon there came a phone call, a news tip concerning several fish found along a Klickitat County roadside, possibly stripped of their eggs.

Stream stockers?

Fishgate?

Time will tell. Meanwhile, we have the cold ribbon of Spring Creek fighting the weeds, with its fly-fisher's paths set between fields belonging to farmers struggling to make it, upstream from creative, if misguided, landowners playing ecology games, upstream from others deeply into ecology politics.

Here's an object lesson in the layers and layers of interests, often competing, with which even tiny corners of land can be burdened. Fish; farms; landowners; racetracks; windmills; tax bases; cities and countryside; peace and quiet.

It struck me that in all of Klickitat County there are few souls making the least attempt to understand the range of interests and to balance them. I think balance may be the only key to a prosperous future.

Lowry, Sam. 2004. Editorial. *The Goldendale Sentinel*, September 23.

Fish, salmon in particular, was a basic food for the native people of the Columbia River basin. Salmon not only provided physical sustenance but also had profound religious significance. Before the advent of white settlers, natives held hereditary fishing sites that guaranteed a share of the abundant fish for ceremonial feasts and for family meals. When white settlers moved into the seasonally occupied land, the federal army suppressed Indian resistance to the newcomers. A treaty signed in 1855 restricted the land held by the Indians, but promised "the right of taking fish at all usual and accustomed places."

None of those who signed that treaty could have imagined that within a hundred years massive hydroelectric dams would drown customary fishing sites, depriving the Indians of their rights under the treaty. Three dams affected fisheries along Klickitat County shores: Bonneville Dam (1938); The Dalles Dam, (1957); and John Day Dam, (1968). At the time they were built, the federal government promised to replace lost fishing sites, but that promise wasn't enforced until 1989, when Congress passed Public Law 100-581, Title IV — Columbia River Fishing Access Sites. That law came about after a century of litigation from 1887 to 1983, and political action seeking to have the provisions of the 1855 treaty enforced. The Corps of Engineers has designated fourteen "in-lieu" sites in Klickitat County, some of them now completed.

The drama of physical and legal conflict over Klickitat's stretch of the Columbia River goes on. Now all who live here are challenged to work together to restore as much as possible of the lost natural treasures of the Columbia River.

Center for Columbia River History.
    http://www.ccrh.org/

Hunn, Eugene S. et al. c1990. *Nch'i-Wana "The Big River;" Mid-Columbia Indians and Their Land.* University of Washington Press.

Title IV: Columbia River Treaty Fishing Access Sites.
    US Army Corps of Engineers.

FISHING THE KLICKITAT RIVER CANYON

Buzz Ramsey

Klickitat Canyon

With only two of our four lines out, my wife, two boys and I had just started our fishing adventure. I was in the middle of wrapping a fillet of sardine to the belly of a banana-shaped salmon plug. Maggie was pouring hot chocolate, while our two boys (each with a donut in hand) were debating whose rod it was that had a spring chinook on the end of its line.

As the fish raced toward the Columbia River, Blake grabbed the rod and struggled to turn the reel handle against the spinning drag. Maggie, while attempting to get the second rod out of Blake's way, spilled her hot chocolate. I dropped my half-wrapped plug in the bait cooler (which now contained a loose donut too) while trying to move too much stuff out of the way to reach the anchor rope quickly. And if this wasn't enough, Wade (the youngest son) demanded that I immediately hand him the landing net; as if the fish was near our boat instead of rocketing downstream faster than a frightened athlete on steroids!

Our fire drill finally calmed after the deck was cleared of extra rods and food and when I finally lifted the anchor, grabbed the oars, and was backing our drift boat toward Blake's first spring chinook of the season. This 25-pound beauty was finally beginning to run low on gas.

We were fishing the roadless canyon of the Klickitat River where trout, steelhead, chinook, whitewater rapids, inspiring scenery, good summer water flow, and an unspoiled 12-mile canyon draws anglers from around the region and world. To many, it is a very special place.

The fishing, boating, and camping season on the Klickitat River begins in the spring and lasts until fall. The best time is April, May, and early June for spring chinook, September for fall chinook, and June through November for trout and summer steelhead.

The Klickitat is a glacier-fed stream that begins its seaward journey high in the Goat Rocks Wilderness. One of its tributaries from Mt. Adams is appropriately named the Big Muddy; it can make the entire river look that way during hot weather that caused the glacier feeding the "Muddy" to release a silt-filled broth. These dirty-water episodes can last for weeks during the summer until cool weather restrains the release of muck, causing the river's water to clear again and triggering a frenzy among the ravenous fish finally able to see well enough to find food.

Much of the canyon, extending from the Leidl and Stinson Flat access points downstream to the confluence of the Little Klickitat, is prime winter habitat for deer and elk and, as such, was scooped up years ago by the Washington Department of Fish and Wildlife. Undeveloped, this river canyon plays host to cougar, bear, bobcat, skunk, coyote, turkey, grey squirrel, bald eagle, rattlesnake, and more.

When I was in my late twenties, I fell in love with the Klickitat River Canyon after a drift boat trip there. I soon bought land nearby where I built a home, got married and raised two boys. The initial draw for me, lurking in the cool riffles of this unique river, was the summer steelhead that always seem ready to pounce whatever fly, spoon, spinner, plug, or bait is placed into the sometimes clearing water.

Most boaters accessing the canyon section of the Klickitat River for chinook salmon use either back-bounce egg clusters or bait-wrapped Kwikfish. We were using Kwikfish the morning the salmon struck before we were ready, and we landed three additional salmon before we ran out of hot chocolate and donuts.

FISHTAILING

Sara Wu

It was a cold winter's day. I left my home above Goldendale with great care, since the roads were visibly icy. As I descended in elevation, they seemed to clear — nice black pavement. But, slowing at a curve, I was suddenly doing a full-circle spin into a tree. The road was covered with black ice.

It took me twice to learn my lesson. The next time was a warm summer's day with just a bit of drizzle after a long dry spell. I was going down a long, straight road and reached over to the passenger's seat to get an orange. I hit the rounded shoulder and went into the steep gravel. I got back on the road, fishtailing madly, and the brakes only made matters worse. Eventually the opposite bank stopped me. Luckily, both times I had my seat belt on, no passengers, and no on-coming traffic!

The roads of Klickitat County are often straight with little traffic. This does not mean that they are without their hazards. Many of the Klickitat County roads have narrow, graveled, rounded shoulders with steep drop-offs. A moment's inattention, such as changing a cassette or reaching for something in the passenger seat, can throw a car out of control.

Many of the roads follow section lines, with corners close to 90 degrees. The recommended turning speeds may seem slow, but such sharp turns justify them.

The roads are especially treacherous when they are slick. In the winter, roads at a higher elevation may be obviously slippery, then clear up, only to freeze again at a lower elevation. This inversion of temperature is difficult to see. The pavement may appear black and clear, yet have a cover of ice. Summer should not lull you into a sense of security. After a dry spell, just the slightest sprinkle can make the roads unbelievably slippery.

State Highway 14 and US Highway 97 are notorious for such hazards. The accidents along them also reflect driver impatience and inexperience driving on two-lane, high-speed highways. Although there may be long periods without on-coming traffic, it is still necessary to have an adequate view of the road ahead before passing. The curves and dips in the road that obstruct your view are not always evident. It is vital to obey the "no passing" solid, yellow line.

Unpaved roads present their own challenges. Gravel, dirt and washboards in the road require great caution, especially as one is heading downhill. Brakes may be as useless as they are in icy conditions. Narrow roads used by logging trucks mean that there is less margin of error. The signs which say "IMPASSABLE WHEN WET" mean just that. The mud can easily stop even an SUV. Furthermore, trying to get through the mud seriously damages the roads for use when they are dry.

Throughout the county are rangeland areas where farm animals are free to roam. It is the driver's responsibility to avoid collisions. Even in unmarked areas, animals can get out of fences. Deer leap over fences as if they are not there. It always behooves the driver to expect an animal to jump into the road. Dawn and dusk are especially dangerous times for encountering deer.

Although it seems easy, driving in Klickitat County still requires vigilance. Once a car starts fishtailing or an obstructions appears, it is usually too late. Your own experience may be the best teacher, but this voice of experience recommends slowing down, more than you think is necessary.

The Flying L Ranch near Glenwood got its start in 1945 when Les and Ilse Lloyd were invited by Goldendale sheep ranchers, Clyde and Clara Story, to see the Glenwood Rodeo. The valley's beauty convinced them to buy 80 acres about a mile northeast of town for $8,000. The Lloyds and their three small children, Christina and twins Darryl and Darvel, spent the summer and fall of 1946 in a tent cabin on the property.

Their 4000 square-foot "ranch house" (now larger and called the "Lodge") was designed by Ilse's father and constructed in three years by local carpenters. By the spring of 1947, they had built a kitchen big enough for the family to live in temporarily. The huge kitchen included a walk-in cold room — Ilse was already thinking about the guest ranch business. The next year they completed the large living room, with Douglas fir logs supporting a high redwood ceiling. On one end was a massive fireplace made of Mt. Adams andesite flagstone; the heavy lava rocks were hauled a few at a time in the Lloyds' 1939 Chrysler.

"Flying L" comes from the Lloyd name and the 2,000 foot landing strip that was cleared of trees behind the house. Les was a log buyer in Tacoma and commuted in his bi-wing Waco. State foresters, airline pilots (in their small planes), Justice William O. Douglas (who had a home nearby), and many others also used the airstrip until it was closed in 1970. Les also worked worldwide as a forestry consultant under the federal Aid for International Development program. Ilse and the kids stayed at the ranch, except for the years 1956-1957, when they joined Les in Taiwan.

The ranch finally opened for business in 1960. It was a low-key, seasonal guest ranch for the next 25 years. On a typical summer day, Ilse would cook her famed huckleberry pancake breakfast — still featured in 2005 — for three or four guests. Then she'd pack lunches, do housekeeping, get the horses ready, lead a horseback trail ride to the Klickitat Canyon, cook the evening meal, and tell stories in front of the fireplace. Most of her guests became such good friends that they

THE FLYING L RANCH

Judy Thomas

THE FLYING L
GLENWOOD, WASHINGTON

would never be charged. Later, more buildings were added, and a housekeeper was employed during the summer months.

The Lloyd sons grew up climbing nearby Mt. Adams and other peaks. In 1970 they founded the Mt. Adams Wilderness Institute, one of the first wilderness-mountaineering schools in the U.S. Based at the ranch, eight and twelve-day "mini" expeditions that included plenty of glacier climbing drew people from all corners of North America. Closure of the mountain by the 1980 eruption of Mt. St. Helens brought an end to the program.

Les died in an outrigger canoe accident in 1972. Ilse continued to operate the Flying L until 1985, when Darvel took over the management. He made it a year-round B&B inn and retreat. Darryl joined him a few years later. In the years that followed, the ranch became a well-known getaway for individuals and groups of up to 30 or more. Multi-day workshops and seminars were conducted by artists, musicians, writers, photographers, professors of many disciplines, and others.

In 1997 the Lloyds sold the Flying L to Jacquie Perry and Jeff Berend, who continue to make improvements and operate the facility as a retreat center and B&B. Ilse died in 2000 at the age of 85. A plaque and bench on the ranch loop trail marks "Ilse's Lady's Slipper Preserve."

Interviews and email exchanges with Darryl Lloyd
*White Salmon Enterprise.*1986. Flying L sees bright future.
    April 19.

FRONTIER JUSTICE

Frank Wesselius

Justice in early Klickitat County was a lot different than today.

In those days, there was a saloon running in the town of Columbus in violation of the law and causing considerable disturbance. On one occasion, Thomas Jenkins asked the owner of the saloon to desist from selling whisky to the Indians as it made the town unsafe to live in. The saloonkeeper said he would sell whiskey to the Indians as long as he pleased. Exasperated beyond endurance, a number of citizens desired to put an end to the matter.

A company of men, including Thomas Jenkins, Nelson Whitney, Lewis Parrot, Stanton Jones, and William Higinbotham, planned to enter the saloon and empty out all the liquor. As the members of the party were all respected citizens, they chose daylight to execute their design. It was known that the owner kept a loaded shotgun in readiness, also that he was liable to use it. He was a good customer at his own bar and often rendered harmless by intoxication, but it was nevertheless thought a wise precaution to dispose of the shotgun before anything else was attempted. Jenkins walked into the saloon alone, and taking the gun from the counter, discharged both barrels in the air. Then the others entered, each of whom took a keg or demijohn outside to a hole where a hut had once stood, and emptied out the contents. They kept this up as long as there was any liquor left in the building. All the while, the saloonkeeper had been in a drunken stupor. When he came to his senses and found his saloon empty, he made all manner of threats. In the end, he did nothing and the saloon was never reopened.

The saloonkeeper was identified as one who had escaped a vigilante dragnet in the Idaho gold fields. After listening to his dire threats against the citizens of Columbus, Major Higginbotham informed him that "the climatic conditions for hanging people are just as good about Columbus as they are in Bannock, Idaho." The saloonkeeper left town.

Ballou, Robert. *Early Klickitat Valley Days*. 1938, Goldendale, WA: *The Goldendale Sentinel*.

Family lore

William Chambers, A trip through Jenkins genealogy. Unpublished.

FRUITLESS LABOR

Rachel Gunkel

According to local legend, only one family ever bought property from Sam Hill. Although their stay was brief and their name has long been forgotten, the following story was told many times over the years:

A family who wanted to become orchardists was lured to the Maryhill area by the beautiful color brochure that Sam Hill had produced. The pamphlet advertised Maryhill as a veritable Garden of Eden, where anything would grow in the land where the rain and sunshine meet."

But Maryhill proved to be less rewarding and far more work than the brochure had implied. The family knew nothing about farming. They discovered that the business of creating an orchard was hard work and the isolation of the area was difficult to endure.

Still, they persevered and managed to plant a small orchard. The trees grew well that summer.

Then the weather changed and became cold. Snow threatened. The family was afraid that the little trees wouldn't survive the winter, and could not bear to see their work come to nothing. They carefully dug up all of the trees and put them in a shed, covering them with blankets to keep them warm.

The roots of the young trees dried out, and they all died during the winter. When spring came, the family packed up and moved out, never to be heard from again.

For many years, local people would come to peek in that old shed, where the fruit trees had been stacked like cordwood and were still covered in the tattered remnants of wool blankets. Then they would shake their heads in wonder at the ignorance of city folk and go about their business.

The house and shed burned one year in a grass fire, leaving no trace that the family had ever been there.

George Gunkel (one of my father's favorite stories)

MAMIE AND FRANCIS GADDIS PARK

David C. Duncombe

This rustic, wooded park, named for two public spirited White Salmon citizens, was dedicated in March 2003. Located less than a mile north of White Salmon's City Hall on Spring Street, its seven acres of woodland trails border on south-flowing Jewett Creek. Walkers see a variety of trees, some now with identifying signs.

The Park was acquired as a supplemental water supply for the city of White Salmon in 1963. In recent years, volunteer members of the Jewett Creek Streamkeepers have cleared new trails and worked with the City's Action Parks Team to enhance its educational and recreational features.

The City has developed a long-range plan for

improvement of the Park. Soon to be completed will be a wheelchair accessible trail through the most beautiful part of the woods, a directional/interpretive kiosk, and a boardwalk over a wetland demonstration area that surrounds the old water-holding vault. The old vault is newly stone-clad, with a spillway from which water cascades down to Jewett Creek. A future stage of this million dollar park improvement project will see a new Environmental Education Center and a native plant demonstration area.

White Salmon residents and visitors of all ages are welcome to enjoy the Park.

GARBAGE

Kathleen Goode

The postmaster at Roosevelt is getting ready to order modern post boxes. He likes the ornate old boxes they have now; they look very old fashioned the way they are set in a beautiful oak wall. His problems are increasing demand and the fact that he can't get replacement parts. The increased demand is due to the success of the Roosevelt Regional Landfill. The area is now at full housing capacity, and newly built apartments are filling up fast. The school is dealing with increased enrollments, and the camping area is always full. The current increase in gas prices is adding to the pressure on workers to move to Roosevelt rather than commute to the Yakima area or Tri-Cities. It requires about fifty truckers to do all the hauling required for the facility that is one of the largest rail-haul landfills in the world.

Garbage was a simple matter when I grew up. The whole town dealt with trash the same way; everything that could be re-used was cleaned and saved, everything that could burn was handled in a backyard barrel (the resultant ash was spread in the garden), and the little that remained was hauled to the local dump. It was customary to survey the dump area carefully in case someone left something useful like an old lamp or half a can of paint. Every so often the city fathers would send someone over with a tractor to bury the oldest stuff and scrape out a spot for the new.

Today, garbage is a big deal. We are encouraged to reduce, reuse, recycle, and buy green products. Increasing population makes burn barrels an environmental hazard (not to mention the problem with fire season). Seattle now prohibits paper, cans, cardboard, bottles, and yard waste in the garbage of residential or commercial businesses. They are training Master Composters and providing free curbside carts for yard waste. They even have a band called Garbage! In spite of all this, they are still sending trainloads of garbage (not the band) to Klickitat County.

Why would we be willing to accept garbage from Seattle and other urban areas? It pays our county in the neighborhood of 6 to 8 million dollars a year plus thousands in tipping fees (at $3 per truckload). The Roosevelt Regional Landfill provides jobs, not only at the plant, but also for the crews that run the trains in Wishram and the truckers that haul garbage from the trains to the site up on the hill above the Columbia.

The active area is covered at the end of each day, which may be part of the reason there is no smell, even as close as workers' offices. All that is visible are neatly manicured green fields. I wonder if the band is this smart.

THE SONG OF BERT GEER

Rachel Gunkel

At the time of the 1948 flood, Bert Geer lived in a house close to the banks of the Columbia River, just about where the boat launch is now located in Maryhill State Park. As the water grew higher around his house and began to flood the main floor, Bert retreated upstairs. Then, as water began to pour in through the second-story windows, he climbed onto the roof.

When his neighbors arrived in a boat to rescue him, Bert was found standing on the roof peak, clinging to the chimney with one hand and gesturing at the wild water swirling around and through his house, all the while roaring out the words to "Old Man River:"

> Ol' man river, that ol' man river,
> He must know sumpin', but don't say nothin',
> He jus' keeps rollin', he keeps on rollin' along.
>
> Ah gits weary an' sick of tryin'
> Ah'm tired of livin' and skeered of dyin',
> But ol' man river, he jus' keeps rollin' along.

Bert's house survived the flood, for he'd had the foresight to anchor it with cables and chains to large shade trees. This prevented the house from being floated off its foundation and swept away by the flood.

When the U. S. Corps of Engineers acquired a flowage easement through Maryhill preparatory to the construction of The Dalles Dam, Bert's house was moved away from the riverbank. It was sited a short distance east of the Maryhill Church, where it still stands.

This story was one of my father's favorites
Additional details supplied by Ruth Ferguson and Don
    Robison in March 2005
The Goldendale Sentinel. 1968. Geer Family Reduced by
    Deaths of Two. January 18.

GEOLOGY OF KLICKITAT COUNTY

Sara Wu

The bedrock of Klickitat County is Columbia River Basalt up to 10,000 feet deep. From 17 to 6 million years ago, there was a series of 50 or more major volcanic extrusions in the area of the Oregon/Washington/Idaho border from a fault caused by the tectonic plate moving northward from Baja. The basaltic lava ran 300 miles to the Pacific Ocean — a record distance for lava flows. It is visible as Haystack Rock at Cannon Beach, Oregon.

Between volcanic extrusions, loess (fine-grained rock) would blow over the lava. The result is layers of granite separated by more permeable sedimentary rock, which are present day aquifers. The top layer is loess, more recently combined with volcanic ash. This soil rose several hundred feet above the present day ground level and remains fertile when there is sufficient water.

By ten million years ago, the tectonic plate continued movement northward, causing the flat land of the lava flow to buckle and form the Columbia Hills. The Simcoe Mountains, long thought to be a shield volcano, probably are the result of this folding as well as the eruptions of small shield volcanoes and cinder cones. The volcanic action in the Simcoe Mountains is one of the few places in Washington State to produce obsidian, the black, glassy rock used to make arrowheads.

The tectonic pressure from the south met an immovable plug of granite in the Glacier Peak area. This produced a backpressure so that the Columbia Hills east of Stacker Butte are moving south. Folding and erosion has brought the sedimentary beds to the surface. The 20-foot deep, white-to-tan Vantage bed is the aquifer that supplies the springs and waters the vegetation along the sides of the Columbia Hills. The clay in this bed is slippery, which has resulted in many landslides — notably on and above the parking lot at the Columbia Hills Natural Area Preserve.

One to two million years ago and into the present, the Cascade Mountains have been erupting through the Columbia River Basalt to form many mountains, not just the snow peaks. West of the Klickitat River, the land is covered with these volcanic flows. In Trout Lake valley, the land is topped with a series of lahars, the mudflows which came off Mt. Adams over the past 12,000 years.

The Columbia River area has always had a slight depression. This became more prominent with the rising of the Columbia Hills. The Missoula floods further scoured the area to reveal the Columbia River Basalt as well as depositing rounded river rock on the hills and up the tributaries, far above the Columbia River.

As the mountains rose, the White Salmon and Klickitat Rivers became the primary watersheds of Klickitat County. Both take water off Mt. Adams and feed it into the Columbia River. The White Salmon empties into the Columbia at the county's western border, draining the Trout Lake valley. The Klickitat originates in the Goat Rocks, the eastern portion of the Yakama Reservation, the eastside of Mt. Adams and the Simcoe Mountains, reaching the Columbia River at Lyle.

The Klickitat River cuts through the eastern edges of the Mt. Adams lava flows, forming a dramatic canyon bisecting the county. This delineation designates west-county from east-county, reflecting not only different surface geology and climatic conditions, but also the two primary population centers with their different histories. It is the name, Klickitat, that holds the county together.

Bleakney, Darlene Highsmith. 1992. *Dalles Mountain Ranch.* Lynx Communication Group, Inc.

Harris, Stephen L. 1994. *Fire Mountains of the West.* Mountain Press Publishing.

http://vulcan.wr.usgs.gov/Volcanoes/Adams (2005)

Powell, Jack. 2005. Personal communication

Lee and I and our first two children came to Goldendale in 1943. Lee was logging for Ted Wilkins. Roger was born. Life was good.

Our fourth child, Jarene, was a blue baby. Dr. Leary, newly come to Goldendale, became our doctor, caretaker, and friend when Jarene came home from the Portland hospital, coming many, many times to Jarene's special room to help her frail life. McKinney's drug store let us have medicine always, not knowing if they would be paid.

When Jarene was a year old, a lady from Sunnyside brought a story to Harold Ferrelo, publisher of *The Goldendale Sentinel*, that Johns Hopkins in Baltimore had found a surgery that could lengthen lives of blue babies. Mr. Ferrelo published the story, suggesting that the community raise $3000 (impossible, in our sights!) to send Jarene to Baltimore. We were proud and didn't want to accept. The $3000 was quickly raised by caring people. At that time, a twenty dollar bill was rare — a Mrs. Partchee had several children, one very disabled; she cleaned homes to support her family — she gave $20.00. I want to cry when I think how everyone sacrificed for us.

In September 1951, Dr. Leary, Lee, myself, and Jarene flew to Baltimore. The doctors at Johns Hopkins said that Jarene had too many things wrong with her heart to operate. I stayed near the hospital; Jarene was part-time with me, part-time in the hospital. The last of October, the doctor said she couldn't live long, but they would like to do the surgery, trying to save her and studying what might help them save others. Lee flew back to Baltimore, and Jarene had surgery November 9th. A doctor came to talk to us every 45 minutes or so during surgery. When they had finished the worst problem, her vitals hadn't changed, so they went for the next. They did four things, and she lived. At the time of her surgery, Leo Moore led some people to meet at 4 AM and pray for her until we called that the surgery was over. The people who sat with us during surgery, the Illigs, were Jane Lee's parents (Mrs. Robert Lee). Their son had more surgeries and lived to be an adult.

We flew home with Jarene in December. I took her back by train twice for the doctors to study her case. In Baltimore, I lived part-time with Slim Lickliter's cousins — wonderful people. All this travel was covered by the $3000 given by caring Goldendale people.

GIVING GOLDENDALE

Marie Ritter

Jarene lived 17 months after surgery. What better place to live than Giving Goldendale, the town that takes care of their own.

GOLDENDALE'S CARNEGIE LIBRARY BEGINS

Teddy Cole

The Carnegie Library Fund provided the money to build Goldendale's library, but the library owes its existence to the efforts of a determined band of women led by Louise Dorman.

Dorman learned that the Washington State Library offered a "Traveling Library" consisting of books for children packed in large wooden shipping crates. The boxes were sent out to rural towns all over the state, a program begun by the State Federation of Women's Clubs but taken over by the State Library in 1901. To qualify, the community needed a responsible group to care for the books and return them on schedule.

To form such a group, Goldendale women organized a local Federated Woman's Association on June 10, 1912. At their first meeting, the members voted to establish a library committee and to accept the offer of a room in the elementary school building for a town library. It would be open "once a week, on Saturdays, from 1-6 p.m.., with two ladies in charge." They appointed a library committee that included Mrs. Dorman, Mrs. Lancaster, Mrs. Frederic Wilson, and Mrs. E. R. Morgan, President of the Association.

Under their auspices, the Traveling Library boxes began to arrive. Moreover, many residents of the community donated books, so that the shelves in the schoolroom were soon filled.

Dorman heard about the Carnegie Library Fund, established to provide money for library buildings. To be eligible, they needed to own a lot free and clear, they needed a city resolution guaranteeing support, and they needed a set of plans that could be built within the grant amount. Once funded, the Carnegie officials wanted the project to proceed without further money from them.

The concern of the women was more immediate: where to find a suitable lot and how to raise the money to buy it. October 12, 1912, the city council awarded them an annual allowance of $1,000 for maintenance of the library. The mayor appointed a five-member

Board of Library Trustees, consisting of C.T. Camplan, owner of the State Bank of Goldendale, Mr. E.O. Spoon, a local teacher and businessman, and three women of the original library committee.

In March 1913, Mrs. Morgan and Mrs. Willis went to Portland commissioned to find an architect to design the building. In the meantime, the board was looking for a building lot and developing a campaign to solicit contributions. The following May, they settled on the three lots on the northeast corner of Burgen and Grant Streets owned by James and Amanda Stackhouse; that August they paid in full the $800 for the lots.

We don't know all the ways the women raised that money, but we know they were inventive. They sponsored a special promotion of "Wheat Eats" at the Ledbetter-Wallace store during the annual horse fair, with the proceeds going to the library fund. They operated the Waters-Rothschild store for a day, all the day's profits going to the fund. They organized benefit baseball games between "The Fats and the Thins" and between the Grangers (farmers) and the businessmen. They bought a dozen gross of pencils for the fifth and sixth graders to sell at five cents apiece, with a prize for the class that sold the most.

Finally, after months of correspondence with Carnegie, on July 24, 1914, the officials issued a check for $8,000. The Committee had chosen well, hiring Doyle and Patterson of Portland to design the lovely brick Colonial that is the centerpiece of our present library. Construction was completed by year's end, and the new library opened to the public in March 1915.

A small group of determined women can be a formidable force for good.

Louise Dorman doesn't appear in Goldendale records until the organization of the Woman's Association, and in 1913 she resigned from the Library Board because she would soon be leaving the area. She doesn't turn up again until the 1930 Federal Census, when she and her husband were living in Seattle. The Library Board minutes refer to her as "Doctor," but doctor of what? However, Louise was clearly the motivating spirit behind the library campaign. Thank you, Louise, our Good Angel of the Goldendale Library.

May, Pete. 1982. *History of Klickitat County*. Klickitat County Historical Society.

Larson, Wanda. 1963. Biography of a Library. *Ruralite*. August.

Reynolds, Maryan E. 2001. *Dynamics of Change; a History of the Washington State Library*. WSU Press.

Unpublished documents from Goldendale Community Library files, including Carnegie Corporation correspondence, "Library [Board] Records," Book #1, June 10, 1912-Dec. 2, 1930; misc. historical articles.

GOLDENDALE GRANGE #49

Mary Anne Enyeart

Goldendale Grange #49 was formed in 1911. Their first hall was an old school house that had been moved to town. The Grange gave farmers and ranchers a chance to exchange ideas and consider legislation affecting rural areas. Once a month there was food to share, household hints to pass along, and children were always welcome.

In 1948 a new Grange hall was built in Goldendale at Brooks and Wilber streets; much of the labor and materials were donated. Then in 2002 a new building adjacent to that hall was built, with generous donations and many volunteer hours. These facilities are available for rent and are used in many ways such as by church groups, 4-H groups, community meetings, family reunions, and wedding receptions.

You don't need agricultural ties to join the Grange, just a desire to be part of a grassroots organization that encourages community involvement and understanding the dealings of our legislature. Goldendale Grange #49 meets on the fourth Thursday of each month. Any farm business or the WSU Extension office can tell you who to contact about membership.

GOLDENDALE HOSPITAL STORIES

Joan Telford

On April 1, 1943, Cecil Allyn received a telephone call telling him his fourth child was a boy. Cecil already had three daughters and fully expected another girl, so he believed it to be an April Fool's joke. The Allyns were living in Vancouver at the time, and Frances had returned to Goldendale to have "Grandma" Eva Radcliffe help with her delivery.

(Eva Beeks Radcliffe operated the County Poor Farm

at Cliffs with her husband Emmett until Emmett's death from a heart attack. Eva then returned to Goldendale and converted the house at 528 E. Burgen St. into a maternity/nursing home. Doctors would go to Eva's home to deliver babies rather than to the mothers' homes. Eva became "Grandma" to most of the babies born in Goldendale from 1933 until she retired from Klickitat Valley Hospital.)

The Allyn family was just recovering from the measles, and daughter Joan had a ruptured ear drum, so she accompanied Frances to Goldendale. While waiting for the baby to come, Joan stayed with Velma and Frank Linden, Frances' uncle. Their son, Duane, was a newlywed at the time, and his wife, Betty, always called him "honey." Joan, almost five years old, decided that was his name, and called Duane "Honey" throughout her high school years.

•••

The Goldendale General Hospital was located in the large former residence of Dr. F. H. Collins at the northwest corner of Collins St. and Grant St. Dr. Rosser P. Atkinson had leased the large house from the owner, Mrs. Myrl McAllister, and had converted it into a hospital.

The Allyn children woke up one morning in 1946 with yellow skin and eyes and feeling puny. Jean and Joan were serious enough with yellow jaundice to be taken to the hospital. Joan remembers being in a ward with four beds, just inside the front door of the hospital. The children were given IV fluids and were told they could not go home until they were able to eat. They were lonesome and wanted to go home, so they hid food under their mattresses to make it appear that they had eaten all of their food. Jean remembers hiding burnt toast since, in those days, children were taught to "eat everything on your plate."

One fall morning, 10-year old Sharon Wilson Gisler and her friend, Linda Lundberg Davies, were walking Sharon's heifer to the fair: north on Columbus Ave., then west on Byars St., when Sharon suddenly became violently ill. She left her heifer in the street with Linda, then ran to the Little Klickitat River, where she lay in the cool water until help arrived. She was taken to Goldendale General Hospital, where she remembers being carried to the operating room in the arms of Dr. Atkinson to have her appendix removed.

It wasn't unusual for Dr. Atkinson to carry his patients into surgery, since the hallways of the hospital were so narrow that a standard gurney could not negotiate the turn into the operating room.

The History of Klickitat County, pp 20, 312.
100 Golden Years, p 67
The Goldendale Sentinel, December 15, 1949
Jean Allyn Smeltzer, Emmett W. Miller, Linda Lundberg
    Davies, Sharon Wilson Gisler

GOLDENDALE LOGGING COMPANY

Joan Wilkins Stone

The Klickitat Pine Box Company had for several years employed gyppo or contract loggers to furnish the log supply for their boxes. In 1939, the company decided to go into logging on their own.

The Goldendale Logging Co. was formed with Ted V. "T.V." Wilkins as president, Philip Hingston as vice-president, and Howard L. Lewis as secretary-treasurer. A newspaper clipping found in the family album reported, "Mr. Wilkins is an outstanding contract logger in the district, Mr. Hingston is manager of the Klickitat Pine Box Co., and Mr. Lewis is one of the members of the Lewis-Bean Co. of Seattle, major owner of the Klickitat Pine Box Co."

The company purchased 200 million feet of Ponderosa pine east of Satus Pass, which was about 20 miles from the mill. This was enough timber to supply the mill for 15 to 20 years.

The company had an exclusive contract with Klickitat Pine Box for all of the firm's logging operations, including delivering box shook (parts of a box) direct to box users. Large quantities of boxes were needed for the war effort to package ammunition and supplies. Bill Wilkins, Sr., son of T.V. and CEO of the Wilkins, Kaizer, Olsen Mills in Skamania County said, "Dad had to promise that he would keep logs in the pond 12 months of the year, no matter the weather. He did it for 9 years."

The company purchased an International TD18 diesel tractor for skidding logs to the landing — one of the first of that model to go into logging service in the West. In September of 1943, T.V. was looking for a cat skinner to handle the big tractor. Hoping to find work, Lee Ritter had come to Goldendale with his wife Marie.

Lee and T.V. met each other at the Unemployment Office in Goldendale and struck up a conversation. T.V. needed a cat skinner; Lee needed a job. T.V. hired him with a handshake, and they worked together until the companies dissolved.

"No one surpassed Lee as a heavy equipment operator. He could log the steep ground and maneuver his tractor through treacherous situations and make it look easy," said Bill.

Later the Goldendale Logging Co. became T.V. Wilkins Logging Co., with Roy Kaiser, Ray Wilkins (T.V.'s brother), and T.V. Wilkins, owners. They no longer transported the box shook to customers in Yakima, Hood River, and White Salmon Valleys. They did continue to handle all the logging and transporting of logs to the mill.

T.V. retired from logging in the early 1970s. Farming had always been a part of his life, and he continued to plough the fields and oversee the land into his 80s. He was a steward of the land, whether logging or farming.

T.V. and his wife Vera were born and raised in Klickitat County. Three of their grandsons live in Goldendale: Greg and David Stone, and Scott Wilkins.

The Goldendale Sentinel. March 23, 1939.
Interview with Bill Wilkins, Sr.

GOLDENDALE OBSERVATORY

Kathleen Goode

What do Yakima Community College students, Scout groups, and Klickitat County tourists have in common? They all visit the Goldendale Observatory. Yakima students are sure to visit when they are taking Astronomy 101 (the teacher gives extra credit for visits!) On any given day in the summer, it is not unusual to find a scout group there, especially if they are camping at Maryhill or Brooks Memorial Park.

The focal point of the Observatory is a 24.5 inch Cassegrain telescope, one of the largest telescopes open to the public. Many scopes this size are reserved for scientific observations. This scope was built by four men from Vancouver: M. W. McConnell, John Marshall, Don Conner, and O. W. Vander Velden. They felt that Goldendale would be a good location for the scope because there was little commercial lighting to compete with the celestial view. The 20-foot dome, completed in 1973, that houses the scope was built with donations and a federal grant. The State Parks Commission purchased the site in 1980. The Observatory also includes several other telescopes and was designated as the official headquarters of the National Astronomical League for the Total Eclipse in 1979.

Steve Stout, facility supervisor, is well-versed in astronomy. He gives a talk before each viewing session about what can currently be seen. Call ahead if you have a large group, and be sure to take along a warm coat and hat. The web page http://www.perr.com/gosp.html includes schedules and a Clear Sky Clock to show probable weather conditions.

Washington State Parks "Goldendale Observatory" http://www.parks.wa.gov/parkpage.asp?selectedpark=Goldendale%Observatory&pageno=1
"Goldendale Observatory State Park" http://www.perr.com/gosp.html

GOOSE ATTACK

Rita J. Liska

Tired after a long, busy day, I drove north on Cedar Valley Road wrapped comfortably in my big Chevrolet pickup with full camper and pulling a stock trailer. As I topped a series of small hills, I noticed a pickup that I'd never seen before following a short distance behind.

Ahead in the roadway, I caught a reflection of something in the road. I stepped on the brakes, thinking that a vehicle might be stalled or a buck or elk might be crossing the road, and that I needed to warn the fellow behind me I might have to stop.

When I could see clearly, I discovered two large gray geese standing in my lane, making themselves at home on the pavement. I stopped and waited. They did the same.

That is when I learned that you don't honk at a goose. They honked back, stood up, spread their wings across my lane and the center line, and ran at me like a pair of linebackers. Dumbfounded, I began to back up, forgetting all about the pickup behind me. Fortunately, he had also begun to back up to get out of my way, so here went two large vehicles in reverse being chased by two big birds.

I stopped and waited for a goose attack. The geese

were so close under my vehicle that I could no longer see them.

Knowing I had to move on, I decided that somebody might soon have goose foot soup. I shifted into gear and left the area without incident.

I pulled into my lane, walked several yards to my mailbox, and was reading the paper as I meandered back to my equipment. Looking up, I noticed the pickup coming down the hill and pulling off the road behind me.

I apologized for suddenly going into reverse ahead of him and asked about his delay. He informed me that after I had gotten past the geese, they had attacked *his* pickup too.

It was a dreary midsummer night with just a sprinkle of rain in the early evening. I sat listening to my scanner while devoting most of my attention to the television set.

I recognized alarmed neighbors' voices, a familiar voice from the Department of Natural Resources, voices of people I knew from the Sheriff's Office. Despite this cool evening, we were well into fire season. They were all searching for the source of a fire very near my home. The odor of smoke was fresh and close, but oddly, no one could locate it.

Throwing on my jacket and boots and climbing into my 4X4 pickup, I decided to go see if I could help with the search — and spent the oddest hour of my life in the Simcoes.

The sky was black, the storm stalling above us, but the rain had stopped. The roadway was wet, and my headlights reflected off droplets of water hanging from leaves as I turned from my own half-mile lane onto the pavement. There I met the first fingers of bumper-high fog drifting from Mill Creek straight at me, and with them the odor of fresh smoke.

I crossed the bridge and headed farther up the mountain toward where my friends were searching and watched those fingers of fog turn back on themselves and follow my vehicle as though trying to catch it. Topping the rise on Cedar Valley road, I met similar wisps of fog reaching toward me from the woods at the roadway's edge. I thought of a gothic novel with the

A GOTHIC NIGHT IN THE SIMCOES

Rita J. Liska

fingers of fog surrounding an old coach approaching a distant castle, and I could actually feel the hairs on the back of my neck begin to twitch as I drove through the fog.

I located the various searchers and a D.N.R. water truck. Nobody had any idea where the fire was. All homes that might have built a fire had been checked long before.

No fire was ever located. Crews remained out in the timber long after I returned home. Everyone out there was used to nights in the woods, but all were uneasy over the odd fog.

When I drove down Cedar Valley Road toward home, the fog's limbs leaped out toward my tires as before, followed a short distance behind, and retreated as others took their place. At the bridge, the fog again disappeared, and my nerves quieted as I turned back up my own lane.

I'm a night person. I used to hike, ride, and drive those areas at all times of the night — even helping with searches. But I have never before experienced the feeling I had that night. And, I wasn't the only one.

GRAY DIGGERS

Tom Beck

My wife and I moved to Ponderosa Park above Goldendale in the spring of 2003. We were city folks and not sure what to expect.

One of our first experiences was with the gray digger squirrel. It is not an indigenous species to this area.

We started feeding them along with birds and deer. We soon found out that sharing is not one of their strong suits. They would aggressively keep other wildlife from the food.

We told some neighbors how cute we thought these animals were. They chuckled and said we would soon change our minds. We were told that these creatures would crawl under our house and vehicles and eat the wiring and anything else they deemed edible.

It wasn't long before I purchased a small caliber rifle and made short work of these invaders. I was now the great white hunter.

Summer, 1974, I was the Grayback Mountain fire lookout. Sixteen miles northwest of Goldendale, Grayback was one of a handful of lookouts operated by the Washington State Department of Natural Resources (DNR) in Klickitat County.

The lookout cabin was built on a ten-foot-tall cement block foundation—fourteen feet square, with windows all around extending from two feet above the floor to the ceiling. There was a catwalk circling the cabin with a trap door that could be dropped and latched for security. Amenities included a narrow bunk with drawers underneath, a small table and bench, and a bit of counter. Propane gas powered the compact stove, refrigerator, and heater. The outhouse was a short walk away. The seemingly barren dirt around the lookout was covered with the delicate pink ground-hugging blooms of bitterroot.

After the initial jolt of transition from a crowded college dorm to the absolute solitude of the lookout, the days settled into a pleasing routine. The lookouts signed on first thing every morning via radio. I always imagined our voices cued in the air like planes waiting for permission to land. "Good morning, Southeast. Grayback is 10-8." From then until sign-off late in the evening (and often beyond), my job was to scan my 360 degrees of horizon every few moments.

I quickly learned the names of buttes, ridges, streams, and valleys from the Osbourne Firefinder topographical map placed on a wooden stand smack in the middle of the cabin. The Firefinder is a circular table with a rotating outer ring. A horsehair is stretched between the vertical metal sights opposite each other. When smoke was seen, the lookout rotated the ring to line up the base of the smoke through the two sights, placing the fire somewhere along the horsehair line on the map. Identifying the location was often complicated by wind drift, haze, and the quality of light. As soon as the lookout called in a smoke, the other lookouts in the area swung their Firefinders around to see if they could obtain another compass bearing. Two bearings intersecting on the map would pinpoint the fire.

While fire suppression was in progress, the lookouts kept a brief running log of the radio traffic, noting what units arrived when, progress of the fire, and efforts of the crews. Sometimes a crew would be working "in a hole" where radio transmissions went up but not out.

The lookout then relayed messages between the crew and other units.

During thunderstorms, the lookout watched for lightning strikes, using a grease pencil to mark ticks around the edge of the Firefinder. Those spots would get prolonged scrutiny, since lightning-caused fires often smolder for days before erupting into flame.

The crash of thunder is bone rattling when simultaneous with the flash of lightning overhead! Middle-of-the-night thunderstorms offered spectacular light shows, often leading to morning valleys shrouded in pale pink fog, while Grayback hovered above the clouds with Mt. Adams, Mt. Hood, Mt. Rainier.

Daily, at a given time, we noted maximum and minimum temperatures over the past 24 hours, humidity, wind speed and direction, and cloud cover, and radioed them to the District Office for compiling and assessing fire danger levels. Twice a day, I radioed myself 10-7 (out of service) and strolled a quarter mile east in order to check the ravines in Grayback's blind spot.

In my first week, the clattering of grasshoppers as they scattered ahead of my footsteps startled me. "Rattlesnake!" I thought. But I quickly grew accustomed to the creatures of my solitary home. My first rattlesnake sighting was just a few yards away from the cabin. Both the snake and I froze, then moved carefully away from each other. While the first few weeks felt lonely, by the end of the summer I came to resent the intrusion of visitors.

Today, aerial surveillance prevails, and many of the former lookouts have automated weather stations. Most of the buildings are boarded up, and some have been torn down, including Grayback in 1996.

My summer at Grayback was life-changing. Of all my many jobs since, I would take up fire lookout again in a heartbeat: the scent of pine and sage heavy in the air, the chatter of squirrels in the nearby huckleberry bushes, the heat of late afternoon sun tempered by constant breezes, the wide vistas in every direction. Bliss.

Wall of Water at Wishram

A heavy snowfall on hard frozen ground, then a rise in temperature, a torrential rain, and a warm chinook wind — it was a recipe for disaster. December 1964 is remembered in Klickitat County for its devastating floods.

On December 21, a great wall of water roared through Wishram carrying boulders, rocks, snow, and mud, with "a sound one never forgets," resident and freelance writer Florence Bartholomew recalled. It carved out chunks of pavement from the road into town and filled basements and homes. Townspeople rushed outside to open up snow banks and try to divert the water.

"Is God mad at us?" a little girl asked.

One group of men rushed up the hill with shovels to try to save the entrance road into town. They barely escaped with their lives when a second wall of water and debris roared down the mountain. Quicksand formed, clutching the feet of the unwary.

Roosevelt's Unexpected Guests

Roosevelt, too, was cut off from the rest of the world. Flooding and slides had washed out tracks and closed the highway in both directions, stranding two passenger trains. From December 22nd to 24th, the village played host to 320 adults, numerous children, and the train crews. Local people found accommodations for mothers with babies and beds for the sick, including a diabetic running low on insulin and a very ill ten-year-old boy.

Drinking water at the depot was out of commission due to flood and frozen pipes, and the town's pump worked 24 hours a day trying to keep up with the unusual demand. Besieged by needy passengers, the owner of the town market quickly set up a rationing system.

Fuel was needed fast, as the storage tanks on the train had only enough diesel to last half a day. White-Ott-Atwater Construction happened to be set up in Roosevelt, relocating tracks that would be flooded by the John Day Dam. They came to the rescue, hauling fuel from their big storage supply to the train to keep passengers warm in below-freezing temperatures.

Roosevelt had only one phone booth, and service was erratic with the phone company run ragged trying to keep its lines in working order. Everyone wanted

THE GREAT FLOOD OF 1964

Mary Jean Lord

to call out. Soon the coin box was full and refused to accept any more coins, so no calls could be made. By the second day, supplies of cigarettes and matches were exhausted, and smokers began suffering from withdrawal.

Attempting to add a bit of cheer, "Army engineers flew in and dropped food, necessities, and a Yule tree," Bartholomew writes. "The tree plummeted straight down and stuck in the ground, stood erect and tall for a minute, then gently tipped over on its side.

"A young mother with three children saw the drop and burst into tears. Then, her children, one by one, began to cry."

A chorus was formed, dancers found and entertainment organized. People cheered up. The Roosevelt folk planned a huge potluck for Christmas, but it wasn't necessary. Section crews repaired the tracks and a few hours before the party was scheduled, the town's uninvited guests pulled out.

Klickitat Flood Watch

Meanwhile, the residents of Klickitat nervously watched the relentless rise of the Klickitat River. By 2 a.m. on December 22nd, twenty families had been evacuated. About 200 people sheltered in the high school gym, in the Lutheran Church, or with families on the hill. Everyone carried small valuables and necessities, such as clothing, blankets, and food. Two teenagers brought their love letters. At the gym, the women prepared turkey with all the trimmings.

For three days the town was isolated with bridges out, roads impassable, water supply gone, and telephones dead, and their only communication with the outside world a ham radio operator. The filtering plant was destroyed, and the sewage disposal system flooded out. On Christmas Day people washed dishes in snow water and boiled snow for drinking.

Bartholomew writes, "Though many of us lost homes and property, some of us lost only our dignity, like the lady who, a week after the storm was over, stepped out on the green lawn on a sunny day to hang her laundry to the tune of a chirping robin and promptly sank to her knees in the soft, wet earth."

Bartholomew, Florence. *Ruralite*, March 1965.

THE GREAT SQUAWFISH DERBY

Mary Jean Lord

Endangered species experts have devised many projects to save Columbia River salmon. One of the strangest was the Squawfish Derby, sponsored by Bonneville Power Administration each August in the early 1990s. The Derby was intended to help control one of the main predators on young salmon bound for the ocean.

Northern squawfish have silvery bodies, small heads, a long snout, and a large mouth, and they have an enormous appetite for salmon smolt. BPA set up fish collection stations along the river, including several in Klickitat County, and paid a three-dollar bounty for each squawfish that was eleven inches or longer.

Everyone, young or old, who liked to fish competed for prizes for the longest squawfish and the most squawfish turned in. Bonneville recommended fishing downstream from dams or hatcheries or "wherever groups of gulls gathered."

"Lures that move and look like young salmon work the best," one BPA brochure advised. "A good bet is a white, lime green, black or gold rubber worm on a 3/8 ounce lead bass jig. When all else fails, use worms. Or try something different. Experiment."

Ruralite. August 1992.
Personal memories

GREEN POWER

Barbara Patterson

What does Klickitat County have in abundance over most counties in the Pacific Northwest? Green power!

Green power describes electricity produced by sources that are less harmful to the environment than fossil fuels. These are renewable power sources such as solar, wind, geothermal, biomass, and small hydroelectric.

Biomass is organic material — wood, garbage, and agricultural wastes — which has stored sunlight in the form of chemical energy. The Klickitat County Public Utility District (KPUD) gas-generating station at Roosevelt captures the methane gas produced as garbage decomposes and uses it to generate electricity. Oregon's Climate Trust, an agency that works to promote climate change solutions, states that each KPUD engine at the landfill "removes 342,000 metric tons of CO_2, equal to removing 58,000 cars from the road for a year." More green power is produced at McNary

Dam near Umatilla, Oregon. The small hydroelectric plant is jointly owned by KPUD and the Northern Wasco County PUD. This was the first green power project for KPUD. It was heartily endorsed by fisheries agencies because it corrected a design flaw in the fish ladder, saving smolt (the young salmon migrating from fresh water to the sea).

Wind is no stranger to Klickitat County. Windsurfers love it. Gardeners loathe it. KPUD plans to put it to work by participating in both large and small wind power development projects.

Klickitat County is noted for its clean air and blue skies. That won't change anytime soon. Green power is here to stay.

Klickitat County PUD website http://www.klickpud.com/
    power/default.asp
Svendsen, Tom. 2004. Green Power, Anyone? *Ruralite*.
    August.
Mary Jean Lord, retired KPUD employee

ROSA GUNKEL: THE FLOWER LADY OF MARYHILL

Rachel Gunkel

On November 3, 1926, several thousand people flocked to Sam Hill's mansion on the Columbia River to see Queen Marie of Romania dedicate the still unfinished building as Maryhill Museum of Art.

Rosa Gunkel was there also, but she was present not just to catch a glimpse of the queen. She was there to see how her flowers had been used. Sam Hill had bought Rosa's entire crop of chrysanthemums. Great masses of the colorful flowers, set off by green pine boughs, had been artfully arranged into swags and bouquets to alleviate the starkness of the mansion's rough bare interior.

The decoration was quite a tribute to Rosa's skill as a gardener, and one that brought her a measure of local fame. A year after the museum dedication, Rosa was still receiving complements: "...it was rather embarrassing, she wrote to her daughter, "for so many people would say 'Are you the lady that grows those lovely chrysanthemums?' So you see I am branded!"

Rosa began receiving letters and inquiries addressed to "The Flower Lady, Maryhill."

Publicity and praise fueled both Rosa's ego and her ambition to expand her flower business. "I must have more flowers and better quality next year," she wrote. "It is such a pleasure to raise nicer ones than anyone else."

Rosa learned the value of advertising, placing a small ad in *The Goldendale Sentinel* every season. She recognized the value of word-of-mouth advertising, and made it a practice to give flowers to neighbors and send bouquets to friends in other locations. Her motives were not just monetary, however, for as she noted, "it certainly is delightful to know somebody is made happy."

Rosa developed methods for packing and shipping flowers so that they would arrive fresh at their destinations. Much of her business was relatively local, but she also sent flowers as far away as Nebraska, Colorado, Minnesota, and San Francisco. Her flowers were shipped by parcel post on the train.

Throughout the difficult depression years, Rosa's flower business continued to grow. She became a little indignant with her brother Alfred Softley when he remarked on the folly of buying flowers when people had no money for food. She wrote "Alfred said that it was a shame to buy flowers when so many folks were in need of the necessaries of life. Well, folk will have them, and they most always pay for them. I'll bet none of those people go hungry and would not give money to the needy anyway."

Rosa grew lilies, snapdragons, roses, and many other kinds of flowers in addition to chrysanthemums. She supplied flowers for weddings and funerals, Easter, Mother's Day, and Memorial Day.

"I am like a little kid, enjoying my second youth," she wrote. "I have so much pleasure playing in the dirt planting flowers."

Arthritis finally forced Rosa to cut back on her gardening when she was 85, but her love of flowers remained constant for the rest of her life.

Letters of Rosa S. Gunkel, 1927-1934
"The Flower Lady of Maryhill," by Wanda Larson,
    Ruralite, 1967
Classified advertisement, *The Goldendale Sentinel*,
    October 29, 1929

GUNNING'S JEWELRY AND BOOKSTORE

Joan Wilkins Stone

The Gunning Jewelry and Bookstore was a refuge during my middle school years. I was either hurrying home to go to the farm with Dad, or heading to the bookstore. It was filled with mystery, romance, travel, and times gone by. Each book held a treasure between its pages.

The store was located on the north side of West Main Street. Squeezed between Pike's Drugstore and McKenzie Hardware, the little store stood out only because of its content and warm atmosphere. The earthy color of the walls, the plank flooring, the muted lighting, and the shelves lined with books created an aura of comfort during a time of disquiet, as the war with Germany and Japan raged on.

Mr. and Mrs. Gunning were the owners of the store. Nadine Hamllik McKinney, a lifetime resident of Goldendale, remembers Mrs. Gunning as a really old lady who wore a wig. Of course we were young then, and probably neither was true. Nadine spent many hours browsing through the pages of books. Her Mom bought a ruby ring from the store, and Nadine still has the box and the ring. Inside the box it says, "D. Gunning Jeweler, Goldendale, Washington."

The store was quiet. Customers spoke in hushed voices, even in the small jewelry area. Mr. Gunning would be busy repairing watches or showing rings. Mrs. Gunning, keeping an eye out for the needs of customers, could be found reading to a small child, helping a teenager find a suitable book for a book report, or visiting with a friend.

I think the bookstore was a diversion for Mrs. Gunning. I never saw anyone buying a book; we read them there. Mr. Gunning, his green eyeshade strapped around his head, must have made the living.

Yes, a bookstore can create dreams, calm fears, challenge the mind, and soothe the soul. For many of us of a certain age, Gunning's Bookstore did just that.

Personal experience
Interview with Nadine McKinney by telephone,
    August 2004

Roll On, Columbia is familiar to many, not only in Klickitat County, but throughout America. Thanks to Woody Guthrie's visit to our area in 1941, the Klickitat River as well as the Columbia River is memorialized in this song

During Woody's youth, his family's well-being was ravaged by the Great Depression and family tragedies, such as the death of his sister in a fire and his mothers' institutionalization for Huntington's Chorea. Part of the mass migration from the land, he developed his sense of marginality, a love of the open road, and his political convictions.

Woody came to Klickitat County at the age of 28, compliments of the Bonneville Power Administration. The BPA was updating a film, *Hydro* by Stephen Kahn, its first public information officer, who insisted that the head of the BPA, Dr. Paul Raver, hear Woody sing. Kahn told Woody to "just play your guitar and sing the songs" and not to talk, in order not to appear too radical. After hearing an hour of Woody's folk songs, Raver gave him a 30-day assignment (the longest emergency appointment available) to write songs for their film. Each day, Woody explored a different segment of the river system in a BPA 1940 black Hudson driven by Elmer Buehler, now of Portland, who was to show him the people, the country, the projects, and the river. Celilo Falls was one of his stops.

Woody wrote 26 songs in those 30 days, for which he was paid $266.66. Part of his composing and arranging was in the back seat of the Hudson on the way back from his visits. His most famous song is *Roll On, Columbia*. Thinking the Columbia River incorporated about the most beautiful places he'd ever been, he noted that he was "pretty certain that everybody just first coming into this country has got some such similar song in his or her head." Woody said he used place names so that "people would grab hold of the songs and use them." On April 23, 1985, Woody's son, Arlo Guthrie, performed a special concert at BPA, singing this song and the similarly titled *Roll, Columbia, Roll*. The Columbia River Collection contains these and other songs about the area and its development, including *Columbia Waters* and *Talking Columbia*.

In 1987, Washington State declared "Roll On Columbia, Roll On" (*Roll On, Columbia*) to be the official

Roll On Columbia
(first two verses)
Woody Guthrie/ Michael Loring

Chorus:
Roll on, Columbia, roll on
Roll on, Columbia, roll on,
Your power is turning our
darkness to dawn
Roll on, Columbia, roll on.

Green Douglas fir where the
water cuts through
Down her wild canyons and
mountains she flew
Canadian Northwest to the
ocean so blue,
Roll on, Columbia, roll on.

Other great rivers add
power to you
Yakima, Snake, and the
Klickitat, too
Sandy, Williamette, and
Hood River, too
Roll on, Columbia, roll on.

state folk song, again referring to both the Klickitat River and the Columbia River:

RCW 1.20.073
State folk song.
...The Columbia river is the pride of the northwest and the unifying geographic element of the state. In order to celebrate the river which ties the winter recreation playground of snowcapped mountains and the Yakima, Snake, and the Klickitat rivers to the ocean so blue, the legislature declares that the official state folk song is "Roll On Columbia, Roll On," composed by Woody Guthrie.
[1987 c 526 ß 4.]

The documentary, *Roll On, Columbia* (University of Oregon, 2000), depicts the Columbia River chapter in Woody's life and the history of public power. Through interviews with Woody's children, his second ex-wife, and BPA employees, the viewer learns the story of this radical folk singer, the federal bureaucracy, the Depression, and the river and its people.

As part of the Fort Vancouver Regional Library's *The Inquiring Mind: Living History series* in 2001, Carl Allen performed in Klickitat County and throughout Washington a one-person show depicting Woody Guthrie: the man and his songs. Carl remembers the White Salmon group (where I saw him) as a "great crowd who loved to sing." I remember that evening's experience as another building block in my love of our Klickitat County rivers.

Allen, Carl. Personal communication by email, May 21, 2004
Guthrie, Woody. Columbia River Collection. Rounder Records Corporation, CD 1036. © 1987.
Lyrics for Roll On, Columbia, Sing Out Magazine 1993, p12 as quoted in Allen, Carl, Personal communication by email, May 21, 2004.
Roll On, Columbia, Documentary video, University ofOregon, 2000.
Tollefson. *Ruralite*. Notes from BPA courtesy of Mary Jean Lord
Washington Statutes RCW 1.20.073. State folk song. [1987 c 526 ß 4.]
Woody Guthrie, written and performed by Carl Allen, Inquiring Mind Series, Living History. 2001.

Young Art Hall came to Goldendale in 1887, when he was nine years old, with his widowed mother and seven sisters. On a summer day in 1888, he watched most of the business buildings burn to the ground, including a hotel building, his mother's boarding house, and the fire fighting equipment.

A new hotel, known then as the Central, was built in 1903 at that corner of Columbus Avenue and Court Streets. The new hotel, owned by Charles Albord and A.J. Ahola, was very modern for the times; it had steam heating, and it was the only electrically-lit building in Goldendale. It housed 63 rooms and a bar with an outside entrance. The building was completed the same year that railroad came to Goldendale, and many patrons of the hotel arrived by rail.

Art Hall bought the Central Hotel around 1918 and renamed it the Hall Hotel. Along with sons Harry and Jim, he operated the hotel in what was considered grand fashion until 1946. The hotel's restaurant became well-known throughout Klickitat County and beyond. A Chinese cook named Wong-Kui presided over the kitchen for many of those years.

Dyrk Hall, grandson of Art, told his sons Mark, Keith, and Scott how excited he was as a child when Wong Kui allowed him to go into the cook's own room. It was "dark and scary," with many items displayed around the room that were unfamiliar to a five-year-old. But, he"always wanted to return." The family of Dyrk Hall has an old Chinese scales that Wong Kui used in the kitchen, made of polished wood with brass inlays. Dyrk's widow, Jo Ellen Hall, said, "The scales were given to Dyrk's father, Harry Hall, when Wong Kui returned to China during the Second World War to help his family."

Art Hall retired in 1947. At the time of his retirement, he told of the horse-drawn vehicles which had made their "sliding stop in front of the hotel, with half the population of the town gathered around to see who came on the stage." He felt this was "one of the finest sights in the world." The Hall Hotel is gone now, replaced by a parking lot. A fire in 1978 caused considerable damage to the building and hastened the decision to tear down the building.

The Goldendale Sentinel, Thursday July 17, 1947 p 1 and 4
The Goldendale Sentinel, Thursday , June 29, 1978 p 1

HALL HOTEL IN ITS HEY DAY

Joan Wilkins Stone

MARK HAMILTON, MODERN PATHFINDER

Jon L. Carlson

Modern Pathfinder Returns to Columbia River

As Lewis & Clark Coordinator for the Army Corps of Engineers at The Dalles Dam, I interviewed on November 1, 1999, a modern pathfinder exploring the original trail of the Lewis & Clark Expedition. I escorted Mark, in a small dory he built, from Riverfront Park to Rock Fort Camp across from Dallesport. He told me he was the only living person to have accomplished the entire east-to-west original Lewis & Clark Trail, alone, under his own power, and on the explorers' timetable. Mark is a former literature professor at Ball State University, poet, environmentalist, and explorer.

Mark sent me a post card a month later that read "Arrived safely November 14th at Station Camp near the Pacific; and November 24th at Fort Clatsop. A fine trip: 4600 miles from Pittsburgh, 3400 miles from the Mississippi River. Will plan a return trip to St. Louis, March thru September 2000." On his April return trip, I led Mark over The Dalles Dam with his pack mule, "Old Joe," and guided him to Horsethief Lake (now Columbia Hills) State Park for the evening. The next day, I met Mark and photographed him alongside the Wishram Pathfinder Monument, dedicated in 1926. Fifty-three famous pathfinder names were recorded on the rock, with Lewis & Clark being the first two, and Mark Hamilton deserving to be the fifty-fourth. Mark successfully arrived back in St. Louis at the original trail's beginning in late September, 2000.

Interview with Mark Hamilton, The Dalles Chronicle, November 1, 1999.
Video Discovering Home, an Adventure with Mark Hamilton. Robert McConnel Productions.

HAROLD HILL'S RED BARN

*Mary Jean Lord
as told by Harold Hill*

By 2004, the roof of Harold Hill's big red barn on Knight Road west of Goldendale was no more than a skeleton. Looking at this barn, no one would guess that it was once the setting for a General Motors TV ad. In February 1991 a Portland production company sent scouts into four or five counties of Oregon and

Washington searching for the perfect red barn.

Harold, his wife, Mary, and his mother, Griselda, were sitting around the dining room table when there was a knock at the door.

"Is that your barn?" the scout asked Harold. "That's a very nice barn with all that moss. Can I take some pictures of it?"

"Help yourself."

Harold Hill's Red Barn

A week later, Harold was called out of a PUD Commission meeting to take a phone call. His barn had been selected as one of four possible sites for a commercial. Could a team come look at it? "Come ahead," Harold said.

Soon after, two rented vans drove up, and eight people piled out and began crawling around the barn and taking pictures.

A few days later the producer called to tell Harold his barn had been selected. Better not plan anything else the day of the filming, he warned, because the place would be overrun with vehicles. The crew could also use Harold's help in getting ready.

After that, Harold's phone rang constantly. The woman in charge said the theme of the commercial would be a veterinarian traveling around seeing his patients. He would be shown "birthing" a cow and "doing" a dog.

Harold said, although he had never used the expression, he knew what she meant by "birthing," but he was curious about what "doing" a dog might be.

The props people knew precisely what they wanted, but the right props weren't easy to find. They wanted a wagon load of loose hay, which isn't readily available where hay is baled. Harold thought of pulling apart one of the big round bales belonging to his neighbor, Bob Imrie, which worked fine.

Harold drove the props people around to all the neighbors to gather what they needed. They found a certain kind of tractor at Carl Amidon's and a wagon at Jim Sizemore's.

One day a young man appeared and spent the entire day taking pictures of the barn, starting early in the morning and following the sun, catching the lighting effects.

Two days before the shooting, a couple of big rented trucks pulled up, bringing the painter and the carpenter to clean the barn and "remodel" it for special camera effects. The painter painted "Hill Farm" on the west side of the barn away from the road. The colors matched so perfectly anyone would have sworn it had been part of the original paint job.

On the big day, vehicles began driving up and lined Knight Road all the way to Fairground. There was a 60-foot motor home, six trucks, a food concession pulled in by a wrecker, and a generator brought by another wrecker. The star of the show, a new Oldsmobile, came loaded in its own truck and van.

Bob Imrie brought his three cutting horses. There was a calf, a lamb, dogs, cats, pigs — all borrowed — and two white-faced heifers hauled in from Dufur, Oregon. They arrived in a horse trailer, stomping and mooing nervously inside.

Besides the animals there were 42 actors and production people, including a professional tractor driver, a genuine veterinarian as a consultant, and an animal rights advocate. One fellow's job was to polish the wheel covers on the new car and position them to properly reflect the setting sun. Harold and his neighbors watched in amazement. They hadn't had this much fun in years.

"Now I want those cows brought into the barn over here," the director commanded, indicating the calf stall, "where we can work with them."

"Not these cows," the Oregon rancher said. "These are range cows. I was just told to bring them; I had no idea what you had in mind. They're wild, and they aren't going to let you handle them."

The veterinarian thought about it and said, "I think I could give them a tranquilizer that might calm them down enough to get them into the barn and then a sedative to get them to lie down."

He gave them each a shot, and the farmers formed a line to direct them into the barn. The first cow bolted as she came out, and production people flew right and left to get out of the way. She tore down the road with a couple of farmers after her, but she was gone, halfway to the fairgrounds. The second cow was wobbly, and Harold and his friends half held her up and steered her into the barn. They got her to lie down in the stall.

The director was monitoring the action on a large screen behind the cameras. "Move the horse gasket!" he yelled. The farmers looked at each other. "Excuse me," Harold said. "What did you say?" "The horse gasket, horse gasket," the director screamed, pointing at the horse collar hanging on a peg.

They moved the "horse gasket" to the center of the scene where he wanted it. "Counter-clockwise the cow!" commanded the director.

The fellows caught on: he wanted the cow, which was lying on a bed of straw, turned slightly.

When the commercial was finally shown on national television, the Hill Farm sequence flashed by so fast Harold wasn't sure he had seen it — no more than a couple of seconds of the commercial. It was aired three times.

"I don't know why they'd paint a sign on *this* side of the barn," Harold heard a neighbor complain about the Hill Farm sign. "Nobody'll ever see it."

"Oh, I don't know about that," the sign painter said. "Probably not fewer than 20 million."

HIGH PRAIRIE

Douglas L. Taylor

High Prairie, or Hartland as it was originally called, was mostly farm and pasture for livestock years ago. The area was planted to grain with wheat and barley, and alfalfa was used for a hay crop. The alfalfa hay crop was a thriving business for some years, as it was better quality than the irrigated hay from the basin. Some farmers used wheat hay to feed their livestock before the alfalfa hay came in to wide usage. Some modern farmers are diversifying their crops with canola and peas and experimenting with other crops. Now there are very few farms with crops or cattle; most larger farms and ranches have been broken up into smaller acreage for development.

The area has open prairie with pine and fir trees, white oaks in the valleys and ridges, and many springtime flowers covering the hillsides. In the cultivated fields and along many late damp areas grow wild onions, garlic, and wild carrots. In the early spring we would pick what we called "little salt and peppers" and eat them. They were little disc shaped seed pods, with little black seeds that were very peppery tasting. They have very small flowers, and the sweetest smell — the aroma on a still day is breathtaking.

There is an abundance of wild life including the blacktail deer, (some are crossed with the mule deer,) coyotes, the common ground squirrel, (known locally as the gray digger) and assorted other wild life. I have seen the gray squirrel, flying squirrel, blue grouse, native grouse, Hungarian partridge and both mountain quail and California quail. I have been witness to occasional sighting of red fox, cougar, bobcat, elk and black bear. The wild turkey has established here and is doing quite nicely; it has brought many hunters to the area to try their luck.

When I was growing up there were huge populations of blue grouse and Hungarian partridge; the wild Canada geese would flock to the wheat fields in the fall and early winter. It would look like some of the modern refuges where the geese flock today, with thousands of geese flying in or feeding on the young wheat. There were not many deer at that time. It was quite a sight to see as many as ten deer, but now it is possible to see a hundred deer in a short drive.

There are several man-made ponds and lakes that have produced many hours of enjoyment fishing, boating and even ice skating. The planted fish seem to grow big and taste wonderful. This happens with well managed waters that are not overpopulated.

Some of the old local landmarks are still standing, including the Baptist church and the Hartland post office. The post office was apparently moved from location to location, depending on the current postmaster. The last post office was on the property owned by John and Nellie Taylor. The church is in its original place on the Taylor property.

The Lone Pine Cemetery is still in use. Many early settlers are buried there, and some of the tombstones and obituaries tell quite a history. Some still have descendants living in the area.

HIGH PRAIRIE BEAUTY

Bev Edwards

As we have lived here on High Prairie, above the Lyle-Centerville Highway, the beauty just keeps growing. No matter the season, there is always nature for us to enjoy.

When summer begins, the deer arrive in high areas such as ours. They come to our yard to graze on green clover that we planted because grass doesn't do well here during the dry summer months. This year we have not had to mow since the first week in August; we have the "deer mowers" who do it for us. After eating the clover and anything else they can reach that is not fenced off, they head for a fresh drink of water at the birdbath. Sometimes does and their fawns are drinking at the same time — a beautiful thing to see. As many as eleven deer in a herd will roam through our yard. We stand at our window watching them, amazed that they come so close to the house we could almost reach out and touch them.

In the mornings we awake to the song of the meadowlark, reminding us the birdbath needs to be refilled, since the deer drink it dry during the night. Many species of birds flock to the birdbath at the same time. They drink, bathe, then fly to the nearest perch, be it the fence, a branch, a shrub, or a dried daylily stem, and preen. They love to play in the water from the sprinkler we put out, where the cats cannot get to them.

Sometimes in the evening we can hear the call of the killdeer. Once we heard a different chirping really close by. We went to the dining room window, and there on the fence near the house were two baby goldfinches, with their short stubby tails and their feathers all fluffed up, trying to feed one another. We watched them for several minutes before they flew away. How privileged we felt to witness this!

Sunrises are spectacular, and sunsets are beautiful. Sometimes the whole sky is pink, blue, and lavender, with Mt. Adams in pink tones. Other times the colors are more orange and golden hues. There is the peace and quiet that comes with living here away from crowds, traffic, and sirens.

The neighbors we have met from all over the prairie are a special kind of people. Everyone seems to be willing to help each other when the need arises. We thank God for leading us to this very special place in our world.

Winter and Early Spring Tips
Water your houseplants sparingly in winter, and don't fertilize again until April. They will benefit from a period of slower growth and do better in the spring.

A heavy snowfall can damage shrubs and trees. Brush snow from the limbs with a gentle upward sweeping motion.

HIGH PRAIRIE GARDENING

*Judi Strait,
Master Gardener*

Be careful using de-icers or rock salt on your frozen walks. Most de-icers have a high salt content that can burn plants and turf if not used carefully and can also damage cement walks and steps. Sand is a better alternative.

There are a couple of things you can do to enrich the soil in your garden over the winter. I usually spread 3-4 inches of straw on mine, or plant a cover crop, and just plow them under in the spring. You will need additional nitrogen in the spring if you use straw, since nitrogen in the soil is depleted somewhat as the straw decomposes.

Remember to water plants under the roof overhang and fruit trees, shrubs, etc., on sunny winter days. This will help them, especially if we have a dry winter.

As the new seed catalogs start arriving, it is fun to begin planning next summer's garden on paper. Think about things that didn't work last summer and new things you'd like to try. Late February is a good time to start tomatoes and peppers indoors. All you need are fluorescent lights and an inexpensive timer so they will get 12-14 hours of light per day.

If you haven't done it before, start a garden notebook this year. Keep track of what you plant and when, where you purchase the seeds and/or plants, the date of the last frost in the spring and first frost in the fall, etc. It is really helpful to keep these notebooks and compare year to year.

I've been thinking of ways to use water wisely in gardens and landscape. One way is to build up a 1" to 2" dam of earth around the base of trees and bushes. This keeps the water where it will drain down on to the roots. Another way is to mulch with bark dust, leaves, or even newspaper. The mulch will dry out, but the earth underneath will stay moist longer. Mulch as well around plants such as tomatoes and peppers.

I also really believe in the advantage of drip hoses in the garden instead of sprinklers. This directs the water right to the roots and doesn't water paths and other areas in the garden where nothing is growing. Evaporation of water from heat, sunshine, and wind is also kept to a minimum.

Have you been feeding the birds this winter? I have, and I really enjoy the variety of birds. The evening grosbeaks and red-winged blackbirds have returned in force and empty two feeders per day. It's a good idea to continue feeding them throughout the year, since it encourages them to stay.

I usually start my pepper plants inside towards the end of February and tomatoes in March. When a seed catalog says "65 days" for tomatoes, it's talking about 65 days to maturity from the time you place the tomato plants in the garden, not from the time you plant the seeds.

To bring a bit of springtime into your house, snip a few branches from a forsythia bush and crush or split the lower stems a few inches from the bottom. Place them in water and store in a cool place. Change the water weekly, and you should see beautiful yellow blooms in 2-3 weeks. You can do this with other flowering bushes and fruit trees, too.

When pruning your trees, be sure to disinfect the pruners after each tree. If you don't, you can easily transfer disease from one tree to another. We learned this the hard way and lost some fruit trees. An easy way to disinfect is to wipe the pruners with a Lysol wipe between trees.

HIGH PRAIRIAN NEWSLETTER

Lozetta Doll

The High Prairian Newsletter, brainchild of The High Prairie Boosters, began in 1991 as High Prairie News, later Hartland Times and High Prairie Update. In October 2001 the name was changed to the High Prairian, and it has been published quarterly since. The newsletter is presently sent to some 600 homes and businesses.

A typical newsletter contains community events, upcoming and past local activities, articles of a historic nature, poems by local residents, gardening tips, health and safety updates, local fire department news, wildlife sightings, and articles featuring a worthy community volunteers.

After the reporters write and assemble the articles, a talented graphic artist in High Prairie puts it all together in a readable form, "All the News That's Print to Fit." The completed newsletter is printed by the Klickitat County Economic Development Council, folded by volunteers, labels affixed, and mailed to area residents. Comments received indicate that the newsletter is a welcome addition to area mailboxes.

To view back issues of the High Prairian, or to

read minutes of the High Prairie Community Council, Historical Society or Fire Commissioners' meetings, or for a convenient way to show friends and relatives this community, visit our website: http://www.highprairie.us/high_prairian/

NATIONAL REGISTER OF HISTORIC SITES IN KLICKITAT COUNTY

Teddy Cole

1972 Wishram Indian Village Site, Horsethief Lake State Park
1974 Maryhill Museum of Art, Highway 14
1975 Whitcom Cabin, 100 Wildlife Refuge Rd., 6 miles south of Glenwood
1977 Charles Newell House (Old Red House) 114 Sentinel Street, Goldendale
1978 Rattlesnake Creek Site N.E. of Husum
1982 Goldendale Free Public Library, 131 W. Burgen St. Goldendale
1991 First Day Advent Christian Church, Maryhill
1992 Appleton Log Hall, 835 Appleton Rd, Appleton
1996 Rowland Basin Site, Highway 14, Lyle

Listing received from Klickitat PUD
National Register Information System.
http://nr.nps.gov/

THE HOLE IN THE MOUNTAIN

Rita J. Liska

For years I had heard stories of a small hole that drops straight down and seemingly has no bottom, somewhere in the hanging valley in the heart of the Simcoe Mountain Range. Because of its danger, I had never hunted for it myself.

Several years ago, Adah Johnson and I happened to be horseback riding together, and the subject came up. This is her story as she told it to me.

She and a friend and granddaughter were riding in The Lake Beds with Adah in the lead. Basically they were lost, riding across a lush, grassy meadow and looking for an easy way back down the mountain to their trucks.

Suddenly the hair along Adah's neck began to tingle. She stopped her horse, sensing danger but seeing nothing except good grass. Then she realized that there were no trails anywhere in sight. A locality that should have had heavy grazing by wild animals and cattle showed no sign at all of animal traffic.

She had one of the others hold her horse, and she moved ahead on foot until she could make out a small difference in the look of the grass. Checking it out, she wound up crawling on her belly to the edge of a hole in the tall grass, which, as I remember her story, was about two feet by eight or ten feet long. Although she dropped several small rocks into the hole, she could never hear anything hit bottom, and as far as she could tell, the walls must have been straight down because there was not even a bounce along the sides. This was a story I had heard years earlier, but I have no idea if it was the same hole.

She said she slithered backward until she could get up onto her feet, then they backtracked, using the same trail they'd made entering the meadow until they could get out of the area. From then on, nothing in the world could entice Adah to return to that arm of the Simcoes.

LEE HONG AND JOLLY OUTSMART THE WICKED BANKER

Kathleen Goode

Chinese immigrants faced growing hostility in the West during the late 1800s. The cheap labor that was welcomed for work on the railroads and mines became the target of increased racism. Twenty-five Chinese miners were massacred near Roslyn, Washington in 1880. Five years later, 31 miners in Hells Canyon were murdered, and 28 were lynched in Wyoming territory. There were riots in Seattle; the governor declared martial law, and federal troops were sent in to control the situation.

Against this backdrop, Klickitat County was peaceful and welcoming. There were not many Chinese immigrants in the county; local histories note several "houseboys" and a laundry in Goldendale. The story of one Celestial citizen is very different.

Lee Hong must have immigrated originally to California, because he belonged to a powerful Chinese tong in San Francisco.. He got the attention of Frank Lyons, the "Sheep King" of Horse Heaven, by showing up in full celestial costume riding a Cayuse pony bareback. Lee Hong asked to be hired as a shepherd, driving the flocks up into the Simcoes where they were grazed in the summer. Lyons was not sure that Lee Hong would be accepted in the camp so he left the decision up to his best packer, Sam Sinclair.

Sinclair, who knew about the Chinaman's culinary skills, said he would agree but only if Hong would do all the cooking at camp. Lee Hong agreed to that, and Sinclair helped him train his sheepdog, Jolly, who would only accept commands in Chinese.

A few years later, the market for mutton and wool started to slow down. Lyons asked Lee Hong to take an I.O.U. for his wages until things improved. Lee Hong agreed, but he also checked with the Tong in San Francisco to see what his rights were. They referred the matter to a law firm in Portland who in turn requested an opinion from Winthrop B. Presby, the pioneer lawyer of Goldendale (also of Presby Mansion fame). Presby showed that the shepherd had a labor lien that would take precedence over a mortgage lien. The herder could not leave his job, though, or he would just be one in a long line of creditors. Lee Hong kept a copy of the letter from the Tong with him. He arranged to corral his sheep at the farm of John Sinclair at night; during the day he grazed them in the Simcoe Mountains.

The bankers arrived one day to take possession of Lee Hong's flocks. He responded by showing them the letter from the Tong. The banker was not eager to get into a legal clash with the powerful Tong, so he left. The second time the banker arrived, he told Lee Hong that the bank had decided to pay Lee's wages or $1200 and gave him a check for the full amount. Lee Hong could smell a rat and decided to consult with Presby about it. Presby told him the check was no good and to get back to his sheep right away. Lee Hong was noticed by many of the area farmers as he was riding his Cayuse pony bareback at top speed with his long queue flying in the wind. He got back to the Sinclair ranch in the late evening and was soon fast asleep.

He woke to the sound of Jolly barking. Someone was trying to steal the sheep! It was the banker again with his own hired hands and two dogs. Lee Hong sent Jolly to turn the flock back and went to the corral with a club to dispatch the two rustler dogs. The rustlers shouted at Jolly to stop but of course he ignored them since they were not speaking Chinese. The banker and his men seized the shepherd and were planning to tie him to a tree. Lee Hong started to yell which roused his friend John Sinclair, a civil war veteran, who arrived on the scene with his Winchester rifle and soon sorted out the whole affair, sending the banker and cohort packing.

Presby had been right; the check bounced. The Tong worked out a compromise in which the sheep were sold and the money deposited with the court clerk. The whole affair was settled in court, with Lee Hong winning all his wages. The court trial was a spectacle that drew in a large crowd of flock masters, camp tenders, and herders who were glad to cheer on one of their own. When last heard of, Lee Hong had returned to China with a small fortune that he had saved from his wages.

Ballou, Robert. *Early Klickitat Valley Days*. Goldendale, WA: *The Goldendale Sentinel*, 1938. Note; copyright was by Irving S. Bath who was the owner and editor of the *Sentinel* and commissioned the book.
Hansen, Dan. Asian American Empowerment: ModelMinority.com-Continental Divide http://modelminority.com/printout390.html

Glass Guru: Harry Horn

Patricia Horn

Harry Lee Horn is a child of the west, born in the Santa Clara Valley of California to parents of English and Nordic ancestry. The family settled in Hammett, Idaho, after residing briefly in Oregon and Washington. Harry finished school in California, served in the Army overseas, and became an experimental glass fabricator or glassblower for the National Aeronautics and Space Administration.

When lasers were being developed, he built them from scratch for the experimenters and researchers at NASA Ames Research Center. The smallest apparatus he ever built was a quartz balance to measure electron impacts. The scale is suspended from quartz fibers as fine as three human hairs. By contrast, he also inspected wind-tunnel windows that were eighteen inches across and two inches thick. In between, he built one-of-a-kind glass assemblies and testing equipment for scientists and engineers in the many departments at NASA Ames Research Center. His work supported biologists, biophysicists, engineers, and chemists — any researcher who could give him a simple sketch or a detailed description of what was needed.

Since settling in Goldendale in 1997, Harry has been an active contributor to the art glass movement in the Gorge. He is always glad to demonstrate his craft to schoolchildren or to take part in community festivals. His work is displayed in galleries and private collections.

Oh, the title? One of the world-renowned researchers at Ames was taking a new assistant through Harry's lab and introduced them, saying: "Here's Harry Horn. Anything you want made in glass, he can do. You might call him our Glass Guru."

HORSE RACE

Kathleen Goode

This story was told to me by Elsie David; she was told the story by her mother.

Long ago, the people gathered to race horses out on the flats near where Bickleton is today. One of the women who planned to race found out that her husband was having an affair with another woman. She was very angry, but she did not confront her enemy or her husband right away. Instead, she went off by herself for a while. She got off her horse and looked around her for large, heavy rocks and filled her wapaas (root-digging bag) with them. She tested the bag to make sure she could easily lift it and then tied the top shut carefully. Returning to the gathering, she waited until her enemy entered a race. She entered as well, and when the race started, she easily caught up to the woman. Riding just behind her, she swung the wapaas high above her in an arc and let it slam into her enemy's head, killing her instantly. Elsie says her mom told her that the moral of this story was, "Don't mess around with a married man." It doesn't hurt to own a good horse, ride well, and know how to make a strong bag.

Elsie David

HORSE THIEF PARK

Mary Jean Lord

In the early 1940s, Emmet Clouse, general manager of Klickitat PUD, and Henry Stegman, right-of-way agent, were scouring the county, checking out routes for future power lines. They were especially attracted to an area known by the Indian name "Calwash," or "Colwash Bottom," at the foot of Dalles Mountain.

"It looks like the setting for a western movie, the

kind of place horse thieves might hole up," Emmet said.

They began calling it "horse thief canyon" and referred to it by that name on the maps they made for power lines. Engineers from the state borrowed from the PUD and copied the name on their maps.

After The Dalles Dam was completed in 1964, the U. S. Army Corps of Engineers turned over land bordering the lake behind the dam to Washington State for a park. When the State Parks Director, John R. Vanderzecht, heard the story, he said, "By all means call the park Horsethief. The public will like that name for a park."

The park drew an estimated 5,000-6,000 boaters and picnickers for dedication day, April 19, 1964.

[The name of the park was recently changed to Columbia Hills State Park.]

Florence Bartholomew, "Horse Thief Park," *Ruralite*, July 1964, and interview with Emmet Clouse by MJL.

Huckleberry picking near Mt. Adams has been a yearly ritual for many families. Of course, huckleberries have been harvested by Native Americans for a long time, but for others it has become a very special family time. Sometimes just for the day, or camping for a night or two and carefully storing their precious find, these folks have much fun and often much work.

I asked a determined huckleberry picker how she knew when they were ready, and she said the grapevine told her. Calling the Forest Ranger in Trout Lake is probably better. You can get a map that shows which areas you are permitted to pick in.

Each year pickers come home with lasting memories. She told me one of their most vivid. They had taken the grandkids up to the mountains. Starting to pick in 'their' special places, they were getting quite busy, and they didn't notice that the five-year-old grandson wasn't with them. Along came the forest ranger and asked them if they were looking for a young man who was down on the road directing traffic. Well, the 'lost' was found.

HUCKLEBERRY PICKING

Mary Anne Enyeart

I read some general suggestions I'd like to pass on:

- Huckleberries are usually found at about 3500 feet.
- Look in open or partially shaded slopes or burn areas.
- Huckleberries like moisture, and they like dead trees for nutrients.
- Pick *up* hill so you get a better look at the lower branches on the next bush.
- Carry a map and choose a landmark — you could mark your landmark with a cloth.
- Clean berries by rolling down a wetted blanket or cloth. The dirt and leaves will stay on the wet cloth.
- Some folks prefer not to wet berries before freezing. Others like the water to wash away leaves and stems.
- When adding berries to muffins, roll the berries in flour before adding.

Interview with huckleberry picker Elaine Koenig Bowen, Asta. c1988. The Huckleberry Book. American Geographical Publishing.

EUGENE HUNN, CULTURAL COMMUNICATOR

Kathleen Goode

The best resource for learning about the traditions and history of Native Americans in Klickitat County is a book called *Nch'i-Wana,"The Big River": Mid-Columbia Indians and Their Land.* The book was created through the cooperative efforts of Eugene S. Hunn and the James Selam Family. Hunn is an anthropologist and linguist with the University of Washington. The preparation for this book included Hunn becoming an apprentice to the Selam Family, who are Sahaptin. The collaboration generated an invaluable resource.

Academic research studies are not always known for their readability, but this is an easily read book with numerous illustrations. Hunn has created a local treasure by letting much of the information unfold for readers as if they were there with him, learning these things first hand. The academic research is a solid foundation for the book, which contains a detailed bibliography and a number of useful appendixes on the Sahaptin language and the full text of the 1855 treaty. The greatest value of this book is its gradual unfolding of an ancient culture, still vibrant and alive today.

Hunn weaves the society, science, myth, traditions,

and beliefs together with the numerous factors of the Sahaptin lifestyle to show how the Sahaptin people are keeping their culture alive today. Important plants and animals are identified, with explanations of how each living thing fits into the cycle of the year. Family relationships, religion, and the challenges of modern life are all included.

An example is the description of the peach-leaf willow. Hunn includes both the scientific name and the Sahaptin term for it, discusses its uses and where it is found. He goes on to describe its inclusion in the traditional winter lodge that was built in 1982 at the Yakama Nation Cultural Center. An entry about the Garry oak includes a retelling of the Wasco tale, "Raccoon and his Grandmother."

Reading this volume will give readers a better understanding of the Mid-Columbia Indians, their ties to the land, and the hope for the future. Watch for two books not yet in print but in preparation: *Sahaptin Indian Atlas* by Eugene S. Hunn and Thomas Morning Owl and *In Defense of the Ecological Indian: TEK and the Sustainability of Indigenous Subsistence Systems* by Eugene S. Hunn.

"Eugene Hunn (PhD 1973, UC Berkeley)" University of Washington, Dept. of Anthropology.
http://depts.washington.edu/anthweb/people/faculty/EHunn.php
Hunn, Eugene S. with James Selam and Family. 1990. *Nch'i-Wana "The Big River"; Mid-Columbia Indians and Their Land.* Seattle: University of Washington Press

HUSUM

Jim Tindall

Husum is the small burg that is shadowed in dawn by Tum Tum, the sacred Klickitat knoll. Earlier, it was Nakrepunk, whose most famous soul was Titcamnashat, or Earth Thunderer, or Jake Hunt, shaman of the Waptasi or Feather Cult faith, whose grave reads, "Jacob Hunt died Feb 16, 1913 aged 108 yrs."

The settler community began as Wilkensheim, home of Swiss emigrants Mattheus and Christina Wilkens, who settled to the east of the falls in 1876. In 1880 Volquart Martin and Sophia Thomsen arrived. They pushed to rename the area Husum for a town near the German / Danish border. On March 8, 1880, a post office of Wikensheim was established with

Mattheus Wilkens as postmaster; on August 23, 1880, the post office of Husum was established with Sophia Thompson as its postmistress and discontinued in 1882. Thompson built the first grist mill in the county at the falls known as the White Salmon Falls, now referred to as Husum Falls. The mill was later transformed into a powerhouse by Henry Thompson in 1908.

After exploring the Washington Territory in 1883, aristocratic Welsh travelers Mordecai and Gwennllian Jones put down roots just north of town. In 1896 they built their home, Hunter's Hill. Jones was renowned as a hunter who favored bear and cougar.

A long-standing landmark for this rural village is the Husum Hotel. It was located in the vicinity of the current Husum's Riverside B&B, but was moved south one lot. It is presently owned by the Richard C. Smith family, former principals in a slug ranching venture. In the first years of the 20th century, George W. Carter purchased the Wilkens homestead and soon built the Falls Hotel, which boasted twenty finely appointed rooms. Carter was also responsible for the construction of a brick plant at the falls in 1900, followed by a power plant in 1905, located between the two current bridges over the White Salmon. In the 1940s and 50s the hotel was home to the popular restaurant, the Husum Fountain Lunch, operated by Claire and Vivian Smith, parents of the current owner.

Husum would have been just another isolated and scenic piece of real estate with abundant water if it weren't for the tenacity and regularity of Teunis Wyers and his Wyers Stage Company, serving the White Salmon Valley from 1894 until 1965 in mail, freight, stage, and school bus services. His family expanded into ranching in the vicinity with the establishment of the Wykre Cattle Company in Gilmer.

Timber businesses floated logs down the White Salmon to sawmills below, using rollaway dams to surge the river's flow. Orcharding progressed in the valley in the early 20th century with the area's Apple Boom. Notable was the Mt. Adams Orchard and its plantings of D'Anjou pears, developed in 1910 by Wade Dean of Husum . Wade and Effie Dean and son Earl were innovators in other industries including mining, telephone, and produce and dairy storage with such businesses as the Oregon-Washington Telephone Company, Guler Cheese, and the Glacier Mining Company.

Attwell, Jim. 1977. *Early History of Klickitat County*. Skamania WA: Tahlkie Books.

Collier, Penny, and Bill Collier. 1979. *Along the Mt. Adams Trail*. Vancouver WA: Penny & Bill Collier.

Gardner, Kenny. Personal interview. 9 May 2004

Hunsaker, Frank. Personal interview. 9 May 2004.

McCoy, Keith. 1988. *Cody: Colorful man of Color*. White Salmon, WA: Pahto Publications.

McCoy, Keith. 2003. *Mid Columbia North Shore*. Victoria BC: Trafford Publishing.

McCoy, Keith. 1987. *The Mount Adams Country*. White Salmon WA: Pahto Publications.

McCoy, Keith. 2002. *Rowdy River*. Victoria BC: Trafford.

Relander, Click. 1986. *Drummers and Dreamer*. Seattle: Northwest Interpretive Association.

Smith, Richard C. Notes, archived articles, and photos; Personal interview, 10 May 2004; Telephone interview, 4 May 2004.

Ward, Anne Margraf. Telephone interview, 10 May 2004.

Wyers, Pat Kreps. Telephone interview, 10 May 2004.

HUSUM SCHOOL

Geneva M. Meyers

The old Husum School was a two-story building, with a bell tower, and to me, it was the greatest school ever.

There had been several small schools in the community of Husum from the mid-1800s into the 1900s, including a schoolhouse made of logs. The school of my childhood was built in 1916. I recall that the gym floor was creaky and had some bounce to it, indicating that it had been there awhile. This was in the late 1940s when the building had already suffered 30-plus years of children running back and forth.

To enter the building you climbed 12 or 13 steps (good for playing "Mother May I") to a big porch (good for spanking kids) from which you entered a hallway. A left turn faced you down a long hall, at either end of which were stairways making 180-degree angles down to the gym area. Along the upper hall on the left was a handrail overlooking the gym (good for a balcony view of gym activities).

Our family moved from Vancouver, Washington, to Husum Hills near White Salmon in the summer of

1946. My twin sister and I were in the second grade, and our older brother, Buddy, was in the third. There were two grades per room: two actual classrooms and a third class held on the stage at the south end of the gym. The bathrooms, the furnace room, and the lunchroom were downstairs directly under the two upstairs classrooms.

My first Christmas Program at Husum School was especially memorable. I was in a lineup of little girls, all in our angel outfits, holding lighted candles. We were to step up onto small wooden chairs lined up along the railing, and walk along the chairs while our parents watched from the gym below, then sing some Christmas tunes from this heavenly perch. Well, this little angel, first in line because of size, found the step up onto the first chair an awfully big step, so I managed to touch the lighted candle to my golden locks. Next thing I knew, my teacher, Mrs. Brown, was frantically slapping me on the head — the smell of scorched hair clued me in as to the reason. In the years that followed, all little angels were restricted to flashlights.

The pine trees out behind the school presented lots of entertainment. We braided and played with the pine needles, or swept them around the ground forming rooms for playhouses. The boys played marbles in the dirt areas, making holes for potsies or drawing circles for marble arenas. Occasionally both girls and boys played baseball. There were swings in the playground, but I preferred climbing up the pipes that held the swings, or hanging upside down between the chains that held the swings, trying to keep my dress from dropping down over my head. Sometimes we chased the boys around the school or they chased us; that was always good for releasing pent-up energy. On rainy days, the gym was the play area, with basketball or maybe just running, jumping and screaming (major kid activities).

There were school programs for all occasions: May Day, with the winding of the Maypole; Valentine Day, when we exchanged cards with all our classmates; Thanksgiving, when we celebrated the coming of the Pilgrims to Plymouth Rock; and Christmas, of course. There was always the end-of-the-school-year picnic for kids and families, out behind the school or in the gym when raining.

I don't recall what the occasion may have been, but a Mr. Biesantz (I assume the one they called Billy) came to the school and taught us to dance like Indians. On a number of occasions, Clair and Vivian Smith, Husum locals, came and taught us square dances. Our music teacher, Mrs. Paulson, traveled between the local schools, teaching us songs and how to play a black, plastic, flute-type instrument called the Tonette.

In the late 1940s, there was an earthquake during our recess, and we were so active in the gym that I never really noticed the earthquake (which may have been a good thing). To us kids, the most interesting effect was the dirt-scraped line along the bottom of the front stairs which showed that they had moved backward a couple of inches.

When I left this school in the little community of Husum to attend the higher grades in the big town of White Salmon, school forever lost its charm for me.

Personal experience
Washington State Archives

ICE AGE FLOODS

When geologists first saw the vast Columbia Basin, they recognized that a large volume of water and ice had sculpted the dramatic landscape of canyons (coulees), buttes, dry cataracts, boulder fields, and gravel bars. They assumed the likely cause to be normal flooding and erosion during the Ice Age. However, in subsequent years, two geologists were instrumental in revealing that it had been extraordinarily huge and powerful deluges that had shaped the region.

It was J Harlen Bretz who in the 1920s looked more deeply into this fascinating landscape. As he explored the region, he was astounded by the colossal size and distinctive characteristics of the land forms. He felt that they had to have been formed not merely by normal flood waters, but by massive flows of very fast-moving glacial water.

The source of such catastrophic glacial flooding eluded Bretz. His theories were consequently rejected by his professional colleagues as unrealistic, and decades of arguments ensued with the scientific community.

Earlier, in 1910, another geologist, Joseph T. Pardee, had described evidence of a great ice-dammed lake, Glacial Lake Missoula, that had formed during the Ice

Age in northwestern Montana. However, Bretz didn't see the connection between this lake and the features he described in Eastern Washington. Then, in 1940, Pardee reported on his discovery that giant ripple marks 50 feet high and 200-500 feet apart had formed on the floor of the lake. These huge current features, along with other newly found land forms, demonstrated that Glacial Lake Missoula had suddenly emptied to the west, producing the tremendous erosive forces that Bretz's theories required.

Over the last two million years, large parts of northern North America, Europe, and Asia were repeatedly covered with glacial ice sheets, at times reaching over 10,000 feet in thickness. Periodic climate changes resulted in corresponding advances and retreats of the ice.

About 18,000 years ago, a large finger of ice advanced into Idaho, forming an ice dam at what is now Lake Pend Oreille. It blocked the Clark Fork River drainage, thus creating an enormous lake reaching far back into mountain valleys of western Montana. As the lake deepened, the ice began to float. Leaks likely developed and enlarged, causing the dam to fail suddenly and release the full volume of the lake.

Resembling science fiction more than reality, this towering mass of water and ice, over 2,000 feet deep near the ice dam, suddenly burst forth. It literally shook the earth as it thundered across the Columbia Basin, moving at speeds of up to 65 miles per hour.

Great Glacial Lake Missoula, with a volume of over 500 cubic miles of water — more than Lake Erie and Lake Ontario combined — may have emptied in a mere two or three days. The rate of flow was 10 times the combined flow of all the rivers in the world. The deluge stripped away soil, cut deep canyons, and carved areas of stark scabland. Altogether, flood waters carved out more than 50 cubic miles of earth, depositing some of it to create new land forms while carrying most of it far out into the Pacific Ocean.

Over a period of about 2,500 years, the cycle was repeated many times: the glacial ice would block the valley, the lake would form, and the ice dam would fail, releasing another cataclysmic flood. Then, almost as suddenly as they had arrived, the colossal flood waters were gone, leaving lasting marks across

Montana, Idaho, Washington, and Oregon. The face of the Northwest was forever changed.

Ice Age Floods brochure, published by Ice Age Floods Institute

Hidden behind a wall of growing pine trees, they watch. If they hear, they listen to the wind in the timber that surrounds them, the rustle of water when it rains, and the roar of cascading water and snow as avalanches rip down from the bluff above each spring.

On maps the area is referred to as Indian Rocks. To people who have ventured there, Indian Rocks is a great deal more than a place on the map. This short, shallow cliff, created over vast years of erosion, contains more faces than can be accurately counted. A viewer is left in awe and more than a little shaken by their perfection.

As you first glimpse the rocks, you may see one face gazing downward at you. Move three paces left, and five faces appear. Move six steps to the right, and even more faces seem to look back at you. It may be hard to resist the temptation to look back over your shoulder as you leave the area.

High in the Simcoe Mountains and next to, if not on, the Yakama Reservation, the rocks are hidden by a high knoll to the south. They can be reached in a long day by horseback from either Butler Creek or Devils Creek. But do not go past the Bearing Tree — if it still exists. If you reach that tree you have missed the cliff. Turn back and to the right, and prepare yourself.

INDIAN ROCKS

Rita J. Liska

Willis Jenkins, born 1801 in North Carolina, came from Kentucky across the Oregon Trail with the second wagon train to cross the plains. He and his family left on June 1 and arrived November 15, 1844, to settle on the Luckiamute River in Oregon. He said he could have settled his square mile of land where the future town of Portland would be located, but it was "too hilly to make for good farming." Willis was drawn to California in 1849 when gold was found in the Sacramento River. He and two sons dug out $7,000 of gold in one summer.

WILLIS JENKINS, EARLY PIONEER

Frank Wesselius, great, great, great, grandson

Upon his return he settled with his family near the town of Wilbur, Oregon.

The Willis family was among the original fifteen families to come to the Klickitat Valley in 1859, known as the 59ers. Congress had just opened this area to settlers, and most of the families came looking for a drier climate, grass for their cattle, and "no taxes." Willis arrived with 150 head of cattle and some horses, filing the first land claim in the Klickitat Valley on the Upper Swale area on what was later known as the John Eddings place.

When the military moved from Fort Klickitat, about 8 miles west of present-day Goldendale, to Fort Simcoe in Yakima County, Willis "bought the rights of squatter claimants" on the abandoned fort. The main part of the fort was a two-story blockhouse structure used by about 100 local settlers to keep themselves and their horses safe during Indian attacks. The blockhouse was last used in 1878 in response to an Indian uprising by Chiefs Moses of the Yakimas and Buffalo Horn of the Bannocks.

Acquiring the name "Blockhouse," this area supported a post office, store, trading post, the first school in the county (1866), and a church. When Klickitat County was formed, there were three voting precincts — one in the Jenkins house at Blockhouse. Jenkins received his land patent on the Blockhouse property from President Andrew Johnson on July 2, 1866.

In 1859 the legislature determined that there were at least 15 men over the age of 21 who could qualify for official positions in the area. In the December 20, 1859, election, the settlers voted to form Clickitat County (later spelled Klickitat). Willis Jenkins was appointed as Probate Judge, even though he had little education and no law schooling. The settlers refused to "prove up" on their new county to the territorial legislature, so Clickitat County was not formed and no taxes were levied that year.

In 1860, again a county election endorsed an official county; again the elected officers refused to qualify it. The legislature simply appointed county officers, and Willis was appointed Treasurer.

In 1867, again the legislature appointed a full slate of officials. Again the officials and the people of the county refused to prove up a county — they didn't like the idea of paying taxes or letting the government tell them what to do. Territorial Governor Stephens sent a U.S. Marshal down to the Klickitat valley to collect all the "county officials" and take them to the territorial capital in Tumwater. The settlers were put up in a hotel for the night. One settler exclaimed he had never slept in a feather bed before, and another was surprised to eat dinner on porcelain plates instead of tin. The next day, a territorial judge gave the settlers two options: the local stockade or sign the papers to organize Klickitat County. The settlers quickly signed. Willis Jenkins became, of all things, the first tax collector. This must have been terribly trying for a man who hated to pay taxes.

After selling the blockhouse and the adjoining 80 acres, Willis and his wife Elizabeth owned and operated a cafe in Goldendale. Elizabeth died January 12, 1873, in Goldendale. Willis married a widow named Elvira Pike Cram. Willis himself died on May 26, 1877, in Goldendale. His wife Elvira died December 10, 1894. All three are buried side by side in the IOOF cemetery north of Goldendale in the "pioneer" section.

William Chambers, A trip through Jenkins genealogy.
    Unpublished.
Ballou, Robert. 1938. *Early Klickitat Valley Days.*
    The Goldendale Sentinel.

KIWANIS READING PROGRAM

John Miller

The Goldendale Kiwanis Club is one of several service clubs in the Goldendale area established to provide support to the community. The Club annually offers activities including sponsoring a fund-raising golf tournament, assisting with the AAU basketball tournament, highway cleanup, conducting a reading program, putting up flags in the city each holiday, supporting several youth programs, and offering a graduation scholarship. The reading program perhaps best tells the story of how a service club can influence a community positively.

In the 1990s, Washington State introduced the Washington Assessment of Student Learning (WASL) to measure student achievement of the state's rigorous new academic standards in reading, writing, mathematics, and other core subjects. It is designed to help teachers refine instructional strategies, increase student achievement, and provide data on the performance of schools and districts over time. All fourth, seventh, and tenth graders in Washington's public schools take the WASL in reading, writing, listening, and mathematics.

Early in 2002, a presenter at a weekly Kiwanis meeting gave the statistics for all subjects and grades tested. One particular statistic got the attention of the Kiwanians: Only 52 percent of the Goldendale 4th grade students achieved the reading standard. The state goal was 80 percent. Some members thought that perhaps, just perhaps, Kiwanis could step forward and help. They formed a committee, and soon the club kicked off the"Kiwanis Reading Program" with a free spaghetti feed in April at the Goldendale Primary School. David Gutterson, a noted author, was the guest speaker. The club gave a book to each child who attended.

The goals of The Goldendale Kiwanis"Read Around the World Program" are to emphasize the importance of reading to and with every child 20 minutes each day and to assist every child to read at grade level upon completion of the third grade.

Since 2002, Kiwanis has sponsored several community forums to emphasize reading and given out more than 10,000 books to children in the community. Kiwanis includes a brochure for parents with each book given to a child. The brochure reads, in part,"All children need to understand the joy of reading. The first step is reading to them. The second step is to give them books they can treasure and read again and again. Reading together every day gives your child a significant jump start when he or she goes to school!"

In 2004, the WASL results for the Goldendale 4th graders showed that 80 percent achieved the reading standard. Did the Kiwanis Club and their reading emphasis program make a difference? The members like to think so.

KLICKITAT BASKETRY

Teddy Cole

"A long time ago in the animal world, before the Lataxat (Klickitat) people came, there lived a young girl along the White Salmon River. She was Sinmi, the brown squirrel... . Because she didn't have anything else to do, she would sit and dream in the shade of a particular cedar tree, Nank. Nank would watch Sinmi, and he worried about her... 'That poor girl. She does not know all the things a young girl should know.'"

So begins Nettie Kunecki's retelling of the story of Klickitat basketry. In her introduction, she says, "It was the belief of our ancestors that the cedar tree was one of our spiritual elders that gave them strong roots for their baskets."

Baskets were essential to the Klickitats, serving as containers for huckleberries, camas, and other native foodstuff, and as carriers for water. Before metal pots were available, the Klickitats cooked food in baskets. They put hot rocks in the bottom of a basket of water, and when the water was heated, they added the food to be cooked. No matter how mundane the use, the baskets were beautiful in craft and decoration. Although baskets vary according to the intended use, the traditional Klickitat basket has a flat bottom with sides curved outward and up, with loops around the top for lacing the basket shut.

Klickitat women were taught basket making from childhood by observing and imitating their elders at their work — grandmothers, mothers, and aunts. Some families were famous for their baskets. If a young girl showed special aptitude, she would be given the name of one of their distinguished basket makers.

Kunecki wrote that describing the techniques of basketry with words and pictures was contrary to their traditional method of teaching. The children learned through observing and imitating their elders, who taught by example, silently. However, she felt compelled to write the book so that the techniques would be preserved, since the knowledge was no longer passed on from mother to daughter.

The legend relates how Sinmi learned designs by observation: mountain peaks and valleys, the starry sky, and familiar creatures around her, the diamond of the rattlesnake and the footprints of the grouse. Traditional designs such as these make Klickitat baskets distinctive.

Nank guided Simni until she finally completed a perfectly woven, watertight basket, beautiful in shape and design, but Nank told her that she would never be a skillful basket weaver if she didn't give the first ones away. Although it was hard to do, Simni gave her treasured baskets to the oldest women of her people. Spilyay (coyote) came to see her baskets, and he told her, "From today on, this land called Lataxat will be known for cedar baskets."

Kunecki, Nettie, Elsie Thomas and Marie Slockish. *The Heritage of Klickitat Basketry:*

A History and Art Preserved. Oregon Historical Society, 1982.

Schlick, Mary Dodds. *Columbia River Basketry: Gift of the Ancestors, Gift of the Earth.* University of Washington Press, 1994.

KLICKITAT: ORIGIN AND MEANING

Teddy Cole

Klickitat: it's the name of a county, a town, a tribe and numerous natural features—but what does it mean? Some claim that "Klickitat" reflects familiar sounds, and others say it's geographical in nature. Still others have said that it referred to a characteristic of local natives.

Klickitat legends, as retold by Clarence Bunnell, attribute the name to sounds found in nature. After the great flood washed all the salmon out to sea, seagulls herded the salmon back upriver with a continual cry of "Klick-tat! klick-tat!" "...some of the gulls liked [the upstream country] so well that they implored Koyoda to permit them to stay always. Accordingly, he changed them to Indians and caused them the settle about the base of Pa-toe, [Mt. Adams] whose name was then changed to Klick-tat in their honor." Others compared the sound of "Klickitat" to horses running, crickets chirping, and water flowing over the falls of the Klickitat River.

In the early 1900s, United States Government publications gave the meaning of "Klickitat" as 'beyond', "... That definition may have originated with Lower Chinooks who called the falls near the mouth of the Klickitat river and the Indians living at the falls 'Hladachut,' meaning 'beyond'" Hitchman says. "A corruption of that name, Klickitat, is now applied to the river and to a tribe of Indians."

In local lore, the name Klickitat means "thief" or "horse thief". In his 1927 History of Washington, Meany says, in discussing the wars between the Puget Sound tribes and their Indian neighbors, "Occasionally also they had been troubled by visits of warlike Indians from the Yakima Country whom they called Klickitats, meaning 'robber.'" In *Early Klickitat Valley Days*, Robert Ballou wrote that George Mennenick, a chief of the federated Yakima tribes, said the Klickitats were so called because they were so clever, adept and persistent in stealing horses of neighboring tribes. Ballou continued, "David Miller, full blood Indian…, is grandson of old Chief Klinquit, who represented the Klickitats in treaty negotiations with Governor Isaac Stevens. He says his tribe, the Klickitats, was not a set of robbers and horse thieves. He classifies this characterization of his people as 'Kultus Wa Wa,' meaning 'hot air,' or 'baloney.' "

When Lewis and Clark encountered local Indians on April 23, 1806, at Rock Creek, they recorded their name as "Wahhowpum," which Elliot Coues identified as the Klickitat tribe. On June 20, 1825, the botanist-explorer David Douglas mentioned the tribe as "Clikitats." The Wilkes Expedition, 1841, recorded the name as "Klackatack."

"Klickitat," however, was not the name the tribe called itself. Minnie Marie Slockish, quoted in Kunecki's Heritage of Klickitat Basketry, said, "We call ourselves Whash-why-pum (Xwalxwaypam) and have always been a tribe. We are known to other Indians as Latakat or by the white men as Klickitat, the name of our mountain range and river."

For most of us who live here, "Klickitat" means "home."

Ballou, Robert. *Early Klickitat Valley Days.*
　　Goldendale Sentinel, 1938.
Bunnell, Clarence Orvel. *Legends of the Klickitats.*
　　Metropolitan Press (Portland), 1935.
Cutright, Paul Russell. *A History of the Lewis and Clark
　　Journals.* U. Oklahoma Press, c1976.
Hitchman, Robert. *Place Names of Washington State.*
　　Washington State Historical Society, 1985.
Kunecki, Nettie. *The Heritage of Klickitat Basketry.* Oregon
　　Historical Society, 1982.
Lewis, Meriwether. *History of the expedition under the
　　command of Lewis and Clark,* edited by
Elliott Coues, Volume III. Dover Pub., 1965
Meany, Edmund. *Origin of Washington Geographic Names.* U.
　　Washington Press, 1923.
Neils, Selma. *The Klickitat Indians.* Binford & Mort
　　(Portland), 1985.

THE KLICKITAT HILLS

Patricia Smith

The hills along the Columbia are
As curvaceous as a voluptuous woman.
Round mounds stand erect,
Tempting as a virgin's breasts.
Sensuous thighs meet,
    forming valleys of secret places.
In spring, they wear a frock of gossamer green,
Sprinkled with amethyst lupin and
    white pearls of mountain phlox.
Balsam root flows like golden honey from
    a secluded cleft.
In summer, as passionate as an eager lover,
The hills throb under the fervent sun,
But, like a fickle woman,
In winter, they lie beneath a frigid white mantel,
Covering a heart of stone.

THE KLICKITAT ICE PLANT

Joan Wilkins Stone

It was the spring of 1951. The junior class of Goldendale High School had been collecting newspapers throughout the school year to raise money by selling the papers to the Klickitat Ice Plant. The class loaded the back of the old farm truck within a foot of the top of the truck's railings and climbed on top of the papers. Coach Kindred closed the gate and told the students to "sit tight and hang on." They did.

Some students from the class still remember that ride. Coach knew how to get his "boys" to football games — and his only way was fast. The Klickitat Grade didn't stop him either. They made it to the plant with a few bruises and scraped elbows and started unloading.

The ice plant was built in the 1930s to bottle mineral water from the local springs. This venture failed because the water went flat or blew up before reaching destinations.

Later tests determined that carbon dioxide was coming with the mineral water. Solidified CO_2 forms dry ice, and a market for it as a refrigerant was just starting. Selma Neils writes, "Here the CO_2 came in crevices in the basal rock formation, presumed to originate from, or be produced by, the action of large magmas under Mt. Adams."

The plant produced 18 tons of dry ice per day and became the largest seasonal storage facility in the world.

It ran two or three shifts a day, and local youths were hired to wrap the 80-pound packages with newspaper for shipping around the country. Old-timers of the town of Klickitat reminisce about the annual summer fish feeds, with dancing and beer drinking, held in the 60 by 80 foot storage building.

The owners sold the plant after their son drowned, and it stood empty for many years. The State Game Division eventually acquired it. The only structure remaining is the furnace house, left as a sanctuary for the birds. Many visitors come to see the swallows during the birds' fall migration. The swallows roost among the sagging timbers and chimneys.

I was a member of the junior class of 1951. I remember the farm truck, the newspapers piled high, Coach Kindred, and the ride. I don't know how much money we made, or what we used it for. Guess that wasn't too important back then to us kids.

Neils, Selma.1967. *So This Is Klickitat.* Portland OR: Metropolitan Press.
*The Goldendale Sentinel.*1962. Klickitat Ice Plant. May 27.

Klickitat River Canals

Rita J. Liska

The canals are considered to be legend, but there is evidence of them today. They are well within the boundaries of the Yakama Reservation, so are seldom seen by outsiders. Most people who do see them are unaware of this piece of history.

Somewhere there may still be maps showing when or who planned to withdraw water from the upper Klickitat River and transport it along the southern edge of the Simcoe Mountains all the way to the Bickleton area.

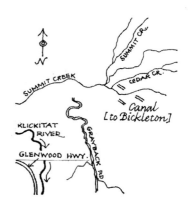

The small sections of canal that can still be located show that it is certainly within the realm of possibility to get water through the Kaiser Butte locality northwest of Goldendale. But, for the life of me, I cannot figure out how anyone planned to cross Rock Creek Canyon and elevate the water 2,000 feet higher than where it originated.

Digging in the rocky terrain with shovels, pickaxes, and horses could not have been easy, and the idea was soon abandoned. So another bit of fact blends into legend.

THE LAKE BEDS FIRE

Rita J. Liska

In the summer of 1994, Klickitat and Yakima counties were bombarded with a series of violent thunder and lightning storms.

One strike landed just to the north and east of The Lake Beds, near the heart of the 5,888-foot mountain. It was soon out of control, despite busy firefighters. Concerned citizens living in the foothills to the south watched the heavy smoke during the day and the pink glow at night grow stronger as the fire spread rapidly in all directions.

Butler Creek Canyon to the southeast already had another out-of-control fire. Only a narrow hogback ridge held the two fast-moving fires away from each other. Another ridge separated those two fires from the heads of Devil's, Mill Creek, and Bowman Creek Canyons which led directly down into communities.

Still another storm struck from the west late in the evening. Local citizens began leaving their homes and driving up to high ridges to watch for lightning strikes and offer help for an already exhausted fire-fighting and dispatch crew.

I sat on Pothole Road watching the storm rip in from the west, swing north along Kaiser Butte Ridge, and charge through The Lake Beds fire and the crews up there fighting it. I did not envy their location as I watched the storm.

Directly to the west, lightning strikes were strong and varied from straight down to various angles. When passing over Kaiser Butte, the strikes became horizontal, bounding from cloud to cloud, but never reaching the ground. The Lake Beds were one of the most horrifying scenes I've ever witnessed as spears of lightning dropped straight down from the black clouds to be met by equal fingers of pink and orange flames reaching up to meet them. Although I do not claim to be a religious person, I could not help but feel that I was watching God throw bolts of lightning directly through the open gates of Hell as the storm settled in that area.

The storm continued east, and I decided to return home. That took a while, because I met neighbors who were also out watching from other locations or manning our local volunteer fire station in case of emergency. We all marveled at the storm.

My mother came as a bride from Norway in 1911. She knew no English when she arrived and didn't have much chance to practice English on our farm east of Goldendale, far from town or neighbors. She had no radio, television, or language textbooks. But she did eventually learn to speak well and always said she learned by listening. Every time the phone rang she would "rubber-neck," as we called it. She would pick up the receiver, whether it was "her" ring or not, and listen in on the party line.

LEARNING ENGLISH ON THE PARTY LINE

Eleanor Dooley as told to Judy Thomas

As far back as the 1930s, the Indian Sliding Rock was a legend. People who had searched for the rock were unable to find it and, although I searched via foot and horseback for almost 20 years, I could find no trace of it either.

THE LEGEND OF THE SLIDING ROCK

Rita J. Liska

Some people thought that, due to heavy logging, the largesliding rock had disappeared, apparently destroyed by equipment and time. But, just last year, the legend became a fact. It actually did exist. For over 70 years, people had been looking in the wrong place.

The story had led everyone to believe the rock must have rested along the bank of Mill Creek in the Simcoes, northwest of Goldendale. But searches concentrated in that area to no avail. In fact, the rock was not on Mill Creek at all, but in a narrow, shallow side canyon just west of the creek and not far from what eventually became the old stage coach and military road to the south.

Earlier, people thought that the rock was used by the Indians to slide down into the water. However, according to my new source, who grew up near the rock and didn't realize it was missing until I told him, that story is untrue. I learned a new legend about the Indian Sliding Rock.

According to the legend he grew up with, the Indians, when getting ready for winter, heavily oiled their clothing. If they had applied enough oil to waterproof their clothes for the winter, they could easily slide down the entire length of the rock and continue on their way. But, if their clothing snagged and stuck to the rock before reaching the bottom, they did not have enough oil worked into it to protect them from the harsh winters, and they could not continue until they had oiled their clothes sufficiently to slide all the way down.

LEIDL PARK

Nancy Barron

Where's the slowest curve on the Leidl grade between Goldendale and Glenwood? Rated at 25 miles per hour, it leads down to the Klickitat River crossing at Leidl Park and Campground. Since we have to slow down anyway, let's pull in to the park and commune a bit with the river.

There is good access to the river on either side of the highway. To the southwest, there are campsites sometimes inhabited by rafters, fishers, or cyclists. To the northeast, there is a beach that might, on a spring afternoon, function as a take-out point for one of the several rafting companies who ply the upper Klickitat. Toilets on either side may provide a welcome break. Picnic tables among the oaks offer good opportunity for a nosh, a chat, or perhaps some reading or contemplation. Swift current around the bend allows some entertaining river floating — then we can cut across the bend and do it again.

Wendlin Leidl and his son, Charles, an engineer, using horses and scoops, improved the Leidl grade during WWI. The area's name honors the family's effort. Son Louis was killed in WWI, and the American Legion post and a memorial at Stonehenge bear his name. Son "Babe" served in the war and returned. After the war, Lisette Leidl, a "Gold Star Mother," although ambivalent about her sons fighting against her homeland, traveled with war mothers to Paris, where Louis was buried. She also obtained permission to visit her relatives in western Germany while on that trip.

Leidl Park is under the auspices of the Washington Department of Fish and Wildlife. Presently, camping up to 14 days is allowed, although a parking permit is required. From a moment to two weeks, Leidl Park is a treasure for us to enjoy.

Interview with Mary Cosner, granddaughter of Wendlin Leidl

In 1803, under orders from President Thomas Jefferson, explorers Lewis and Clark, aided by Indian interpreter Sacagawea, led a group of men in search of a water passage from America's heartland to the great Pacific ocean.

In 1805, while traveling down the Columbia River, they observed on the cliff walls an array of intriguing rock carvings of human images and, in the distance, a large conically-shaped, snow-capped mountain. Here, for the first time, they tasted barbequed salmon and wapato, one of Sacagawea's favorite foods, and traded for beautiful coiled and twined baskets, one of which was covered with designs of giant condors and 20-foot-long fish called sturgeon. On April 22, 1806, they came back to this area and walked across the bluff at the top of the cliffs.

Where is this place? Where can you see all of these things today? In Klickitat County, at Maryhill Museum.

What else related to Lewis and Clark can you see there? Lots of Native American artifacts; a print from Captain Lewis's branding iron bearing the inscription"U.S. Capt. M. Lewis;" a scenic overlook with interpretive panels of passages from the Lewis and Clark journals; and Osage orange trees. There is even a bronze relief sculpture of Sam Hill created by Alonzo Lewis, a descendant of Meriwether Lewis.

LEWIS AND CLARK AND SAM HILL

Lee Musgrave,
Maryhill Museum of Art

Oscar, the Lewis' woodpecker, first came to visit one fall day. I noticed Oscar sitting on our transformer pole, hunched up and watching the surroundings. I thought he was just a visitor resting and that the next day he would be gone. But every day at about 10 o'clock, there sat Oscar. This went on for a week or so, then one day as I saw Oscar sitting on the pole, he flew off and headed for the pine tree next to the church building on our High Prairie property. He was obviously getting things to eat, as he would come back to the pole to sit and peck at something until he took off on another flight.

One day as I was sitting down for lunch, I noticed Oscar flying back and forth from a nearby pine tree to his perch, getting his own lunch. Once when he flew off, a Steller's jay landed on the pole. Oscar promptly flew up to the pole and chased off the jay. Mr. Jay

LEWIS' WOODPECKER

Douglas L. Taylor

decided that no woodpecker would tell him what to do, so he promptly returned to one of the cross braces on the pole. Oscar again chased the jay off. This time the jay did not return, and Oscar held possession of the pole. Sometimes you wonder how birds determine the 'pecking order'. The Steller's jay looks the bigger of the two, but apparently the Lewis' woodpecker was the tougher.

By the middle of February, days were getting longer, and spring was in the air. Oscar did not stay on his perch as much as when it was colder. He would just come with an acorn and peck on it till it was eaten and then go out searching again. I noticed that robins and other smaller birds could come and light on the pole without the usual objection from Oscar. He might have been out courting, as I saw another Lewis' woodpecker in the area. This bird was not allowed to sit on the pole; Oscar would charge back to the pole and put the intruder on the fly.

After defending his perch all winter, Oscar disappeared the last week of April. His disappearance left me wondering if he finally found a mate or if a raccoon found his night time roost and had Oscar for a snack. Then in May, down at my father's house just a quarter mile from my own, I noticed a Lewis' woodpecker and its mate flying together. It particularly enjoyed claiming the yard transformer pole as its own and was not afraid of people walking around in the yard. I wanted to think that it was Oscar, that he found a new home and started a new family, and might return again to his pole in our yard.

Audubon Watchlist — Lewis' Woodpecker
http://audubon2.org/webapp/watchlist/viewSpecies.jsp?id=123

Klickitat County Library Service *Teddy Cole*	1912	"For the Uplift of Goldendale....": Local women organized the Goldendale Woman's Association and began a library in an elementary school classroom with donated books and the State Library's "Traveling Library".

1914-15 The Carnegie Library: The Association raised money to buy three city lots on the corner of Burgen and Grant Streets, the City pledged $1,000 to maintain a city library and appointed a Library Committee for oversight. The Carnegie Foundation granted $8,000 for the construction of a library building. The new library opened to the public in March 1915.

1920-29 Big Boxes and Substations: With financial support from the County Commissioners and books from the Traveling Library, the Goldendale library provided the beginnings of county-wide service. Librarians shipped boxes of books by truck to library sub-stations — often homes — in Bingen, Hartland, Husum, Lyle, Timber Valley, Trout Lake, and White Salmon. In 1929, Governor Hartley terminated the Traveling Library service and ordered all books returned to Olympia.

1929 White Salmon Library in City Hall: The White Salmon Woman's Club started the White Salmon Library in the City Hall. Nordby's Mill donated the lumber, and the high school Manual Training Class built the shelves. "Books were donated by local residents and loaned from the 'County Library' in Goldendale." (*History of Klickitat County* Washington, 1982)

1972-73 A Rural Library District: County voters in the unincorporated areas approved a measure creating a library taxing district. The County Commissioners of Clark, Skamania, and Klickitat Counties then signed an agreement to expand the Fort Vancouver Regional Library District (FVRL), organized in 1950, to include Klickitat County.

1973 Advent of the Bookmobile: Vans carried books, magazines, and audiovisual materials to Klickitat County's outlying schools, homes, and villages from Goldendale and Stevenson Libraries, with visits scheduled for each stop twice a month.

1976   Building a Network: The Washington (later, Western) Library Network organized "with 15 member libraries and an automated system designed by Boeing Computer Services under contract to the Washington State Library." FVRL's membership in the network expedited interlibrary loans to residents of Klickitat County.

1982-85   Goldendale Expansion: the Building Committee pieced together the $1.2 million necessary from State and Federal agencies, corporate donations, legacies, gifts from local businesses and organizations, and door-to-door solicitation. Wilson and Callan, architects who had graduated from Goldendale Schools, created a design that respected the original building and expanded its usefulness.

1992-93   Automated Catalog and the World Wide Web: The automated catalog allowed keyword, partial title, or author searches in addition to the conventional author, title, subject entries. Soon full-text magazine articles were added, followed by pages from on-line reference books. Best of all, the catalog was available from home computers, making it possible to place holds on materials even when the library was closed.

The capacity to search the Web was added to the library terminals, bringing a wealth of information and opening library catalogs around the state and the world.

1995   Bingen Joins FVRL: A spirited campaign garnered the votes necessary to bring Bingen into the Library District at long last, unifying service for all Klickitat County residents. The White Salmon Library became the White Salmon Valley Library to celebrate its enlarged service area.

2000   White Salmon Valley Library Gets A New Home: April 28th the Library moved from its cramped quarters in an old bank building into an expansive new home of over nine thousand square feet with a magnificent view.

Onward: The world of information awaits at our Klickitat County Libraries.

Goldendale Public Library documents, unpublished

May, Pete. 1982. *History of Klickitat County,*Washington. Klickitat County Historical Society.

Minutes of the Board of the Goldendale Public Library, unpublished

Minutes of the Goldendale Federated Woman's Association, unpublished

Western Library Network website www.liebscher.org/ liumaterials/lis565/lecture3.html

LIGHTNING ROD SALESMAN

Wayne Eshelman as told to Teddy Cole

In 1898 my grandfather built a new barn and in 1903 a new house. A barn in the valley had been set on fire by lightning, so when a salesman came around selling lightning rods, he signed up.

The lightning rod came, but my grandfather was unaware that when he signed the paper he'd also signed a note for $500 for the salesman. The fellow had gone to the bank and sold the note, and there was nothing my grandfather could do but pay it. Of course, he had to pay for the lightning rod, too.

LION ON A TREE LIMB

Rita J. Liska

After my husband's death, I lived alone at the end of a long lane for years. Because of an old sow bear with two cubs that liked to play with the screens in the spring, I often carried a rifle with me whenever I went to check our piped water source. Because the brush was thick and the trail narrow, I did not want to find myself between mama and babies without some form of protection.

The evening before, my mare had gone nuts, racing across the pasture and refusing to let her foal go to the creek for water — something they'd done from the time he was born.

As I closed the pasture gate, both of my dogs raced past me and out of sight up the trail. As usual, my cats were following, so we meandered up the trail toward where I'd last seen my dogs. I had not heard a sound from either of them.

About a third of the way up the trail, I looked to my right and saw both dogs through the brush, sitting underneath a thick fir tree, looking up. Supposing they had cornered a porcupine in the tree, I began wading through brush toward them. I could see nothing in the tree, so I moved back into the brush to check the other side.

Something caught my eye as I studied the fir, and I took a closer look at a stunted pine just a few feet away. There, lying among thick growth on a sturdy limb, was a half-grown cougar looking right back at me.

I never did find the hole in the brush that I must have made going in. But a month later, when I went with a helper to clear out and widen the trail, you still could have ridden a bicycle through the hole I made coming back out.

LIPIZZAN HORSES

June Boardman, co-owner of White Horse Vale Lipizzans

"Hello, June. Are you and Leonard still interested in buying a Lipizzan mare?" my friend's voice asked through the phone.

"Yes, we are still looking, but haven't found anything." I replied.

"You won't believe it, but twenty-four Lipizzans are going to auction in February at the horse sale in Hermiston, Oregon."

Indeed, it was hard to believe. At that time there were only about 3,000 of these rare and exquisite horses in the world, and we had been searching for one in the United States for four years. Expecting to buy just one mare or filly, my husband and I drove to the sale in one of the coldest Februarys in years. When we came home that night, we owned three mares and two fillies. One of the mares was in foal. Instantly, we were in the breeding business.

The Hermiston sale was in 1985. Today, twenty years later, our farm White Horse Vale Lipizzans in Goldendale, is one of the largest Lipizzan breeding farms in the country. Each spring sees the birth of six to nine new foals, each of them a special treasure to help assure the future of this rare breed.

Although most Lipizzans are gray/white in color, foals are all born dark and gain their silver coats as they mature. Usually they will be pure white by the age of six to ten years; however, a small percentage remain black or bay their entire lives.

The Lipizzan breed was founded in 1580 for the exclusive use of the Hapsburg royal family and other nobility of the Austro-Hungarian Empire. Throughout its 425-year history, the Lipizzan has always been a rare jewel among horses. It was used for elegant parades, warfare, and fine carriage driving.

Lipizzans have been best known as the "dancing white stallions" of Vienna's famous Spanish Riding School where they continue to carry on the art of classical dressage to this day. After the fall of the Empire during World War I, the imperial horses were dispersed among several countries that were carved out of the old Empire. In Hungary, Czechoslovakia, and parts of Yugoslavia, the Lipizzan was bred for agricultural use on mountain farms. Today in the United States and Europe, Lipizzans are used for competition dressage, carriage driving, and pleasure riding. Their gentle, intelligent natures make them an ideal choice for many equestrians.

To help us and other breeders reach our goals and preserve the Lipizzan horse, White Horse Vale has hosted five bi-annual breeding stock evaluations and breeder's seminars conducted by Dr. Jaromir Oulehla, who was director of the Spanish Riding School and the School Stud Farm of Piber for eighteen years. Our goal is to produce classical baroque type Lipizzans, similar to the ones used in Vienna, with competitive dressage ability. Horses from our farm, ridden by amateurs and professionals, have won many awards, testifying to the success of our efforts.

This year, 2005, not only marks the 425th anniversary of the breed, but also the sixtieth anniversary of the rescue of the Lipizzan mares held captive by Adolph Hitler during World War II. General George S. Patton agreed to send troops behind enemy lines to bring the entire herd of Lipizzan mares into American protection. If it had not been for the brave action of his troops, there would be no Lipizzans today.

We at White Horse Vale entertain visitors interested in Lipizzans from around the world. Anyone wishing to learn more about Lipizzans, or choose one for their own, is invited to make an appointment to visit our farm.

{Some of the stories in this book written by Rita J. Liska mention locations that are not shown on most maps of Klickitat County. You should be able to find those locations on this map.}

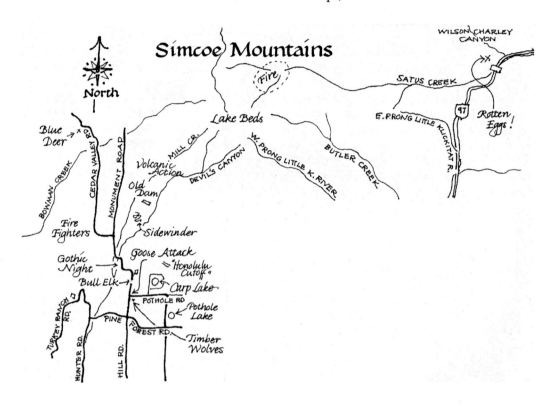

LOCAL DIET

Kathleen Goode

Native American populations in our county based their traditional diet on a wide variety of fruits and vegetables, nuts, wild game, and salmon. They made regular treks from the Columbia to Mt. Adams, from Mt. Adams to the valleys, and from the valleys back to the Columbia. There was also travel to visit relatives in neighboring tribes, travel for celebrations, and travel for trade. They were strong, lean, and healthy. Every aspect of their lifestyle would be considered sustainable living.

Today, nutritionists encourage us to eat more fruits and vegetables and include in our diet good sources of Omega 3 fatty acids, such as wild salmon. We read warnings about the additives in processed foods and the hormones and antibiotics in meat. Doctors encourage us to get more exercise, and the best exercise, they say, is walking. Environmentalists warn that we are destroying the ecological balance of the planet and encourage us to use more sustainable methods of producing energy, housing, and food.

THE LONG NARROWS

Teddy Cole

The Long Narrows: a stretch of the Columbia River approximately three miles long between present day Horsethief State Park (now Columbia Hills Park) and The Dalles Dam. It was named the long narrows on maps drawn by the Corps of Discovery in 1806. The long narrows formed the eastern border of the peninsula once called "The Grand Dalles" ("the big flagstone gutter") because French explorers thought it resembled the gutters of Paris lined with flat rocks. It formed a bottleneck where the river, which had been a half-mile wide, was compressed into less than 200 feet. In Emory Strong's words, the river was "literally turning on edge" in a channel hundreds of feet deep.

This area was the gateway between two distinct geographical regions and two language groups: the Chinook to the west and the Sahaptin to the east. The ease of catching fish in the narrow channel drew many to fish and others to trade. Amateurs and profiteers disturbed the sites and removed many relics, but archeologists found indications dating back at least 2000 years. The sites were not completely excavated and studied before the area was drowned in the waters behind The Dalles Dam. However, a road cut on the opposite side of the river revealed evidence of continuous occupation of 10,000 years, the oldest in the United States.

One artifact that endures is the face above the site of the ancient Wishram village: Tsagaglalal, "She Who Watches." William Least Heat-Moon writes, "There is a chance she will still be watching when dams, like Roman aqueducts, are relics of an empire that prized technology over vision and natural harmony, creations of a mechanically clever people who in only a couple of hundred years, give or take a day or two, worked consciously to turn a zoggledyteen-million-year-old river valley into a great memaloose."

Heat Moon, William Least.1999. *River Horse: the logbook of a boat across America*. Houghton Mifflin.

Spranger, Michael S. 1984, reprinted 1996. *The Columbia Gorge, a unique American treasure*. WSU Cooperative Extension and the U.S. Department of Agriculture.

Strong, Emory M. 1976. *Wakemap Mound: and nearby sites on the Long Narrows of the Columbia River*. Binford & Mort.

LOVE FOUND ON THE WHITE SALMON RIVER

*Talia Norman
(guest, then employee,
at Wet Planet Rafting &
Kayaking, Husum WA)*

Whitewater Rafting

I will forever dearly love the White Salmon River. I was working at a vineyard in the Willamette Valley and had been on my way to Joseph OR for a wine tasting. My truck broke down, and I waited in the hot sun all afternoon to get a tow and get back on the road. I had missed the tasting completely, so I headed toward home. By nightfall I found myself in Hood River looking for a hotel and trying to keep my spirits up after missing the event that featured the wine that I helped to make.

After settling in, I decided to make the most of the weekend and go whitewater rafting. I grabbed a brochure from the hotel desk and called the Wet Planet Whitewater Center in Husum, far too late in the day to expect an answer. To my surprise, someone picked up, and I scheduled a trip on the White Salmon for the next morning.

When I arrived at Wet Planet, I noticed that I had an eye for one of the guides who was kayaking along with the trip. I did my best to avoid him, because he made me nervous — especially while I was walking around in a body hugging wetsuit! I couldn't tell whether the butterflies in my stomach were from the upcoming whitewater trip or him. Once we got on the water, though, all anxiety was lost and I was enthralled with the beauty of the Northwest. I still am, every day.

The trip was phenomenal. One other couple and myself were on the trip, and we were the only people on the river that morning. There was a slight mist in the air, it wanted to rain, and the fog creeping across the banks to the river was breathtaking. Mergansers and harlequins flocked to nearby boulders as we floated along downstream, and an osprey eyed us from its perch high above the river (I've since seen a bear and a bobcat in this river canyon). Small waterfalls cascaded down over the basalt cliffs, and the rapids drenched us in chilly glacier water. I was hooked.

After the trip, I felt so peaceful and good about myself that I decided to ask that good-looking kayaker out for lunch. We got married in August.

EARLY LYLE TALES

Mary Jean Lord

In 1901 Tim Wall lived on the big curve of land that juts out into the Columbia River below the town of Lyle. He had come to Lyle with his mother, who cooked for railroad crews. When Mary Morgan, a writer for *Ruralite* magazine, interviewed him in 1974, he was still living in the same house.

In the early days of the 20th century, the house was located on Main Street, Lyle. Boats docked nearby. The town boasted two livery stables, two hotels, three merchandise stores, a barber shop, tobacco store, drug store, restaurant, school, and numerous saloons. It all came to an end when a fire bug set the town on fire. Afterwards, the town moved to its present site.

The saloons did a brisk business. One time, Wall recalled, a fellow who had had one too many tumbled into the one-holer behind the saloon and had to be rescued by the sheriff, who hauled him off to the river to soak.

Another drunk, "mistaking his own shadow for a lurking enemy," accidentally rushed off the bank into the river. His yells for help woke up Gus Haleburg over on the Oregon shore, who rowed across the river and pulled him out.

M. V. Frank Morgan, *Ruralite*, September 1974

LYLE POINT

Teddy Cole

The native Klickitats called Lyle Point Nanainmi Waki 'Uulktt: "Place where the wind blows from two directions." A traditional fishing ground, "It was a good place to live," according to Chief Johnny Jackson, "because the people could dry fish in a hurry. If an east wind wasn't blowing downriver, a west wind was blowing upriver."

Lyle Point curves into the Columbia east of the mouth of the Klickitat River and south of the unincorporated community of Lyle. The first European-Americans who settled on the Point in 1859 called it Klickitat Landing. Since then it has been trading post, riverboat landing, farmland, town, railroad freight yard, and, most recently, the proposed site of a residential development.

In recent years the residents of Lyle have been affected by several Federal laws, among them the Endangered Species Act of 1973 that protected the mouth of the Klickitat as breeding habitat of the bald eagle. In 1986, the Columbia River Gorge National Scenic Area Act restricted expansion of the town. However, it designated the Point, then owned by the Burlington Northern Railway, as a Gorge Urban Area, a rare piece of undeveloped Columbia River frontage.

In 1990, Henry Spencer purchased Lyle Point from the Railway for $1.2 million. After much effort and expense, he completed the permitting and environmental impact process and began developing an upscale residential complex that he named Klickitat Landing. In September 1993, several Klickitats who had been accustomed to fishing from Lyle Point and who had been assured of access by the terms of the 1855 Yakima Treaty, upheld by subsequent judicial decisions, arrived to find a gate barring their way.

"I am a quiet person. I do not like to fight," said Margaret Flintknife Saluskin. "I could not permit a blue metal gate to separate me from my ancestors, my way of life." She organized a protest. Although Spencer pledged access, Saluskin worried about the residents who would move into the development. "Our rights to fish cannot depend on the kindness of strangers," she said. Saluskin had unleashed a whirlwind. The local Klickitats and, as news spread, activists of various ethnicities and causes, came together in protest. They erected tipis, a sweathouse, and a longhouse, and they lit a flame that they vowed to keep alive until the developer withdrew. The Columbia Gorge Audubon Society entered the fray, having discovered that the State's environmental report had omitted reference to the protected bald eagle habitat at the Point.

August 27, 1994, the sheriff arrived to remove the non-Natives for trespassing on private property. Eventually, the structures erected for the camp were demolished and the flame extinguished, but Spencer, after years of work and his money gone, had had enough. He gave the Trust for Public Land an option on the property, which they bought for $1.86 million in 2000.

The Trust hoped to sell the land to the state or national park service to be developed as a park, but the county commissioners re-zoned all Gorge Urban Areas in Klickitat County to keep them available for future development, thus forestalling placing a park at Lyle Point. As one resident said, "We don't need another park; we already have parks! We need housing."

As of 2005, the Trust holds title to the land and pays property taxes on it. The Klickitats continue to harvest fish at their customary place, which was added in 1997 to the Federal list of "in-lieu" sites, providing an extra measure of protection. The uneasy winds continue to blow over Lyle Point.

Burkhardt, Jesse. 2000. Urban overlay ordinance adopted by Klickitat County Commissioners. *The Goldendale Sentinel*. June 8.

Hollander, Zaz. 1994. Fishing clashes with windsurfing Western Roundup. July 25. High Country News.org, www.hcn.org

Lyle Washington Early History. http://community.gorge. net/lyle/History.htm

May, Pete, ed. 1982. *History of Klickitat County*, Washington. Klickitat County Historical Society.

Public Law 99-633, Columbia River Gorge National Scenic Area Act. November 17. 1986.

Sexton, Barbara, Lyle resident. Personal conversation, May 25, 2005.

Stevens, Isaac I. Yakima Treaty of Fort Stevens, Article 3, Walla-Walla, June 9,1855.

Williams, Marla. Spring 1999. River Land for River People. The Trust for Public Land, www.tpl.org/

LYLE-BALCH CEMETERY

Barbara Sexton and Teddy Cole

The Lyle-Balch Cemetery is the final resting place of a well-known writer, Frederick Homer Balch. He spent part of his short life in this area, writing *Bridge of the Gods* and *Genevieve,* and a granite boulder marks his grave. Leonard Wiley's biography of his life, *The Granite Boulder,* written in 1970, is titled for this unusual marker.

The Lyle-Balch Cemetery was first used as a burying place as early as 1883, when Mrs. Sarah James was buried there. She is the great-grandmother of Frank Hewitt and Alta Hewitt Shields, both presently of Lyle. The cemetery, originally the Pine Tree Cemetery, is located on what was government land.

In 1902, the Lyle Cemetery Association registered Articles of Incorporation with the State of Washington. This gave the Association authority to acquire title to the site and up to 20 adjoining acres. Thomas Whitcomb served as the first president, with Philip Eirich, Herbert F. Hewitt, and Hester Daffron as other officers and trustees.

During the organization period, E.W. Jones had taken up 160 acres as a homestead, which included this land. He refused to release the entire twenty acres, but finally he relinquished the two and a half acres covering the land of the former Pine Tree Cemetery, where scattered interments had been made. Further attempts to secure the entire twenty acres allowed by the state proved fruitless.

In 1904, Mr. Jones transferred his homestead to a Mrs. Armstrong, a widow. She in turn transferred it to Mr. Ralph Hood, who bought the land at $1.25 per acre. Ironically, two charter members of the Lyle Cemetery Association signed as witnesses of the transaction. As soon as Hood received the patent for the land, he demanded that the Association pay $100 per acre. The association offered to pay fifty dollars for five acres, but that was refused. Later, Hood transferred his ownership to a brother, Victor Hood, who demanded payment of $100 for two and a quarter acres. No records remain to show how this dispute was settled. Either the warranty deed was deemed valid, or the Association paid the demanded $100.

Originally, ownership of lots was given for payment of twenty-five cents annual membership dues. This custom led to complications, and the method was finally abandoned. However, titles remain uncertain to many unused plots for which as little as twenty-five cents had been paid.

Volunteers who care about their ancestors and families give many hours to tending the cemetery. They hold an annual workday and groom the grounds for the Memorial Day guests coming to pay homage to loved ones. Generous gifts and bequests have made possible a directory sign, an enlarged area, an improved water system, and a building with storage space and restrooms.

The cemetery has been renamed the Lyle-Balch Cemetery in honor of the author. It is a beautiful, rustic cemetery, with wildflowers abounding, oak and pine trees scattered here and there, and a commanding view of the Columbia River.

Lillian Hamm

Lucy Palmer Maddock was the daughter of Ed Palmer, a banker in early Salem, Oregon. She met Frank Maddock when he arrived there on a wagon train. The young couple soon married, moving to eastern Oregon where they homesteaded. Frank started a trading post and mercantile store. He was also elected the first sheriff of Umatilla County. Frank and Lucy had five children: Frank Jr., who died young of tuberculosis, John, George, Louis, and Birdie.

In 1865, while serving as sheriff, Frank received a letter from The Dalles informing him that the notorious horse thief HankVaughn had stolen two horses and that the writer thought Vaughn would try to sell them in Umatilla. Sheriff Maddock set out to find him. Unfortunately, Hank Vaughn saw the sheriff coming and shot him in the cheek. Frank died several years later from complications resulting from this bullet wound.

After her husband's death, Lucy moved to McMinnville, where her children could complete their educations. Frank had been a prosperous merchant as well as sheriff and left his family financially independent.

Son John Maddock bought property at Columbus and farmed there for a number of years. John was also a banker, a founder and the first president of the First National Bank, Goldendale's first bank. Lucy often came to Columbus to visit John and his wife Ida, staying in the boarding house of Caroline Hope. She became well acquainted with the community and its residents.

When the prominent Goldendale attorney W. B. Presby went looking for a backer to finance the purchase and planting of wine grapes at the Presby Ranch in Columbus, Lucy loaned him the money. She foreclosed when Presby was unable repay the loan. Lucy was not able to manage the Presby Ranch herself, so she leased it to local farmers. After Mrs. Maddock's death, her daughter Birdie and son-in-law, the Reverend W.T. Jordan, successfully farmed the Presby Ranch for twenty-five years.

LUCY PALMER MADDOCK

Rachel Gunkel

Ruth Jordan Peterson. 1982. This Land of Gold and Toil. Caxton Printers, Ltd.
The Illustrated History of Yakima, Klickitat and Kittitas Counties. 1904. Interstate Publishing Co.
U.S. Federal Census, 1900.

Mary Jean Lord

In the early 1980s, motorists driving along Highway 14 near were sometimes startled by a surreal vision of airplane-like rotors rising and falling above the brow of the cliff. Intrigued, some turned up the Maryhill grade and drove the country road twelve miles east. It was worth the trip. From a high perch in the Goodnoe Hills, the sleek white towers of the three largest windmills in the world soared skywards.

Built by Boeing for the Department of Energy (DOE), the MOD-2 experimental wind machines drew a steady stream of visitors from all over the world. The towers reared 200 feet in the air, their two outstretched arms measuring 300 feet from tip to tip. A fortunate visitor might be standing nearby when first one, then two, and finally all three windmills sprang to life. The sound was unforgettable — a whir like a spinning top and a sharp whip crack as the blades swept round.

Important guests were escorted inside one of the towers and up in the elevator to the nacelle, the boxcar-sized room at the top that held the gearbox and other machinery. The most daring ventured outside onto a narrow catwalk for a giddy view of Mt. Adams, Mt. Rainier, and most of Klickitat County.

Those were the windmills' good days, which, as Goldendale residents were all too aware, were few and far between. During the years between their dedication in 1981 and their removal in 1987, the windmills were silent for months at a time, the ground littered with house-sized chunks of rotors in various stages of being dismantled or put back together. Only rarely did anyone see all three MOD-2s operating at the same time. They were, after all, experimental.

When something in one machine broke or developed a crack, all three were shut down on the assumption that what had happened to one could happen to all. There were no spare parts. NASA, the agency that managed the project, had to call the factory that made the part, which might be in Denmark or Sweden, and order three new ones manufactured and shipped to Goldendale. In the meantime, the giant work cranes, leased and brought to the site from Portland at a cost of thousands of dollars a day, sat idle.

Eventually, most of the bugs were worked out, and, for a few glorious months, the windmills churned happily, generating lots of electricity for the Bonneville

Power Administration power grid. Wind experts arrived from NASA and EPRI (Electric Power Research Institute) to conduct tests. They lit colored smoke bombs and studied the patterns set up by the spinning blades, working out guidelines for the efficient configuration of wind farms.

In 1987, the DOE announced that it had completed testing and no longer needed the MOD-2s. Since no utility wanted to run windmills that were so costly to maintain, they were broken up and sold to a Portland scrap metal dealer.

A charming metal sculpture of Don Quixote, created by three Bonneville Power Employees, had captivated everyone at the small Goodnoe Hills visitor center. Bonneville Power presented the sculpture to Klickitat PUD on the condition that it be placed where the public could enjoy it. The horse doesn't gallop, and the arms of the windmill no longer turn in the wind, but Don Quixote can still be admired at Vern Markee Park near the north entrance to Goldendale, the only memorial to Klickitat County's magnificent wind machines.

MAIL ORDER BRIDES I

Mary Jean Lord

In the late 1880s a group of young men from Germany came to America to avoid compulsory military service and to seek their fortune. Upon landing in New York, they heard about the homesteads to be had in the West and put to sea again. Sailing around the Horn and along the coast to California and Oregon, they eventually made their way up the Columbia River to Fort Dalles. Florence Bartholomew, in the January 1966, *Ruralite* magazine, tells their story.

"One day," Bartholomew writes, "one of the men struck up a conversation with a settler who had come to town for supplies. The gentleman extolled the beauty and fertility of his homestead farther north.

"He could grow potatoes as big as his two fists, he boasted, and cabbages as large as a barrel head. The wild hay grew rump high, he said, and the game was so plentiful you had only to step outside your door for meat."

The young men used most of their remaining resources to purchase horses and supplies and followed the man across the river. He led them past Lyle and through the Klickitat gorge, up the mountain and through the forest, descending finally to a valley with "a large lake and rich meadows heavy with wild hay."

"'Is this the place?'" they asked.

"'This is the place,' the man answered proudly."

The young men spread out, and each found and filed on a piece of land. Only one thing was missing in their little paradise — women. They decided to send to Germany for wives.

After months of hard work, they raised enough money for tickets to bring the brides over. In a long letter to Germany, each man described the kind of woman he preferred, tall or short, dark or fair. One man is supposed to have written, "I don't care if you are homely as a cow, just so you're strong!"

The men were cleaned up and waiting in Fort Dalles when the bride boat finally arrived. The men looked on silently while the women walked down the gangplank single file. Suddenly a man called out in German, naming his choice.

With that, Bartholomew writes, "A war-whoop went up from the men and they surged forward engulfing the women. In a matter of moments, all were paired off. And, while a few drunks had to be fished out of the Columbia, all seemed well satisfied."

Some of the descendants of these men and their brides still live in the beautiful valley at the foot of Mt. Adams known as Glenwood.

Florence Bartholomew. 1966. Glenwood Brides. *Ruralite*. January.

MAIL ORDER BRIDES II

Toni Stencil

About 100 years ago, two young brothers, Leo and Alex Kirbish, came over from Austria to homestead on Oak Ridge Road just above Husum, Washington.

The women were scarce back then, so the brothers purchased mail order brides through a catalog. When the mail order brides, who were sisters, arrived, Leo the eldest said that he would get first pick. So, of course, he picked the best looking of the two.

Leo then took his bride and moved up to the base of Tum-Tum Mountain. He called himself the 'King of Tum-Tum'. Alex stayed in the homestead on Oak Ridge Road with his new bride.

Leo's beautiful bride was a bit unsettled and enjoyed going to town to party. Leo, discouraged with her desire for town life, sawed off the high heels of her shoes, hoping to discourage her trips to town. Sad to say, it didn't work. She ended up running off with a boot-legger. So the story goes. However, Alex and his bride lived happily ever after.

Town legend

MARYHILL LOOPS HILL CLIMB

Robert Bush

The Maryhill Loops Hill Climb, a sports car hill climb race up the historic Maryhill Loops Road, was held annually from 1955 through 1963. On one weekend each summer, Goldendale would come alive with the sounds and sights of the latest sports and racing cars as drivers from throughout the Northwest arrived in Goldendale to participate in this challenging race which received national recognition in automotive magazines of the day including "Road and Track."

The winter weather during the winter of 1963-1964 caused extensive damage to the road, effectively closing it and putting an end to the event. However, with the resurfacing of a large part of the road in 1998, the road's fortunes improved.

The hill climb event was revived in 1999 by the Society of Vintage Racing Enthusiasts (SOVREN). Many local organizations assisted, including the Maryhill Museum of Art, the City of Goldendale, Klickitat County, the Greater Goldendale Chamber of Commerce, the Goldendale Motorsports Association, and the Yakima Valley Sports Car Club (which had started the original event in 1955). This revival is true to the original, bringing back many of the same cars, including Jaguars, Corvettes, Austin Healeys, Porsches, and Allards, and some of the drivers who actually raced up the hill from 1955 through 1963.

The original weekend event incorporated a car show on Saturday afternoon. The main street in Goldendale was blocked off, and the race cars and sports cars were put on display. When the event was revived in 1999, the car show was moved to the grounds of the Maryhill Museum of Art, and was no longer limited to sports cars but included all models of cars. At noon on Saturday, the race cars drive down Highway 14 and arrive at the

Museum in a thundering mass to join the car show for the afternoon.

The road and the surrounding area have not been spoiled by development or other changes. Everyone can enjoy this truly vintage event brought back to life as it was in the late 1950s and early 1960s.

MARYHILL MUSEUM OF ART

Kathleen Goode

One of the most impressive estates in Klickitat County is Maryhill. It was built by 19th century tycoon, Sam Hill. He originally intended it as his palatial home and the focal point of a new agricultural community, but things turned out rather differently.

The estate overlooks the Columbia River, one of the largest rivers in the United States. High on the bluff, you could not ask for a grander setting. It is surrounded by beautiful grounds, complete with wandering peacocks and a sculpture garden. The grounds are maintained much as they were in Sam Hill's day, but with a small army of volunteers completing the yearly weeding and planting of annuals.

The mansion has become an art museum. In truth, the place is much more than that. The art collection includes things as varied as American paintings, French fashion figures, and a large chess collection. There is a special collection of works by the French sculptor, Rodin, and a spectacular collection of Native American items. There is something seldom seen in American museums, a room dedicated to royalty; Queen Marie of Romania donated most of these items when the museum opened.

The Maryhill Museum of Art is the kind of place you take your visitors to see. It is also the kind of place you go to once or twice a year just to check out the new exhibits, especially if you like art. The place is even more than that. It is the setting for weddings and, occasionally, a high school prom. It is a place to listen to a music concert under the stars, with children dancing and friends visiting. The grounds are a good place to learn about what will survive here and what plants create happy combinations. It is a place to explore history and learn about Native American plants. Once a year it becomes a perfect setting for Dias de los Muertos — the Days of the Dead celebration. On another night, there might be a formal dinner and dance. There have been living history presentations, storytellers, hands-on art projects, lectures, tours, auto shows, and, once, even a train. Maryhill is an art museum, but it is also what Sam Hill originally intended it to be, a beautiful, central part of community life.

Personal experience
Museum web site at http://www.maryhillmuseum.org

MARYHILL WINERY

Joy Bradley

What in the name of Sam Hill is happening in the Columbia Gorge? Maryhill Winery entered the 2002 West Coast Wine Competition, along with 100 producers of California Zinfandel, and walked away with Best of Class. Gold. Gold from a harvest picked before Craig and Vicki Leuthold broke ground on October 11, 2000, for the winery, tasting room, and amphitheater that overlooks the mighty Columbia River. The tasting room opened its doors in May of 2001. Four years later — with gold, double gold, and platinum medals — Northwest Wine Press declared Maryhill Zinfandel not only the best Zin in the state of Washington, but the best Zin anywhere.

Annual records show that 60,000 visitors a year have walked through the tasting room doors, and another 12,000 have enjoyed the concert events. You'd think that most of these visitors would have questions about the wines, or the 80-plus acres of vineyards surrounding the winery, but that is not the case. The most often asked question is about Potter, who greets them when they arrive.

Potter, a Great Pyrenees, is the winery dog. People come just to see Potter and are disappointed if he's not on the grounds to greet them when they arrive. On his birthday, declared Dog Days, you will see 10 or 15 dogs and masters there to help Potter celebrate. Cookie biscuits are available for all four-pawed critters, and a supply is kept behind the bar year round.

The second most frequent question is,"Where did you get the bar?" The magnificent bar dates back to the late 1880s. It's an old Brunswick, originally ordered from a Sears Roebuck catalog and shipped around the Horn to Juneau, Alaska, where it remained through the Gold Rush days. In the 1960s, it moved to the Old Fort Spokane Brewery and stayed there until the brewery's closing in December 2000. Craig and Vicki Leuthold placed a bid, acquired the bar, and instructed their architect to build the tasting room around the bar. The wine, once tasted, speaks for itself. The medals for awards won rest around the necks of wine bottles crowded on display behind the bar.

So, will your first question be about Potter or about the award-winning wines?

Personal experience
Conversations with Craig and Vicki Leuthold

KLICKITAT COUNTY MASTER GARDENERS

Joan Wilkins Stone

The redtail hawk swooped down and nabbed a bite of breakfast for her young. Nestled high in the locust tree were the babies, in a home of twigs and other debris pilfered from the leftovers of earlier growth. Again and again, the mother hawk searched for grubs and insects to feed her open-mouthed babies.

Below, a group of Centerville School children walked the nature trail, looking for praying mantis and other small insects, and watching the hawk care for her babies. Marilyn Sarsfield, retired Centerville School teacher and active Master Gardener, said the children always ask, "Can we go on the trail?"

A group of Master Gardeners, including Marilyn Sarsfield, Valerie Berry, Glenda Bowdish, and Paula Ransom, provide their services to the Centerville School once a week during the spring season. Along with the children, they have built raised beds and planted flowers and vegetable seeds. The students help with watering and weeding.

Kristin Cameron, a fifth and sixth grade teacher at the school, suggested creating the nature trail. Gardeners, teachers, and students went to work The trail meanders through the back areas of the school. A pond was added, dug by the children. A resident snake makes his home there.

The Master Gardener Program in Klickitat County began in 1994 under the direction of Washington State University Extension. There were 45 members in the first class. The classes are held once a month for nine months. The members are to fulfill their obligation to become a Master Gardener by attending classes, completing tests, and volunteering 90 hours of service in horticultural education. Directly involved in the program in Klickitat County are Susan Kerr, Extension Education and Chairperson, and Linda Williams, 4-H Program Coordinator.

Master Gardeners helped develop the Lewis and Clark Memorial Garden at the Maryhill Museum and participated in the garden's dedication. They are involved in Earth Day, informing people about plants and gardening techniques. They carry out many after school programs. The plant diagnostic clinic, staffed by volunteers during certain hours, handles fellow gardeners' problems.

Marilyn Sarsfield says, "To be a Master Gardener is a process of learning and having fun for all involved." Marilyn continues the story of the redtail hawk and her babies. One day the mother hawk leaves the nest and doesn't return the whole day. The babies squawk loudly. The next morning the nest is empty, and the younger students worry. The Master Gardener explains the babies have flown away and are on their own.

The redtail hawk returns to her home in the locust tree. The children are taught another lesson in the cycle of nature.

Interview with Marilyn Sarsfield

THE MEADOW LARK INN

Rachel Gunkel

One of the buildings that Samuel Hill constructed for his planned Quaker community of Maryhill was the Meadow Lark Inn. The inn, originally called the St. James Hotel, stood where Stonehenge is now located. When Hill decided to construct Stonehenge in 1918, the site of the hotel was determined to be the best location for the memorial. The hotel was moved north a couple of blocks and renamed at that time.

The Meadow Lark Inn was a handsome, two and a half story wooden frame building with a wraparound porch on two sides. Hill occasionally stayed at the inn when he was pursuing his business interests in Klickitat County. He had envisioned the inn as an elegant setting in which to wine and dine friends and politicians, thereby gaining their interest and support

Meadow Lark Inn

for his many projects, and as lodging for travelers, an essential element in his grand scheme to make the Pacific Northwest more accessible. The Meadow Lark was also used to house engineers, craftsmen, and other highly skilled employees of Hill who were in the area to construct dams, roads and buildings.

Sam Hill became acquainted with Clara Carter and Lucy Leatherby in Victoria, B.C. in 1921. The two Englishwomen, inseparable friends since childhood, had come to Victoria to attend the wedding of Clara's sister. Hill hired them both to work in his Seattle mansion; Clara as cook and Lucy as housekeeper. They remained in Hill's employ until his death in 1931.

Hill's will gave the two women a life interest in the Meadow Lark Inn, and they operated it for the next 22 years. The Meadow Lark became a famous landmark throughout the Mid Columbia. The restaurant business kept Clara and Lucy busy, and the inn earned a reputation for serving good food. A few people also lodged at the inn, and their clientele included regulars who returned year after year. When Lois Davis Plotts visited her childhood home of Maryhill in the early 1950s, she stayed at the Meadow Lark and recorded Lucy saying that people came there "to lose the cares of life among the everlasting hills, to regain perspective from the songs of the meadow larks."

Clara and Lucy were affectionately known as "the girls" by their neighbors in Maryhill. A favorite story, repeated often over the years, concerned Clara and Lucy's unique method of driving. "The girls" owned an old car, and the efforts of both were required to operate it. Clara steered the car, and Lucy shifted the gears. Neither woman ever learned to drive the vehicle without the assistance of the other. When their neighbors saw Clara and Lucy on the road, they would prudently pull over and wait for them to pass.

Clara became ill in 1953, and the restaurant business at the Meadow Lark Inn ceased. When Clara died in August of 1955, Lucy moved to Goldendale. Lucy's own health declined rapidly after the loss of her life-long friend, and she died the following year.

The Meadow Lark Inn sat abandoned for several years until a raging grass fire swept across the hillside on July 11, 1958. Driven by a 40-mile-an-hour wind, the fire destroyed everything in its path for miles. One of its victims was the Meadow Lark Inn.

"Rites held here for Clara Carter, Maryhill resident,"
   The Goldendale Sentinel, August 11, 1955, p. 1;
"Death comes to Lucy Leatherby, native of England,"
   The Goldendale Sentinel, August 2,1956, p. 1;
"Grass fire sweeps over six mile strip along Columbia,"
   The Goldendale Sentinel, July 17, 1958, p. 1;
Sam Hill: the Prince of Castle Nowhere, John E Tuhy, Portland:
   Timber Press, 1983;Maryhill,
Sam Hill, and Me, Lois Davis Plotts, Camas, Washington:
   Post Publications, 1978.

THE MEMALOOSE ISLAND GRAVE MARKER

Mary Jean Lord

Travelers in the Columbia Gorge often wonder about the marble monument jutting from an island in the middle of the Columbia River west of Lyle. The island is named Memaloose, a Chinook word meaning "to die." When Lewis and Clark came down the river in 1805, they noted numerous grave sites on this and other islands in the river.

Marble monuments were not the custom of the native Americans, however, who honored their dead by burying objects with them that they had enjoyed in life and would need in the afterlife. The monument on Memaloose marks the grave site of a white man, Victor Trevitt, of The Dalles.

Trevitt, a printer, came to The Dalles in 1853 and opened a saloon. It was known as a "gentleman's place" because Trevitt didn't tolerate drunken rowdies. He did extend credit, however, which eventually led to his having to give up his bar.

Trevitt was elected a state senator in 1866. Whether as a result of his experiences in the legislature or in the saloon business, he became thoroughly disillusioned with "dishonest white men." He made friends among the Wasco and Klickitat tribes and determined that he wanted to be laid to rest on Memaloose Island, a sacred Indian burial ground.

After he died, about 50 of his friends gathered on Memaloose Island to say farewell. Not long after his burial, surviving tribesmen began gathering the bones of their ancestors, relocating them to Wish-Ram Cemetery in Washington. By 1857, only Trevitt was left on the island.

Ruralite. October 1992.

MAN OF MANY TALENTS: BRUCE E. MEYERS

Geneva M. Meyers

Musician, lapidarist, marqueter, carver, carpenter, cabinet maker, sketcher, oil painter, hybridizer, writer, Bruce was a man of many talents. He executed all these talents with excellence.

Bruce Edward Meyers was born at Mt. Adams Orchards in 1924, to Lawrence and Dulcie Meyers. He started school in the old Gilmer schoolhouse (still standing today on the Kreps' Family Ranch property). In the early 1930s, the Meyers family moved to BZ Corners where, Bruce recalled, he and his two brothers cut and carried brush to help clear land for their new home. Bruce finished school at Husum Elementary and Columbia Union High School in White Salmon. His graduation in 1943 fell during World War II; he was drafted into the army air force where he served as an airplane metal worker.

Self taught, he played lead guitar in local musical groups. He took up rock hunting with his aunt and uncle, created a huge cabochon and cabinet-specimen collection and several pieces of jewelry, and wrote articles for Gems & Minerals Magazine. He was a builder and woodworker, hand carving works of art inlaid with marquetry. He was a master at drawing and painting, his favorite medium being oil paints. He painted on a number of surfaces: canvas, wood, conks (bracket fungus), plastic, and porcelain.

He dabbled in photography for a short time, which led him to an interest in wild flowers. He became acquainted with local native plant club members and was introduced to the art of hybridizing. He made a number of hybrid crosses with his favorite wild flower, the Penstemon, his most famous being the Mexicali Penstemon. As an active member of the American Penstemon Society, he sent seeds from his hybrids to the seed exchange for several years. His seeds went to members around the United States and abroad, including Australia and New Zealand. His hybridizing projects were left unfinished when he died at his home in White Salmon on August 10, 1998.

The following is an excerpt from Clive Gandley of Devon, England, written on September 6, 2004. "For over thirty years the late Bruce Meyers of White Salmon had amazing success in crossing the native penstemon, particularly with his strain of the Mexicali Penstemon. His work although recognised in the USA was more appreciated in England and over two hundred of his crosses were taken back to Britain. By invitation the Mexicali Penstemons flower in the gardens at Highgrove, the residence of HRH the Prince of Wales (Prince Charles). What an amazing legacy for my great friend."

Bruce forever remains one of the most interesting people I have ever known.

Coyote Canyon is little more than sand and sagebrush. It lies at the far northeast corner of Klickitat County, a remote area well suited to the old farm trucks and sturdy off-road bikes that traverse it.

The area just south of the canyon stands in profound contrast. It is filled with green fields, thriving vineyards, and the diversified crops of Andrews Farms and Mercer Ranch. Andrews Farms is known for its grapes, apples, beans, and peas. Neighboring Mercer Farms raises tonnage crops of sweet corn, garlic, beans, peas, potatoes, carrots, onions, kale, spinach, grapes, apples, pears, and cherries. Their produce is shipped as far away as the Pacific Rim, and much of it goes to commercial processors such as Del Monte and Con Agra. Together, Andrews and Mercer Farms represent 10,000 acres of irrigated land.

Mercer Ranch was range land for sheep when the family began building its holdings in the 1930s. Following World War II, the sheep industry was no longer as profitable, and many farms went under. Mercer Ranch converted to cattle ranching and put in the first irrigation system in the area in order to raise hay for their herds. When the John Day Dam was built in the 1960s, Mercer Ranch gained an irrigation resource. They have continued to grow and adapt, trying new crops, developing new markets, and creating many jobs. Mercer Ranch has about 55 full time employees with an additional 30 people hired on a seasonal basis.

Mercer Ranch developed a carrot processing plant that uses about half of the carrots grown there. Some of the production is dedicated to the baby-peel carrots that are so popular now. The processing plant is a major employer with over 200 people working there in the peak season. The plant was sold to Bolt House

MERCER RANCH

Kathleen Goode

Farm, a company from Bakersfield, California, but is still in full production. The successes of the ranch and the processing plant have brought new life to the small town of Alderdale. Like Roosevelt, there is a building boom as more people want to live near the area where they work.

Federman, Mike. 1999. Mercer Ranch bears fruit in
    Alderdale. *Ruralite Country*, September.
Interview with Mercer Ranch Agronomist, Todd Crosby

MIDDLE OF NOWHERE

Kathleen Goode

People often complain that this county is in the middle of nowhere. I live in the middle of Goldendale, which is right in the middle of the county, and I think it's the middle of just about everything. We are in the middle of our family with children in Denver, Seattle, Hawaii, and California. They all live close enough to visit, and no one feels slighted because we moved closer to one kid than another. According to them, we are a million miles from anywhere.

Quilting taught me that we are in a pretty good spot. North is Yakima (what a beautiful drive in the fall!), Ellensburg, and Spokane. The last is an overnight trip, but Yakima is only about an hour and a half away and has several great quilt shops, plus one of the oldest community colleges in the state, the Yakama Cultural Center, and a wonderful arboretum.

East is the Tri-Cities, which has two fantastic quilt shops, a very good old-fashioned toy store, and a beautiful river-front park. On the Oregon side of the highway, there is Pendleton (another quilt shop and the famous blanket factory) and the Blue Mountains. South is the road to Bend and Sisters that goes through quite a few small towns. The first time our quilt group drove down for the famous Sisters quilt show, it took us nearly the whole day. Normally it's about a three or four hour trip but we had to explore every place our husbands had refused to stop. My husband says it's a guy thing; they want to get from point A to point B and only stop for emergencies. Seems to me you miss half the fun that way.

Southeast is the nearest town and the one I visit the most, The Dalles. It is less than an hour away, and the drive is along the beautiful Columbia River. There is a tiny quilt shop there and another, slightly larger one in Hood River, just a bit down the road. The Dalles is home to Klindt's — one of my favorite bookstores. West are the two largest cities in the area, Vancouver and Portland. They have tons of quilt shops, another old-fashioned toy store (yes, I have grandchildren), the airport, a huge privately owned bookstore (Powell's), and the regional library. The highways in each of these directions are excellent. The most scenic drive is on the Washington side between Klickitat County and Vancouver. It is a little longer than the trip on the Oregon side but is worth it for the view. There is very little traffic and the roads are seldom blocked by anything. Now, if the price of gas would just go back down.

MICKI AND THE NAVAJO-CHURRO SHEEP

Kathleen Goode

Micki Jones decided to be a little different. She and her husband, Steve, moved here from Southern Oregon and started Dry Creek Ranch near Bowman Creek. They had raised cattle, but this property was not suited for that, so Micki decided sheep would be a good alternative. They were small enough for her to manage and would still be good producers. She looked at many different breeds and finally settled on a rare breed from the Southwest, the Navajo-Churro.

This primitive breed of sheep was the first brought to the United States. It is an ancient Iberian breed brought to the New World by the Spanish in the 16th century. They thought it would be useful to provide both food and clothing for the armies of the conquistadors and Spanish settlers. The decision was a sound choice because the Churro is a hardy breed that can endure with less water and grass than other breeds. The meat produced is delicious and lean. The wool is a favorite with hand spinners. These qualities made it an attractive choice for the Navajo. The Navajo saw the Churro as a gift from the creator, one that would provide them with food, clothing, and commerce.

Today, Churro wool is available in white, tan, brown, black and red (and about every shade in between). It is a favorite of hand spinners but of little use to commercial mills. The breed was nearly made extinct because of a bad policy decision by the U.S. government. They forced the Navajo farmers to replace their favorite breed with one that might be more attractive to commercial mills. This was a disaster. Today, small independent farms have helped bring the breed back to at least a point of recognition. Micki now serves on the Board of Directors for the Navajo-Churro Association.

Micki decided on her sheep before she learned to spin, and she is glad of the choice. She always admired the designs and culture of the Navajo weavers. Today she has over 100 sheep, some from as far away as New Mexico, and her youngest daughter, Jessica, is following in Mom's footsteps with a herd of her own. The Churro meat and wool are of such excellent quality that their farm receives top dollar for both animals and fleeces. Micki weaves wool bags reminiscent of the Navajo style she so admires, and sells them through galleries and special shows. Steve works for the county, but he also shoes horses and shears sheep. The family continues to demonstrate what made successful pioneers: willingness to take a chance and try something new and then to share their knowledge with others.

Interview with Micki Jones
The Ark USA. Navajo-Churro Sheep.
Navajo-Churro Sheep Association. http://www.navajo-churrosheep.com

MIGAKI FAMILY FARM

The Migaki Family with
Sissy Gorgus

In 2005, Masashi and Mary Migaki celebrated their 65th wedding anniversary, the culmination of years of hard work, dislocation, and the development of a family farm. Mas, from Rowena, Oregon, and Mary, from Eatonville, Washington, had met at the Portland market where Mary worked and Mas brought produce to sell. They married in 1940, and after living in Rowena for a short while, bought property in Dallesport, the first part of their current farm. The couple, his parents, and their new daughter lived in a log cabin there.

Although Mas and Mary were American citizens, because they were of Japanese heritage they were sent to an internment camp in 1942. They had to pack one bag each and report to a certain check point within 24 hours. Forced to leave their home, they had no idea when they would be able to return. After being interned in Pinedale, California, then Tule Lake, California, they were given early work release and worked for Mr. Woods on his farm in Ontario, Oregon. In 1944, during the time they were in Ontario, their second daughter (writer of this story) was born.

In 1945, the family was finally allowed to come home. They were among the fortunate, because John Dickey worked their farm as well as his own while they were gone, and he paid the taxes on their property, so, unlike many other people of Japanese heritage, they did not lose their property due to unpaid taxes.

When they came back, Mas and Mary worked their land and raised their family, adding acreage and housing and birthing two sons. In the early years, the family would harvest and pack the produce during the day, and Mas would haul the produce to market in Portland every night. That was before the freeway, I-84, was built. It made long hours.

But it wasn't all just hard work — they met many nice people who became friends. Some would come from as far as Montana just to have Migaki tomatoes, corn, and peaches.

They retired from the farm when Mas was about 75 and Mary about 73. However, as the family points out, this is difficult to pinpoint, since farmers do not really retire — they just gradually slow down!

In 1995, the four kids (Janet, Becky, Roger, and Gerry), with their respective spouses, formed a corporation and leased the farm from Mas and Mary. The corporation turned the produce farm into a cherry orchard. Mas and Mary still live on the property. To date, they have four children, six grandchildren, and 12 great-grandchildren who enjoy the fruits of their hard labor.

MILITARY ROAD

Teddy Cole

The Old Military Road no longer crosses the Klickitat Valley but, just as a vivid image remains after a dream, traces of the road lie deep in Klickitat soil. For a quarter-century, the military road provided passage for horse-drawn wagons between the Columbia River — the

Territory's primary transportation corridor — and the great Yakima Valley.

The road ran north from Rockport (now Dallesport) over three mountainous ridges. It was first a route for army wagons loaded with arms and provisions to Fort Simcoe. Later, freighters carried supplies for settlers and the Yakama reservation, and stages transported passengers and mail between Central Washington and the steamboat docks on the Columbia River.

The story of the Military Road is a cumulative tale wherein one thing leads to another, as in the House that Jack Built:

New settlers, encouraged by the Federal Government to move into the Pacific Northwest, demanded that more land be opened. This led to the 1855 treaty signed at Walla Walla. The treaty provided for a division of territory between the native people and the incoming settlers.

Some natives believed that their leaders had been hoodwinked into signing away their lands. A band attacked a party of miners moving into the Kittitas Valley, and another group murdered Indian agent Andrew Bolon as he crossed the Simcoes heading back to Vancouver.

General Waller led an expedition to punish the people who had murdered the miners and Agent Bolon, but met resistance from the Yakama Nation. Waller's troops retreated into the Klickitat Valley, where they built a defensive stockade, "Fort Klikitat," near present-day Blockhouse.

The Army built Fort Simcoe in the Yakima Valley and established a garrison to quell hostilities and protect the settlers, but its isolation required a supply route from Fort Dalles on the Columbia. Captain Frederick Dent undertook the task, and began work the year following the signing of the treaty that was the cause of the trouble in the first place.

The road began at the Rockport ferry dock, crossed the present-day airport, and climbed the Columbia Hills. It descended into the Klickitat Valley, passed the stockade, and climbed the Simcoes, crossing the Toppenish Ridge, eventually descending into what is now known as the Yakima Valley.

The Yakamas called the valley where Fort Simcoe was built "Mool-Mool." It was their favorite wintering place, and the name referred to its many bubbling springs. From there an ancient Indian trail called "Ah-soom," (Eel Trail) led to the Columbia River, passing just to the west of the Wahk-shum, the spring where Bolon was murdered.

Winter weather closed the route by the end of October. Frequent deadly blizzards on the high passes led to a Native belief that an evil spirit, a "chil-wit," lay in ambush for anyone so foolish as to try crossing the Simcoes in winter.

After the Yakima Indian Wars ended in 1859, the Army pulled out from Fort Simcoe, and the site became headquarters for the Federal Indian Agency. The military road continued to serve the needs of reservation and settlers alike even after the Army abandoned it in 1867.

As the military road deteriorated, the newly organized county government undertook to establish a new road from the county seat in Rockport to the northeastern county boundary on the Yakima River. The road ran through Centerville to Klickitat Creek (the area that eventually became Goldendale), climbed to Alder Creek (now Bickleton) and on over the Simcoes to Cock's ferry.

The Military Road is long gone, but the memory is embedded in deep ruts on private land that was once a public thoroughfare and a lifeline.

McKensie, Mickael. 2002. *Lessons from an Old Road: Frederick Dent's Route from Fort Dalles to Fort Simcoe. Columbia*, publ. Washington State Historical Society. Fall.

McWhorter, Lucullus Virgil. 1994. *Tragedy of the Wahk-shum*. Donald M. Hines, ed. Issaquah WA: Great Eagle Publishing Co.

Maps, including

Standard Atlas of Klickitat County, Washington, G.A. Ogle, 1913.

Klickitat County, K.D.P. Enterprises, 1975.

Official Map of Klickitat County, Klickitat County Road Dept, 2002.

MINNIE AND THE MOUNTAIN LION

Barbara Purser Voreis

My Grandmother, Minnie Purser, told me this story.
One day when Minnie, George and their family were living in White Salmon, George was ill. He was not well enough to walk the seven miles to Minnie's homestead to feed the chickens; Minnie went. In a trap which George had set to catch the animal that had been stealing their chickens, Minnie found a mountain lion. She killed the mountain lion, put it into a sack, trap and all, and took it back to show her husband George that she could take care of herself!

I was 15 when Grandma Minnie died. I wrote this story down just as Grandma told it to me. I am the oldest daughter of John Cleburne Purser who was born in White Salmon on August 30, 1911, the youngest son of George and Minnie Purser.

Unfortunately, I know no further details about Grandma and the mountain lion. I know that Minnie and George Purser were married in Vancouver, Washington, June 27, 1899. They moved from White Salmon in 1918.

Minnie Gertrude Elliott Purser

THE MISSING HOWITZER

Jo N. Miles

A story has been told for years about a missing howitzer (cannon) buried by soldiers in the Yakima Valley during the 1850s. During a retreat after a deadly ambush by hostile Yakamas, the surviving soldiers abandoned the heavy howitzer in order to escape to safety. Legend persisted that the artillery piece was never recovered. Many people tried to find it without success.

Written records left behind by military officers who were present during the incident reveal the following details about the story:

During the first week of October in 1855, Major Granville O. Haller and two companies of soldiers set out from Fort Dalles into Yakama country to seek out and punish the murderers of Indian Agent A.J. Bolon and miner Henry Mattice. Haller's troops brought with them an artillery piece known as a mountain howitzer, carried by a mule using a special harness. Bolon and Haller traveled a frequently used trail from The Dalles, passing northwest of Goldendale near present day Monument Road. The path then passed over the Simcoe

Mountains, snaking its way down to lower elevations where it was known as the Eel Trail.

The soldiers proceeded north over the Simcoe Mountains until they descended into a valley near upper Toppenish Creek. (The site is approximately three miles from the place where Fort Simcoe was established the following year.)

At Toppenish Creek, the soldiers were ambushed by a large force of hostile Yakamas and allies under the direction of Chief Kamiakin. After a three day running battle, the soldiers fought their way back to Fort Dalles, suffering 5 killed and 17 wounded. During the retreat, the harness carrying the howitzer broke, forcing Major Haller to bury the artillery piece along the trail, expecting to retrieve it later.

The howitzer was buried in a dry creek bed somewhere between the Eel Trail and the Yakima side of the summit of the Simcoes. Major Haller's diary and military records confirm that he did in fact return the following year as part of a large expedition under the command of Colonel George Wright. Colonel Wright personally recovered the howitzer in August of 1856 and safely returned it to Fort Dalles.

Legend persisted that a howitzer still lay buried somewhere in the foothills of the Simcoe Mountains despite confirmation by Major Haller that a single howitzer was brought into the field and Colonel Wright's report that it was successfully recovered. Philip Sheridan's published memoirs, which stated that Major Haller buried two howitzers, may have kept the idea alive. Sheridan wasn't with Haller at the time the cannon was buried. Sheridan did serve briefly in the Yakima Valley during November of 1855, returning to Fort Vancouver before the cannon was dug up the following August. Sheridan may have mistaken the number of howitzers because of Lt. Col. Steptoe's similar battle and retreat that took place near Rosalia in May of 1858 — Steptoe was forced to leave behind two howitzers. Colonel Wright also recovered Steptoe's artillery pieces in September of 1858.

Haller, Granville O. "The Indian War of 1855-6 in Washington and Oregon", Part 4, accession #3437, box 2, folder 5; "Kamiarkin in History", folder 6; Haller Diary 1855 — 1856, microfilm (Manuscripts,

Special Collections, University Archives, University of Washington Libraries, Seattle); Report of Oct. 16, 1855" by G.O. Haller, Records of the War Department, Office of Adjutant General file No 2076239 (Relander Collection 42-11, Yakima Regional Library)

McWhorter, L.V. *"Tragedy of the Wahk-shum"* edited by Donald M. Hines, Great Eagle Publishing, Inc., Issaquah WA 1994

Wright to Mackall, August 24, 1856, National Archives, M567 R545

Sheridan, Philip H. *"Indian Fighting in the Fifties in Oregon and Washington Territories"* Ye Galleon Press, Fairfield, WA 1987, p 42 (Originally published as "Personal Memoirs of P.H. Sheridan" vol. I, Press of Jenkins and McCowan, New York, 1888)

Steptoe to Mackall, May 23, 1858, Sen. Exec. Doc. 32, 35th Congress, 2nd Session, SS 984, pp 60-1

Wright to Mackall, Sept. 24, 1858, no. 19 — 20, Sen Exec Doc #1, 35th Congress, 2nd Session, SS 975, pp 399-400

MOPAR LIMO SERVICE

Kathleen Goode

1948 DeSoto

There are a lot of old cars on Main Street, but the coolest one is usually Dr. Ogden's. He became interested in old cars as a kid growing up in Castle Rock. The hot cars in those days were Mustang convertibles, but Jim Ogden was coveting a 1934 Ford coupe owned by a friend of the family. He never did get to buy the Ford, but he did buy a 1949 Dodge that was the proud possession of another family friend. It was his first classic car purchase, and it cost him a whole 50 dollars. That was pretty exciting, but he couldn't stop there; he eventually bought a 1947 Plymouth and then a 1948 DeSoto. Along the way, he learned a lot about how to restore classic cars and keep them running. Unlike most classic car owners, he doesn't keep them just for show. They all earn their keep.

He takes the cars everywhere. When Ogden isn't walking to work, you'll see one of his classic cars decorating the street next to the office. He drives them all over — to Portland, Spokane, and Seattle. The Plymouth was his ride for a trip to Missoula, Montana and back. This still wasn't enough, so ten years ago he became the president and CEO of Ogden's Mopar Limo Service. The company motto is "Fast, Friendly, and Free." The CEO says that the fun of having these old cars is using them to help people make memories.

The Limo Service takes people to weddings, anniversaries, proms, and other special occasions. The busiest time for the business is during the county fair, when they become a radio-dispatched taxi service. The dispatcher is Loleta Zumwalt, who has been with them from the start. She is a retired telephone operator and celebrated her 92nd birthday last January.

Interview with Dr. Ogden

As you drive south from Goldendale on Highway 97, the loops of brown ribbon you see laid out on the hills on your right are the Eddieville racetrack.

The track hosts motorcycle and ATV races from February through December. Racers compete in a variety of races, from 4-hour team races on the 6-1/2 mile long grand prix track to 15-20 minute events on the 1-1/2 mile motocross track. There is also a 10 to 15 mile long track located nine miles to the west at Starvation Ridge, with races lasting anywhere from 1 to 25 hours.

The soft dirt tracks emphasize curves and jumps and can be used by riders of varying skill levels. Events are scheduled for beginners to pros. Winners receive trophies or, in the expert and pro classes, cash prizes. The majority of riders come from the western states, but a few have come from as far as Europe. The World Off-Road Championship Series has drawn nearly a thousand riders over two days.

The event organizers are a group of local volunteer enthusiasts called the Over The Bars Gang. They developed the Eddieville site in 1998 and the Starvation Ridge track in 1999 with the goal of promoting challenging racing in an atmosphere of family fun and camaraderie. There is a peewee track used by riders as young as five years.

The competition is intense, but the organizers like to inject a lighthearted element. The Starvation Ridge track runs through an abandoned farm house and a barn. It also skirts some of the 20 ponds on the 800-acre site; riders who end up in a pond are asked to sign the life preserver kept in the track office.

Interview with Scott Doubravsky
www.overthebarsgang.com

MOTORSPORTS — EDDIEVILLE AND STARVATION RIDGE

Judy Thomas

In the late 1950s, the people of Roosevelt received notice that their little town was about to be condemned. Construction was starting on the John Day Dam, and by about 1967, when it was completed, the Columbia River would rise and cover the town of Roosevelt.

Following normal procedures, the Corps of Engineers offered to purchase the property, then sell back the buildings as salvage to anyone who wanted to move them. The 38 families who were being displaced began meeting to decide what to do. Most agreed that they wanted to hold their community together. They quickly elected the unstoppable Winifred Flippin, wife of the ferry boat operator, Ben Flippin, as their chairman.

The next question was where to move the town. Railroad employees already knew they would be moving to new homes the railroad was building next to the highway. A few business owners decided to join them, wanting to be conveniently located for passing traffic. The majority voted 25 to 13 to accept Dewey Beeks' offer of property on the bluff above the river. As Winifred said, "We wanted to be up high where we could look out and see what was going on."

The new town needed a water system. The Corps could pay individual homeowners for their wells, but they could only pay an official government entity for a community water system, and Roosevelt was unincorporated.

They looked into incorporating the town, but the state required a population of at least 500 people. They investigated the possibility of forming a water district, but the law required petitioners for a district to live on the property, and no one could live in the new Roosevelt without water, a Catch-22 situation.

Winifred approached the Klickitat County PUD's manager, Emmet Clouse, who, like Winifred, never knew a problem that couldn't be solved, and a legendary team was born. The PUD was an official government body that could receive payment on behalf of Roosevelt.

As Winifred recalled in a 1965 interview for *Ruralite*, "At one point, it looked like we were stymied on water supply, so we decided not to wait for government action. Five of us threw in a total of $350. We hired a dowser, struck a flow of 900 cubic feet per second at 322 feet down, and were in business. Then we made a deal with Klickitat PUD to service the pump and system."

The old Roosevelt had been on septic tanks, but the state health officer refused to permit installation of septic tanks in the new town. People might not think so now, he declared, but by denying septic tanks, he was doing them a favor for which they would someday be grateful. State law did not give PUDs authority to operate sewer systems.

The story of Roosevelt's heroic struggle to move the town attracted the news media throughout the state. With the help of Senator Al Henry, Klickitat County's powerful representative in Olympia, carefully phrased legislation was adopted to allow certain PUDs to operate sewer systems. It was no accident that Klickitat County PUD was the only one to qualify.

Though willing to help, the Corps couldn't pay for the new sewer system so, in 1968, Winifred, Emmet and company turned to Congresswoman Catherine May. After introducing special legislation, she asked Winifred and Emmet to travel to Washington, D.C. to plead their cause before the Appropriations Committee. The pair must have performed well, because the Committee approved the funds and the sewer system was built.

Thus Roosevelt moved to higher ground, and Klickitat PUD acquired its first water and sewer system. Through their determined efforts, Winifred Flippin and the people of Roosevelt saved their community from disappearing under the flood waters. Though divided in two, Roosevelt lives on, stronger than ever.

Ruralite. 1965. Moving Roosevelt. November.
Interviews with Winifred Flippin and Emmet Clouse

MOVING TO MISERY

Kathleen Goode

Linda moved away one day; packed up her boat and her sewing machine, put the two children in the back of the car, and prepared for the very long drive to Misery. At least, that's what we called it. It's a town in the South where her husband found a new job. She and her family didn't want to move, but the aluminum plant closed. Hundreds of people lost their jobs; many had to move; some found ways to hang on here, but it has been hard. The plant has been the focus of a boom-and-bust economy in the county for many years. The final (maybe) death knell for the place was the high price of electrical power. This seems very ironic for a county that is adjacent to two hydroelectric dams. A further irony is that a power plant was built in town to serve the aluminum plant. When the decision was made to build the power plant, it was noted that wind power was not an option — currently there are several wind power plants being developed. Meanwhile, the plant on the bank of the Columbia remains closed, a sort of industrial ghost town.

My friend Linda was a special part of the community. She learned to quilt while she was here, and she gave the art a very modern twist. Often made with exotic batiks, her quilts were technical marvels. Linda loves math and encouraged all the kids to excel at it. Her great sense of humor kept all of us laughing. Linda encouraged us to start walking and inspired us to do great things when she ran the Portland Marathon. She was the cool mom, the Cub Scout leader, and the classroom volunteer. She and her husband, Rob, escorted the senior class rafting trip and introduced lots of kids to water skiing. Rob was a community volunteer as well, especially if it had anything to do with engineering. Both of them added a lot of fun and vitality to our town. They hate the new town and want to move back to the Northwest, but it won't be here. There are still very few jobs, especially jobs that require mathematicians and engineers. Our community lost a lot when Linda moved to Misery.

Conversations with Linda MacDonald and various articles in the paper

MOUNT ADAMS — NO LONGER FORGOTTEN

Keith McCoy

The bulk of Mount Adams lies outside Klickitat County, but we consider it 'our' mountain. Its towering, glacier-clad beauty is visible from many parts of Klickitat County, and access to the peak is through the Trout Lake and Glenwood valleys on Klickitat County roads.

Though Mount Adams is the second highest peak in Washington and Oregon, its remoteness from population centers has resulted in minor development compared with Mt. Rainier and Mt. Hood. Mount Adams is larger in bulk than the other two; in fact, of the Pacific Coast peaks, only California's Shasta is heftier than Mount Adams. The surrounding Yakama

Indian Reservation and Mount Adams Wilderness have minimized access and development.

Now a spotlight has fallen on our mountain. In 1981 the United States Geological Survey (USGS) began a study to determine the mineralization of the mountain wilderness. For the next ten years, a team of professional geologists spent part of each summer on and around the mountain examining, mapping and dating the lava flows that have created this many-glaciered stratovolcano. (A stratovolcano is a tall, conical mountain composed of both hardened lava and volcanic ash.)

They soon learned Mount Adams was so complex that it merited an expanded study of "How a Volcano Works." The final study report and maps were ready in 1995 and have been of special interest to professionals and others with an interest in strato volcanos. The study not only details the growth of the 12,276 foot peak, but explains the side eruptions that created such spectacular features as the Aiken lava flow on the southeast slope of the mountain and the deep-channeled White Salmon River.

Mt. Adams

William E. Scott et al. 1995. Volcano hazards in the Mount Adams Region, Washington. U.S. Dept. of the Interior, U.S. Geological Survey.

MUD

Gladys Hodges

What sticks about Klickitat County is the mud. A stranger can be stuck in the mud — that is, if the person is foolish enough to venture off a main road. The ground may appear to be solid, but it is deceptive, and he may soon be sucked in over his boot tops.

Our first experience came about when a realtor failed to meet us at the property we were planning to purchase. When we arrived there, driving a Ford F250 pickup and towing a twenty-four foot travel trailer, we found ourselves on a dead end road with no place to turn around except an open field.

My husband walked around in the field, and decided the ground was firm. To his surprise, we had only gotten the front wheels of our truck off the road before it was buried in sticky goo halfway up the tire.

What could we do? We didn't have a shovel or a tow chain with us. Fortunately, we had an abundance of tree limbs — oak and pine — and, of course, lots of rocks.

We placed rocks and limbs under the front tires, hoping to get the truck back on the road. That didn't work. Our next move was to unhook the trailer.

Four hours later, we were still putting rocks and limbs under the wheels when our future neighbor drove up in his four-wheel drive. Soon our truck was pulled backward onto the road, hooked to our trailer, and we were on our way back to town.

We learned that day that people in Klickitat County are neighborly — and we also learned about mud.

MUSHROOM HUNTING

Judy Bane

Grover always started out a mushroom hunt at the house with a little ceremony of going into the bathroom and carefully folding up some toilet paper to put in his pocket. "Can't go into the woods without your tickets," he'd say.

Then Grover would go find a spot that had been logged off in the last two to five years. "Always go after it has rained some; not before mid-April and not after May. The nights have to be a bit warm, not freezing. Skid trails where the dirt has been stirred are a good place to start."

When he found a likely spot, he got out and walked into the woods. "Can't hunt mushrooms from a car window. People who try to do that are called 'would-be hunters' — they 'would be' hunters if they'd get out of the car and get into the woods."

Morels look like a dark brown pinecone, "but they stand straight up, they aren't lying down. When you find the first one, look around, there will be more. Stand still, or squat down and just look. Take your time. You'll see more."

They can be colored dark or light brown. Only pick them if they look fresh, no dried-out ones. Grover always said, "If you have to look at it twice, throw it back."

Pinch off the mushroom a little above the ground. Don't pluck up dirt, root and all; leave some to propagate more spores. That way you have no extra dirt in your bag of mushrooms, or 'weeds,' as Ma Riley always called it.

When you get home, cover your mushrooms in cold, salted water, a few tablespoons of salt to a gallon of water, to soak out the bugs and dirt. Rinse a couple of times — gently, they are fragile — then cut them in half vertically and place in clean water. Drain, cook, and eat!

You can blanch them briefly, drain well and freeze, or you can dry them. I like them frozen better. To eat mushrooms, I like to fry a steak in a cast iron pan and quick fry the mushroom to serve as the steak comes out of the pan. But my very favorite recipe is to shake them up in flour, fry in bacon grease or butter, and scramble eggs over them. Num, num!!

Sometime in the mid-1970s there were so many mushrooms that we filled an eight-foot wide Mr. Turtle swimming pool. That's a lot of mushrooms to clean. We called friends and told them to bring a sack. They would bring a little bitty bowl or something, and we would take them outside and say, "No, no, please take a great big sack!" I have never seen them that thick ever again.

Grover Riley

"Teaching piano is a rather lonely profession because you don't see anybody else to talk to about what is going on with your work or your students," said Jackie Erland Ladewig, who taught piano lessons in Goldendale from 1956 to her retirement in 2004. This loneliness changed in 1978 when music teachers from the Mid-Columbia District, which included Goldendale and White Salmon, were invited to attend a meeting in The Dalles to discuss joining the Oregon Music Teachers Association. The Oregon group encouraged the Mid-Columbia District Music Teachers to band together and join OMTA. A small group joined, but for several years Jackie was the only one from Goldendale. At present, there are five Goldendale members: Kay Kimmel, Betty Fahlenkamp, Lorelie Lammers, Sandee Marshall, and Jackie.

The goals of the organization are to improve teachers' skills, implement professionalism, and maintain high standards. To become an OMTA member, one must have a degree in music or prove

MUSIC TEACHERS ASSOCIATION

Joan Wilkins Stone

ability to teach by presenting a number of students in several levels to participate in syllabus exams. Passing the exams requires competence in applied theory and repertoire representing all eras: Baroque, Classical, Romantic and Contemporary. Listening skills, reading skills, and rhythm are also tested. "It was a thrill when I completed the three-year provisional membership and earned active membership," stated Jackie.

The group holds several meetings throughout the year to promote fellowship. "Only private music teachers understand the joys and frustrations of our profession." Workshops are held to bring in experts to teach, share ideas, and broaden knowledge. Events promoted by the workshops are: Baroque Festival, Ensemble Festival, Federation Festival by the National Federation of Music Clubs, the joint recitals, and the Piano Playathon.

For Jackie, belonging to the OMTA "opened up a whole new level of professionalism." It enhanced her skills and broadened performing opportunities for the students.

Interview with Jackie Erland Ladewig

MYSTERY WALLS

Teddy Cole

Who built Klickitat County's stone walls? None more than three feet high, made of loose rocks piled together, they ramble across the high plateau above Lyle like the trail of lovers out for a stroll.

Just as water seeks its own level and nature abhors a vacuum, mysteries beg for solutions. The mysterious stone walls have more than their share. One theory says that farmers tossed them off to the side when they cleared the land, just to get them out of the way.

Another story is that farmers hired Chinese workers from the railroad to build the walls. The problem with that one is that the local railroad didn't have any Chinese workers. A variation on the theme is that farmers hired Indians who sent their wives to do the work, but the men showed up to get paid when the work was done.

A shepherd built the walls to contain his sheep; a man whose only skill was constructing rock walls built them; native Americans piled them to be handy for ammunition in case of attack; youths stacked them as part of the requirements of their vision quests.

An unidentified man reported that scientists had made carbon tests at the site and found the rocks dated back thousands of years, a statement as enigmatic as the walls themselves. (*Ruralite*, 1962)

Whatever the truth may be, the fact is that the walls exist, an anomaly on our landscape. If the Indians know anything, they aren't talking.

(For a related article and photo, see: "Enigma Unsolved: California's East Bay Walls" By Andy Asp http://www.forteantimes.com/exclusive/caliwalls.shtml)

Bartholomew, Florence. *Mysterious rock fences of Klickitat County*. *Ruralite*, December 1962.

Fish, Byron. 1972. *60 Unbeaten Paths, An Unusual Guide to the Unusual in the Northwest*. Superior Publications

THE MYTH OF THE VANISHING INDIANS

Kathleen Goode

The place now called Klickitat County has been the home of many Native Americans for many thousands of years. There is a persistent idea that most, if not all, of these tribes have either moved away or ceased to exist. Historians often refer to the various tribes and bands of the Columbia River in the past tense. Ruby and Brown delineate a specific decline among the Wishram and the Klickitat, leaving the reader with the impression there are only a handful of Native Americans left in the region and they will soon vanish into the pages of history. There is a historic foundation for their pessimistic outlook.

The arrival of fur traders, missionaries and pioneers created successive waves of illness, all with lethal results. There are realistic estimates that place tribal losses at nearly ninety percent. Treaties and the Dawes Act eroded their lands to a fraction of what was once their home. Children were forced to attend boarding schools where the goal was complete eradication of their Native heritage.

Assimilation failed, but not without causing great suffering.

Casual observers might look at the places Lewis and Clark identified and conclude that the historians were right. The large trade center at the head of the

(continued on page 198)

Take me back moss-covered boulders
To the day you rolled from stone-boat
To wall or field-side
Resting more than a hundred years

You saw their pioneer faces
Their rough, strong hands
You heard them speak in phrases
To horses Queen and Maud

And you old charred pitch-post
Where front gate once swung
On a long, tapered hinge
Forged with hammer and fire

What you witnessed there please tell
Of family members going in and out
Getting serious jobs done
That's what it was all about

To the west see Jim approaching
On a Percheron-Mustang steed
Through the gate he passes
Without missing a beat

Jim was the ramrod, a real cattleman
Branding with the 15 iron
And waving his old black hat
Took them through town

See sister Jeannette on sidesaddle seat
Like a lady poised and neat
But Indian-like she rode all day
Wearing angora chaps the color of bay

To the east a farm house, new
Drop-siding painted white
Old mother Sara stands on the porch
Like a pillar strong and bright

That's Charlie at the grinding stone
Where water turns the wheel
He also learned to drive a truck
And irrigate the fields

Tom and George were loggers
And helped them get their start
This family is like a six-horse team
All did their part

Look south, a handsome barn is there
Hand-hewn beams rising from the ground
Through barn boards voices speaking
For ages such a haunting sound

Listen, you might hear a story
Of Johnny like a monkey swung
Under the carriage to fix the wheels
Across the barn's highest rung

A doughboy fought in WWI
The old-timers say
Had more fun fighting
Than working in the hay

Around the barn zigzagging
A split-rail fence seven high
Split from old-growth logs
To one hundred a day

Look north beyond a mile
A ditch up the canyon does stretch
To tap the water of Rattlesnake Creek
Since 1899 in Miners inches did fetch

In hard rocky ground it was carved
With grub-hoe, shovel and pick
Grub-hoes still in a pile
How many backaches provoked?

Now don't lie
You know how Jim hated a lie
'Dom liar, Dom bureaucrats!'
He would sometimes say

Because pioneer life wasn't easy
Always a challenge to success
Whenever something was gained
A parasite was there to suppress

A little gruff on the outside
These pioneers appeared to be
But even little children
Their hearts of gold could see

One day each year — the Fourth of July
They decided to have fun
Standing around eating ice cream cones
Take Me Back, so I may have some

Joy Markgraf

The Myles family — mother Sara and six children — homesteaded near Husum in the early 1890s. The site is recorded on the original survey map of August 13, 1896. Joy Markgraf married a descendant.

Take Me Back

(continued from page 195)

Long Narrows is now underwater. The north side of the river is now Columbia Hills State Park where tourists go to see the ancient petroglyphs. There are no"Indian Villages" visible in Klickitat County; there are no cedar canoes on the river, and no great summer gathering or colorful figures putting on Wild West shows.

Sometimes the explanation is that they all"moved to the reservation." This is partly true; many tribal members were forced to choose between one of three reservations: Yakama, Umatilla, or Warm Springs. No matter what an individual decided, they were certain to be separated from their ancestral homes and some of their family members. Not everyone agreed to live on the reservation. Some families used allotment money to buy homes near where they once lived. Fishing continued, root gathering continued, and fruit harvesting continued.

Things were not the same as they had always been, but the River People survived. They overcame many problems through the wise leadership of their elders. One of these leaders was Kis-ëam-xay, who convinced Congress not to break up the Yakama Reservation. She is honored among the people as a great warrior, healer, and historian. The River People today are improving their lives the same as everyone else. They push their children to study hard and get a good education. There should be a joke that asks"Where have all the Indians gone?""To court," would be the answer,"where they can fight to prove they still exist." They struggle with the problems of healthcare and alcoholism, best use of resources, protection of their legal rights, and the survival of the salmon. They build longhouses, museums, and libraries to save the heritage and knowledge of their elders for future generations.

The government is, in some ways, keeping its promises and even beginning to see the great value of the culture and history of the First People. The State of Washington is on the verge of requiring Native American history to be taught in every school. I hope that Kis-ëam-xay will be one of the people students learn about; she embodies a powerful lesson about freedom, responsibility and self-determination. Native Americans have not disappeared from our county. Thankfully, they are a growing population, and we are

all richer when we begin to understand their heritage
and history.

Personal experience
Hunn, Eugene S. with James Selam and Family. 1990. *Nch'i-*
Wana"The Big River"; Mid-Columbia Indians and Their
Land. 1990. Seattle: University of Washington Press.
Ruby, Robert H. and John A. Brown. A Guide to the Indian
Tribes of the Pacific Northwest, revised edition. 1992.
Norman OK: University of Oklahoma Press.
Uebelacker, Morris L. Time Ball: A Story of the Yakima
People and the Land. 1984. Yakima: The Yakima
Nation.
Ferolito, Philip. 2005. Tribute of a Tribe. *Yakima Herald*
Republic, June 8.

THE NAME GAME

Kathleen Goode

Nixlúidix was a large village at the head of the Five-Mile
Rapids. The people belong to the Upper Chinookan
language group and were known as the wišxam
or "Wish-ham" as they were named in the Yakima
treaty. This village is also featured in a Coyote legend,
Tsagaglalal, known as "She Who Watches." The name
of the village was changed to "Wishram," an English
misspelling of the name "wišxam." The Indian village
of Wishram was made famous by Washington Irving's
romantic description of it in his popular novel "Astoria."
Wishram (at least Irving's version of it) became the best
known Indian Village in the United States. The railroad
company decided that such a popular name would
be beneficial for their new rail stops, and in 1926 they
changed the name of Fallbridge to Wishram.

Nixluidix became known as Speedis, after a popular
Native resident, Martin Spedis. He was one of the
Wishram people photographed by Charles Bell about
1876, and he became a leader in Yakima during the 1930s
and 1940s. One of the unique images in Columbia River
art is known as the Spedis owl. Eventually, the Spedis
area became known as Spearfish—it is still shown this
way on some maps. There was more serious change to
come.

Disaster struck in the name of progress when The
Dalles Dam was built in the 1950s. It raised the water
level above both village sites. Wishram was the site of
hurried activity as amateurs volunteered their efforts
to excavate Wakemap Mound. "Wakemap" is an

anglicized version of the word "woq'emap;" it means "old woman." The people at Spearfish worked to save the petroglyphs. The River People mourned the passing of a way of life that extended back thousands of years. Many of the fishermen left their nets and equipment at the river as Celilo Falls was drowned. The area above the village of Nixlúidix now became known as "Horsethief Park"; named by two workers from the U.S. Army Corps of Engineers. They thought the area resembled sites seen in the 1950s westerns, and they noted that local Indians kept horses there. It is now a state park and was renamed "Columbia Hills State Park" in 2003. There are petroglyphs preserved here, including the Spedis Owl. If you take a tour, you can see this as well as the county's most famous image, Tsagaglalal — through it all, She Watches.

Atwell, Jim. Early *History of Klickitat County*. 1977. Skamania, WA: Tahlkie Books.

"Columbia Hills State Park" http://www.parks. wa.gov/parkpage.asp?selectedpark— Columbia+Hills&pageno=1

Hunn, Eugene S. with James Selam and Family. *Nch'i Wána "The Big River"; Mid-Columbia Indians and Their Land*. 1990. Seattle: University of Washington Press.

Strong, Emory, Editor. *Wakemap Mound and Nearby Sites on the Long Narrows of the Columbia River*. 2nd edition.1976. Portland, OR: Binford & Mort. 1st edition published in 1959.

ARTHUR C. NEWBY, BENEFACTOR

Keith J. McCoy

Although Arthur C. Newby never lived in Klickitat County, he often visited relatives here and greatly influenced their lives. Ronald Richardson, who grew up in Goldendale and was at one time editor of *The Goldendale Sentinel*, told the story of how Newby's generosity helped sixteen Klickitat County youths go to college.

Newby was an industrialist in Indianapolis. He saw an early bicycle chain in France, and the United States patents he obtained for the device were the foundation of his fortune. He is also one of the four men who conceived and built the "Red Brickyard" that became the Indianapolis Speedway.

In his later years, Newby had no family other than a few widely-scattered cousins, some of whom lived in

Klickitat County, hence his visits here. When Newby died in 1932, his cousins and their families received a generous bequest which eased many depression woes and made it possible for sixteen young people to go to college. I remember the story well. I was one of the lucky sixteen.

Newcomers to East Klickitat County

Sara Wu

For many people, the move to east Klickitat County is the culmination of a dream come true. The rural nature is a tremendous relief from the city. The community, recreation, beauty, and rural life-style lead to a very fulfilling time. Retirees often say that they do not know how they had time to work, they are so busy now. Others feel sorry for their "isolated" city friends. In a small community, it can be easier to find kindred spirits. But some newcomers are stunned by the changes in their lives.

The wind can seem to blow one's brains out. The frequent question "How long have you lived here?" can make you feel like an outsider, when you do not have generations of local residents in your background. The hills may seem a bare, dull brown. The lush gardens and woods of west of the Cascades may feel like a lost ideal.

But with time, the joys of east Klickitat County can overcome all these negatives. Many residents are relatively new and also looking for connections. The long-time families appreciate the input from newcomers. It is possible to get involved with many community activities. All community organizations and activities need help, and it is heart-warming how residents pitch in, when asked. Some people find that driving where there is more traffic is a real incentive to get back to east Klickitat County.

When spring explodes in its riot of flowers and birds, it is hard to imagine anything more beautiful. The rest of the year, the graceful flow of the hills contrasting with the rocky outcrops above the rivers, topped with snow peaks in the distance, becomes a new definition of beauty. No dense forest of trees blocks the views!

The sky is astonishing both day and night. The mountains and wind shape the clouds into fascinating forms. Sunset colors are often brilliant in all 360 degrees of the big sky. When the moon comes up or the stars blaze through the clear air, east Klickitat County can be seen as a little bit of heaven.

Conversations with Marilyn Sarsfield

NOTHING TO DO HERE

Kathleen Goode

The common lament of kids growing up in a rural area is "There's nothing to do here!" When my own children try this, I either question their ability to read or invite them to do a few more chores. Still, I am amazed whenever I hear the comment, because there are actually too many things to do here; no one kid could do them all. In case your children are singing this all too familiar refrain, here are some of the things they could be doing. Most of these require parental involvement in some way.

Always number one on my list is reading, the ultimate summer excursion. There are books to trade with friends, books at the library, and at the library book sale. Don't live in town? Find out when and where the bookmobile stops. I like to keep a good supply of reading on hand and will almost always buy my kids books. When too many books pile up, you can set them free at bookcrossing.com. Teach a younger sibling to read or share a favorite book with them. Challenge yourself to only see movies after you've read the book, and start your own list of the world's 100 best books.

Building things is a traditional country activity that honors the spirit of the pioneers. Start with a bench or a bookcase. Try building a fort, or go small and build a dog house or even a bird house. Be an adventurer, and build a raft. A young friend of mine built one out of empty milk cartons sealed with melted wax. Read Tom Sawyer and Huckleberry Finn, and then set out on your raft on the Little Klickitat. The distance from one side of Goldendale to the other is about right. You can also try the same journey on a large inner tube.

Try visiting every river in Klickitat County, and find out what is so great about each one. Save up money to take river rafting lessons. Get a license, and go fishing. Start a bait stand. Start a bird list — you're going to see a lot of them while you're out fishing. Go swimming, hiking, kayaking, skiing, snow boarding, spelunking, rock hunting or camping. If you are really wild (and a very strong swimmer), take a class on how to sailboard. Parents won't let you do anything that risky? You can still learn something new.

Learn to ride a horse. If you don't own a horse, try trading chores for lessons. Take art lessons with Felicia Gray, and enter your best work in the County Fair. Take music lessons to learn or improve your skills in voice or an instrument. Learn karate, gymnastics, or dance. Join 4-H and learn to sew, raise an animal or train your dog. Learn to knit and donate blankets to Warm Up America. Learn about local history at the museums or at a Pioneer Picnic. Learn about the Day of the Dead at Maryhill Museum. Learn about the stars at the Observatory and by attending Star Parties.

You love music? Attend a summer concert Under the Stars at Maryhill Museum or a jazz performance at the Presby Museum for Christmas; hear the Gorge Winds play at the Library Ice Cream Social in August, or attend a street dance during Community Days. If you play an instrument, join the concert band and/ or the jazz band. Start a rock and roll band. Join the Old Time Fiddlers, if you think you can keep up. Find more groups while you are just hanging around at the County Fair.

Save at least a few summer mornings for picking berries — huckleberries at Mt. Adams, blackberries everywhere. Learn to make a berry pie, and you'll be instantly popular. Gather your friends together and go to the carnival, a rodeo, the dirt bike races, or see a movie at the library. Make a movie of your own or rent a few for a movie night. Document life around you with your own photographs.

Write.

Walk or run during the summer to stay in shape, and join a sport during the school year. Some choices for sports include baseball, basketball, football, golf, softball, soccer, tennis, track and volleyball. You could become a cheerleader, or build school spirit as the mascot or as a team manager. Sports not your thing? Try getting involved in the school paper, working on the yearbook, joining the drama club, the business club or the chess club. If you've done all of these things and you're still bored, go climb Mt. Adams, or do more chores! Remember, time to be bored is a luxury for most of us.

NOXIOUS WEEDS

Teddy Cole

Noxious weeds are plants designated by a Federal, State or county government as injurious to public health, agriculture, recreation, wildlife, or property. A noxious weed is also commonly defined as a plant that grows out of place. Invasive plants include not only noxious weeds, but also other plants that are not native to this country. Plants are considered invasive if they have been introduced into an environment where they did not evolve, show aggressive growth habits, and have no natural enemies to limit their reproduction and spread.

The web site www.klickitatcounty.org/weedcontrol/ has links to photographs found on the Washington State Noxious Weed Control Board web site. Some weeds are classified "A" — to eradicate; others are classified "B" or "C" — to control. Many of these plants have lovely flowers. For example, "A" includes several thistles; "B" and "C" include such plants as St. Johns wort and ox-eye daisies. Noxious is not necessarily noxious county-wide; some plants are noxious except when they are within 200 feet of the Columbia River or when they grow in certain ranges of the county. Knapweed and kudzu are among the most pernicious. All landowners have the legal responsibility to identify which plants are noxious in the area of their property and to eradicate or control them.

Klickitat County Noxious Weed Control Board, klickitatcounty.org/weedcontrol/

Klickitat County Noxious Weed List, leaflet updated annually by Klickitat County Noxious Weed Control Board

Noxious Weeds in Washington State: an introduction to Washington's Weed Laws, undated leaflet published by Washington State Noxious Weed Control Board

Sheley, R., J. Petroff, M. Borman. 1999. Introduction to Biology and Management of Noxious Rangeland Weeds, Biology and management of noxious rangeland weeds / edited by Roger L. Sheley and Janet K. Petroff. Corvallis OR: Oregon State University Press.

Westbrooks, R. 1998. Invasive Plants, Changing the Landscape of America. Fact book. Federal Interagency Committee for the Management of Noxious and Exotic Weeds (FICMNEW) Washington, DC

U. S. Bureau of Land Management, http://www.blm.gov/weeds/

Oaks in Klickitat County

Robin Dobson,
Botanist/Ecologist,
US Forest Service, Columbia
River Gorge Scenic Area

The Garry oak, or Oregon white oak, is the only oak species found in Washington State. This majestic tree can live for hundreds of years, becoming gnarled and full of hollows when growing in dry, windswept places. In moist, deep soils, its straight trunk can rise over a hundred feet high.

The oak woodlands are a unique habitat, home for a wide diversity of plants and wildlife. Their large acorns feed the introduced wild turkeys, are important winter feed for deer, and are the mainstay for many birds, such as the Lewis' woodpecker. Oak leaves provide food for butterfly caterpillars and hundreds of different insects, including the gall wasp (whose larvae induce the oak to produce a protective dome around it for protection). As old branches fall off, the hollows left behind become homes for flying squirrels, raccoons, or screech owls.

More remarkably, and less known, about 90% of the oak woodlands in the state are located in Klickitat County. Most of the oak habitat in the western portion of the state has been lost to farms, homes, and urban development. In more forested areas, timber management has long regarded the oak as a weed, with little appreciation of its beauty and importance to wildlife. Douglas firs are promoted, while the oaks are felled or left to languish under the shade of the taller firs. When fire ran free over the landscape, the firs were removed, and the oaks flourished into the magnificent legacy. Those of us who live in the oaks of Klickitat County have inherited a beautiful tree that often graces our yards and brings birds, such as the orioles, close to our lives. In reverence we cherish this most magical tree and the wonders that hide within its spreading branches.

Ode to Charlie

Tom Doll

Ol' Charlie Horse came a-calling last night,
Left a tight wad in my muscles before daylight.

Can you imagine the sky turning
    dark blue in the moonlight
As I lumbered out of bed to turn on the PUD light.

The silence was suddenly broken by the
    calls of Wiley Coyote
As he prepared to wow his love out of sight.

I listened for the sounds of those who slept,
But my moaning and groaning was all I heard,
As I groped for my 'Myoflex' in the cabinet drawer.

Expecting some relief from the white cream that
    I was led to believe
Foretold the years of ancient past as I rubbed
    the trail of his pain before.

The journey of Ol' Charlie's death has now begun
But what is dying and death of Ol' Charlie
    before daylight?

For haying and climbing these hills, he will be reborn
    another day
As we live and age in a life of strife.

For our cycle of life can be remembered by Ol' Charlie
    crying in the night.

DR. OGDEN

Kathleen Goode

Jim Ogden is a Doctor of Optometry. Of course, that's just the tip of the iceberg. He plays a host of other roles also, some of them well known, some less obvious. He was nominated for a 2005 Jefferson Award, a community service award for which he is well qualified. Most days you can find him at work in his office at the corner of Columbus and Main in Goldendale. It is part of Goldendale's historic past, the part of Main Street that was rebuilt in brick after the big fire. Dr. Ogden is not one of the old-timers, in fact, he is a relative newcomer to Klickitat County, having arrived in the mid 1970s. His path to Goldendale and his career in optometry all started in the little Washington town of Castle Rock.

The town where Jim Ogden was born and raised is right next to Mt. Saint Helens. His great grandparents emigrated to the Northwest from Nova Scotia. His grandmother attended the Munsell-Martin optometry program, graduated in 1911, and had a practice in the Portland area until she married a dairy farmer. The grandparents moved their dairy to Castle Rock in the 1920s. Jim Ogden made the decision to study optometry when he was 16, and his grandmother was very pleased. After completing his education, he served as a Lieutenant in the Navy. He was stationed in Charleston, SC and says that his two years on the east coast gave him a much greater appreciation of the west.

Finished with his service, he was looking for a place to settle down when he saw an ad for a practice in Goldendale. After taking ownership of the practice, he bought a house on Burgen Street. He has been here ever since and plans to stay "until Daryl Erdman [of Erdman Funeral Home] takes me away." In 1976, he and Jan were married; three children and almost thirty years later, they are still happily married. Ogden says he always tried to find ways to entertain the children in the evening to give his wife a break. When they were young, he would take them to the grocery store where he had to use two carts; one full of kids and one for the groceries. He also worked hard to help them acquire an appreciation of music. Ogden played the accordion to entertain the residents at the nursing home. He took his daughter Nancy along in a backpack when she was little. This routine didn't last too long though; as she got bigger he noticed that the combination cut off the circulation in his arms and his hand went numb! These days, the children are grown, and now he is playing the accordion on his own for one-man concerts, funerals, and Sunday services at the county jail. Ogden feels that it is important to help the inmates, especially if they are trying to do things that will help them avoid returning to a life of crime. In addition to Sunday Services, he also gives them rides home or to a bus station and collects clothes for them. This is pretty typical of the kind of things Jim Ogden does; low key projects with little cost that might make a huge difference in someone's life.

There is a bigger project that he is well known for: missions. The missions to third world countries started when his first child was adopted from Colombia in 1984. He packs up his equipment and puts together a team that will spend a month in a poor area, giving free eye exams and providing glasses. The team is made up of volunteers, and they all raise the money for their expenses. One year Pam Reed was part of the team; she was taking quilts to an orphanage in Rumania. She did this even though her house had just burned down. Fund raising sometimes takes the form of a talent show and dinner with people donating whatever they can afford. It's always a fun evening and for a very worthy cause. The simplest way to donate is to give him your old eye glasses; there is a basket at the office for them.

When he isn't off on a mission, playing the accordion somewhere, or working, you can often spot Dr. Ogden walking. He claims to only get in about a mile and half a day, but in 2002, he walked from here to Castle Rock for his 35th high school class reunion. That is a 185 mile walk to party with the Rockets. Wow. The most spectacular day of his trip was crossing the blast zone at Mt. Saint Helens; it took 9 hours to go 20 miles on the trail and he didn't see another person for 7 hours of that. Ogden has also made a habit of climbing Mt. Adams; he's been to the summit nearly every year. This year he will be singing his way up the mountain along with the other members of a quartet; Gary Erickson is planning to videotape the whole thing. One thing is certain, when you get an eye exam here you can find out about all sorts of interesting things.

[See also MOPAR LIMO SERVICE]

Interview with Dr. Ogden
General knowledge.

OLD LOCKUPS STORY

Mary Jean Lord

Nanna McCann grew up in the town of Columbus in the late 1800s and early 1900s, before Columbus was renamed Maryhill. In 1962, she wrote for *Ruralite* magazine about her early memories of the First People in Klickitat County. Old Lockups and his wife Queenie, who lived near the Columbia River, were familiar figures to her from her childhood. She had heard from his half-brother what a brave man Old Lockups was and how he triumphed over his enemies, the Snake River Indians.

McCann had heard many stories of Indian battles. "The last one occurred on Miller's Island, just below Columbus, when the Snake River Indians surprised the Columbia River Indians and a terrible massacre ensued. One old fellow, the last survivor of that massacre, lived until 1957.

"I have often looked upon the grim evidence of that slaughter — scores of skeletons which had lain bleaching upon the sand until 1894, when the great flood washed all those bones away. That summer the

Columbia reached the highest watermark it was ever known to reach."

Old Lockups and Queenie, whose camp was next to the river, were forced to move their camp twenty times as the flood rose.

"I have vivid memories of that camp." McCann continued. "They used to keep several dogs that barked savagely as we rode by. Toward the last of their lives the whites took matters in hand for them and killed the dogs. The Indians would not kill them, though the dogs would steal their food right out of the frying pan. I can almost smell that old Indian camp yet, with its mingled odors of fish and campfire smoke."

The life that Old Lockups led was "a far cry" from the lives of present-day Indians of Klickitat County, McCann declared, though in 1962 she could say that "a few remain who follow the ancient ways."

She described Old Sallie as "the best known of any of the Columbian Indians," a woman of proud bearing and a sense of humor. "It is a common sight to see Old Sallie, her daughter, and her granddaughter working side-by-side around the camp. Long may she live to enjoy their feasts of salmon, camas, and huckleberries!"

She remembered seeing Old Lockups looking imposing "on his black horse, wearing a blue army overcoat, with a wicked-looking knife thrust in his belt. He was short of stature, had been blind for years; his skin was seared and wrinkled as though with the wear and tear of centuries. After his blindness was total, he used to walk out from his tent holding onto a rope. Seeing him groping about thus, and contrasting his appearance with what it must have been when he was the intrepid brave of whose prowess his half-brother used to tell, I would exclaim to myself, 'How are the mighty fallen!'

"I myself had seen quite a falling off in his fortunes, for when he used to ride through the hills before blindness came upon him, he had an air about him, a native pride, even when stopping at our house to ask for bread. Calmly stating that he had had no food for three days, when food was given him, he would take it with a certain dignity and, not deigning to taste it in our presence, would wrap it up and ride away."

McCann, Nanna. *Ruralite*, April 1962.

In 1977, I started to remodel a small bedroom in our rented home near the old Forry Stables. The wall paneling was badly scratched, and when a sheet was pulled away I could see the original pine board wall that had newspapers glued over the cracks. The old newsprint was yellow with age and very brittle. After a few tries, I managed to remove a piece about 10" x 3". It was part of the front page of *The Goldendale Sentinel*, Klickitat County, Washington Territory, March 4, 1886." On the back of this fragment were the tops of articles of local interest. One column was headed "Bickleton Items" and described the beautiful early spring they were having. The other column was titled "Held Up," and this is the story:

"Last night between 8 and 9 o'clock, as Dr. F.C. Miller was returning from a professional call to the first ward, an attempt was made to rob him by a highwayman. At the point near the slaughter house, while the doctor was riding at a brisk run, a man entered the road ahead of him, and brandishing a revolver over his head, called on him to 'stop'. Taking in the situation at a glance, Dr. Miller dropped his body for-...." The old newspaper is torn and missing at this critical point of the story, like the old serial movies, only we'll never know the ending, even if we come back next Saturday.

I still have the paper.

The Goldendale Sentinel

"Sacrifices now are being made to the heathen god of war"

— original Stonehenge Memorial consecration, July 4, 1918

Sam Hill was a builder. Today we would call him a developer. He came to Klickitat County to create a self-sustaining community near the present town of Maryhill. His community never thrived or grew to the scale he had dreamed of. Nevertheless, he did leave us two of Klickitat County's most recognizable man made landmarks: the Maryhill Museum and Stonehenge.

Sam Hill was also a Quaker. The Quaker church was founded over three hundred years ago on the principles of pacifism, that is, opposition to war. Carrying on that tradition in the dark times of World War I, Sam Hill set out to build a memorial to the soldiers and sailors from Klickitat County who, in his words, were "sacrificed to the heathen god of war." He chose to replicate the original Stonehenge in the belief that it had originally been the site of human sacrifices in ancient times.

The Stonehenge memorial has been pictured on postcards, calendars, and even the phone book. It has become a minor tourist attraction as well as the scene of solstice celebrations. Yet, its origins and intentions are often overlooked by those of us who live in its midst. The Stonehenge memorial was built to remind us of the solemn cost of war. It is also a very visible symbol of the tradition of pacifism and the moral opposition to war that has deep roots and a prominent place in the history of Klickitat County.

From an informational display at the 2004 Klickitat County Fair presented by the Goldendale Citizens for Peace

THE PARTY LINE

Joan Wilkins Stone

Loleta Zumwalt began her career as a telephone operator in Goldendale in 1946; in 1949, she became chief operator. The telephone office was one room on the second floor above the old Post Office, which was located on North Grant Street. "There was one person working a shift with 4 hours on, 4 hours off, and back again for another 4 hours. All training was on the job."

The office had the old type switchboard with operators punching in the numbers. "A receiver above the operator's head is what you talked into, and the caller's voice responded with the number they were calling," explained Loleta. The operator would then punch in the two lines. There were about 10 customers to a party line. The caller would pick up the receiver, listen to hear if the line was free, and call the operator. Each household had its own long and short rings, but all calls rang into every household on the line.

Listening for the family's ring became a way of life, and eavesdropping was as easy as picking up the phone. Loleta recognized the voice of everyone in town, if they used a telephone, because of her work. Privacy was scarce, and most people knew what was going on with their neighbors. Two ladies of the town, on the same party line, would make appointments with each other to pick up their phones at a given time — no rings. Hopefully, this insured some privacy.

Dial service was offered in Goldendale in 1949. The advent of dial service ended the ringing of calls into each household on the same line. The switchboard would light up only when customers needed to speak to an operator. This was necessary for long distance calls, to report a fire, asking the time, or to verify why a line was still busy. The operators rang the noon whistle each day or warned of a fire by pushing a button on the switchboard. Eileen McCredy remembers that some people would ask the operator to dial for them. One excuse was, "I misplaced my glasses." The operators would oblige the customers and place the call.

In the early 1960s, a three-minute cutoff was established. A beep warned that the call would be terminated in thirty seconds. Some callers discussed ahead of time which one would call back in hopes of continuing the conversation.

Wade Dean was founder of the original company, which was known as the White Salmon Valley Telephone Company. Wade and Effie, his wife, ran the first switchboard, located at the Carter Hotel in Husum, 24 hours a day. In 1908, Wade purchased the Goldendale Telephone and Telegraph Company and two other small companies. In 1913, the companies were merged to form the Oregon-Washington Telephone Company. The motto "friendly service" and the name stood until 1965, when the name was changed to United Telephone Company of the Northwest. Wade Dean retired in 1958, and his son, Earl, became president of the company. Wade Dean lived to see the establishment of direct distance dialing. He made his company's first DDD call on November 14, 1959, to the governor of Oregon.

The Goldendale telephone office was moved to new quarters on Grant Street, facing the Court House, in October 1962. The office closed on June 11, 1964.

A booklet presented by the Board of Directors and
    employees of United Telephone Company of the
    Northwest in memory of Earl R. Dean, 1984
Interview with Loleta Zumwalt
Conversations with Eileen McCredy

Old-timers in Klickitat County tell a joke that goes something like this: "Does the wind blow all the time? No, there's a barbed wire fence off to the west that cuts the wind — but it's down right now."

Do you feel the wind upon your face? The Columbia River Gorge, formed by millions of years of erosion, of water relentlessly forcing a passage to the sea, provides a channel for more than water. It also acts as a funnel for the wind, and this nearly incessant movement of air is one result of its existence.

Two volcanoes are landmarks in Klickitat County, although not located within its borders: Mount Adams and Mount Hood. These peaks in the Cascade mountain range were formed millions of years ago when subterranean reservoirs of magma spewed to the earth's surface.

Residents of Mid-Columbia have always depended on these mountains for orientation.

Farmers and gardeners have used the snow line on the mountains and foothills as planting guides since the days of the pioneers. Today my neighbor told me that I was working in my garden too soon. "The snow is still on the Simcoes," she warned. The snow line is only a rule of thumb, however, and hardly infallible. With the exception of the much milder microclimate of the gorge itself, killing frosts have been known to occur in Klickitat County during every month of the year. M.R. Enyeart humorously summarized the capricious nature of weather in Klickitat County: "Every frost before July 1 is a spring frost; every frost after July 1 is a fall frost."

Do you feel the sunlight warm upon your shoulder? The sunny weather is also attributable to the Cascade Mountains that divide Washington State. The Cascades wring most of the moisture out of the clouds on the west side, leaving the east side of the mountains sunny and dry.

Have you noticed the huge granite boulder on the basalt plateau about a mile east of Maryhill Museum? White Rock Farm was named after it. That boulder did not originate there. Geological studies indicate that granite boulders like this one were scattered across Washington and Oregon by the Missoula floods. Stonehenge and Maryhill Museum are built on basalt bedrock scoured clean by those floods.

Human activities have also shaped the landscape.

PAST PRESENT: A PERSONAL GEOGRAPHY

Rachel Gunkel

That berm in the village of Maryhill, straight as an arrow and apparently without purpose, has been a part of the landscape since 1909, and was once the raised bed of the railroad track. The railroad had to be moved north to make the eastward ascent more gradual after John Day Dam was built. That wide flat spot just east of the crossroads in Maryhill was once a busy railroad depot, transporting both passengers and mail. Orchardists used to ship their fruit to market by parcel post on the train.

Just across the street from the little Maryhill Advent Christian church built in 1888 is a big rosebush. It's an Austrian Copper, and every spring its exuberant display of orange and yellow blossoms stops more traffic than the stop sign ever has. The old service station and the house next to it belonged to I.C. and Gladys Robison. To the west of the rosebush is the Leloh house. Built in 1864, it is the oldest surviving house in Maryhill. Mr. Leloh was a Civil War veteran who came west by wagon train. Then there's the old general store/post office built by George and Edith Goss and the little cottage that the community built for Aunt Ella Stark when her house burned.

Above Maryhill, the faint ghost of Rattlesnake Road is still visible on the hillside. Those ruts were made by the heavy iron-wheeled wagons that the farmers used to haul wagonloads of peaches and apricots from Columbus to Centerville. From the Centerville valley, part of the Rattlesnake Road is still drivable.

Have you heard how Mortgage Flats got its name? In 1896, Ira and Oscar Henderson mortgaged the ranch that their parents had homesteaded in order to invest in a large flock of sheep. But during the financial panic of 1898, they couldn't even sell their wool at a profit, and the bank foreclosed. Many neighbors were in the same position, and that section of land came to be called Mortgage Flats. Sam Hill bought these properties, and they are now part of the Maryhill Museum ranch.

It is a habit here to refer to people and places that have not existed for many years or even generations. It is in part an easy way to identify a specific location or direction, such as the stand of poplars "across the tracks," or the vineyard at "the Burgen place." It is also an acknowledgment of the part that people and events from the past continue to play in shaping our landscape and our lives. Their stories are indivisible from the land and form the background that gives shape and substance to the present. Klickitat County resonates with the past, and it is visible to those who have the desire and perception to seek it.

McKee, Bates. *Cascadia; the Geologic Evolution of the Pacific Northwest.* 1972. NY: McGraw-Hill

Alt, David. *Glacial Lake Missoula and its Humongous Floods.* 2001. Missoula, MT: Mountain Press

PAUL BUNYAN STORY

Ray Gosney as told to Mary Anne Enyeart

Did you know that Paul Bunyan came through Klickitat County?

I was told that it was a hot day, and he was looking for gold. Nudging his sizable shovel in the ground, he took out a shovelful of dirt and threw it over his shoulder. He didn't find any gold. So he took a step or two and filled his shovel again. Tossing the dirt, it landed close to the first shovelful. The result was Pothole Lake, Carp Lake and Jack Knife Butte which has two bumps.

(Jack Knife Butte used to be known as Coulee Butte, but it was traded for a jackknife.)

Legend

PEACOCK AND HEN

Sara Wu

"Those two wild turkeys have pompoms on their heads. They must be peafowl." I had no idea where they came from, and they were not exactly what I expected when I drove into my place in the woods. Oh, I knew that Maryhill Museum had peacocks, but that was 20 miles and the Columbia Hills away.

Neither the sheriff nor my neighbors knew of any missing peafowl, so I settled down to enjoy them for a bit. It was fall, and they weren't making their screeching calls. They were quiet except when the neighbors' dogs came to visit. Then they would fly to the roof. When the dogs left, they would walk to all sides of the roof and yell out, "hoo-hoo, hoo-hoo". When that didn't bring on a bark, they returned to cleaning up the seed under the bird feeders.

Once a flock of wild turkeys came to visit, but the peafowl would have no invasion of their space. The pair herded the turkeys away and down the hill, not returning for two hours. It took more than a year for the turkeys to return.

The peafowl only seemed to have a couple of drawbacks. First, they really liked the white insulation around the concrete slab on which my cabin is built. I didn't appreciate the holes, although it did give me an idea for recycling Styrofoam. The birds didn't seem to be bothered by it, and it was not evident in their poop.

It was this poop, however, which set me against them. Being "peacocks," they liked to admire themselves in my windows that looked out onto the porch. The calling cards that they left behind made the porch unusable.

With winter coming and no way and no urge to care for them, it was time to find them a new home. An ad in the newspaper offering them "for the taking" did bring a response. The catch was that the responders wanted me to catch them. They wanted peafowl to keep the rattlesnakes down at their place east of Goldendale. So, I had to figure out how to become the mighty peafowl catcher. I started by putting a mirror and food in a large dog crate. The birds could stretch their long necks in without stepping in. Next, I put a log in the front of the cage and suet up at the top in the back so they would have to step in. With a couple of false starts, I got them into the crate and a cardboard box. I thought that they would be very upset, but actually they were very docile once caught.

When I called the responders to say that the "birds were in the bag", there was a pregnant pause. Then they said that they would come and get them. I graciously replied that I would happily deliver them. I didn't want there to be any chance that the peafowl would find their way back.

The new keepers gave them a fine home and even welcomed more from another source. They, too, had to barricade their porch that had windows looking out on it. Unfortunately, the next spring brought out the peacocks' raucous calls that the neighbors did not appreciate. Even more, the neighbors didn't like the way the peafowl used their sports car as a mirror and a roost. Now, the birds may have just gotten wanderlust again, but they weren't there for very long that spring.

Bird watchers across the river in Oregon first spotted the fire at Maryhill Museum of Art and reported it. They feared for the building and its treasures.

If they had only been watching the right birds, they could have identified the culprit who started the fire in their binocular sights. The groundskeeper discovered a charred peacock that had tangled with a power line, causing sparks that set dry grass ablaze. Fortunately, the fire only burned through a vegetable garden before being put out.

The fire happened in June 1992. Since this was the first and only recorded instance of a peacock starting a fire at Maryhill Museum, the museum director, Josie de Falla, refused to ban the birds. Maryhill peacocks are a favorite of museum visitors, especially in the spring, when the males spread their tails in a magnificent display of beautiful feathers.

Ruralite, July 1992

PEACOCK STARTS FIRE

Mary Jean Lord

The flowering plant named Penstemon is indigenous to the North American continent. It cannot be found in the wild on any other continent. It is a flower that all of us have seen, but not all will recognize by name.

There are several varieties of penstemon growing alongside the highways and out of the sheer rock bluffs that hang above highways and roadsides. There are varieties that grow in the open prairie lands as well as in the high alpines.

Klickitat County's most notable penstemon is the Penstemon *Barrettiae*, which is described in a botanical reference as being "narrowly endemic to the east end of the Columbia Gorge" meaning that it grows nowhere else in the world. In fact, the three largest colonies of Penstemon *Barrettiae* can be found in Klickitat County. The three locations are the Roland's Lake area, the Klickitat River canyon, and above and below the upper falls on Rattlesnake Creek. It is truly a beautiful, showy, and colorful plant.

Bruce Meyers, a White Salmon native, spent years hybridizing the various species of penstemon with the goal of developing the perfect plants for flower gardens. His documented hybridizing of the penstemon ranged from 1968 to 1998, the year of his death. In 1995

PENSTEMONS

Geneva M. Meyers

Bruce received the Glenn Viehmeyer Award from the American Penstemon Society for developing hybrids of merit. One of his hybrid crosses, which used the *Barrettiae* Penstemon as one of the parents, is an albino variety displayed at the Longwood Gardens in Kennett Square, Pennsylvania. Bruce's favorite cross, the *Mexicali*, can be found in various seed catalogues today. Some of his original hybrids can still be found in friends' gardens around White Salmon.

Bruce Meyers' notes

PETROGLYPHS

Mary Anne Enyeart

Tsagaglalal
"She Who Watches"

Petroglyphs and pictographs were most evident in Klickitat County before The Dalles Dam backed up the Columbia River. The Native Americans had "chipped or ground into rock to depict tribal legends, hunting scenes, and mysticism" to make petroglyphs. Some of these were created as long ago as 8,000 to 10,000 years. The pictographs were paintings on basalt boulders. These may date back 300 years. Before the dam completion, there were thousands of drawings in the area. It was known as Petroglyph Canyon.

When The Dalles Dam was finished in 1957, the rising river covered many of these rocks. The year before, in 1956, a rubbing rush was on. The National Park Service granted funds to the University of Washington to record these ancient images. Many of these image rocks were moved and placed at The Dalles Dam park and tourist area. Rubbings were made of those that couldn't be moved. A rubbing was made by using cloth and paper, with oil paint carefully rolled across the surface of the paper so as not to damage the rock surface. Many of these required much effort; sometimes one had to lean out over the river two or three feet to reach the rock. The Skamania Lodge in Stevenson recently purchased a number of these petroglyph images and hung them in the lodge.

Many petroglyphs that were taken to the dam are now displayed at the Columbia Hills State Park (formerly Horsethief Lake State Park) and other local points of interest. The most famous pictograph "She Who Watches" or Tsagaglalal, in native language, still graces the rimrock on the Washington side of the river across from Celilo Falls. To prevent vandalism, she can be viewed by appointment only by contacting Columbia Hills State Park. Federal Law prohibits removal of archaeological resources from the site.

These special rocks may be found in other areas in our county as well as along the Columbia. Care should be taken to only look and not damage. Most are on private property, and permission is required before viewing.

Richard, Terry. 2001. 'She Who Watches' pictograph worth a gander. *The Sunday Oregonian*, July 15, sec. T.

Richard, Terry. 2004. Gorge petroglyphs moved to place of honor. *The Sunday Oregonian*, March 28, sec. T.

Muldoon, Katy. 2004. Preserving a past, finding a future. *The Sunday Oregonian*, August 1, sec. A.

PHOENIX FESTIVAL

Teddy Cole

Trout Lake is perched on the flanks of a volcano, but it only rocks once a year, and that's when the Phoenix Festival comes to town.

The Northwest's answer to Nevada's "Burning Man," this twenty-four-hours-a-day long weekend (three to five days) has erupted near Trout Lake since 2000. The Festival organizers create an eighty-acre tent village complete with commons, marketplace, medical station, and multiple performance stages. Stallings (Seattle Weekly) called Phoenix Festival "…an immersive experience of amplified sound." It is promoted as "the largest outdoor non-commercial, cooperative, community based underground music and arts festival of its kind in the Northwest."

Jan Nelson, a Trout Lake resident, said that the locals had no complaints except for the 24/7 loud music — especially hard on those living closest. The odd-looking people wandering around Trout Lake for several days did raise an eyebrow or two. The organizers gave free passes to the local businessmen, who reported seeing nothing objectionable when they visited.

The folks attending the festival had to provide their own water, as well as other necessities, because none was supplied on the grounds. A few Trout Lake ladies handed out free water at the festival.

The organizers emphasize the importance of maintaining good relations with the communities where the festival is held. "The key to being able to have a freaky arts festival in a small town without any corporate backing is to make sure that our presence within these communities is positive and well intentioned. We have been successful with this in the past, and intend to keep it up."

Interview with Jan Nelson
Phoenix Festival Web site: http://www.phoenixfest.com
Stallings, Ariel Meadows. 2002. Raving in Klickitat. Seattle
    Weekly. July 11-17.

PIKE'S SODA FOUNTAIN

Joan Wilkins Stone

The soda fountain inside Pike's Drugstore was the place to congregate during the 1940s and 1950s. The red padded stools bolted to the floor were seldom empty.

Clifford and Eula Pike treated customers of all ages as if they were guests in their own home. Browsers and buyers were given the same respect. Business men and farmers, in for supplies, would stop for morning coffee and the news of the day. "They flipped a coin to see who would be paying that day," said Barbara Adkison, a clerk at the store in the late 1940s.

Ladies stopped by in mid-afternoon to test the newest perfume or pick up a prescription. They joined each other for a dish of ice cream and a cool drink at the fountain. The group checked out and commented on patterned dresses and saucy hats worn by the ladies. A dab of nail polish was often seen on a stocking as a lady checked to see if her seams were straight. Nylon hosiery was scarce because of the war, and fingernail polish would stop a dreaded run.

By 3:30, the stools at the fountain would be empty. The chrome fixtures and granite counter were wiped clean, and the girl behind the counter would take a quick break, but not for long. School was out.

In came the high school girls, dressed in sloppy joe sweaters and pleated skirts with matching anklets and wearing penny loafers. The lucky ones, or so they thought, showed off a boy's ring dangling on a chain around their neck. Out came fuchsia lipsticks from the plastic shoulder bags, and the preening in front of the mirror began. That mirror was the backdrop to the fountain, running the full length of the bar.

"The fountain clerk had to know all of the recipes and be able to move fast," said Barbara. Phosphates (fizz water, flavoring, and milk), sodas, chocolate or cherry flavored Cokes, suicide Cokes (a combination of cherry, vanilla, chocolate, and lemon flavorings), malts, sundaes, and banana splits were some of the favorites.

When speaking with people who remember the soda fountain, they usually smile and wish it were here still. People who don't remember the place might wish it were, too.

Interviews with Barbara Adkison, Betty Rogers

PINE MARTEN

Kathleen Goode

The woodlands of Klickitat County were once home to a small creature sometimes referred to as the American Sable: the Pine Marten *Martes americana*. This small, cat-like creature was trapped nearly to extinction for its fur; today its curious nature leads it into traps meant for other animals, such as gophers.

The citizens of Washington State voted to eliminate most animal trapping and commercial sale of pelts in 2000. A bill before the State Legislature this year may rescind the earlier protections. The Pine Marten also faces loss of habitat. Clear cutting, or even clearing to reduce fire danger, may render an area uninhabitable for the Pine Marten.

People over 65 seem to be well aware of the Pine Marten as a local species, while people under 30 seem never to have heard of it. My first (and only) close observation of a Pine Marten was at the Goldendale Art Gallery. The Pine Marten was on a small branch above the door and had been artfully preserved by Bob Butts, a local taxidermist.

The small, nocturnal animal is related to otters and weasels; I think it looks more like a Red Panda. The long body and bushy tail are dark brown, with lighter coloring marking the face and chest. It has large eyes, rounded ears, and sharp claws. The martens are excellent climbers, which helps them hunt squirrels and avoid predators. They also hunt on the ground, making use of brush piles and fallen logs as cover. The animals are not often seen, being nocturnal, and might be noticed more readily by their footprints. Tracks usually show all four feet close together. There is a good example of a single paw print at http://www.bcadventure.com/ adventure/wilderness/animals/marten.htm and an excellent photo by John Marriott at http://raysweb. net/wildlife/pages/08.html. Being very sensitive to changes in the environment, the pine marten is used by scientists to monitor the health of certain areas. I think it should be one of the poster critters for saving old growth forests. If people can't relate to the plight of a rare snail or even the spotted owl, they might be attracted to this shy forest resident.

Ellis, E. 1999. Martes americana, Animal Diversity Web, http://animaldiversity.ummz.umich.edu/site/accounts/information/Martes_americana.html

Distribution map of Martes americana in Washington state, http://wdfw.wa.gov/wlm/gap/gapdata/mammals/gifs/maam.gif

Marten: Martes americana or Pine Marten, American Sable, http://www.beadventrue.com/adventrue/wilderness/animals/marten.htm

News-The Fur Trade Today 03/17/05, Source: *Seattle Post-Intelligencer*, 03/08/05, http://www.bancrueltraps.com/news?p=70&more=1

PIONEER BRIDE

Frank Wesselius

America Jenkins was the last of seven children born to Willis and Elizabeth Jenkins, early pioneers of Klickitat County. The first six Jenkins children were born east of the Mississippi river, while America was born in Washington County, Oregon, on March 31, 1846, just a year after her parents had crossed the plains on the Oregon Trail.

America moved with her family to Klickitat County in 1859. (The 15 families that settled on the slopes of the Simcoes at that time were known as the 59ers.) She spent her teenage years at the Blockhouse ranch about eight miles west of Goldendale.

When America got married, services were held in the Blockhouse and conducted by her brother Henry Clay Jenkins, the local Methodist minister. Of course the reception and dinner was also held in the family home. The wedding day was August 14, 1867.

America was the first white woman married in Klickitat County, married in the first permanent structure in the area and by the first minister of Klickitat County.

Klickitat County Historical Society archives
William Chambers, A trip through Jenkins genealogy. Unpublished.

Each year on the second Saturday in June, the community of Cleveland, five miles west of Bickleton, is filled with campers and motor homes in anticipation of the weekend to come. This tiny community has a few homes, a cemetery, and a park with a carousel nearly a hundred years old, a grandstand, and a rodeo ground. What began years ago as a memorial service by Bickleton area folks for those who have passed on is now that plus much more. For two days friends and neighbors, former residents, and passersby enjoy the sights and sounds of a good old fashioned get-together.

The rodeo on Saturday and Sunday afternoons draws cowboys from far and near. Professional cowboys and cowgirls entertain and share their skills. Local organizations have food booths where a good old hamburger with grilled onions and homemade pie and ice cream suit the palate to a tee. The carousel with beautifully restored rocking horses and the fun chatter of old friends and new acquaintances make the day complete. Saturday evening includes a dance and Sunday morning a cowboy church service. I have attended this weekend for the last 10 years or so, taking Grange Pies to sell. It's a just a treat to take part!

PIONEER ROSE
"HARISON'S YELLOW"

Rachel Gunkel

On a breathtakingly hot Memorial Day, I walked up the hill past the Maryhill cemetery to the site of Marion and Lavinia Wren's house. Several chunks of concrete were embedded in the dry soil, barely visible. These remnants were all that was left of the house's foundation. There was no other sign that anyone had ever inhabited this desolate hillside.

As I walked through the cheat grass and star thistle, something stabbed my bare legs with unusual ferocity. I looked down and parted the brown grass.

Straggly branches were entwined among the grass. Brown, thorny, and nearly leafless, the most robust stem was pencil-thin and no taller than my knee. But the real surprise was a single luminous blossom.

I circled the foundation and discovered that rose suckers had entirely surrounded the perimeter of this old homestead. They were everywhere. I dug a bit of earth away from the base of a cane and used my shirttail to grasp its thorny stem. I pulled. Dirt clods and cheat

Harrison's Yellow Pioneer Rose

grass flew. A foot-long section of root lay exposed, and I used a sharp rock to sever it.

I took my rose start home and planted it. Regular watering soon had this exceptionally hardy rose growing madly. By the following year, it had reached four feet in height and bloomed profusely. The rose turned out to be "Harison's Yellow," a variety that dates back to 1830. Pioneers cherished this rose and brought starts of it with them on wagon trains.

There are many old homesteads in Klickitat County that still have "Harison's Yellow" roses growing around them. If you would enjoy growing a living piece of Klickitat County history in your own garden, be sure to get permission from the landowner before digging a sucker or taking a cutting.

Phillips, Roger, and Martyn Rix. 1993. *The Quest for the Rose.* New York: Random House.

PLEASANT VALLEY SCHOOL

Joan Wilkins Stone

"I don't think I learned how to study in those days. The teachers mostly let us work in the areas we liked. Dad tried to help me with math, but he did it differently than the teachers." So begins Beatrice Schuster Miller's recollection of her school days at Pleasant Valley School.

The schoolhouse that is now Pleasant Valley Grange was built in about 1917. The old building that housed the school before was bought by Beatrice's granddad. He hauled it home and made a garage out of it.

Bea started first grade in 1925 when she was seven years old. She had two classmates. The first six weeks she walked to school, about a two-mile walk. Her dad warned her not to ride with anyone she didn't know because that was the main highway to Yakima. Later she rode horseback.

There were nine grades and two teachers in the school. The school day began at 8 AM and ended at 4 PM. Water was drawn from the well by a hand pump.

School subjects were reading, writing, and arithmetic. "None of the extras like we have today," said Bea. But some things never change; recess was the highlight of the day. In the winter months, kids with saddle horses would tie a sled to the saddle and tear around the school yard, one student in the saddle and one on the sled. When their enthusiasm got the best of them, they would race down the road. The teacher would furiously ring the school bell to call them back.

The year Bea was in the third grade, her Granddad built a horse-drawn two-wheeled cart. She rode in it with her sister, Ruth, and brother, Art, who was the driver. It was pulled by their old saddle mare. They were getting ready to go home from school one day when they heard a racket on the road. It was a neighbor, with a four-horse team, carrying a load of wheat. "Art should have put the bridle on that mare first. He didn't do it, and the mare got scared and ran around the schoolhouse, maybe more than once, and ran into the swings, which tore the cart all up."

It took the Schuster kids about thirty minutes to get to school in the mornings, but longer coming home in the afternoons. They went across the fields to grandma's house. She always had a warm pie ready in the kitchen.

A barn on the school grounds housed all the students' horses during the school day. Numbers on each stall indicated where each horse was to go. It has been hinted that two well-known matrons of today stole the numbers off the stalls in an earlier time.

No hot lunches were served in those years; the students brought their lunches. Bea's aunt made her a cloth bag with a strap that she put over her shoulder to hold her lunch pail. One icy morning her mare slipped on the ice and fell, taking Bea with her. The container and lunch were crushed. Bea was more concerned about the lunch than her scrapes, scratches, and torn stockings.

There were many celebrations and gatherings at the school during the school year. The folding doors separating the two classrooms were opened to accommodate families and friends. Bea remembers Valentine's Day as the 'big one.' Everyone made their valentines and exchanged with everybody in the school. Bea filled a scrapbook with all of the valentines and kept it for many years. It was ruined when she and her husband's basement flooded during the heavy rains of 1996.

Bea's vivid memories bring to light the story of a small country school. So many things have changed, and yet, some are just the same.

Interviews with Beatrice Schuster Miller

PONDEROSA PARK

Bev Anderson

Ponderosa Village, Ponderosa Park, or just Ponderosa — mention any of these in Goldendale, and you get an immediate response. There have been many stories told about Ponderosa Park: stories of people dancing naked before the full moon, of witches and solstice celebrations, of a commune of hippies and tree-huggers. It has been told that a group of townsfolk went out to check on these stories and found ten naked men with chainsaws cutting trees (what a frightening thought!) Some feared and were convinced that it had connections to the Rajneesh cult in Oregon.

Perhaps some of these stories have a grain of truth. Ponderosa is a community of diverse people, most of whom have fled the cities seeking quiet in the midst of nature. Having come from larger cities, they may be a bit more liberal than many of the townsfolk. Those coming have walked their own path and created the living environment they wanted, seeking a more sustainable lifestyle. They have blended in with their surroundings, making the environment work for them with "Good Sense" homes, dome homes, straw-bale homes, and earth-berm homes. A few have met the challenge of living off the grid.

The Park was started in 1977. Larry and Meg Letterman and Meg's brother, William Kershaw, purchased 1,089 acres that had been a cattle ranch. They began the arduous task of dividing the land into 5-acre parcels. Meg drove each corner property marker in herself, as the wildlife looked on. It was to be a community of like-minded, self-sufficient folk, people who would work together. The natural environment was to be preserved, and wildlife given a safe haven.

Ponderosa Park is a homeowners association, complete with by-laws, rules, and regulations that were developed early on by the residents and founders. Yearly dues are collected and used for road repairs and other community needs. Two community wells were put in by the founders. The water system was designed by Larry Letterman and one of the other residents. A number of residents helped install much of the water system as well as the reservoir. The community initially managed the water system, and in August 1998 turned it over to Klickitat PUD to manage. Especially in the early days, people helped each other with building their homes. Some of that cooperation still exists, especially when a new straw-bale structure needs mudding.

As Ponderosa Park has grown, change has occurred, and yet the sense of community is still strong, the surrounding beauty is still preserved and protected, and the monthly community pot-lucks and the solstice celebrations continue.

Conversations with William Kershaw and Meg Letterman, cofounders of Ponderosa Park

History of Ponderosa Park by Meg Letterman, Klickitat County Historial Society archive

WE CREATED A HAVEN FOR OTHERS: PONDEROSA PARK

Meg Letterman

Long before my husband Larry retired, we decided cities were getting crazier every day and we wanted out. So we began searching for land in a rural area. While a new locale held appeal, we worried that we'd end up being "outsiders" there the rest of our lives. The solution, we decided, was to buy a large enough piece of land that we could attract other "outsiders" and build our own friendships. That's why we bought a 1,089-acre cattle ranch five miles north of Goldendale, Washington. That was a lot more land than we'd intended to own! So now what? The answer was to subdivide it into 5-acre parcels. That was back in 1977.

Larry and Meg Letterman

We call our subdivision Ponderosa Park.. We feel like we are a community, not just a subdivision. We know and help each other with projects on our properties. We lend each other tools, invite one another to dinner, and cooperate with our neighbors in every way possible. It is a pleasant living area based on environmental consciousness, voluntary cooperation, self-responsibility, and respect for others.

And our early worries about being treated as outsiders by the local folks? It turned out to be absolutely groundless! The "natives" around here are friendly and neighborly. Now in 2005, there are about 75 households living in Ponderosa year around as well as many vacation cottages. All this adds to the tax base, business for local businesses, talent for various jobs, members for local organizations, schools, and volunteer services.

[Editor's note: Meg Letterman died in April 2005, shortly after submitting this piece for the book.]

POWER POLE STORY

Judy Bane

My Dad is Luke Enyeart. He farmed in Klickitat County for 30 years, from the 1940s through the 1970s. As a young man, he would work a day job and then farm after work. One of his early day jobs was helping construct the electric power line through the county. My Uncle John Strange also worked on this job.

Sometime in the 1980s, my husband, Everett Bane, got a temporary job with a crew to go butt-test the wooden power poles running down the Klickitat Canyon. The Klickitat Canyon, with the Klickitat River in the bottom, is a wild, rocky area.

The first night Ev came home from work, he said the digging was mighty hard in some of those holes. They had to dig out two sides of the pole down to a couple feet, test the wood and treat it, cover the hole, and dig out the other two sides to repeat the treatment — Lots of hand digging with shovels. Ev decided that the installers must have dynamited the holes where the soil was nothing but rock, and backfilled with the rock. Mighty hard digging.

Well, a couple days later, Dad called to visit. He had since "retired" to the coast (translation: bought a dump truck, backhoe, and loader and went into the excavation business). I told him what Everett had said about dynamiting the holes in solid rock and backfilling with rock.

And Dad said, "Yup, that's just what we did."

THE PREACHER, PROHIBITION, AND THE TOKAY RANCH

Rachel Gunkel

After Lucy Palmer Maddock's death, her children inherited the Presby Ranch at Columbus. The three sons in the family were all well established, and they relinquished their interest in the property in favor of their sister, Birdie Maddock Jordan, and her husband, the Reverend W. T. Jordan. Jordan, a Baptist minister in Portland, lived with his wife and two daughters in genteel poverty. Their struggle to make ends meet had long ago grown old.

Hoping for a more prosperous life, the Jordans decided to try farming. In 1909 they refused an offer from Sam Hill to buy the Presby Ranch. They moved to Columbus, where they were determined to till the soil, convert the Indians, and "live the Christian life as an example to all."

As a preacher, the Reverend Jordan had spent many years fighting "liquor, gambling, prostitution, card playing and dancing with all the fire and brimstone [he] could muster." He should have rejoiced when Washington State adopted prohibition in 1916, followed by the rest of the nation with the passage of the Volstead Act in 1920.

Prohibition probably did make the Reverend Jordan rejoice. While the law made the sale and distribution of alcohol illegal, it permitted the consumption of wine made at home. Commercial wineries went out of business, but the number of home winemakers multiplied. The demand for wine grapes boomed, and the price of grapes soared. Growers of wine grapes grew prosperous during Prohibition.

Regardless of the law, it seems that the Reverend Jordan should have felt torn about the morality of growing wine grapes, given his personal stance on liquor. Evidently the family did feel uneasy, for Ruth Jordan Peterson wrote that the wine grapes that her family shipped were packed in a manner to avoid detection. "Prohibition was in force, so all of the grapes were packed in basket crates, the top row wound into tight bunches to hide the stems, and mostly shipped for table grapes or juice." It was common knowledge that the grapes were sold for making wine.

Some of the Jordan's neighbors were harshly judgmental. Rosa Gunkel wrote the following scathing comments in a letter dated September 25, 1927: "I am disgusted with Mr. Jordan. He went and planted a lot more wine grapes south of the railroad track, you know, in that peach and cherry orchard. I had supposed they were table grapes. He certainly does not deserve a blessing and the grapes are surely cursed."

Sam Hill called Jordan a "damned bootlegger" during a quarrel. It was an accusation the Reverend Jordan claimed he could never understand.

In the end, the business of growing wine grapes was too profitable to abandon. Jordan was transparently delighted with prosperity. He boasted to the *Klickitat County Agriculturist* that he had cleared over $4000 a year from grape sales alone throughout the 1920s. This was a far cry from the paltry $500-a-year salary he had earned as a preacher.

The Jordans even renamed their property to honor a variety of wine grape, calling it the Tokay Ranch.

Irvine, Ronald, with Walter J. Clore. 1997. *The Wine Project: Washington State's Winemaking History.* Sketch Publications.

Peterson, Ruth Jordan. 1982. *This Land of Gold and Toil.* Caxton Printers, Ltd.

Klickitat County Agriculturist. 1935. The Tokay Ranch at Maryhill. July 26.

Klickitat County Agriculturist. 1932. Childhood Memories: Columbus and Vicinity. June 17.

Letters of Rosa S. Gunkel, 1927, unpublished

Journal of Ralph D. Gunkel, 1933, unpublished

THE PRESBY LIGHTING

Naomi Fisher

It's the beginning of December. The holiday season is upon us.

Crunching through the snow, we all converge on the old mansion in the center of town. For hundreds of townspeople, this is the official beginning of Christmas: the lighting of the lights at the Presby Museum.

We arrive and join the crowd on the porch, talking with old friends, meeting new ones. Inside, folks are lining up for hot cider and cookies, all laid out with elegance and care by the generous members of the Klickitat County Historical Society, caretakers of the museum. We walk around, enjoying the delicious snacks and taking in the beautiful decorations. Many tour the cold upper floors of this Victorian mansion, others huddle in the parlour, enjoying the warmth there. Soon the music will start. There's always music to enjoy; years ago it was carols sung with enthusiasm, now it's lively jazz played by talented local music students.

As darkness falls, the announcement is made and we go outside to watch and wait. We can see our breath in the cold light of the street lamp across the way. More people come out onto the porch and walkways.

There is a brief flicker, then suddenly the grounds are illuminated with thousands of white lights, hanging from every eave and post, lining windows and even the old steam tractor on the lawn. I'm overcome with a warmth in my heart that matches the glow of the lights, and for me, the holidays have arrived!

[Sadly, the holiday tradition of the Lighting of the Presby Museum in Goldendale ended in 2003. Time has taken a toll on the old house, and I'm told that it was deemed too dangerous to the integrity of the eaves, porch and other parts of the house to bear the annual hanging of the lights. Volunteers have done an admirable job in opening the house each winter for the community, but the preservation of the house is by necessity their utmost concern. The celebration still happens, but spotlights illuminate the mansion instead of the many strings of white lights. I thank the Historical Society and all the volunteers of the Presby lighting for the years that we have been able to enjoy this event.]

W.B. PRESBY'S VINEYARD

Rachel Gunkel

Presby Mansion

Few people know that W.B. Presby, the man who built the Presby Mansion in Goldendale, also had a role in establishing one of the first wine vineyards in Klickitat County.

W.B. Presby's much older cousin, John W. Presby, was one of the early pioneers at Columbus. Like many of the other settlers, "Uncle John" raised fruit. The Presby Ranch was one of the largest and most successful fruit-growing operations on the Columbia River.

It was at Uncle John's urging that young Winthrop Bartlett Presby moved to Goldendale in 1887, following his graduation from Dartmouth College. Intelligent, ambitious, and energetic, W.B. Presby was determined to succeed. He became an outstanding attorney, active in local and state politics. W.B. also wanted to live in a luxurious style that reflected his status and taste.

W.B. Presby was reputedly fond of good wine. After acquiring the Presby Ranch at Columbus after his cousin's death in 1902, he decided to add the role of viticulturist to his accomplishments. Only the finest varieties of European wine grapes interested him and would fulfill his ambition.

In spite of his reputation as Goldendale's richest man, W.B. Presby was already financially overextended by the time of his cousin's death. Earlier that same year, he had begun building the largest mansion in Goldendale. W.B. could not afford to go to Europe and buy the thousands of grape cuttings needed for his vineyard, so he borrowed $10,000 from a wealthy widow named Lucy Palmer Maddock.

The trip was made and the grape cuttings bought. W.B. Presby planted his vineyard at Columbus with Rose of Peru, Tokay, Muscat of Alexandria, and other varieties of wine grapes.

Unfortunately, W.B. Presby was not able to repay Mrs. Maddock's loan. She foreclosed and became the owner of the Presby Ranch.

The Wine Project: Washington State's Winemaking History by Ronald Irvine and Walter J. Clore, Sketch Publications, 1997;

This Land of Gold and Toil by Ruth Jordan Peterson, Caxton Printers, LTD, 1982;

Klickitat County Washington Birth and Death Records by Jean Smeltzer, 1976;

"The House Next Door" by Thelma Jane Van Vactor Norrie, *Klickitat Heritage*, October 1992;

"The Man Who Built the Presby Mansion,: *Klickitat Heritage*, 1997;

"W.B. Presby Called," *The Goldendale Sentinel*, June 25, 1914

PUCKER HUDDLE

Mary Jean Lord

In 1901, William A. "Billy" Biesanz bought five acres of land near the mouth of the White Salmon River next to his friend Merle Fox's strawberry fields. He was so busy clearing the timber and brush and getting ready to plant that, when winter came, he hadn't built a cabin, and Merle invited him to hole up with him in his 10- x 12-foot cabin.

Having plenty of time on their hands, the young men kept busy building weird rope and pulley constructions — ropes that opened and shut the windows, opened a door to reveal a ladder to the attic, pulled curtains over blank walls, and opened a trap door in the floor. Pleased with their work, they held a dinner party and invited as many guests as they could squeeze in. Everyone exclaimed over the contraptions, but nobody cared for the food — mashed potatoes laced with honey, gravy seasoned with vanilla and a pink cake iced with salt instead of sugar.

As they sat crammed into the little room, Billy remarked, "You can see why we didn't invite the girls out here to do any spooning. It's so crowded you couldn't even pucker, let alone get in a huddle."

After that folks called the cabin "Pucker Huddle," and soon began calling the district by that name. Newer residents tried to suppress "such a silly name," but before long they started to enjoy the laugh they always got when they said they lived in Pucker Huddle, and the name stuck.

Bartholomew, Florence, "Pucker Huddle and why," *Ruralite*, Dec. 1964

QUIET COUNTRY LIFE

Kathleen Goode

Elizabeth bought five acres in Klickitat County with the dream of a quiet country retirement. She put up a feeder and bird bath. She and her two cats were delighted with the entertainment, but the trouble soon began. Spilled birdseed attracted mice, squirrels, raccoons, and skunks. Mice got in the pantry, squirrels tore up insulation under the house and ate all the seedlings in the garden, and raccoons came through the pet door to steal cat food. The presence of rodents attracted a coyote that began lurking around. Elizabeth felt this was all part of the beauty of country life. She sealed the foundation, put food in jars, and quit growing vegetables.

The bird baths also attracted butterflies, bees, and wasps. The wasps built a nest in the kitchen fan. Deer came for a drink. Elizabeth found the deer enchanting until she found herself threatened by an angry doe (a newborn fawn was a few feet away.) The cats brought prey in the house, especially lizards and mice. Elizabeth turned on her light one evening and found a bat hanging on the wall. The indoor wildlife was a problem, but the outdoors was just as dangerous. Dogs stalked Elizabeth and chased the cats. Cats came to fight over territory. One day Elizabeth stepped out the door to get the mail and saw a bull come charging into her yard. It was her introduction to the meaning of "open range."

Late one summer a pair of skunks decided to set up housekeeping under a shed. A neighbor came and shot them, but one managed to crawl under the shed before it died. Elizabeth is now finding life in the big city to be rather quiet!

In the early 1900s, Columbia River and Northern Railroad Company purchased right of way for a rail line into Goldendale. The track followed the Klickitat River from Lyle through Klickitat, then up Swale Canyon into Centerville and Goldendale. Following completion of track to Centerville, the first load of grain was shipped in 1903. Grain was shipped from Goldendale when the line was completed. Transportation by rail became the valley's lifeline for supplies and travel for these communities.

At a celebration of life recently, stories were shared about when the Finnish Church in Centerville had a National Convention in 1921, with people coming by rail from as far away as Michigan and Finland. Meals were served in the recently torn-down granary which sat beside the track. It had been decorated with greenery to smell good (pieces of greenery were still in the loft of this recently torn-down building). Young and old attended, but Louise Mattson told how she and her siblings stayed home from the last meeting, so mama could enjoy the meeting, and later lamented "and *they* got to have ice cream."

Wayne Eshelman told the story of a championship basket ball game in 1926 with Goldendale at White Salmon. Goldendale Merchants paid $350 to hire a steam locomotive and a few cars. Passengers boarded in both Goldendale and Centerville. Gals sold eats as they traveled, and buses transported the folks from Bingen to White Salmon and back.

Candy Magnuson told a story of her grandmother Jessie Mattson, about renting half of a box car to move their belongings from Centerville to Kelso. Even a piano can ride the rails!

Alvin Randall told how many wives got their money by selling cream and eggs by rail. Wayne Eshelman said that when a woman got a 5-gallon can of cream or a case of eggs, it would be set at the landing, waiting for the train to pick it up and deliver it to Portland or Vancouver. The cost to send the cream was 18 cents.

Don Ritzschke told about those cream cans. He said nearly everyone had them. His dad died young, and his mom, who lived with her family, milked 5 or 6 cows. He said there were lots of cans at the train station. The empties would come back to be picked up, and they were quickly gathered and filled with water to put out fires. New school teachers would go to the rail station and look over the names on the cans to see who their new students would be.

Wayne also said that, up until WWII, you could mail an order to Sears and Roebuck in Seattle or Montgomery Ward in Portland on Monday and the item would return on the Wednesday train. The mail went out on the train and was sorted on the way.

Wheat and lumber were shipped until the early 1980s, when trucking became more convenient and less costly. Especially after floods, upkeep was heavy on the rail line down the Swale canyon and along the Klickitat River. An old notice from September 1966 announces that the passenger train had just completed its first run after the December 1964 flood.

Locals say it really wasn't a passenger train towards the end. You had to ride in the caboose, but it was often used as a way to get into town or back home if the time was right. More than one young man had ridden in with a farmer from Centerville and was able to catch the late afternoon train home after meetings or games.

Looking around, you can still see places where a rail line was removed. The old Goldendale station has been moved and made into a home. The grade from Lyle to Warwick is now the Klickitat Trail. But many memories remain.

Stories told by Neva Shelton, Stan Crocker,
    Tony Sarsfield, Don Ritzschke, The Randalls,
    Wayne Eshelman

RAIN SHADOW

Keith McCoy

Klickitat County, sprawling for 84 miles along the north shore of the Columbia, has several distinct rainfall zones.

As water-laden clouds drift eastward from the Pacific toward the Cascade Range, they rise to cross the mountain barrier, causing heavy precipitation on the western flanks. An effect called the "rain shadow" is apparent when that barrier is crossed, and precipitation diminishes. The range of foothills that extends from Underwood Mountain to Trout Lake Valley, skirting the White Salmon River, is the breaking line.

The United States Weather Bureau keeps close track of rainfall, as does a special department at Oregon State University. They revise the rainfall figures every 25 years; those currently available cover the years 1977 through 2000.

Portland International Airport reports an average annual rainfall of 37 inches, while Troutdale reports 46 inches as the Cascades begin to rise. At Bonneville Dam, near the north-south line of the Cascade Crest, the rainfall is 79 inches per year. Some 20 miles east at Hood River-White Salmon, as mountain heights reduce and the "rain shadow" line is reached, rainfall is down to 37 inches.

The decline for the next few miles is not as rapid as might be expected; the Snowden-Appleton plateau, at approximately 2300 feet elevation, reports 33 inches. Then, very few miles eastward at The Dalles, annual rainfall is reduced to 14 inches. Goldendale, across the Columbia and somewhat higher in elevation, reports 18 inches. Moving eastward, precipitation drops rapidly as clouds cross the Columbia Plateau.

Alderdale, at the extreme east end of Klickitat County, has an average rainfall that is reduced to about nine inches. Alderdale has no reporting station, but it is between Oregon's Arlington and Boardman, both of which have nine inches per year. McNary Dam has an average precipitation of eight inches.

The rain shadow phenomenon has everything to do with the types and density of timberlands and agricultural possibilities. Obviously, the nine inches of rain at the east end of the county makes artificial irrigation necessary — and fortunately Columbia River water is available to support the orchards and other agricultural activities there.

U.S. Weather Bureau
Oregon State University

RAISING PIGS

Eleanor Dooley
as told to Judy Thomas

I got started with pigs because of pneumonia. My husband, Paul, and I had been raising a few pigs each year, but the summer piglets usually came down with dust pneumonia and died. Paul suggested that we give up on the summer litters, but I decided to see if I could pull them through. I moved our four sows to a shed with a board floor and gave them each a private suite and lots of TLC. The floor kept the piglets away from dust, and the partitions reduced the chance that piglets would be crushed or lost. All the litters survived, and I was in the pig business!

Pigs are a lot like humans — they do best when they have a varied diet. I gave my pigs grain grown and ground on our ranch, but also beans, buttermilk, whey, potatoes, pears, apples, squash, sugar beets, corn, watermelon, cantaloupes, day-old bakery goods — and more beans. Each food had its own story, especially the beans.

I drove my truck to Othello once a week, picked up 8 tons of beans, and brought them back to our farm near Goldendale at the top end of the Maryhill loops. We cooked the beans over a wood fire in a 500 gallon tank set on cement blocks. This was so much work that we began looking for an easier method. A friend helped me build a cooker, still fired by wood, but with a wheel inside for stirring, a 30 ft. smoke stack, and a 6 inch valve to drain the soup. I got an electric car used to move merchandise in warehouses and had it fitted with a tank to hold the soup. I used the car, my "Yellow Hornet", to deliver the soup and pump it into the feeding troughs.

Getting the other foods involved a lot of driving. I got buttermilk from the Goldendale creamery until it closed, then started going to a Portland cheese plant once a week to fill the two 500 gallon tanks on my truck with whey, sometimes also loading up with bread, cake, cookies, and fruitcake. In the fall I made trips to Hood River and Bingen three times a week to pick up fruit culls. I enjoyed making these trips and got a lot of my "brain waves" — ideas about how to improve my operation — while driving those miles.

I loved my trucks. During the first seven or eight years of our marriage, my husband and I had no farm machinery and no electricity. So, when we got our first tractor, I just fell in love with it. When we got electricity, Paul suggested that we get a freezer, but I said a loader for the tractor would help me more. That Ferguson tractor was my right hand for fifty years, and I practically wept when I sold it.

If the tractor was my right hand, my left hand was a pickup. For my birthday and Christmas presents one year, I had a machine shop fit the back of the pickup with storage compartments for tools and a generator. I grew up learning and enjoying the traditional feminine skills of cooking and sewing, but everything to do with machinery became my true love.

Pigging (farrowing) every month meant that the weather was involved — piglets born in freezing weather can die in an hour. In the coldest months I would park my station wagon at the barn and, leaving the engine running, would sleep for an hour and then get up to check on the sows. If one was pigging I would wait, then put the new piglets under a heat lamp.

When the pigs weighed about 225 pounds and were ready for market, I would haul them to Goldendale to be shipped to a special market in Seattle. Because of the way they were raised, my pigs had more meat and less fat than most, and they made a nicer pork chop. For a while, I trucked 10 hogs to Portland every Sunday night.

In about 1980, I decided to get out of the pig business. Domestic animals are completely dependent on their humans, and I began to doubt that I could handle the job myself were I ever left without hired help. Also, our cattle and farming operation took a lot of my attention. I gradually sold off the animals until I was left with just six sows. Those were my last pigs.

RATTLESNAKES

Kathleen Goode

The local tribes believed that if you killed a rattlesnake, its mate would seek revenge. The rattlesnake, or wah'k-puch, was a very powerful spirit. One who controlled such a spirit was a very powerful medicine man and could communicate with the snakes and cure a bite from one. Most people were careful not to bother the wah'k-puch, and few Yakama were ever bitten, even though the snake was present in very large numbers in the grass meadows.

Klickitat County is rattlesnake country from one end to the other. Pioneers had to deal with them constantly, at least until the arrival of mechanical harvesters that could literally kill the snake in the grass. Perhaps the largest collection of rattlesnakes in the county was found by Mark Crawford when he was 12 years old and living at what is now the Dalles Mountain Ranch. He was hiking in the spring and suddenly found himself almost entirely surrounded by rattlesnakes. Somehow, he had the presence of mind to escape them and go get his father. They shot 45 rattlesnakes that day, but it was only the beginning of their war with the snakes. The rattlesnake den was destroyed by dynamite years later.

Rattlesnakes seldom attack people; bites are most frequent among male teens who attempt to pick up the snakes. Normally, avoiding rattlesnakes is just a matter of using common sense: wear boots when out hiking, and look where you are putting your feet. Carrying a walking stick is also a good idea. If you do come across a snake, slowly back away. The number one rule if you are bitten is to remain calm and remember that rattlesnakes rarely inject venom when they strike. Remove shoes or jewelry near the bite, and get to a doctor. The good news about rattlesnakes is that you will probably never encounter one in the wild. Dr. Ogden has walked all over the place for 30 years and has never seen a rattlesnake outside of a zoo.

Askham, Leonard R. Extension bulletin 0984: Rattlesnakes
http://cru.cahe.wsu.edu/cEPublications/eb0984/eb0984. html

Bleakney, Darlene Highsmith. 1992. *Dalles Mountain Ranch: Museum of Natural & Cultural Heritage of the East Columbia River Gorge*. Salem OR: Lynx Communication Group.

Hines, Donald M. 1993. Magic in the Mountains — The Yakima Shaman: Power and Practice. Issaquah WA: Great Eagle Publishing.

Hunn, Eugene S. with James Selam and Family.1990. *Nch'i-Wana "The Big River": Mid-Columbia Indians and Their Land*. Seattle: University of Washington Press.

RECIPE FOR A GRAND BICYCLE ADVENTURE

Nancy Allen

Gather several bicycling, wildflower, bird watching enthusiasts. Stir together on a sunny spring day. Meet at the Warwick trailhead of the Klickitat Rail to Trail. Mount your bicycle seat, and ride into the wilderness of Swale Canyon. It helps if you are unaware of the rough trail surface conditions ahead, although you will soon learn the truth of your situation.

When I watched the redtail hawk soaring overhead, I forgot the headache suffered while crossing the first bridge of railroad ties, spaced just far enough apart to make it very rough. The orange and purple carpet of balsamroot and lupine covering the hills was enough incentive to continue the gradual descent deeper into the canyon. The beauty of the creek and the majestic hills is beyond description. But, I discovered the danger of looking at the beauty for more than a split second when I hit an oversize rock with my front tire and sprawled on the trail, with my bike doing the riding on my small body. With a few minor scrapes, I remounted to continue the adventure.

It is impossible to list the large number of wildflowers and birds seen on this four-hour ride from the prairie at Warwick through the wildness of Swale Canyon, along the wild and scenic Klickitat River, to Lyle. Don't miss the spectacular view of the river from Fisher Hill Bridge. Of course, I stopped in the small town of Klickitat for ice cream to refuel.

OLD RED HOUSE

Mary Jean Lord

When the Old Red House was built about 1890, it was "out-in-the-country." Today it is surrounded by neighbors and within a few blocks of the post office and city hall. Though often thrown into the catchall category of "Victorian," architecturally the Red House is more like a tall, anorexic Swiss chalet.

Charles Newell built it for his wife Mary. He scandalized the good people of Goldendale by painting it barn red, a color applied only to outbuildings. The three-story house has ten rooms and boasts leaded and stained glass windows imported from Europe.

Some folks say Mary was half-Indian and Newell promised to build her the finest house in Goldendale to make up for the slurs she had received from prejudiced townspeople. Others say Mary didn't have any Indian blood, and the story grew out of the fact that Charles spoke the local Indian language fluently, and acted as lawyer and mediator for the Native Americans.

The Newells didn't live in the Red House long, but moved to Toppenish where Newell, such a successful horse trader he was known as "the Horse King," had invested in a hotel. Their only child, Major Howard Newell, became a lawyer and moved to Washington, DC.

Perhaps because the house lay empty so long, many believe it to be haunted. When it was still in the country, children feared to walk past at night. People reported lights flickering through its tall, narrow windows, and an old lady was said to sit in a rocking chair on the second floor.

A bungalow-type white house was built a few blocks beyond it, and youngsters believed there was a secret tunnel between them where horrible, unmentionable things went on. When the white house burned to the ground one night, the stories multiplied.

Another tale was that a photographer tried year after year to get a good picture of the house, but the developed film was always blank. The Rev. Ralph Barber painted a picture of the Old Red House at twilight with the rays of a dying sun shining eerily through the windows. The family who owned the picture had to remove it from above the fireplace because it frightened the children so.

The house was neglected and desolate when Franklin Miller bought it in 1949 and began a loving restoration that lasted the rest of his life. He tried renting it once, but was so upset at the renters' lack of respect that he never allowed anyone else to live in it.

Miller pooh-poohed the stories of ghosts. There wasn't a rocking chair in the house, and the idea of a secret tunnel was ludicrous. He once spent the night in the house himself and saw or heard nothing out of the ordinary.

The Old Red House is one of the most photographed and painted buildings in the state. In spite of its charms, this house that was once considered the height of modernity is hopelessly out of date today.

Bartholomew, Florence. 1964. Old Red House. *Ruralite*.
    February.

Old Red House, Part 2

Alexander Rush-Hallak

It was mid-October 2003 when we first saw the red house. My wife and I had recently moved to Seattle from New York City, so that our daughter could grow up near her grandparents. We had heard of Sam Hill's Stonehenge replica and decided we should come up to see it. We stayed at the Ponderosa Motel for three days. All three days were rainy and miserable. We decided that, before we left town, we would go have lunch at Sodbusters Café.

We saw Clark's Floral and went in to see if we could find any postcards to send friends. There my wife found a greeting card which had a picture of the red house on the front. Being lovers of Victorian houses, we were drawn to it and decided we should see it before we drove back to Seattle. We got directions and made our way to Sentinel Street. On the way, we joked that it would be funny if it were for sale. Turning the corner, we saw it standing tall and proud, beautiful and mysterious; better yet, it was for sale. We grabbed a listing, because we wanted to know more about this house. We saw the realtor's office wasn't far away, so we drove over to see if we could see the inside, partly out of natural curiosity; the other part we considered for a moment that maybe we could move up here. Within moments, we were driving back with the realtor; now we were wondering what it might look like inside. We saw that it was built in 1890, so we were concerned about the interior condition. To our surprise, it looked beautiful — the stained glass windows, hardwood floors. One look and we knew two things: this house was well-loved, and we wanted it.

It took another two months until we made the move from Seattle. On a late cold winter night, only a few days before the snowstorm, my wife, my six-month-old daughter, and I moved into the old red house, built out of love by Charles Newell for his half-Indian wife over 100 years earlier.

Please note: We do understand that people admire and love this house; however, it is private property, please respect that when coming to view it. We do not currently give tours. The house is available, however, for film projects. If you are interested in the house for such a project or would like to take a virtual tour, please visit www.oldredhouse.com.

RIVER'S-EYE VIEW

Nancy Barron

1 Down to the ri-ver's eye view, leav-ing the dry-lands and dri-ving be-
2 Wield - ing our pad-dles with glee, snug in our raft, we are off to ex-
3 Out from the ra-pids, we cheer! Now we can laze while we're float-ing down-

- low, hill - sides, the pen-sta-men bloom. Sce-nic and wild, see the
- plore. Ea - gles and her - on and gulls claim this as home as do
- stream. Af - ter the har-row-ing piece come a few qui - et spots

Klick - i - tat flow. Val-ley fra-ming sky, wit-ness-ing peace. Earth and wa-ter
ou - zels near shore.
where we can dream.

bal - anced, hold and re - lease. *Fine* Rush-ing and roa-ring, the nar-rows con - verge,

out-crop-pings grasp-ing at us as we flee. Holes suck-ing whi-irl-pools in - to the

D.C. al Fine

flow, bould-ers ap - pear-ing, must stay with the Vee.

ROAD SIGNS OF KLICKITAT COUNTY

Sara Wu

Some road signs that reflect the rural nature of Klickitat County:

Impassable When Wet

Primitive Road, Not Maintained Next "X" Miles

Entering Range Land
and
Leaving Range Land
But are there equal numbers of each sign?

No Gas for "X" Miles
"50 miles" on US Highway 97 going north from Goldendale
"82 Miles" on State Highway 14 going east from Highway 97
"65 Miles" on the Bickleton Road going east from Goldendale

Electrical Signs (the only ones in the county)
Red and amber flashing sign (beacon) in Bingen on SR 14, removed in 2004 *
Red and amber flashing sign (beacon) in Roosevelt on Highway 14
Red, four-way, flashing stop signs in Goldendale— three, one block from each other
First multiphase traffic light installed in 2005 at the Hood River Bridge and SR 14.

* The beacon in Bingen was installed in 1947 where the street from White Salmon came into SR 14. When SR 14 through Bingen was widened in 2004, WDOT decided that the beacon was no longer needed. There was some local resistance, since it had been a landmark for such a long time.

Personal communication with Gary Weiss, WDOT, Vancouver (2005)

ROCK HUNTING

Geneva M. Meyers

Rocks such as agates, jaspers, petrified wood, and opal are found in Klickitat County. I have fond memories of walking across a field on a warm summer day, breathing in the fresh air, and searching for collectable rocks.

Shortly after we married, my husband, Bruce, taught me the art of rock hunting. We spent many weekends walking the fields of Lyle and High Prairie, picking up rocks and loading them into our rock-sacks to carry home. We would drive around, hoping to find a freshly-plowed field where the rocks had been surfaced by the farmer's plow. The best time was after rain had fallen, exposing the agates. Once the rain has washed off some of the dirt, the agates and other jewelry-grade rocks shine from the reflection of the sun, making them easier to spot. We had several favorite fields where we had been granted permission from the property owners to remove all the rocks we desired, which, over the years, was a lot of rocks. You do have to get your eyes "tuned" to spot the rocks, however. I picked up a lot of dog rocks (rocks you might throw at your neighbor's dog) before learning to spot the right ones.

Once we got the rocks home, Bruce, an experienced lapidary, would cut and polish them to form cabochon and cabinet-specimen collections as well as pieces of jewelry. We always had more rocks than we could ever do anything with. Half of the fun was in the finding.

In other parts of the country, rock locations are called 'diggings', because you must use a pick or shovel to extract rocks from the ground. Also, you are digging for one particular type of rock, perhaps thunder eggs filled with agate or with pastel jasper, chunks of jasper or agate or picture rock, certain types of petrified woods, obsidians, geodes, etc. In Klickitat County, rocks are found on top of the ground, and are usually a mixture of rock types — you never know what you may find! We have agates that resemble almost any kind of agate you might find elsewhere. Our rocks are often water-worn, having traveled through a lot of moving-water-activity in the distant past.

The opal found in Klickitat County is generally in large chunks and far from jewelry grade. However, Bruce found the rarest of all finds in our Klickitat rocks — a fire opal! It was small and crumbled apart, so he imbedded the chips into a plastic form for a paperweight. The opal was not gem quality, but was a true novelty for our local area.

ROOSEVELT LANDFILL

Judy Thomas

Peregrine Falcon

Where in Klickitat County can you find caravans of trucks delivering material destined to be guarded by birds? The place is the Municipal Solid Waste landfill, the material is garbage, and falcons are the hired guns. The landfill, located at Roosevelt in the east end of the county, is the final resting place for garbage from the northwest U.S., as well as British Columbia and Alaska. The majority of the waste arrives at Roosevelt by rail; it is trucked approximately five miles from the rail yard to the site. During the day, garbage is dumped and compacted at the 200-foot working face of the landfill. During the night, the face is covered with soil to eliminate odors and to discourage seagulls, rodents, and other scavengers.

The gulls, ever-present at most landfills, are particularly difficult. They bombard workers and machinery with their droppings. They quickly become accustomed to deterrents such as noisemakers and plastic owls. However, the managers of the Roosevelt facility have found a solution: falcons. They have hired a local falconer to bring his birds to the site and fly them around. The gulls want nothing to do with these predators — even the sight of the falconer's car approaching is enough to send them scattering! A falcon reminder several times a week keeps the gull population near zero.

The landfill began operation in 1991. The site is permitted to accept 244 million cubic yards of waste. When that limit is reached, perhaps in about 40 years, the landfill will be closed, and the entire area can be returned to agricultural use.

The landfill location was chosen because the natural features and low rainfall of the area make it possible to build a facility with minimal environmental impact. The basalt and naturally occurring layer of low-permeability clay located beneath the site provide good separation from the local aquifers. Several layers of man-made membrane, clay, and gravel are laid down before the waste is deposited. The liquid produced from the garbage is collected by a system of pipes and re-circulated through the landfill to encourage rapid decomposition and accelerate methane production. The methane, a potent greenhouse gas, is collected by another pipe system and is used to create electrical power at the on-site H.W. Hill Landfill Gas Power Plant, operated by the Klickitat County PUD. The landfill is expected to eventually generate enough power for 30,000 homes.

Visitors can observe the landfill operation from a viewing gazebo. They must sign in at the office when arriving. A virtual tour of the power plant is available at www.rabanco.com. The falcons, however, are available only on site.

Phone interview with Arthur Mains, landfill staff
Rabanco web site www.rabanco.com

ROUSH CORNER GROCERY

Joan Wilkins Stone

In the 1930s and 40s, on the corner of Grant and Allyn streets stood an old two-story house, its exterior faded gray with age. School children walking from the Goldendale Primary School would never have noticed it except for one thing: the magic within.

The sign above the door read "Roush Grocery." A bell tinkled as the door was opened. Penny candy filled a glass display case that stretched almost wall to wall. Jaw breakers the size of ping pong balls, candy cigarettes painted red on one end, Guess Whats, wax lips, bubble gum cigars, and licorice pipes were for sale, a penny apiece.

Boys in overalls and girls in jumpers and white blouses stood in line clutching a few pennies that were dutifully saved, snitched from their mom's penny jar, or bartered from a younger sibling. Mrs. Roush greeted each child, counted out their pennies, and listened carefully to their choices as if this were her purpose in life.

Parents had no idea their children were making this stop. No one would have dared to walk downtown to a store, because walking straight home was the rule. However, a little jog on the way didn't seem to be a problem.

In retrospect, how could parents not have known? Bubble gum-smeared faces, teeth tinted red, black tongues… Keeping it a secret probably stopped all the haggling for pennies!

Personal experience and interview with
    Nadine Hamllik McKinney (2-26-2004)

C.E. RUSK: MOUNTAINEER

Keith McCoy

When Claude Rusk was growing up in Goldendale, he was fascinated with Mount Adams, but could only wonder — and worship — from afar. When he was fifteen, he came closer to realizing his dream. His parents bought the Wetemis Soda Springs on the Klickitat River and developed a rustic resort called Rusk Springs Resort. Even so, young Rusk had to wait until he was seventeen and hired as a teacher in the Camas Prairie school to achieve his objective. In 1888 he climbed Mount Adams and circled its glaciated mass by trail. His love affair with the mountain deepened.

C. E. Rusk went from teaching to journalism, and for a time he was editor of *The Goldendale Sentinel*. Then his career took him to Yakima, where for many years he was receiver for the U. S. Land Office.

Climbing was never far from his mind, and his favorite mountain was nearby. He pioneered several treacherous east-face routes. He was a leader in the Yakima Cascadians. In 1901 he was a charter member of the prestigious American Alpine Club, in which he became known as one of the most expert and daring climbers in the West, having climbed all the snow-capped peaks in Northern California, Oregon and Washington, and many in British Columbia and Alaska. Perhaps his most publicized venture was in 1910, when he led a group of Mazamas in an assault on Mount McKinley. His *Tales of a Western Mountaineer* is a classic in mountaineering libraries.

It is fitting that on his death in 1931 his fellow Cascadians placed his ashes in a cairn atop the Castle, the towering promontory that dominates the Great East Face of Mt. Adams. From this point one looks directly down on Rose Glacier.

McCoy, Keith. c2003. Mid-Columbia North Shore: "odds 'n ends". Trafford.

Rusk, C. E. 1924,1954. Tales of a Western Mountaineer. Seattle Mountaineers.

SAM HILL'S DAM

Rachel Gunkel

In 1909 Sam Hill began the construction of a dam intended as a source of water for his planned community of Maryhill and as an irrigation source for the hundreds of acres of fruit trees and vineyards on his estate. He built this dam in a canyon several miles north of Stonehenge, between Highway 97 and the Maryhill Loops Road.

The dam was built with a reservoir capacity of 80,000,000 gallons, reported the *Klickitat County Agriculturist* in March 1911, and Hill installed an irrigation system designed "to carry the water to the land in pipes, offering a minimum of loss through evaporation and providing water for domestic and fire purposes as well as irrigation." The buildings at Maryhill had indoor plumbing, and the town had a sewage system. Fire hydrants were installed, at least two of which remain in their original locations. Hill planned to pipe water to each ten-acre plot at Maryhill in order to attract purchasers to his planned Quaker community.

Sam Hill

But the dam was a problem from its inception. Local farmers told Hill that the dam's rock and clay floor wouldn't hold water, and they were right. Not only did the water constantly leak, but so much dirt washed down the hillsides that the reservoir soon filled with silt.

The construction of the dam also cost an enormous amount of money. Hill told the *Agriculturist* that his irrigation system would cost at least $100,000 when complete, but problems and delays in construction undoubtedly escalated that figure. A law partner of Hill's, Charles Babcock, warned Hill that the cost of the irrigation project would considerably exceed that of the land. Lois Davis Plotts, who grew up in Columbus, wrote that the dam was rumored to have cost Sam Hill a million dollars.

Like Hill's other plans for the community of Maryhill, the dam just didn't work out. The leaky reservoir and pipelines were abandoned and eventually forgotten.

The Christmas flood of 1964 destroyed much of the dam. Enormous chunks of concrete were torn from the middle of the dam and swept down the canyon. The sections of the dam that remain standing are badly cracked and out of alignment.

The remains of Sam Hill's dam can be glimpsed from Highway 97, or a closer view may be obtained from the Maryhill Loops Road. The Maryhill Loops are open to walkers and bikers year round, thanks to generosity of Maryhill Museum.

Sam Hill and Me, Plotts, Lois Davis. Maryhill, 1978. Post
    Publications.
Prince of Castle Nowhere, Tuhy, John E. Sam Hill. 1983.
    Timber Press.
The Klickitat County Agriculturist. 1911.
    Klickitat Intelligence. March 25.
Klickitat Heritage. Summer 1979. Babcock, Edgar as told to
    Pete May. Maryhill: Columbus Transformed.

SANDHILL CRANES

Judy Thomas

In traditional lore, cranes were known as messengers of the gods and symbols of vigilance and discipline. Today, wildlife biologists might use the terms fidelity and responsibility when describing these intriguing birds that mate for life and share in the raising of their young.

Greater sandhill cranes, which nest at Conboy Lake and a few nearby areas, are tall, stately birds with long legs and neck and a thick body with bustle-like feathers. Standing four to five feet high with a wingspan of five or more feet, the cranes are one of Washington's largest birds. Their apparently bulky bodies are surprisingly lightweight — the males average 12 pounds and the females 9-1/2 pounds. They are gray except for white cheeks and a bare reddish forehead. They frequently preen with vegetation and mud and so appear reddish brown rather than gray most of the year. Sandhills make a variety of sounds, including a remarkably loud and penetrating call generally described as a "garoo-a-a-a" that can be heard for over a mile. Their unusual looped windpipes allow them to make this trumpeting call.

The cranes are opportunistic feeders. Though they may eat fish on occasion, their diet normally consists of a wide variety of plants and animals, and they often dig several inches below ground in search of a morsel. Animals such as snails, crayfish, worms, mice, birds, frogs, snakes, and insects are consumed. They also devour acorns, roots, seeds, and fruits and browse vegetation.

Cranes are famous for their dance. They bow, jump, and toss sticks. This behavior is often associated with mating, but young, unpaired birds will also dance, suggesting that dancing serves other functions as well.

When settling down to raise a family, sandhills generally are attracted to isolated, open, wet meadows or shallow marshes on the edges of rivers or lakes.

They are very territorial — each family, parents and young called "colts," may actively protect as much as 250 acres. They build large nests, two to six feet in diameter, constructed of vegetation pulled from the nearby area and formed into a mound just inches above the water. The female lays two eggs, and both parents share in incubation duties and rearing of the young. Survival rate is low, however. In a given year, most pairs fail to raise a fledgling to adulthood. In the fall the cranes become more sociable, forming into flocks for the flight to their wintering grounds. They may fly at 50 miles per hour and as high as a mile above ground during the migration. The Conboy Lake cranes winter in California's Sacramento Valley.

Sandhill cranes return to the same nesting locations year after year. When a pair flies north, they are usually accompanied by the offspring that they so carefully protected the previous year. However, these youngsters are in for a rude awakening, since shortly after arrival on the nesting ground, the adults drive the young out of the area. For the next several years, these youngsters will roam rather unpredictably in loosely knit flocks. Eventually they find partners and establish territories of their own. Finding an available territory is not easy, however; habitats suitable for cranes often appeal to humans as well.

Conboy Lake National Wildlife Refuge brochures
Interview with Harold Cole, manager, Conboy Lake
   National Wildlife Refuge
Washington Dept. of Fish and Wildlife web site,
   http://wdfw.wa.gov/

Between 1908 and 1940, 100,000 families ordered their homes from Sears, Roebuck and Company. The catalog offered more than 450 different models of "kit" homes ranging in price from $145 to $5,140. The average house had 30,000 parts, not including nails and screws.

Each home included everything but the lot and foundation. The precut pieces were perfectly shaped, no sawing was required, and all parts were number-keyed to a blueprint. The kits were packed in crates and shipped by rail car to buyers across the country, thus the name Box Houses.

*A SEARS BOX HOUSE
IN GOLDENDALE*

Joan Wilkins Stone

Sears Box House

Many homeowners have no idea they are living in a Sears Box House. Rosemary Thornton lists nine ways to identify such a house in her book, *The Houses That Sears Built*. Roger Telford found one of the easier ways. He bought the home at 301 South Columbus, Goldendale, where Klickitat Valley Realty is now located, in May of 1981. While checking out the contents of the garage, he found paperwork that identified the house as a Sears catalog home.

Joan Telford said that walls were removed and other changes made in the interior of the home, but there were no structural changes to the exterior. The gabled roof and the three small windows under the peak of the roof are representative of the catalog homes.

The sale of Sears Modern Homes boomed in the 1920s. Each catalog offered more than 90 different house designs, in addition to garages, outhouses and chicken coops. If a water system was not available, you could purchase an outhouse for $30. There was no paperwork to apply for a mortgage; an applicant simply listed his vocation. For one dollar, buyers could receive full blueprints and a materials list. When an order was placed for the kit, the dollar was credited to the buyer.

So goes the saga of Sears Box Houses. For some, it has become a challenge to prove the authenticity of their box house. It is another connection to the past.

Thornton, Rosemary. 2004. The Houses That Sears Built.
    Alton IL: Gentle Beam Publications.
Stevenson, Katherine Cole and Jandle, H. Ward. 1986.
    Houses By Mail. NY: Preservation Press.
Klickitat County Assessor's Office
Interview with Joan Telford

SEED POTATOES

Sara Wu

The old adage, "don't eat your seed potatoes," is not consistent with modern potato-growing practices. Potatoes can only be free of viruses through a complex process of germinating minute amounts of potato in sterile conditions, that is, in Petri dishes. Several steps are necessary to produce potatoes that can be used as seed. The final step for growing seed potatoes is done at the Dan Hathaway Farm in Glenwood.

Dan's great grandfather, Crocket Castle,

homesteaded in Glenwood about 1880. He would have returned to Virginia, but his wife wanted to stay in Glenwood with her Hinton brothers. So, they began a family farm.

In the 1960s, Dan's father, Ray, was looking for a way to diversify the farm. With the encouragement of WSU Extension Service, he got into the seed potato business. Glenwood was isolated from the major potato growing areas, so its soils were not infected with potato viruses. Still, it was closer than other seed potato farms to the potato growing area around Pasco WA.

Glenwood used to have five farms in the seed potato business. The farms would have other enterprises as well, but would put 30 to 80 acres into seed potatoes. As large corporations entered the market, the small farmers could not compete. The hassle of virus-free certification, brokers' fees, and transportation cut into the profits. Young people are no longer willing to work on the farms, so labor has to be imported. Dan came back to the farm in 1980 when his father wanted to retire. Now he is looking forward to following his father and the other farmers, and retiring out of the business. His is the last of the seed potato farms in Glenwood.

Keeping its farmland is one of the great challenges for Klickitat County. As land prices rise from the pressure of people escaping the city, farming becomes less viable economically. When pristine farmland is lost, this resource is irretrievable.

Personal communication with Dan Hathaway

The Simcoe Mountains are restless, despite their impressions of innocence. Earthquakes happen often in the Simcoes, for the most part gentle shakes that simply rattle dishes and windows and do little damage. But, when a geologist at the Vancouver WA U.S. Geologic Survey Office told me that what I described was not an earth quake but a land quake, I could not help but be a bit unnerved. A land quake rolls above ground and does not register on a Richter scale. I must have been very near the source of the event, she said, because I had heard the "mountain walk."

First I noticed a dull thud, like snow falling off trees after a storm, but the sound stayed the same, never

SHAKERS

Rita J. Liska

getting louder or nearer. I noted a three count between each thud. The cat, asleep in a chair next to the wood stove, sat up, listening. My dog had jumped from my lap, down onto the rug, looking aroused, searching. I switched off the TV remote, thinking the TV was going gunnysack.

Suddenly, something hit the wall hard behind me, and everything in the kitchen began to bang and rattle. I twisted in my chair thinking someone had stormed in through my back door.

Instead, I saw some type of force ripple across my kitchen floor and go underneath my living room rug, making it look like rows of dominoes moving under it. Then it went up my wall; my television set, wall clock, and windows all went out of focus. It was like looking at heat waves shimmer on a hot summer day, except that this was mid-January 1994. When it hit my ceiling, it left my house, and I heard one more dull thud as it continued toward the southwest, then total silence.

The cat was now standing upright with eyes as big as saucers — probably reflecting the size of my own eyes. My poor dog was trying to keep three feet in the air and get the fourth one up as well, looking horrified.

I called my nearest neighbors to ask what just happened. They had heard or felt nothing and obviously thought I was crazy — until the snow began to melt in the spring, and they found tools and cans dumped off shelves and heavy lawn items no longer in place.

There have been "shakers" (small earth quakes) occasionally during the years in between, but only once have I heard the mountain walk. I hope never to hear it again.

SHOPPING CENTER SIGN

Teddy Cole

A traveler who strays into Goldendale from Route 97 will encounter a sixty-six-foot long banner sign astride Columbus Avenue at the intersection with Main Street proclaiming "Shopping Center" in letters three feet tall. The traveler will surely be puzzled. "Where's the shopping center?" and, "Why the sign?"

The "where" is the two or three blocks of businesses and offices stretching along Main Street, and the "why" is because the street once bustled with a variety of shops and busy shoppers.

For decades, travelers through the Klickitat Valley passed through Goldendale's intersection at Columbus and Main on what was known as Road 8. Most stopped to dine or shop before continuing on their way. Traffic increased when the road over Satus Pass opened in 1931, making the trip between Yakima and Portland faster and easier.

About the time Road 8 became Route 97 and the Sam Hill Bridge over the Columbia was built, an ambitious entrepreneur decided to capitalize on the increased traffic through the center of town to build a "mini-mall" on the south side of town.

The downtown merchants wouldn't hear of it. "This is Goldendale's shopping center," they said, and they arranged with the PUD for the purchase and installation of an illuminated sign that would make that message clear. The sign was installed August 3, 1964, and paid for through the merchants' monthly electric bills.

Within ten years, Route 97 was moved to bypass Goldendale, and now an abundance of services welcomes travelers at the two exits from the highway. Local people drive to the Costcos, Home Depots, and Fred Meyers of larger cities or place orders online. Agencies and secondhand shops lease otherwise empty storefronts downtown.

Banner signs like Goldendale's were popular in the nineteen-fifties, along with other roadside curiosities. One of the most famous is the arched sign over Reno's main strip, "The Biggest Little City in the World." Many others have been taken down as cities widened and modernized their streets. This one remains as a reminder of a bygone era when residents could buy most anything they needed at Goldendale's Shopping Center.

Conversations with Jim Allyn, Harold Hill, Joan Stone

The Goldendale Sentinel, August 6, 1964

The Sam Hill Bridge, photo caption, www.angelfire.com/
   wa2/hwysofwastate/

State Roads As Established by Legislature, 1893 to 1935.
   Washington State Dept. of Transportation

SIDEWINDERS?

Rita J. Liska

There is only one snake in the world that I know of that makes a track like half a tractor tire, and that's the sidewinder rattlesnake.

I have said for years — since 1978 to be exact — that these tracks can be found in the Simcoes. Therefore, the snake making that peculiar track also must be in northern Klickitat County.

The first track I saw was along a dusty road just west of Devil's Creek in 1978. The second, a much smaller track, was in 1989 along Honolulu Cutoff.

I have talked to others and learned that, although these snakes are rare and the snake itself has not been seen, the tracks regularly have been noticed in the dust around Jones Canyon and Grayback. Now I am hearing stories about people noticing and questioning this track east of Highway 97.

Is it a sidewinder? If so, how did it get started in the Simcoes? Is it a true sidewinder, like those found in the southwest? Whatever it is, it could be deadly, so watch where you step in the Simcoes.

SKUNKS

Kathleen Goode

The first summer I lived in Goldendale was very hot, and after the children were tucked in bed, I liked to take a book out on the porch to read in the cool night air. I used a small book light so that I could enjoy looking up at the stars occasionally. One night, just as I opened the screen door, a great big skunk ambled around the corner only about two feet away. Quietly closing the door, I prayed it wouldn't be startled enough to spray. The skunk was unperturbed, waddling off the porch and down the sidewalk as if he had an important engagement. Reading indoors was suddenly a smarter idea, but I began to observe the nightly parade.

Most evenings the skunks could be seen, often walking right down the middle of Main Street. Neighbors told me this was common during the hottest part of the year. The skunks normally lived higher in the foothills but came down to the river in the summer heat, spending the days hidden under houses or sheds. A local grocer told me there were once so many skunks in town that it made a national paper.

Several years ago, there was a story around town

about a poor fellow who had just remodeled his kitchen when a skunk came in through the pet door and ruined everything. One evening we returned home from a shopping trip and saw two skunks in our yard, eating something in the grass; we just backed slowly out of the driveway, and they ambled away soon after. Often I have wondered how people manage to walk home from the local bars without being sprayed — perhaps it's because they are usually making so much noise.

Indian legends describe Skunk as the younger brother of Coyote. The older brother was a great trickster and used Skunk's powerful scent to kill game. This trick worked until the people realized what he was up to and refused to come near.

There are a number of tricks for getting rid of skunks; some work better than others. When a skunk family sets up residence under your house, you might be willing to do just about anything to get them to move. The most frequent suggestion is to put mothballs under the house. I can tell you from experience that this will drive out the skunks, but it isn't an improvement; mothballs stink.

The next idea is to use a live animal trap; check with animal control to see if they have any available. People tell me the best bait to use is peanut butter. Once trapped, the skunks are usually drowned. I'm not big on killing animals, so my favorite is this suggestion from William Wood: wait till the skunks leave the house at night, and then light up the under-house area. Skunks want to hole up in a dark spot, so they will be repelled by the light.

The best solutions are to keep your foundation well sealed so that skunks cannot get in, lock your pet door at night, and control food sources such as mice, fallen fruit, and open garbage. Oh, and if you want to read outside or watch the stars, just wait till the little critters wander down to the river for the evening; they'll be gone for hours.

Personal experiences, rumors and local wisdom

Hines, Donald M. 1998. *Where the River Roared: The Wishom Tales*. Issaquah WA: Great Eagle Publishing.

Wood, William F. Living with Skunks. http://www. humboldt.edu/~wfw2/livingwskunks.html

Slashed Portrait of Tsar Nicholas II

Lee Musgrave,
Maryhill Museum of Art

Commissioned in 1910, the portrait of Tsar Nicholas II hung proudly in the Russian Embassy in Belgrade, Serbia, before the onset of World War I and the Russian Revolution. As the mob fought past the guards and into the embassy, no one thought to remove the magnificently framed, life-size painting of the man who was fated to become the last monarch of Russia.

In an act of defiance and anger, the mob slashed the portrait, and someone killed the minister. At that moment, the painting transcended art and became a historic document. Where is it today? In Klickitat County, at Maryhill Museum of Art.

How did it get there? Years later, the minister's daughter arranged to have the painting donated to the Museum. It now hangs in a gallery with many other artifacts associated with the Tsar and his cousin, Queen Marie of Romania.

Are You Sleeping Tonight With a Boa?

Rita J. Liska

I've argued with old-timers, newcomers, and herpetologists about the Simcoe Mountain boa constrictors, and most thought I was nuts until I showed them the snake that coexisted with me in the Simcoes.

It is known as a hog-nosed boa, a northern boa, or a rubber boa (the most common name). It is actually a constrictor, though that part of the name is rarely used. Its adult length is supposed to be 18"-20", but on my place I have handled them at 6" up to 24-plus inches. I have not found them to be dangerous.

These interesting snakes are rarely seen, so most people don't know they exist in North America. Even some people who spent their lives prowling the Simcoes had never seen one until I showed them a snake.

The boas are difficult to see because they are dark brown without distinguishing marks, resembling a dark buck-skinned limb. They will stretch out and freeze in position like an old limb when they feel that danger is near. They are round at both ends, and I've even gotten off my horse and down onto my hands and knees to figure out which end is coming and which is going. The tiny one I played with simply wadded up into a ball beside the trail and, because of its coloring, just looked like a small knot off the side of a tree.

I do have an unanswered question about these boas. All the larger snakes I've seen had a pale green belly like the moss that grows on the trees. But, the little one's belly was a bright pumpkin orange. I'm guessing the difference is because of age or, perhaps, time of year. I cannot think of any other factor, but can't rule one out.

Ben Snipes is a legendary name in the Klickitat Valley. Back in the 1850s, when the valley was all wavy bunch grass with not a fence in sight, Ben came, looked around, and felt it was a perfect place to start a cattle ranch. He purchased cattle in the Willamette Valley and brought them here.

Ben settled along the Little Klickitat River southwest of Goldendale. For a few years, all went well. Then the winter of 1861-62 permanently changed farming in the valley. Before that, the snow had not been deep, and the cattle could still eat the tall bunch grass. But this was a long winter with many snows, and ice on top. The cattle were cut by the ice, and with no hay to feed them, they simply starved to death. Ben and other valley residents lost most of their herds. After that winter, folks started cutting grass and storing the hay for winter feed.

Ben rebuilt his herd. (It was sometimes said that Ben's men had taken Grandma's milk cow for his herd.) As more people moved into the Klickitat Valley, Ben moved on to the Sunnyside area, then on to Okanogan country.

With time, Ben's herd numbered nearly 120,000 head. Ben and his cowboys would take part of the herd to Canada to sell to gold miners. This journey required crossing many rivers, where a 10% loss at each crossing was expected. But, they sold the animals at a good price, so it was all worthwhile.

Ben Snipes eventually bought property in downtown Seattle and a bank in eastern Washington. The depression of 1893 led to his financial demise.

Snipe's Butte southwest of Goldendale carries the family name, and on top is a monument for his parents, who are buried nearby. Ben is buried in The Dalles.

Local lore
Sheller, Roscoe. 1957. Ben Snipes: Northwest Cattle King. Portland OR: Binford & Mort.

BEN SNIPES, CATTLE RANCHER

Mary Anne Enyeart

Snowbound in Goldendale, 1879

Teddy Cole

For a young officer fresh from West Point and Maryland society, 1879 Goldendale was a bleak place to be snowbound. Charles Erskine Scott Wood entered West Point because his military father expected him to. Wood disliked the required science and math and spent his time socializing, flouting regulations, and seizing every opportunity for artistic experience.

Following graduation, due to his mediocre record, he was assigned infantry duty on the western frontier at Fort Vancouver, W.T. In 1877 he was present at the surrender of Chief Joseph at Bear Paw and wrote down Joseph's words of surrender, preserving them for history. Wood was enthralled by the vast open spaces of the west and recorded his experiences in poetry and prose.

February 8, 1879, Wood left Fort Vancouver to join Capt. Winters at Fort Simcoe. He met up with Major Canby, Lt. Pickering, and the major's brother, escorting a group of Indians to the Yakama Reservation. They arrived in Goldendale at four o'clock on the 10th to find the way north blocked by snow. The following day he began writing his impressions in his personal journal: "Snow nearly waist deep on the level…. The landscape of Goldendale might now be easily drawn by putting a few gables and chimney tops on a blank sheet….

"All communication is shut off, and all business seems suspended. There are no signs of life in the village save the yells and struggling figures of some two dozen young men that shift from one corner to another of the main street, tangling perpetually among each other in snowball fights. Wild huzzas greet every fresh sally.

"Meanwhile, we sober and staid members of society sit around the tavern stove and talk cattle, morals, markets, rabbit hunting, and being snowed in. Landlord promises us — no beef, no eggs, no milk, no cheese, but we shan't starve. Canby plays solitaire. The Major reads anatomy, and Pickering writes letters, presumably love letters, since he has taken off his coat to the task. Snow measures 2 feet on a level, fears are entertained on the roof breaking with the weight.

"Out side, save the snow revellers, not a living thing is in sight — oh yes — one melancholy cow. Not a petticoat have I seen except that worn by our tall bright-eyed waiting maid. — The dinner bell!"

February 12th, when the mail carrier arrived from The Dalles, he was complaining about the meanness of people hereabouts. Mr. Canby said, "The world is about alike." The carrier proclaimed, "I believe there is more cussedness and meanness concentrated right here in Goldendale than anywhere else."

Wood entertained himself by planning a play: "I conceive the brilliant idea of writing a comedy termed 'Blocked by the Snow.' I pace the floor to stir up the afflatus but Major Canby joins me and speaks practically of the trails, etc., and I never get beyond the title...." That evening he sketched out the idea more fully.

February 13th, desperate for entertainment, Wood proposed a dance in the hotel dining room. "Begins at 8 p.m. Have much trouble hunting up two fiddlers. More trouble in getting girls. The Methodist church is in full blast, and all the members of the church frown on dancing.... Dance ends at midnight. Have coffee and dried peach pie for refreshments."

On the 14th, Wood wrote a valentine to his new wife and made up his mind to be on his way the following day. February 15th, he "made arrangements, laid in two days' provisions, crackers, cheese, bologna.... Some tea.... Get a coffee pot and hatchet from French's." Thus equipped, he started out, accompanied by a Corporal Rasmusson and Deputy Sheriff Conrad. They camped three nights in the snow, arriving at the Fort Simcoe Indian Agency on February 18th.

The hotel where the officers stayed was the Palace, owned by W. H. Chappell, on the corner of Grant and Main. Most likely, the "tall, dark-eyed waiting maid" was one of Chappell's daughters.

Bingham, Edwin, ed. 1997. *Wood Works: the Life and Writings of Charles Erskine Scott Wood*. Oregon State University Press.

Oregon Historical Quarterly. C. E. S. Wood, "Private Journal, 1879." June, 1969. Vol. LXX, #2.

"Sadie Chappell Baker, Pioneer, Tells Her Story," *The Goldendale Sentinel*, reprinted in *Scrapbook of Early Klickitat County Washington*, edited by Townsend, Homer, n.d.

Wood, E. 1978. Wood, Erskine, *Life of Charles Erskine Scott Wood: a Renaissance Man, by his son*.

SNOW STORY

Rita J. Liska

When Charlie and I moved into the Firwood area of Klickitat County in the spring of 1981, a couple of major snow winters had already occurred. We had our first major snowstorm in 1981 on December 16th and, although we had two crawlers with blades, it took us both plowing every day to keep our half-mile lane open to traffic.

By late March 1982, it appeared that our winter was over. We were busy building cross-fences in our pastures with our shirt sleeves rolled up. Then came April 3rd.

The day began with sun, but quite cool. By late afternoon, we both had our winter coats back on and were dividing our time between building fence and watching the sky.

We had been leaving tools outside at night, but decided we had better haul everything in and get it under cover. I drove the tractor and backhoe in, gassed it up, and put it into the shop for the night while Charlie loaded tools into the trailer, hooked it onto the crawler, and headed up the lane.

By the time he reached the house, it was already dark and beginning to spit snow. While he filled the gas tank and put tools away, I returned to the house to build a warm fire in our wood stove and start supper.

The next morning, I woke up to find Charlie watching a program on TV, so I began making breakfast, taking my time because he appeared to be in no hurry. I kept watching the clock and waiting for it to get daylight. It didn't.

Finally I could stand it no longer. I opened the door and stepped out onto our back deck, to find two feet of overnight snowfall rising from the railing almost to the roofline.

I called our two elkhound dogs and could see Mykey's curly tail and the tips of her ears as she tried to hop through the snow. I also saw her give up and return to her dog house. A few seconds later, I could see the tip of Cassie's nose, both ears, and her tail as the larger dog used both shoulders to plow a path through to the front porch. About three feet behind the end of Cassie's tail came the little curly tail as Mykey followed Cassie's plowed trail.

Needless to say, we didn't build fences for a few days, and our records show that between December 16th and April 3rd, we had 103 inches of snow.

At the north edge of the town of Klickitat is a recently completed fish ladder. Attractive to the eye, healthy for the watershed, this project is intended to restore salmon access to Snyder Creek. This effort exemplifies cooperation of the Mid-Columbia Regional Fisheries Enhancement Group and the US Fish and Wildlife.

In-depth information on the efforts to regain and maintain the health of the Klickitat and Little Klickitat watersheds can be found at the Columbia Basin Fish and Wildlife Authority web site, http://www.cbfwf. org/ (Go to the bottom of the page to "find a province by subbasin" and select "Klickitat." In this case, a "province" is similar to a watershed and a "sub-basin" indicates which part of the Columbia River Basin.)

SNYDER CREEK FISH LADDER

Nancy Barron

On the bluff high above the Columbia River, where the Klickitat River joins it, sits an old farmstead with a fascinating history.

Lewis and Clark likely camped here when it was an Indian village. Later, in the 1890s, an English nobleman, Sir Thomas Balfour, bought the property and developed an extensive farming operation.

A century later, the family that owned the property was known for its vast collection of vintage-model cars and trucks — all derelict — which adorned the hillsides. The old farm was also known for its unmended fences — through which a wide assortment of animals escaped from time to time to cross the road, presumably to find better pickings on the other side.

Every weekend in the early 1990s, my husband and I turned up Old Highway 8 out of Lyle to drive to our property near Appleton. We drove cautiously around the big bend, never knowing what to expect.

With the motor idling, we once waited while a mother duck made her way through a hole in the fence and waddled across the road, followed, single-file, by her brood of ducklings. Another time, there might be five or six playful young goats out looking for a good time. These animal parades included chickens, pigs, sheep, and the occasional cow.

One afternoon, a frantic woman flagged us down at the intersection of Old Highway 8 and Canyon Road, just north of the farm. She enlisted our help in chasing a stubborn black cow back down the old highway to her

SOMETHING STINKS IN THE GORGE

Barbara Patterson

property. The cow ran this way and that, avoiding our shouts and maneuvers. Finally, tired of the game, the cow allowed itself to be herded back to the farm and through the opened gate.

About this time, in the fall of 1991, the Management Plan for the Columbia River Gorge National Scenic Area was adopted by the Columbia River Gorge Commission. The Federal Act which established the National Scenic Area mandated that each county within the area adopt regulations to implement the Management Plan. The plan included guidelines to protect the scenic, cultural, natural, and recreation resources of the Gorge.

The new guidelines did not appear to impress the owners of the old farmstead. We noticed they were developing a big gravel pit on their property just off Old Highway 8, an area considered a "key viewing area" of the National Scenic Area.

One Saturday a new sight caught our attention. Just east of the Klickitat River Bridge on Highway 14 was an 8 by 12-foot, boldly-lettered sign stating "SOMETHING STINKS IN THE GORGE." On the sign was a crude drawing of a skunk, complete with radiating "fumes." The words "Columbia River Gorge Commission" were also highly readable on the sign. It was obvious that this particular farm family, and presumably some others in the area, did not hold the Columbia River Gorge Commission, or its mandates, in especially high regard. Perhaps the rules and regulations outlawing the development of gravel pits within the scenic area did not suit their views of private-property owners' rights.

The morning we saw the enormous slaughtered pig hanging from a wooden beam between two trees on the bluff overlooking Highway 14 and the river, we knew that things must be heating up.

Some time passed. In the spring of 1994, we heard the farm property — all 358 acres — had been purchased by the U.S. Forest Service in a $870,000 deal that likely smelled a lot sweeter to the family than the peculiar odor they'd been detecting in the gorge.

As for the vintage vehicles strewn about the property, which were undoubtedly giving the Gorge Commission bouts of anxiety, due to the rusted relics' decidedly unscenic appearance, the family may have gotten the last word — their "nyah-nah-na-nah-nah" to the Gorge Commission. Lined up along the edge of the same bluff where we'd seen the hanging pig, were two dozen or more of the old derelicts. They formed the final parade of many we'd come to expect on those weekends in the early 1990s.

The "something stinks" sign found a temporary home just west of The Dalles, highly visible on a property off Interstate 84, until Wasco County ordered its removal some years later.

Today, the old farmstead is gone. In its place is the Balfour Klickitat Day Use Site, a U.S. Forest Service park, complete with restrooms, picnic tables, and paved paths. The ducks are still around and can be seen splashing about on the Klickitat River. The gravel pit off Old Highway 8 has been restored to a natural appearance that blends with the surrounding landforms.

The park is a beautiful, peaceful place to visit, providing an entirely different kind of entertainment than that of the former tenants.

Personal experience;
Pam Campbell, Columbia River Gorge Office re: sale of
    property;
Joan Frey, Klickitat County Commissioner re: former
    property owner's views of National Scenic Area and
    Gorge Commission;
Columbia River Gorge Scenic Area Web site re:
    Management Plan;
Balfour Klickitat Day Use Site and history

SPINNING MEMORIES

Kathleen Goode

Summertime is coming, and I will get my spinning wheel out of storage. It has been hidden there to protect it from a toddler granddaughter. Children can't seem to resist this contraption; they spin it until the tension cord falls off and the loose wool is tangled in the bobbin hooks. When they are old enough, I let them have a go at it, but they can seldom coordinate their efforts to keep the treadle going while smoothly feeding in the wool. They have better luck starting out with a drop spindle. There is always a magical moment when the realization hits that they have just turned a bit of fluffy wool into a length of yarn. Few stay with it; the only young spinner I know is Jessica Jones, and she raises the sheep that produce the wool she spins.

My spinning wheel looks like some ancient creation

that came out with the pioneers. In a way, it did. We were visiting a farm in Redmond to buy a pet lamb for my young niece in 1976; it was a way to celebrate my sister's long awaited move to country life. I noticed a beautiful spinning wheel in the farmer's front room. He told me it was his mother's wheel and he had brought it over when he emigrated here from Norway after the war. The wheel itself was carried on his lap during the flight to New York; he was afraid it would be damaged in the cargo hold. It was one of his most precious possessions.

My husband started cooking up a surprise for the following Christmas. He went to visit the farmer Olav Kyte and asked him to build a spinning wheel just like the one I had admired. Olav agreed to try, and my husband paid him $10 a week toward the purchase. It took many tries to get the wheel just right. There were challenges every step of the way, but the man persevered. His wife painted beautiful flowers on the base for me, and they added a simple bobbin holder for twining the wool. It took nearly until Christmas before the wheel was ready, but there it was under the tree — of course it is now one of my most precious possessions. I took lessons at a nearby museum the following summer and learned to clean and card wool, to spin it, ply it, and dye it with natural materials.

My spinning was dreadful! Hours of effort would result in lumpy yarn, full of blobs and over-twists. Weavers wanted it, and I was glad to give it away just so I wouldn't have to look at it. The wheel was still a treasure and remained a focal point in my home. Then came many years of children underfoot and the wheel was often carefully stored away. When I wanted to spin, I used a drop spindle, but it was very slow going. After we moved to Goldendale, I met Micki Jones at the County Fair. She showed me how to oil my wheel and set the tension in order to spin an even yarn. What a difference!

My favorite time to spin is in the summer, when I can take my wheel outside on the porch. Spinning is a great stress reducer; maybe it's the feel of the wool or the steady rhythm of the treadle and the smooth rotation of the wheel. I often think about the women who used wheels like this for hundreds of years to provide warm clothing for their families. Many of the nation's immigrants and many pioneers must have brought spinning wheels with them, carefully guarding them against damage. Spinning is not as popular as quilting, but it is not a craft that will die out soon either. People like Micki Jones and her daughter Jessica are keeping this ancient art alive and well.

Salmon is a sacred gift of the creator, given to the people for food and provided in such rich quantities that the People of the River were wealthy enough to trade for goods from other areas. Salmon helped them develop a rich and enduring culture. Then the white man arrived and built fish wheels, overtaxing the supply that had been a cornerstone of the local culture for thousands of years. Canneries were set up so that the salmon could be shipped to large markets on the West Coast. The Native People signed treaties to ensure their right to harvest salmon. This story is best told in *Empty Nets* by Roberta Ulrich, which describes the experience of Nelson Wallulatum, the Sohappy family, and others. Native determination, courage, jail time, and a small army of lawyers were required to protect that right of access.

With the Boldt decisions of 1974, there was no longer a debate over who has the right to harvest salmon. However, by then another problem had become painfully clear: there might not be salmon for anyone to harvest. Hydroelectric dams and over-fishing had almost completed the end of salmon history on the Columbia River.

Four of the tribes most affected by the diminishing number of salmon decided to work together to ensure salmon recovery. The Nez Perce Tribe, the Confederated Tribes of the Umatilla Indian Reservation, the Confederated Tribes of the Warm Springs Reservation of Oregon and the Confederated Tribes and Bands of the Yakama Nation came together in 1977 to form the Columbia River Inter-Tribal Fish Commission (CRITFC). This organization combined the wisdom of the tribes with the latest scientific information to come up with a salmon restoration plan called Wy-Kan-Ush-Mi Wa-Kish-Wit, or Spirit of the Salmon. The tribes collaborated on many projects to help solve this complicated problem. They worked on restoration of streams and flood plains, removed blockage and

SPIRIT OF THE SALMON, WY-KAN-USH-MI WA-KISH-WIT

Kathleen Goode

debris, conducted assessments, acquired and improved habitats supporting watersheds, and improved the natural production and healthy river systems. Like the new longhouse at Celilo, the CRITFC combines the best of the old and new to ensure that the rivers are alive for future generations.

Columbia River Inter-Tribal Fish Commission (CRITFC) web site, www.critfc.org

Ulrich, Roberta. 1999. *Empty Nets; Indians, Dams, and the Columbia River.* Corvallis OR: Oregon State University Press.

SPRING WHITLOW GRASS

Ruth Miles Bruns

If you are out walking in March in Klickitat County and you're crossing a field that has recently begun turning bright green with new grass, you are likely to discover Spring Whitlow Grass, one of the tiniest wildflowers of them all. Its white blossoms are less than a quarter inch across and are closed to pinhead size unless the sun has been shining on them. Its threadlike dark red stems are seldom much more than an inch long, and there's a small rosette of inconspicuous leaves at its base. If it didn't grow in "groves" a few inches to a few feet across, you might never notice it at all.

Who would think that such an important-sounding name belonged to such a wee little flower?

SPRING WILDFLOWER HUNT

Kathleen Goode

Armed with a new digital camera, my husband and I set out to capture a few images of Klickitat County. We were especially interested in finding spring wildflowers currently in bloom. Our first stop was at a spot we call "Dead Man's Curve." We call it that to impress upon our children the fact that one should drive very carefully here, especially during icy winter weather. This, however, was a fine spring day, and we pulled off the highway into a tiny gravel area. There were wildflowers aplenty. Within just a few moments, I was able to photograph Balsamroot, Long-leaved Phlox, and Death Camas, all in full bloom.

Just as I snapped the last shot, my husband called

to me, in exactly the same voice he would use to point out an interesting new plant, "Here's a snake." He was standing calmly a few yards away, and as I walked toward him, he pointed to the grass nearby, telling me, "It's right here. It stuck its tongue out at me a minute ago." I thought it must be a garter snake. As I looked to focus the camera, my ears informed me that I should calmly back away. The annoyed creature was a rattlesnake! Luckily, it was no more interested in prolonging the encounter than we were. We moved automatically to the car and got out of there before we met any of its relatives. Next time we go hunting wildflowers, we will carry a big stick. With luck, the noise will warn such creatures away, but if not, the snake can bite the stick instead of us.

Personal experience
Lyons, C.P. *Wildflowers of Washington, 2nd edition revised.*
    1999. Renton WA: Lone Pine Publishing.
Askham, Leonard R. WSU Bulletin # EB0984, Rattlesnakes.
    Washington State University. http://cru.cahe.wsu.
    edu/CEPublications/eb0984/eb0984.html

Square Dancing on Horseback

Judy Thomas

"Allemande left with your left hand, a right to your honey and promenade the land."

Those words usually bring to mind stomping cowboy boots, but in the 1940s and 1950s in Klickitat County, you might have heard horses' hooves instead — the No. 12 Riding Club square dancing on horseback.

The No. 12 Riding Club was started in 1945 by a group of Klickitat County Sheriff's Posse men who wanted to do something together that included their families — and their horses. They fixed up the abandoned No. 12 schoolhouse near Goldendale to use for their monthly meetings and for dances and potlucks as well. The group also went on trail rides, trucking their horses to sites in the nearby mountains and setting up camp. Those who didn't ride would go along to help and to enjoy the company. Mary Ann Miller remembers what fun all these activities were for the kids, and she especially remembers attending a Rock Creek tribal ceremony; the club had become acquainted with the Rock Creeks and was allowed to ride on their land.

No one seems to remember just where the square dancing idea came from, but for people who loved riding and loved dancing, it must have seemed like something they had to try. They started practicing in the schoolyard with one of the members as the caller. They performed regular square dance routines, with the added complication of getting eight horses to cooperate with their plans. Soon they were performing at rodeos such as Moro, Wasco and Glenwood, doing a show at the Saturday rodeo, going to the Saturday night dance, and doing another show on Sunday. Eleanor Dooley, who along with her husband Paul was one of the original members, thinks that the growing popularity of TV in the 1950s was a factor that led to an end of these performances.

The No. 12 schoolhouse, still standing, is used now as a multipurpose building at the home of Claudia Young.

Interviews with Eleanor Dooley, Mary Ann Miller and
    Claudia Young
Mid-Columbia Saddle Clubs Assoc. Horse Show and Race
    Meet.1948. Official program.

Star Parties

*Phil Reid for the
Star Party Committee*

August 11, 2004, saw the initial Klickitat County Star Party. This event was the kickoff for Klickitat County Star Parties, an annual series of public astronomical observation sessions for northwest amateur astronomers, students, and families — that is, anyone interested in the stars and planets.

The first Star Party was attended by eighty individuals and dozens of telescopes, featuring Stan Seeberg and his infamous telescope. Stan speaks to the evolution of astronomy and provides an excellent tutorial for all, young and old, amateur to professional.

The Star Party site, some twenty acres located between Skyview Acres and Whitney Oak Gardens, eight miles northeast of Goldendale proper, offers excellent dark skies for astronomical observation. The area will allow expansion of accommodations to handle upwards of a thousand participants.

Hopes are high that the Klickitat County Star Parties will eventually become the Northwest's premier events for astronomical observation.

An advertisement in the 1929 Goldendale High School Annual touts the excellence of the Star Theatre, "The best of the talking pictures, reproduced by our Masterphone and Beaded Glass Vocalite Screen, always a good program at the Star."

The place to be for young people in the 1930s through the 1950s was the Star Theatre. For many of those years, the Star played four different movies a week. There were few latecomers because a cartoon began each feature. Newsreels ran every night, giving the news and social events of the day.

The feature movies were on Friday and Saturday nights. Many of the films of the 1940s had a war theme. Audiences were glued to the screen. Fact and fiction were often mixed up in their minds. Jack W. Janual writes in his article "Those War Films — Fact, Fiction, Impact" from the book *V for Victory*, "By combining fact and fiction, the studios produced many dramatic films to bring to life the conflict for audiences."

The Sunday and Monday movie, with a matinee on Sunday, would feature films for all ages, and families would throng to the theatre. The Tuesday-only movie was a grade B thriller or an older western. They always played a cliffhanger to bring the crowd back the next Tuesday. Weekday presentations were often double features.

Barbara Adkison remembers seeing "Gone With The Wind" in the late 1940s. "It cost 25 cents, and that was a lot in those days. I lost my quarter on the way to the theatre, and I had to go home and ask for another one. The movie cost more because it was so long. There was an intermission halfway through." A few people thought it was over and left.

By the 1960s there were fewer movies played each week. The owners had added a popcorn machine and sold pop. A Saturday matinee was popular with the children, and many parents happily sent their children off to the theatre.

One Saturday, Greg Stone and Brad Wilkins went to a matinee. "We were seven or eight, it was about a dinosaur, and we were so scared we hid under the seats. The usher finally took us to the lobby and called our parents. I saw the same movie years later and couldn't help laughing." said Greg. David Stone remembers the Captain America serial that played week after week "drawing all of us in."

The Star Theatre building sold in the 1960s. A move to another location on Main Street was short-lived.

Interviews with Barbara Zumwalt Adkison, Ruthe Layman Wilber, Greg Stone, David Stone.
The Simcoe, Goldendale High School Annual, 1929.
Cohen, Stan. 1997. V for Victory: America's Home Front During World War II. Missoula MT: Pictorial Histories Publishing Company Inc.

THE STONE HOUSE

Judy Thomas

Once a cozy cabin, the stone house is now a ragged shell. Many stories have been told over the years to explain this intriguing structure located on the north side of highway 14 near the entrance to Columbia Hills State Park. One story had it that years ago, before the coming of the railroad or highway, four rich men from the city regularly came to the area to hunt. At first they camped out in a tent, but later built themselves a stone lodge. An equally untrue but more romantic story was that the house was built by a young man suffering from tuberculosis who came to bask in the summer sun in hopes of regaining his health. A story popular with children is that the house was a fort or a jail.

The true story seems to be this: In 1925 Laurence McNary had the house built near where he lived as a child. McNary's parents had homesteaded on land south of where the stone house now stands and had moved to Oregon when two of their daughters died during a diphtheria epidemic. Laurence became a lawyer in Portland, but at age sixty and in poor health, he longed to spend time near his childhood home.

McNary bought 40 acres of land adjacent to the old homestead. He hired stonemason Joe Studenecker to build a cabin for him from stones found on the property. The stones were dry-stacked, then chinked with concrete. Studenecker wanted to dress the stones but was overruled by McNary, who wanted a rustic effect. The house was about 12 by 16 feet, with a fireplace at the north end, two small windows, and a large skylight topped by an iron grating (possibly the source of the jail story). The floor was tamped earth. The mason carved "Rockland", an old name for the Dallesport area, into a large boulder that sits at the base of the road leading to the house. McNary came on the train about once a month to spend the night, occasionally accompanied by his wife.

As recently as 1962, the house was described as being "in excellent condition", but today all that remains are broken walls, fallen timbers, and the memory of a man who built a weekend retreat so he could enjoy the simple life of his childhood and the beauties of the Columbia Gorge.

Bartholomew, Frances. 1962. *Ruralite*. July.

History of Oregon, Biographical, Vol II. 1922. *The Pioneer Historical Pub. Co.*

STONEHENGE: THE MAKING OF A MEMORIAL

Rachel Gunkel

During the early part of the twentieth century, it was commonly thought that the Druids had used England's Stonehenge to sacrifice captives to heathen gods of war. This belief led Sam Hill to replicate Stonehenge as a war memorial. "The central thought," he explained, "being that the nature of humanity never changes, and that, though many centuries have passed since the days of Stonehenge, the world is still making sacrifices to the god of war."

Hill decided to construct the nation's first World War I war memorial on his property at Maryhill. Building the memorial proved to be more challenging and problematic than he had anticipated. Like many of Hill's other works at Maryhill, Stonehenge almost ended up as yet another unfinished project.

Professor W.W. Campbell of Lick Observatory helped Hill choose the best location for the memorial. The St. James Hotel stood squarely in the way. Hill had it moved.

Hill planned to construct the memorial of stone. The Italian stonemasons who had worked on the Columbia River Scenic Highway came to Maryhill to carve the monoliths and pillars of Stonehenge from local basalt. Lois Davis Plotts wrote that Hill "set his stone masons to work on the central altar. It was discovered almost immediately that local rock could not be used as planned." Along the rocky outcropping below Stonehenge, a huge piece of basalt, perhaps the original altar stone, lies partially covered by dirt and rocks. A half-dozen stone pillars, unmistakably man-made, trail down the hillside, looking as if they had been shoved over the bank in mingled frustration and fury.

Since the memorial turned out to be more difficult, expensive and time-consuming than planned, Hill decided to make the altar stone of concrete and finish the project at a later date. The altar stone was consecrated in a public ceremony attended by scores of dignitaries and members of the public on July 4, 1918.

At a meeting of the Klickitat County Soldier's and Sailors' Memorial Association, the trustees (Sam Hill, W. G. Collins, Charles Babcock, E. N. Hill, and J. C. Potter) determined "to proceed with the erection of this Memorial with all due diligence." In fact, no further work was done on the monument for another decade, perhaps for the lack of a highway from Lyle through to Pasco or perhaps for lack of money and labor during the war years.

Sam Hill finally returned to Maryhill to complete the memorial in the fall of 1928. He had decided that the entire memorial would be constructed of concrete. "Instead of rock, steel reinforced concrete that is imbedded in the solid rock will be used," announced *The Goldendale Sentinel*. Aesthetically, concrete was not the ideal building material for Stonehenge, but care was taken to make it resemble hand-carved stone. The forms in which the concrete was poured were lined with crumpled tin so that the pillars would simulate the shape and texture of hewn stone.

When workmen finally began digging the holes for the foundation, they disturbed many nests of hibernating rattlesnakes. At least one man was bitten.

The Stonehenge Memorial was finally completed in the spring of 1929, and a dedication program arranged for Memorial Day. The well-attended ceremony involved much fanfare and publicity.

The reasons for Stonehenge's existence are just as relevant today as in the early decades of the twentieth century. It remains an evocative monument, both a sober reminder of the human costs of war and a celebration of the human spirit.

Tuhy, John E. Sam Hill: *The Prince of Castle Nowhere*. 1983. Timber Press.

Lois Davis Plotts. *Sam Hill, Maryhill and Me*. 1978. Post Publications.

Consecration of Soldiers and Sailors Memorial (Dedication
    program), July 4, 1918
The Goldendale Sentinel. 1918. Dedication at Maryhill on July
    4th. July 11.
The Goldendale Sentinel. 1918. United States Trust Company
    Holds Meeting. July 11.
The Goldendale Sentinel. 1928. Soldier Memorial Will Be
    Finished. October 11.
The Goldendale Sentinel. 1928. Maryhill column.
    October 25.
The Goldendale Sentinel. 1928. Maryhill column. November 8.
The Goldendale Sentinel. 1929. Stonehenge Dedication on
    May 30th. May 23.
The Goldendale Sentinel. 1929. Memorial Dedicated at
    Maryhill. June 6.

WILHELM SUKSDORF, PLANT COLLECTOR

Marty Hudson, Klickitat County Weed Control

Klickitat County became home to German immigrant Wilhelm Suksdorf, who was an avid plant collector. He would collect ballast (soil) off of ships in Portland and put it in his fields or garden at Bingen WA, to see what would come up. Some of the county's most notorious noxious weeds were first recorded in Washington State from Mr. Suksdorf's collections out of his garden in Bingen, including yellow starthistle and diffuse knapweed.

He also collected flora extensively from the Columbia River Gorge and surrounding areas, especially near Mt. Adams. This was a great contribution to the botanical collections for the state of Washington and the west. Mr. Suksdorf frustrated many botanists, as he would only record his botanical observations in German and with his own version of shorthand, so some of his observations passed with him, and one can only guess what some of his writings mean.

He donated his significant library of collections — over 30,000 specimens — to Washington State University, where he received an Honorary Degree in Botany.

Catherine Hovanic, Washington Native Plant Society

Wilhelm Nikolaus Suksdorf Papers, 1867-1935,
    http://www.wsulibs.wsu.edu/holland/masc/
    finders/cg315.htm

SUNBONNET GIRL

Rita Liske

This rock formation cannot be ignored once you have met her. She rests against the cliffs next to I-84 and is visible as you travel east between mileposts 91 and 92. She patiently watches as traffic moves east on its customary return trip to Klickitat County from The Dalles, Oregon.

A perfect little Sunbonnet Girl, this creation of Mother Nature occasionally finds her skirt engulfed by wild sunflowers, but most often someone honors her with plastic flowers according to the season. I've never seen whoever graciously places those flowers at her feet, but I hope they realize their honor to the Sunbonnet Girl is appreciated by many who are aware of her presence.

SUNDAY DRIVES

Barbara Patterson

Scenic highways and byways abound in Klickitat County. Pack a picnic lunch, camera, binoculars, and a wildflower identification guide and set out for a delightful sight-seeing trip. From the lush foliage and tall evergreens at the west end to the vast open expanses of wheat and cattle ranches in the central and eastern regions, there is much to explore in this beautiful and diverse area.

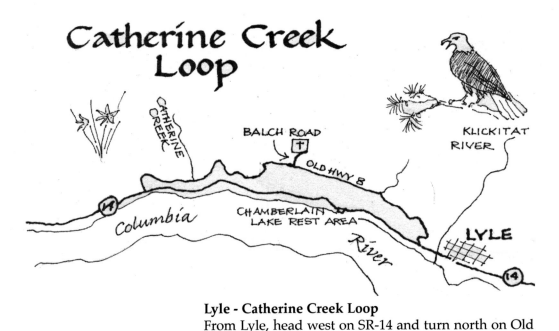

Lyle - Catherine Creek Loop
From Lyle, head west on SR-14 and turn north on Old Highway 8 (county road 1230), just past the Klickitat

River bridge. Drive one-quarter mile to the Balfour-Klickitat Day Use Site. Turn right into the parking lot. Restrooms and picnic tables are provided. This U.S. Forest Service site provides unique views of the Klickitat and Columbia Rivers and opportunities for bird-watching. In the spring, wildflowers are abundant on the hillsides and bluffs. Handicapped-access paved hiking trails lead down to a fenced area above the Klickitat River where one can watch ducks paddle along its shores. From there, the trail follows an upward incline to the bluff overlooking the Columbia River, the likely site of a Klickitat Indian village visited by Lewis and Clark. The day-use site was named for an English nobleman, Sir Thomas Balfour, who developed an extensive agricultural operation in the 1890s. Little remains of that venture today.

Next, drive about 2 miles on Old Highway 8 to Balch Road and turn right. This short diversion will take you past an old schoolhouse with a bell tower, built around 1900 and now serving as a family residence. You will pass Balch Lake, which provides habitat for many species of wildlife. Continue through groves of pine and large Oregon oaks. Atop a grassy knoll lies the Lyle-Balch Cemetery. Stop a moment at the iron gates and look south across the Columbia River for a spectacular view of Mt. Hood. A stroll through the cemetery reveals a bit of the history of the area, if only through the names of Lyle area pioneers and later residents who now reside there. At the back, behind a fence, lies an Indian cemetery; its graves, in typical Indian fashion, are covered with everyday objects placed to help the departed on their journey to the afterlife.

Leaving the cemetery, drive back to Old Highway 8 and turn right (west). For the next several miles, the highway affords excellent river views, particularly of Memaloose Island, site of a sacred ancient Indian burial ground. Bald eagles are often spotted along this route.

Travel just under two miles to the parking lot on the north side of the road at the Catherine Creek recreation site. South of the road is the Catherine Creek Universal Access Trail. This U.S. Forest Service day use area abounds with botanical treasures. Over 90 species of wildflowers blanket the open grasslands and oak woodlands in succession from late winter into July. Grass widows cover the surrounding area in sweeping drifts of purple blossom as early as February.

Be prepared for breathtaking views of the Columbia River and Mt. Hood.

Continue one mile on Old Highway 8, past Rowland Lake to SR-14, where you will turn east toward Lyle. Drive 3.7 miles to the Chamberlain Lake Rest Area, a perfect place to find a table, spread out the picnic, and enjoy the close proximity of the Columbia River. Barges transporting wheat and wood products travel west to Portland while upstream barges carry fuel to the eastern regions of Washington and Oregon. White double-decker cruise ships are seen occasionally, carrying passengers on this scenic river route to and from Lewiston, Idaho, and points between.

From the rest area, it is a short 1.7 miles back to Old Highway 8, the starting point of the Catherine Creek loop trip.

Klickitat ~ Appleton Road ~ Fisher Hill Road Loop

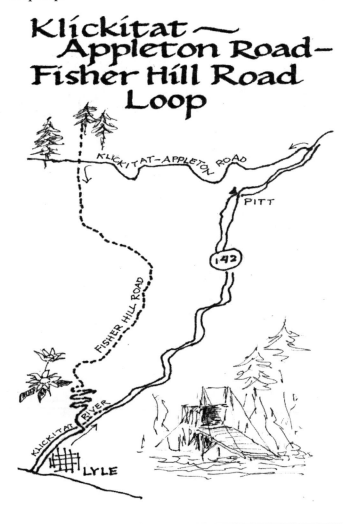

Klickitat-Appleton Road - Fisher Hill Road Loop

Begin this loop trip on SR 142 North, just west of Lyle. Drive 11.8 miles along the nationally designated Wild & Scenic Klickitat River.

This glacier-fed river stretches approximately 100 miles from Mt. Adams, its source, to the Columbia River. It cuts through rugged hillsides and steep canyon walls, tumbling over boulders and around log-jams.

The Klickitat is noted for healthy runs of chinook salmon, silver salmon (Coho), and Pacific Northwest steelhead. From late April until early June, the mountain runoffs are at their peak, making white-water rafting and kayaking popular activities on the upper stretches of the river.

At mile 10, the highway crosses the river at the tiny community of Pitt, a former Spokane, Portland, & Seattle (S.P.&S.) Railway town. The railroad shipped lumber milled at Pitt and at the town of Klickitat, three-and-a-half miles upriver, to Portland and points east.

At 11.8 miles, turn left on the Klickitat-Appleton Road. This steep, two-lane paved road with stout guardrails was once a trail that led to Appleton, before becoming a road in 1911, known as the Durkee Grade. The flood of 1933 took out all the bridges the length of the river, except for the one at Fisher Hill Road. The only road open to the townspeople in Pitt and Klickitat was the Durkee Grade, but continued rain made it all but impassable. Selma Neils, who wrote *So This Is Klickitat,* said the county WPA crews were put to work on it, cutting branches and piling them in the ruts until the road became known as the "Evergreen Highway" by the mail and provision truck drivers.

The approach to a spectacular river valley view pullout, at mile 13.4, can be literally breath-taking. For several seconds, it seems the road ends and you will drive straight into oblivion. This illusion passes quickly, and soon the wide pullout is visible.

From this vantage, the Klickitat River valley stretches out far below, a spectacular, world-class sight. In the foreground, where the highway crosses the river at Pitt, the houses and outbuildings look like pieces in a Monopoly game and the highway a narrow gray ribbon winding alongside the blue-green river. Beyond the bridge at Pitt, the Klickitat makes a wide bend along a flood plain before continuing through narrowing canyon walls to Lyle and emptying into the

Columbia. In the far distance, hazy blue hills lie south of the Columbia River Gorge in Oregon.

Continuing up the grade, the Ponderosa Pines and Oregon White Oak which have covered the hillsides are gradually replaced by a forest of towering Douglas-fir mixed with pine. The Klickitat River is recognized as the ecological dividing point of the county. East of the river, as average rainfall diminishes, pine and oak forests make way for sagebrush desert land. West of the river, rainfall gradually becomes more abundant, as evidenced by the lush growth of ground covers, shrubs, and large stands of Douglas-fir.

At mile 16.4, turn left (south) on Fisher Hill Road. Follow this good gravel road just under one mile to Pleasant Hills Cemetery. In summer, pink blossoms of wild sweet peas cascade freely over the fence-line. Beyond the tall wrought-iron double gates sits a whitewashed chapel. Gravestones in this quiet place bear testimony to pioneers and their descendants who once lived in the surrounding area.

Continue two miles along Fisher Hill Road to view a picturesque farmhouse surrounded by acres of alfalfa and pasture, with Mt. Hood prominent in the background.

A bit further along, notice the massive timbered barns of the old Shippey homestead, which remains a working farm. With the gradual drop in elevation along this road, pine-oak woodlands replace the Douglas-fir forest.

A pullout on the left, at mile 21.4, marked by gnarled and weather-beaten oaks, provides another high-vantage overlook of the Klickitat River valley, this time to the east.

After the pullout, look again for superb views of Mt. Hood, which looms surprisingly large beyond the sloping fields.

At mile 23.1, the three-and-one-half mile descent begins into the Klickitat River valley to SR 142. A series of switchbacks winds along the steep canyon walls, where wildflowers grow abundantly beginning in early spring and lasting through July. Predominant among the many wildflowers are phlox, lupine, balsam root, and mustard-family species.

Stop at a small parking area at the base of Fisher Hill before driving across the Fisher Hill Bridge.

The bridge provides the perfect place to observe the Klickitat River as it flows into a turbulent chute called the Narrows. Assembled precariously on the cliff-face walls, just above the rapids, are scaffolds, where Native Americans dip-net for steelhead and salmon journeying upriver.

Spanning the river directly above the Fisher Hill Bridge is a four-trestle railroad bridge, eventually to become a part of the Klickitat Trail. This trail follows a 31-mile abandoned railroad corridor extending from Lyle to Goldendale.

Crossing the bridge, SR 142 is at mile 26.6. Turn south, and drive one-and three-quarter miles to Lyle, to complete the loop.

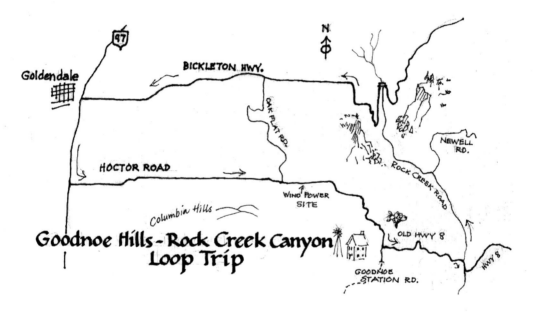

Goodnoe Hills - Rock Creek Canyon Loop Trip

Goodnoe Hills - Rock Creek Canyon Loop

Start the Goodnoe Hills loop trip at the intersection on SR 97 and Broadway (SR 142), in Goldendale. Drive 3.6 miles south on SR 97 to Hoctor Road and head east. This stretch of paved road is dotted with farmhouses, cattle, and acres of alfalfa fields. In the north distance the Simcoe Mountains rise above 3,000 feet. Nearer, to the south, are the Columbia Hills.

Just beyond Oak Flat Road, about 12 miles out, is an old homestead with a two-story house, water tower, outhouse, corrals, and barn — all abandoned years ago and now weathered gray. A giant oak grows next to the house, once providing welcome shade for the residents, as well as a handy escape from the second story, should a fire have threatened.

Drive 13.1 miles to the Goodnoe Hills wind demonstration site at an elevation of 2,540 feet. Here Sen. Henry M. (Scoop) Jackson of Washington proclaimed the Pacific Northwest the "windmill capital of the world" at a May 1981 dedication ceremony when he signaled the start-up of the MOD-2 experimental wind generators at Goodnoe Hills. Eventually, the machines were dismantled and the parts sold at auction to a Portland scrap metal dealer. An anemometer tower remains at the site to measure wind velocity and direction from two sensors located at 50 and 192 feet on the structure. The tower is operated by Oregon State University Energy Resources Research Laboratory.

From this high vantage point, look south for a view of the Columbia River Gorge and beyond to the wheat fields in Sherman and Gilliam counties in Oregon. To the northeast is Rock Creek Canyon, a pronounced ravine that runs up to the Simcoe Mountains.

Drive beneath the BPA power lines, turning south at mile 15.7, and continue on Hoctor Road to the descent into the lower Goodnoe Hills area. This section of road was built in the 1930s by Work Projects Administration (WPA) workers. In spring through early summer, wildflowers cover the green hillsides, presenting a glorious palette of yellows, reds, pinks, and blues. By summer's end, an overlay of golden-brown velvet appears to blanket the Columbia Hills.

The pullout at mile 16.6 delivers a spectacular view of snow-capped Mt. Hood and of Mt. Jefferson, further south. In the distance, the John Day Dam stretches across the Columbia, providing hydro-power to electric utilities across the Pacific Northwest.

The Hoctor Road grade levels out to what locals call the Goodnoe Hills "second bench" land. This seven- to ten-square-mile area stretches from two to four miles north of the Columbia River to just west of Rock Creek and rises about 1,000 feet above the river.

On the right, approaching the junction of Hoctor Road and Old Highway 8, lies an old almond orchard, a reminder of the "orchard boom" of 1908-1918, when 2,000 acres were purchased by Portland interests, platted in five and ten-acre tracts, and sold to investors as ideal land for growing not only apricots, peaches, and grapes, but English walnuts, almonds, and watermelons.

Getting water to the orchards was a problem. Homesteaders used horses to haul water in barrels on sleds from Sand Springs on Rock Creek to their farms. Eventually wells were dug for household and livestock use. Plans for irrigating the orchards through the sale of bonds came to an abrupt halt with the outbreak of World War I. Most of the orchards were later taken out and supplanted by wheat, leaving only a few areas where apricot and almond trees still blossom and bear fruit.

At mile 18.1, on the northeast corner of Hoctor Road and Old Highway 8, sits an old and weathered, highly photogenic two-story wooden house. A windmill on the property bears testament to the strong winds which regularly visit the area.

At this point, Hoctor Road ends and Goodnoe Station Road starts. This road winds down to the Columbia River and the site of the former Goodnoe Station, where trains brought in mail and supplies until 1963.

Continue south one-half mile on the graveled Goodnoe Station Road to visit the abandoned general store and post office. This building also provided rooms for boarders in the "orchard boom" days. Musa Geer, who served as postmaster for over 45 years, recalls a dance hall upstairs where "we used to dance all night and go home in the morning."

The schoolhouse, built around 1895, is another quarter-mile down the road. A bell in the tower atop the building summoned children back to class after recess and lunch and could be heard across the Goodnoe valley. The school closed in 1963.

Drive back to Old Highway 8 and turn right (east) at mile 19.5. In 1906, a farmer named Tom Watson, who lived along this stretch of road, developed a special variety of watermelon available today in heirloom seed catalogs. This melon has a tough rind which made it excellent for shipping and was a popular dessert served in railroad dining cars.

At mile 20.2 the descent begins into Rock Creek Canyon. Drive two miles along Old Highway 8 and cross Rock Creek Bridge. Continue one-half mile on

Old Highway 8. Many families from the Confederated Tribes of the Yakama Nation once wintered in this area. In summer, they hiked to a camp in the Simcoe Mountains, north of Goldendale.

To the right is the Rock Creek longhouse, an impressive concrete-block building built in 1981. The longhouse replaced a wooden structure built in the 1950s. Prior to that time, root festivals were held in a large tent set up for the event. To honor the annual return of the salmon and to celebrate the coming of the first camas and wild celery roots, a pow-wow is held each March at the Rock Creek longhouse.

At this point Rock Creek Road turns south and meets SR 14. Old Highway 8 continues east.

Turn back on Old Highway 8. Just before the Rock Creek bridge, turn right (north) on Rock Creek Road at mile 23.3. This graveled road winds nine and one-half miles along the creek to the Bickleton Highway. Growing along the creek are black walnut, alder, and willow trees. In fall, wild sumac turns a brilliant red. At mile 27.3, at Newell Road, another creek joins Rock Creek. Cross the bridge, continuing on Rock Creek Road. Along this creek route towering basalt cliffs attract the eye with multi-faceted surfaces and subtle shades of gray, brown, green, and orange.

At the Bickleton Highway, mile 32.7, turn left. Drive 15.9 miles to Broadway (SR 142) and turn right. Travel two-tenths of a mile to SR 97 to complete the loop tour. Total travel miles are 48.8.

Columbia Gorge Scenic Area Web site

KPUD 1971-72 Annual Report. The 'Uncommon' Schools.

Mary Jean Lord re Goodnoe Hills wind demonstration site history

OSU Energy Resources Laboratory web site re continuously operating wind sensor tower; *History of Klickitat County*, by the Klickitat County Historical Society

Frank and Betty Wesley re Indians at Rock Creek, life in Goodnoe Hills

The Goodnoe Hills and Musa Geer, as told to Pete May by Musa Geer, 1961

Tourism@co.klickitat.wa.us

Klickitat Trail Web site: www.klicktat-trail.org;

Fishing: http://www.worleybuggerflyco.com;

SP&S Postcards, Clatsop Beach, Second Issue home.att. net/~spsrailway/spsissuedclatsop2.html

Neils, Selma. 1967. So This Is Klickitat.

"swale: [origin unknown] (1584) a low lying or depressed and often wet stretch of land"

THE SWALE

Teddy Cole

Merriam-Webster's Collegiate Dictionary, tenth edition, Merriam-Webster, c1996.

Three miles south of Simcoe Drive, Highway 97 dips down to cross Swale Creek. Most people wouldn't notice the crossing, but the Swale played an important part in Klickitat County history.

When the first cattlemen crossed the Columbia Hills to enter the Klickitat Valley, bringing their livestock to feast on the expanse of tall grass, they settled along the Swale. John Golden came first, in 1859, followed by John Burgen in 1860. The abundant bunch grass provided the grazing they sought, and the surrounding hills promised refuge from harsh weather.

Newton Burgen, the first white child born in Klickitat County, was born on the Swale. The first school in the county opened on the Swale in 1860, on the property of Louis Parrott, followed in 1866 by a second school on the John Burgen homestead.

Swale Creek meandered across the valley floor and, in a wet season, rose to cover a thousand acres. Natural reservoirs held the water and allowed it to soak slowly into the clay soil, sustaining the grass and refreshing the aquifer below.

Homesteaders moved in and soon wheat fields surpassed the grazing area. As wheat production grew, the spring melt and seasonal heavy rains washed soil from the plowed fields. By the 1930s, "the County's Central section was losing tons of topsoil a year." (1982 History) The newly organized Soil Conservation Service tackled soil erosion and flood control problems. With workers from the Civilian Conservation Corps (CCC), they built dams, planted trees, and restored stream banks.

On the Swale, the Service straightened the stream's meanders and deepened its channel. In times of heavy runoff or heavy precipitation, instead of pooling and seeping slowly into the high prairie as it had done for thousands of years, the water became a torrent racing through Swale Canyon into the Little Klickitat and Klickitat Rivers.

Through much of the year the Swale is a graceful sweep of green, but nothing remains to mark its place in Klickitat history, not even a sign on the bridge crossing the creek.

Wayne Eshelman, personal memories
Illustrated History of Klickitat, Yakima and Kittitas Counties.
Interstate Pub. Co., 1904.
May, Pete, ed. *History of Klickitat County*. Klickitat County
Historical Society, 1982.

TEAM WRITING
FOR RURALITE

Mary Jean Lord

The Klickitat County edition of *Ruralite* magazine,
mailed to every Klickitat PUD customer, publishes
an article each month about one of the local residents.
These stories, accumulated over 50 years, have become
a treasure trove for historians.

The most prolific of all those who have collected
and written articles about Klickitat County have been
husband and wife teams. Florence and Alba "Bart"
Bartholomew, of Wishram, set an early example. A
descendant of Klickitat County pioneers, Florence's tales
of the early days were especially popular with readers.
In a period of ten years, starting in 1962, Florence wrote
more than 200 *Ruralite* pieces for Klickitat PUD and
neighboring Wasco and Hood River Electric Co-ops.
Most were illustrated with Bart's photographs.

Considering herself a musician rather than a writer,
Florence, at the age of thirteen, played piano for silent
films in White Salmon. Later, she composed eighteen
songs for a play, "The Winds Blew West, presented in
The Dalles in 1966. In 1952, she also wrote five songs
for the centennial pageant, "The Mount Adams Story"
in which the entire community of White Salmon
participated. CBS sent a crew from New York to record
the production, and it was played on 205 stations and
on the Voice of America.

In a sidelight, Florence's parents were the first couple
to be married in the new White Salmon Congregational
Church in 1905. The day after they celebrated their 50th
anniversary in the church, it was torn down to make
way for a new building.

Mary and Dick Morgan, who wrote about Klickitat
County for *Ruralite* from 1972 until the mid-1980s, were
the next husband and wife team. Mary, who signed her
pieces as M.V. Frank Morgan, specialized in interviews
of the elderly, recording their talents and life experiences.
Dick took the photographs. Thanks to Mary and Dick,
many valuable stories were written down that would
otherwise have been lost. Although they lived in

Oregon, Mary and Dick came to know Klickitat County well and made lasting friends wherever they went.

Rick and Kristi Steber, who followed the Morgans, had a different working arrangement. Rick traveled, interviewed, and took photographs. Kristi, who worked or stayed home with their young family, would sometimes help with writing up Rick's notes and polishing the pieces. In addition to writing for *Ruralite* and other magazines, Rick published dozens of short stories of the West, which were sold in restaurants, mini-marts and tourist stops.

Mario Milosevic and his wife, Kim Antieau, don't usually collaborate on their writing. They are both published writers and rely on one another as critics and sounding boards. Mario, who drew out wonderful stories about local people for *Ruralite*, is a poet, while Kim has published several novels, including *The Jigsaw Woman* and *Coyote Cowgirl*.

Although their working methods and writing styles differed, all of these writing teams believed in *Ruralite*'s philosophy, as expressed by Emmet Clouse, Klickitat PUD's first general manager, that "...no citizen is too uninteresting or undistinguished to be covered in *Ruralite*. Every man or woman has at least one good story in him or about him; and the true strength of our country lies in the good sense and good citizenship of its millions of ordinary citizens."

M.V. Frank Morgan, "Now It's Florence's turn...", *Ruralite*,
    June 1972
Personal knowledge of *Ruralite* writers

Temani Pesh-wa Project

Kathleen Goode

Teepees blossomed on the grounds of Columbia Hills State Park as tribal elders gathered to celebrate the return of sacred images. The spring gathering in 2004 was the culmination of a project that took nearly eight years and the cooperation of many groups to complete. Temani Pesh-wa means "Written on Rock". The occasion marked the establishment of a special display area for 43 rocks that are carved with numerous petroglyphs. The stone artifacts had been taken from Petroglyph Canyon before the rising waters of The Dalles Dam covered the area. They were then placed along a wall of the fish ladder; unfortunately, this was a site where birds perched and the images became covered with dung.

The U. S. Army Corps of Engineers, who operate The Dalles Dam, contributed $100,000 toward the project. Their efforts were assisted by the Yakama Nation, the Confederated Tribes of the Umatilla Reservation, the Nez Perce Tribe, and Washington State Parks. The rocks were carefully moved and cleaned by J. Claire Dean of Portland, who is considered one of the top ethnographic conservators in North America. The process was completed without mishap, and the art works were placed in the newly established 300-foot trail. Park authorities have set up surveillance cameras to help protect the art. Eventually, petroglyphs from the Roosevelt area will be displayed here as well. This site is intended as a place of prayer and reflection and should be treated with respect.

Personal Experience, info from Park Rangers at Columbia Hills State Park and:

Bonneville Power Administration "Transmission Business Line" http://www.transmission.bpa.gov/aboutTBL/Tribal_Affairs/pic_archive.cfm?page=horse

Richard, Terry. *The Oregonian* — Gorge petroglyphs moved to place of honor. Sunday, March 28, 2004. http://www.oregonlive.com/columbiagorge/oregonian/related.ssf?/columbiagorge/oregonian...

THANKSGIVING AND THE SEARCH FOR HOME

Bruce Howard

I had taken the holiday week off, rented a car in San Francisco, and packed one bag of clothes. I expected to do some hard and fast driving. When you're seeking an elusive prey, you have two choices: stay quiet and wait for it, or run hard, holler, and flush it out. I only had a week, so I chose the latter. I was after the great American dream, that most elusive prize of all — a home. I was looking for a certain type of town. I didn't have a clear idea just what type that was, but I was certain I'd know when I saw it. So I drove fast into every little town along the route I'd chosen, and I drove just as fast out the other side.

The main route leaving California for Oregon was restricted to traffic with chains or snow tires. I had neither, but the map showed a small highway, 97, going north, so I backtracked and found it in a town named Weed.

Highway 97 quickly became a vague, thin path of tire marks through new snow. Lucky for me the car had front wheel drive and new radials, because the snow got heavier and my progress slower. I passed two unlucky people watching a tow truck winch their car from between two trees. I became cautious — my insurance wouldn't warm me if I skidded off the road into white oblivion.

Late on the eve of Thanksgiving, I stopped at a motel in Biggs, Oregon. I was tired, beat, disappointed. In the morning I ate breakfast at a café. The man next to me at the counter started talking. He lived in a small community up the Gorge. Because the aluminum plant had closed, his neighborhood had turned into a ghost town. He didn't mind that so much.

"But what I don't like," he said, "is that everything is brown. If I was to move anywhere in the Northwest," he told me, "I mean Idaho, Wyoming, Utah, Oregon, or Washington, I'd move to Goldendale. It's got mountains and green and water and grain — like an oasis in a desert."

"Where's Goldendale?" I asked.

"Oh, just another ten miles or so north on 97."

Now, it seemed strange to me that this man didn't have his own plans for moving to Goldendale. This made me suspicious, but also intrigued. After breakfast that morning, I drove up Highway 97 to see the oasis. I expected to find a mirage.

The Gorge had been brown, but Klickitat Valley was white with new snow. The snowflakes melted on the pavement, so I easily followed the wet, black line of South Columbus straight into town. Maybe it was the old man's words, maybe it was the quiet snow, but I drove slowly, respectful of the wintry scene that recalled where I had grown up in Ohio. I drove around the courthouse park, out to the fairgrounds, and on my way back I had to stop and look.

The Little Klickitat River was dressed in winter, prettier than any greeting card. A boy wearing a colorful stocking cap, big jacket, mittens, and rumpled pants had black snow boots with metal buckles flapping loose. Snow clung to his clothes and he carried an old Flexible Flyer sled over his shoulder. That could have been me, thirty years ago. This was no mirage, a dream perhaps, but not a mirage. I'd found the all-American town, or at least a reasonable facsimile.

At the real estate office I asked if they paid a man to eat at a café in Biggs and tell any elbow acquaintance about Goldendale. I wish I had gotten that man's name, the one at the café in Biggs, I'd like to thank him. Maybe he moved here, too. After all, it was his idea.

THAT'S NOT A DOG!

Icey Sheeran

On a sunny Saturday morning in May, I slept in an hour later than usual. While I dragged myself to the kitchen to brew coffee, my husband Nayland went to the door to take our Jack Russell terrier for his morning constitutional. I glanced out the kitchen window and noticed a big dog lying beyond the back deck. It was just lying there, its back to me in the tall grass, watching a herd of deer grazing at the bottom of the hill. Coffee carafe in mid-air, I looked closer at the dog's head. It was strange, very large and round, with low-set ears. I hollered to Nayland that there was a cougar outside. The cat heard our voices and turned to look our way. Folks, I was awe-struck — totally spellbound. Its face was absolutely beautiful. The sun was fully up, shining directly into the window, so the animal probably could not see us due to its reflection. The cougar's face and neck were a bright blend of so many brown and cream hues. It was unafraid, very relaxed, and obviously not on a hunting expedition. To think that we used to pay big bucks to see cats like that at the San Diego Animal Park!

I whipped out the binoculars to see it really close up. I could practically count the whiskers and nose hairs at 25 feet. We wanted to get some great photos of this back yard wildlife but alas, my personal photographer found himself without a camera in the house! He had put all the camera equipment in his car trunk the night before. His saying has always been, "If it isn't photographed, it never happened."

After watching awhile, Nayland decided to sneak out the front door and try to get a camera. As he was putting on his shoes, I was still getting an eyeful of cat when I spotted a movement near its head. Another cougar! They were both curled up together, just like big domestic cats. One had been sleeping with its head down. So now this is really a big deal, and we have to get a picture, right? No such luck, though, as the moment Nayland went out the front door, they got up and walked into the trees.

That is our cougar story for High Prairie friends and neighbors. We have no photos to show off, but the sight of those awesome animals will forever be etched in our memories.

THE THINKER WITH ONE FOOT

Lee Musgrave,
Maryhill Museum of Art

The Thinker, Auguste Rodin's most celebrated sculpture, has come to symbolize his art, and indeed, intellectual activity itself. However, creating the contemplative and soul-searching expression on the face of the sculpture wasn't very challenging for Rodin.

What was? Well, the feet, of course. Rodin felt that the mood of the sculpture could best be summed up in the gesture of the feet. So he tried several different shapes and positions. The right foot on one of the versions especially displeased him, so he cut it off.

Where is that sculpture today? In Klickitat County, at Maryhill Museum.

How did it get there? Modern dance pioneer Loie Fuller, a friend of both Rodin and Sam Hill, made it possible for the Museum to acquire several dozen original sculptures by the famous artist.

TIMBER WOLVES

Rita J. Liska

Environmentalists, conservationists and our game department may tell you that there are no timber wolves in this part of Washington state and may recommend that some be introduced. Locals may just shrug, grunt, and go on about their business with a grin, neglecting to say that they see wolves regularly.

I watched a big, reddish male with a gray female come in behind my house to eat apples, every fall for years.

One time a friend and I stopped along Cedar Valley Road and watched five big grays dig for mice or gophers in a neighbor's hay field. One wolf finally became aware of us through the brush and, within seconds, all had disappeared into the timber and brush at the edge of the field.

Just a couple of years ago, a neighbor nearly wrecked her car when she rounded a curve and found a big gray ambling across the road ahead of her.

We have coyotes too — lots of them. But make no mistake, anyone who lives among these creatures certainly knows the difference between a coyote and the much larger wolf.

THE TIMMERMAN HANGING

Kathleen Goode

Jochim Henry Timmerman is perhaps the best known scoundrel in the history of Klickitat County. He is the only man ever sentenced in court to death by hanging. Unlike many tales of the Wild West, this one did not include a lynch mob, but instead, a carefully conducted investigation, trial, and even an appeal to the State Supreme Court. It all started with a grisly discovery in October of 1886 by a shepherd who was tending his flock in the Horse Heaven area. Martin Peck found the dead man, fully clothed except for his boots and hat, in a shallow grave. The body had been partially devoured by coyotes. A later autopsy confirmed that the man had died of four bullet wounds to the back of his head.

The victim was William Sterling of Walla Walla. Timmerman and Sterling had been traveling together from Yakima and were seen by a number of witnesses. Mrs. Sterling identified the body, and Sheriff Lesh of Yakima soon had a warrant out for the arrest of Timmerman. Col. Eugene B. Wise, an ex-Union Army officer, was the sheriff of Klickitat County. He received the warrant when the trail was already cold but decided to start his investigation at the ferry where the travelers were reported to have been heading. Timmerman had been seen and remembered; it was not long before Sheriff Wise had him in jail at Alkali. Timmerman was caught in possession of the dead man's hat, gun, boots, money, team, and wagon. Throughout his trial, Timmerman repeatedly claimed he was innocent. The jury disagreed, finding him guilty and sentencing him to be hung. The Territorial Supreme Court confirmed their conviction and sentencing in February of 1888. Justice was slow and measured in this part of the territory!

Timmerman predicted that the whole town would be burned down and that vile misfortunes would affect everyone connected with his trial. He even claimed he would rise from the grave to make sure these misfortunes were carried out. That spring, the gallows were built on a hill overlooking Goldendale, not far from the cemetery. On April 6th, Henry Timmerman had a hearty breakfast and drank nearly a quart of stout whiskey. He was quite jovial on the way to the cemetery, riding on top of his own casket. A large crowd gathered to observe the sentence being carried out by the sheriff and his deputies. Timmerman was buried in the cemetery, and the town set about putting the memory behind them.

Three months later, many of the town's residents were at a community picnic, far from town. A fire broke out in the livery stable, and soon most of the downtown area was in flames. The citizens were able to rescue the one prisoner who was in the jail — he was never seen again. The fire caused devastating losses, but the pioneers did not quit easily; they soon rebuilt the downtown area, this time in brick rather than wood.

Two years later, some boys were fishing in the Little Klickitat and found a human skeleton hidden in the bushes. This was about the same time that the sexton of the cemetery reported that Timmerman's grave had been opened. The coroner returned Timmerman's skeleton to his grave.

Today, we have a well-supported volunteer fire department, and town picnics are held on the courthouse lawn.

(Note: the last town picnic was advertised on the "Shopping Center" sign.)

Ballou, Robert. 1938. *Early Klickitat Valley Days*. Goldendale WA: *The Goldendale Sentinel*
Angie Hoffman, member of the Historical Society, who first told me the story

TIMMERS

Michelle Krause-Cooper

Having lived at 511 N Columbus only a few months, I have learned that many fascinating stories go with the house and property. It amazes me that so many people have visited, lived here or knew the owners of this house. Dr. Gerard and Maria Timmer were not a founding family, preserved in history; however, they had quite an influence on the local community. From the stories told me and found in the Goldendale Library, the following picture appears.

Maria and Gerard Timmer

The Timmers were both from the Netherlands. They moved to Goldendale with their six-year-old son, Bernard, where Dr. Timmer began his practice in 1957 on Main Street. They became citizens in White Salmon in 1960. Through all the places they visited and lived, they loved the northwest.

Previously, Gerald and Maria lived in many places including Everett WA, Kansas, South Africa, and other foreign countries. They loved Indonesia, where Dr. Timmer set up a much-needed office and hospital. You can see the love for the Timmers in the photographs of the children and staff at the hospital.

Maria was responsible for organizing the bar codes on all the books in the community library in anticipation of a computerized system. A memorial plaque in the library garden reminds us of her dedication. She was kind-hearted and welcomed everyone as a friend.

Gerald and Maria bought the Red House at 511 N. Columbus and later bought the Golden House on S. Columbus, both houses built before 1900. The Timmers extensively remodeled both properties.

With Gerard's drive and Maria's gardening and talent for decorating, they created lovely homes and showplaces for the art they had collected around the world and created themselves. Maria took photographs of beautiful flowers and birds in all their travels. She organized a gardening club that met and shared ideas on plants and creating a natural feel to a flower garden. Gerald loved carving items out of wood, from little spoons to large artwork, for example, the "Madonna," mounted on the front door of the "creek house," the North Columbus Red House. They donated many art pieces and paintings to the Maryhill Museum of Art.

They shared a love for classical music. Their home often served as a place for recitals. The Timmers played musical instruments, including the piano and violin. Maria sang in the choir at church and sang solos at home.

Gerard and Maria designed and built a home called "Happy Acres" on Highway 97. It included a sunny studio for Maria's art projects where she enjoyed weaving at her loom. The Timmers donated Happy Acres to the Greek Orthodox Church for a monastery. One of the buildings now serves as a gift shop and bakery selling fresh pastries made within the monastery.

Gerald and Maria made Goldendale their residence for the remainder of their years. They loved spending time with their friends, children, and grandchildren Casey and Seagrin.

Communities are made by the people who settle there. Some leave us appreciation for music, art, and architecture, as did Dr. Gerald and Maria Timmer.

TIPS FOR COUNTRY LIVING

Kathleen Goode

The commissioners in Klickitat County have heard it all. They seem to get complaints and requests from a lot of newcomers and, in order to make life a little easier for everyone, they put their best advice together in a pamphlet called "Tips for Country Living." They emphasize the fact that an important element of country life is self-reliance. The gist of the document seems to be that if you are new to the county, please do not call them for every little thing that comes up like snow-blocked roads, wild animals clawing at your door, or neighbors you think are up to no good. (Unless it's something illegal and then you should call the sheriff!) What follows is my own interpretation of the highlights (the commissioners were much more polite).

Buying property is no guarantee that you can build, and you may not be happy if you do. Permits are required, even if you buy land in the back of nowhere, and they cost money. The land may not "perk", that is, be suitable for a septic system. Some entity may be able to build a road, install power lines, or run a sewer line right through your land. The neighbors might cut down all their trees, there may be large livestock with a right of way through your front yard, and the road might be blocked up with snow for the better part of a month. The county will not plow your driveway, shoot that annoying neighbor's dog, or keep the deer off your back deck. If you buy land that is involved in a homeowners' association, don't come whining to the commissioners about it. There may be a power plant built directly blocking your view. Plans to build anything near water may come up against a brick wall. If you build in the back of beyond, don't expect the ambulance to be able to get there in a jiffy! When you decide on that great new manufactured home, make sure it can fit down your narrow country lane.

There is so much more that you really should read it yourself, but here are a few of my favorite lines:

"Gravel roads are not always smooth."

"North facing slopes or canyons rarely see direct sunlight in the winter."

"In general, it is best to enjoy wildlife from a distance."

"Dogs, cattle, horses, pigs, goats, ram sheep, etc. can attack human beings and other animals without warning."

"It is generally understood in agricultural areas that farm animals produce manure. . . "

And finally, . . . "we encourage you to be vigilant in your duties to explore and examine those things that could cause your move to be less than you expect."

All joking aside, this is a very handy little booklet to consider if planning to buy rural property just about anywhere. You can download a copy at the web site http://www.klickitatcounty.org/Commissioners

Klickitat County, Tips for Country Living
http://www.klickitatcounty.org

TIRED, NUMB, AND DUMB

Rita J. Liska

I had been in the saddle since early morning, trying to take care of three different jobs in one day. I finally came down off the mountain to let my horse rest and have some brunch, but something happened and I didn't take time to eat before climbing back into the saddle to trek 7+ miles south to pick up a herd of cattle, bring them back north, and turn them loose on open range for the summer.

Once at the owner's corrals, the cattle had to be run through a chute and checked out, then the entire herd was re-gathered, turned out of the corrals, and the push continued. Cattle aren't worked quietly. So, when the owner mentioned, as the cattle were being released to continue the drive, that there should have been another herd in a pasture adjoining those corrals, it stood to reason that there were no cattle in that pasture, or they would have been at the corrals to see what was happening.

We made it about a quarter of a mile, following a pickup through the brush, when we approached a steep canyon. I saw the pickup slam on its brakes as we pushed the herd through a gate. Within seconds, we had two cattle herds joined together and two bulls, both larger than our horses, on the fight.

It was getting so late that I couldn't read ear-tags from the saddle, and we returned to the corrals with both herds — one supposed to be kept in the pasture, the other supposed to be high up on the mountain.

It was already dusk by the time we were able to continue. We arrived at the release gate well after dark to find that, while someone had left one gate open so the herds could join, someone had also closed the one gate that should have been left open until our herd was released.

The herd hit the fence and scattered, and I spent half my time chasing noises in the brush before finding out I was after a kid on foot instead of a cow. By the time we finally got the herd through and the gate closed behind them, we had to depend on the taillights of the pickup to get us back through brush and boulders to the corral and pavement.

The other rider and I parted company at Cedar Valley Road, and even though my horse was a little gelding that would have died before he ever quit, he was concentrating on just putting one foot ahead of the other because he was so tired.

I was also tired, and when the sun went down the temperature dropped, so I'd lost all feeling in my hands and feet despite gloves and taps*.

Charlie had gotten worried about me, so he drove down to meet me, giving me a flashlight so Boots and I could at least see where we were going that last mile home.

He turned on the yard light, helped me fall out of the saddle, and carried it down to the shed while I took care of my horse. By the time I got to the house, he had a hot fire in the stove and a mixed drink waiting on the hearth where I would be sitting to warm up. Then he went to bed.

I'm not a drinker by nature, but that one tasted wonderful as I sat with my back to the fire and nursed it while watching a television program. But, when I got up to let the dogs out for the night, I was in trouble. Every time I reached for the knob, it did a loopy-loop around my hand, and I could not catch it.

It was only after getting the door open and the dogs out that I turned around and realized the whole house was askew and that I'd had nothing to eat since early that morning. Had it not been for our two chairs, the kitchen counters, stove handles, and the walls on each side of the hallway, I know I never would have made it to bed that night.

I never pulled that stunt again.

*"taps" = tapederos or tapedera, leather covers on the stirrups in a western saddle to protect the rider's feet.

TOWBOAT LIVING

Teddy Cole

Barge on the Columbia River

Out of my window looking in the night,
I can see the barges' flickering light.
Silently flows the river to the sea,
And the barges too go silently.

Campfire Girls Songbook

Crews on the tugboats that tow barges on the Columbia River include a captain, a pilot, and usually two deck mechanics, with a third man for the largest barges. The crews work six hours on, six hours off, around the clock.

Each crew works half of the month. The day prior to crew change, off-duty personnel call in to learn what boat they are assigned to and approximately where it will be the next day at noon. Because the boats work non-stop, the location for boarding may be anywhere from Lewiston ID to Astoria OR. Crew members make arrangements with each other for safe storage and retrieval of their personal cars.

When a man (and almost all are male) climbs aboard at the beginning of duty, he will stay on the boat for fifteen days. Food and laundry facilities are provided. For personal items, he must plan ahead, because a quick trip to the pharmacy or convenience store is not possible. If he didn't plan well, he will do without.

When a new hire reports to work on a tugboat, he begins a rigorous two-year training. He will need a communications card because talking on a radio is a large part of the job. He must complete courses in handling hazardous chemicals and treating spills, extensive safety training, and training with an automated external defibrillator. Safety is the number one concern. No other industry discusses and practices safety more thoroughly than towboating.

Life on board requires other skills: the crews prepare their own food, keep the vessel clean, and share cramped quarters. Contrary to the campfire song, a new man must get used to the constant noise level and be able to sleep through intense vibrations that feel like an earthquake.

Working close to the river's edge, crews see animals of every kind: deer, coyotes, mink, beaver, all types of birds, mountain goats. They observe bald eagles and osprey learning to respect each other's territory. River workers know where to watch for the new goose chicks and the baby fawns. They know when the young osprey will try its wings. Farther down river, they watch for seals trying hitch a ride on board for a nap on the deck.

If a stray dog or cat turns up at any dock along the river, all the crews soon know about it. They save table scraps, and before long their new friend will be waiting to get his next meal. Usually there's enough to last until the next boat arrives.

The work, hazards and pleasures of the towboater's life are far from the romantic vision of the campfire song, but for some it has an irresistible lure all its own.

"Barges," Makin' Music with Camp Fire. Camp Fire Boys
    and Girls, n.d.
Marvel, Ken. Personal experience.
Oregon Public Broadcasting, Oregon Field Guide #410,
    "Gorge Tugboat."

Towboats on the Columbia

Teddy Cole

Towboats are a vibrant part of the river panorama along Klickitat County shores. They add more than color to our landscape; they support our economy as well.

From the shore a towboat looks small. The tug pushes or pulls four or more barges, and one might guess that it is 200 feet long altogether. In reality, a tug with its tow is 84 feet wide and 650 feet long, longer than two football fields end to end. Its speed is about eight miles an hour.

A tugboat runs twenty-four hours a day, 365 days a year. The tugboat's systems work together to make it self-sufficient. Each of the two 1500 horsepower engines uses 55 gallons of diesel and burns two quarts of lube oil every hour. Seventy-five sensors connected to the boat's "brain" ensure that all systems are working properly, that fluids are at proper levels, and that smoke in any compartment is immediately detected. Any abnormal condition will trigger an alarm.

Tugs have electric winches, while barges have the hand-cranked type. Barges are strapped together with 1-1/8 inch cables. Usually, six cables are used to connect two barges; four barges take eighteen to twenty cables.

Navigating a tow takes years to master. The pilot operates the boat from the wheelhouse, 45 feet above the water. Modern technology has introduced new tools to help with the job: global positioning systems (GPS), depth indicators, swing meters, wind gauges, radar, and more. An on-board computer is part of the company's network; at any time the main office can locate any boat in the fleet.

An observer on shore watching several boats pass will notice that all boats travel the same path. This is the deep channel of the river. Buoys, range markers, and the GPS help the pilot keep the tow in this channel. During spring runoff or heavy rainfall, water flowing down the Columbia River travels at 300,000 cubic feet per second; this rapid current creates only one of the problems a pilot must learn to handle. Others include fog, wind, rain, ice, snow, bridges, and dams. People also present potential hazards when fishing, windsurfing, and pleasure boating take them into the deep channel.

The complete trip between Portland OR and Lewiston ID takes about 48 hours. The boat will pass through eight dams, four on the Columbia and four on the Snake River. The dam locks are a maximum of 650 feet long and 86 feet wide, a tight squeeze for the largest tow. When a tow enters the locks it is roped to eight large floats set into the lock wall; they hold the tow in position as it is raised or lowered. John Day Dam has the highest lift, 100 feet.

Wheat is the primary cargo downriver. Wheat from Lewiston and other upriver locations is brought down to Portland, Vancouver, Kelso, and Longview, where it is loaded on ships for overseas ports. Fifty-three per cent of the wheat produced in the United States is transported down the Columbia River: forty percent by

Columbia River :

1st   Bonneville Dam, completed in January 1938 (new locks completed in March 1993)

2nd   The Dalles Dam, completed in March 1957

3rd   John Day Dam, completed in May 1968

4th   McNary Dam, completed in November 1953

Snake River:

5th   Ice Harbor Dam, completed in October 1962

6th   Lower Monumental Dam, completed in April 1969

7th   Little Goose Dam, completed in May 1970

8th   Lower Granite Dam, completed in April 1975

barge, thirteen per cent by train. River barges are the most efficient method of transporting wheat, because a tow of four wheat barges will carry 14,000 tons of wheat, or 28 million pounds. It would take 140 railroad cars or 560 trucks to carry the same amount.

Tugboat companies also transport scrap metal, wood chips, paper products, petroleum products, and garbage, among other cargos. Forty-two-foot-wide barges carry one million gallons of petroleum, while jumbo barges, 84 feet wide and 247 feet long, with thirteen and a half feet of barge under water, will carry 2.2 million gallons of petroleum.

Marvel, Ken. Personal experience.
Oregon Public Broadcasting, Oregon Field Guide #410,
    "Gorge Tugboat."

TRAILIN' COWS

*M.L. "Charlie" Shattuck
Daughter of Russell
and Marie Kreps*

Trailin' cows is nearly a lost art. With the coming of trucks and stock trailers, many have found it convenient to load and haul. We have portable loading chutes for the trucks, making it easy to load and unload almost any place. With a stock trailer, all that is needed is a couple of panels. It helps if the cattle are not too wild.

My memory goes back to the late 1930s, and I must have been about 8 years old, when my father trailed cows from Gilmer 20 miles to spring pasture in the hills above White Salmon-Bingen. In late May, the cows were gathered and trailed back to Gilmer. Riders were many, and we kids were always ready to go.

Going to spring pasture was early and not too hot. We would leave Gilmer at daylight, resting the cows before we got to the highway at Husum. From there to the pasture, we had traffic to contend with, plus tired cows and cowboys. The trailing down Main Street in White Salmon was a thrill for me. Once the cows got lined out, they would trot, and at times they would see their reflection in the store windows. It was always a relief to be through town, knowing that soon we would be in the pasture. We would ride back through town to grandfather's (Tune Wyers) barn on Oak Street. This barn had lots of stalls, since it was a delivery stable in the early days. After a meal at grandmother's, we loaded the horses into a truck and went back to Gilmer.

The two-year-old steers, summered in Camas,

Cattle Drive

were driven first to Gilmer, then on to Bingen to the stockyards, where they were loaded on the train and shipped to the commission yard in Portland. Going from White Salmon down the hill to Bingen was a challenge, especially the yards without fences. Yards were not a good place to leave horse tracks. Traffic in those years was a concern; however, most drivers were used to livestock on the road, and there were not that many vehicles.

In early June, about 1950, when I was home from Washington State College, Father, Chip, and I hauled our horses from Gilmer to the Locke Place (on the Columbia River). Father helped us gather about 30 pairs and start across country, then he went home. Chip knew the way, "over the top — Snowden area — and come out at Husum, then up the Oak Ridge Road to Gilmer." It was my first and only trip across the top. Darkness set in when we were about three miles from home; the cows were tired and wanted to stop. Chip and I were happy to see lights coming. It was Father. We left the cows, loaded our horses, and headed for home. We were back at daylight to gather and continue on to Gilmer.

My last trip helping to move cows from Gilmer to White Salmon Hills was in the early 1960s. I was married and living in Toppenish. A friend from Seattle (Dr. Bert Hagen) went with me. The first day we trailed from Gilmer to Northwestern Lake, where Father used Ernie Child's pasture for the night; the second day was on to pasture. This allowed the herd to go through town in the early morning — hopefully before most people were out and about. My sister Marguerite Kayser came to help with her kids — I remember seven-year-old Nancy impressed Bert by always being ahead of him in returning an animal to the herd.

Now my Kreps nephews haul the cows; there's too much traffic and too many people who are not used to the animals using the road like in the "good old days."

THE TRAVELING HENDERSONS

Teddy Cole

Robert W. Henderson's time in Klickitat County was brief, and came near the end of a restless life. He arrived in Goldendale sometime around 1877, worked as a butcher, and died before Washington Territory joined the Union.

Robert was born into a traveling family. His father, Ira Baxter Henderson, was a man on the move. By 1823 Ira and his wife, Margaret Wilson, had settled in Ohio where Robert, their oldest child, was born. They didn't stay long. In the early 1830s, they were off to Cass County in Michigan Territory, traveling with the Fulton and Wilson families.

By 1840, Ira and his family were living in Porter County, Indiana. The Oregon Trail opened in 1843, and the West was calling. The Hendersons started out for Oregon Territory, but in 1849, disaster struck. An epidemic of cholera swept through the States from 1848 to 1853, one of a series of worldwide pandemics. As the entourage made its way through Illinois, Ira was stricken. They stopped while he suffered through the first bout and moved on when he improved. So it went: camping when Ira got worse, traveling as he was able.

Cholera causes profuse, effortless and painless diarrhea, leading to dehydration. It's beyond imagination how, given their primitive living conditions, Margaret was able to care for her sick husband while keeping the disease from spreading to the rest of the family. The wagon train kept going in slow stages, committed to the belief that once they reached Oregon their lives would be better. In 1852 they arrived in Atchison County, Missouri, and halted near the banks of the Missouri River. Ira died in July, leaving his wife with nine sons and daughters, five of whom were in their 20s or late teens, with one as young as eight.

Two daughters married and moved to Texas. Robert and his brother, James, had land claims in the Oregon Territory. Undaunted that in three years they had traveled less than a fourth of the distance to Oregon, in 1853 the Hendersons and related families set out again, this time with Margaret's brother, James Wilson as their scout.

Somewhere in eastern Oregon an ox fell sick, and once again they were stranded, but help was on the way. The Rev. Wilson Blain, who had married Margaret's sister, Elizabeth, and settled in Oregon several years earlier, heard that the caravan was coming. He took supplies and a few oxen and came to meet them. He found the train resting, with all the teams exhausted.

The sick ox had died, and Wilson put his fresh oxen in its place and helped the train to move forward once more.

In 1853 the travelers reached their destination at last, Union Point, Linn County, Oregon, and there they settled down on their various land claims to build a community. Margaret took up her husband's claim, and she used her needlework skills to work. Her granddaughter wrote, "She made her family's living by making fine linen shirt bosoms for the dressy men of the community. In those days, fine white linen shirts were very fashionable. When worn they were starched stiff as a board."

Robert married Margaret Ellen Sanders in 1858, and they had seven children. Robert's reason for leaving his homestead and moving his family 225 miles northeast to Klickitat County is unknown. Perhaps it was simply because Washington Territory was still relatively open. Robert settled in Goldendale, where he worked as a butcher. Here two more daughters were born, and two were married, and here he died. The children scattered, most to California. Daughter Vitrella grew up to marry a Methodist preacher who served several parishes in Washington and Oregon, a marriage ensuring that the family's traveling ways lived on.

The restlessness of the Henderson family means that few records are available to document their story, but such families were a vital part of the western expansion, including the settlement of Klickitat County. Their lives embody optimism, the belief that something better is just beyond the next hills.

"Cholera," Encyclopedia Americana, v. 6, pp. 624-625, Grolier, c2000

Denis, Linnea, "Robert W. Henderson; Genealogy"

"Overland from Indiana to Oregon: the Dinwiddie Journal," edited by Margaret Booth. Missoula, MT, 1928 (Sources of Northwest History,...Historical Reprints No. 2, State University of Montana.) 14p, 24 (Thought to have been written by either David or John Dinwiddie.)

"Pioneer Stories of Linn County, Oregon: WPA Interviews," Leslie L. Haskins, et al. Compiled and indexed by Nina L. Williamson and Richard R. Milligan. Linn County Historical Museum, Volume 3; pp. 22; 23

THE TREATY OF 1855

Kathleen Goode

During the summer of 1855, many tribes or their representatives assembled in a great meeting at Walla Walla. They were there to negotiate a peaceful settlement with Territorial Governor Isaac Stevens. The State of Washington did not exist yet, nor did Klickitat County. The treaty agreement brought together, among others, 14 different tribes and bands to create the Confederated Tribes of the Yakama Reservation. Under the terms of the agreement, the Yakama Nation ceded 10.8 million acres of land to the United States and kept control of 1.2 million acres that would be for their exclusive use (the reservation). They reserved the right to gather foods in all their traditional places; this included fishing rights as well as other food gathering rights. The United States, in exchange for the 10.8 million acres, agreed to build schools and a hospital and to protect the rights of the tribes as they were defined in the treaty. The treaty was exactly like those signed with other tribes in the Oregon Territory; it was designed to allow for the coming influx of white settlers.

Portions of the treaty were violated almost immediately. Whites were allowed to cross over Indian lands and to graze cattle and sheep there. The allotment act resulted in large portions of the reservation being sold to whites, including the town sites for Toppenish, Wapato, and Parker. Hydroelectric dams destroyed the salmon runs and Celilo Falls. Promises regarding schools and hospitals were not honored. One hundred and fifty years later, the court battles continue, but many of those battles have resulted in the courts upholding the rights of the First Citizens. The Yakama Nation gathers in June to celebrate Treaty Days; perhaps this will be the year there is more done to honor the treaty than to try and defeat it.

The Treaty of 1855 was a legally binding agreement between two sovereign nations. The United States sought to gain control of land for new settlers, and the tribes sought to preserve their lives and traditions for the future. One hundred and fifty years later, some might say the agreement has proven to be effective. The legal system has upheld the promise of the treaty, though often after a great deal of time, money, and training were devoted to answering challenges. Perhaps this will be a turning point, where both the letter and the spirit of the law are put into practice.

Ferolito, Philip. 2005. Treaty rights, wrongs. *Yakima Herald Republic*. May 29.

Hunn, Eugene S. with James Selam and Family. 1990. *Nch'i-Wana "The Big River"; Mid-Columbia Indians and Their Land*. Seattle: University of Washington Press.

TREE HOUSE LOOKOUT

Sara Wu and Mary Anne Enyeart

How awesome! A fire lookout in a living tree!

The J. Neil Lumber Company needed to watch for fire at its railroad-logging site, so it used an available tower, a Ponderosa pine. In 1944 four men with the Department of Forestry including Dewey Schmid, Phil Dean, and Fred Steinbach, constructed this lookout on Meadow Butte, also called Shaw Mountain. The tower was ready-made, so the task was to hoist the materials 86 feet above the ground, through the branches.

The lookout was turned over to the State as part of their fire watching system. It was then equipped with a fire finder, radio, and other equipment. Richard Smith, a Washington State Department of Natural Resources employee, remembers that it was a real pain using ropes to get this equipment up and down each year.

There were special challenges at this lookout. Guy wires could only partially stabilize the natural sway of the tree in the wind. A ladder was built three feet out from the trunk for access. Climbing the ladder on the side next to the tree gave some sense of security, but did not ease anxiety for everyone. The last lookout left her post at the end of summer with hands bandaged and bleeding from having gripped the rungs of the ladder so tightly.

The lookout person was usually a high school or college young woman who would stay for the summer. There was a cabin at the base for sleeping and cooking, but without electricity or running water. Nevertheless, the beauty and quiet of the place often brought the same lookout back for several summers. In 1958 it was decommissioned and replaced by a new, 40-foot tower on Nestors Peak west of Husum. The tree house lasted into the 1980s, but now this remarkable construction is gone.

Richard C. Smith, with the Dept. of Natural Resources 1957-1984, said, "Whenever I visited Meadow Butte, I only climbed to the actual lookout when I had to. Built in a tree, it had a homemade ladder built so that when you went up the tree, you were facing outwards with your back to the tree. I recall it was built with saplings with a 2x4 nailed to them. You entered the lookout through a trapdoor in the floor.

"At the time it was decommissioned, it was in the most beautiful spot of any lookout I had ever visited, not because of the view, but because of the site itself. It was a park-like setting with a beautiful one-room cabin on the ground. We moved the cabin to the Department of Natural Resources compound in Glenwood and used it for storm shelter."

Kresek, Ray.1985. *Fire Lookouts of Oregon & Washington.* Ye Galleon Press.

Personal communication with Richard Smith, 2003.

Spring, Ira and Byron Fish. 1981. *Lookouts: Firewatchers of the Cascades and Olympics. Mountaineers.*

TROUT LAKE, AN ORGANIC VALLEY

Pat Arnold, with Monte Pearson

The Organic Valley cooperative wasn't named after Trout Lake, but we are an organic valley whose farmers produce organic milk, herbs, and other crops. The native animals, herbs, grasses, mushrooms, and other plants, including the famous huckleberry, have always been harvested and enjoyed in their original, organic form long before there was "organic" labeling.

The most enduring form of agriculture, other than timber, has been the dairies, introduced to the valley by the first white settlers who brought a dual-purpose breed of cattle, for both meat and dairy. Peter Stoller presumably had dairy on his mind when he brought twenty cows with him to Trout Lake in the spring of 1880. The open meadows around the lake with their abundance of wild grass probably suggested an ideal dairy environment. However, the weather didn't cooperate. Only seven cows survived the unusually long winter that followed, in spite of the family's efforts to keep the cows alive by gathering moss from the rocks in the creek and sacrificing the straw in their mattresses.

After that rocky start, dairy farming did take hold. One of the area's natural features, caves formed by ancient lava flows, lent itself to the dairy industry. The caves provided cool storage for butter, ideal humidity and temperature for curing cheese, and a source of ice for keeping milk cool.

According to Joe Wood, who for years delivered milk from Trout Lake Valley to the processor, there were as many as 50 dairies in the Valley. Many of these were very small, perhaps 10 cows, and most went out of business as the industry changed.

By the 1960s, the number of dairies had declined to about 25, although the quantity of milk produced continued to rise. In 1971 there were 12 dairies, and now, in 2005, there are three, all organic.

Before bulk tanker trucks started running, milk and cream were delivered in 10-gallon cans, weighing nearly 100 pounds (80 for the milk and 20 for the can). The trucks picked up about 80 cans a day for delivery to the creamery in White Salmon and later to Hood River for transportation to Portland. Milk was cooled by spring water running through coils over which the milk was run. The cooled milk was put into cans which were placed in troughs through which ditch water circulated to keep the milk cool until the truck arrived.

Dairies now cool milk to 38 degrees in refrigerated tanks almost immediately after milking, and hold the milk within a degree of that temperature for every-other-day pickup for transport to Portland, McMinnville, or Springfield. In 2005, the three organic dairies are producing 60,000-80,000 pounds of milk every other day.

The three surviving dairies are thriving because of the skill of the farming families and the switch to organic production. The national dairy industry has been using bovine growth hormone, a move that Trout Lake dairyman Monte Pearson, who co-owns Mountain Laurel Jerseys with his wife Laura, believed would put unreasonable stress on his cows. He faced the choice of using growth hormone to boost production, or finding a way to get a better price. He began exploring the organic option with Organic Valley cooperative.

It took about a year to make the transition. The dairy's farmland could qualify for organic since no prohibited material had been used for the previous three years. All the cattle feed must come from fields that are chemical-free for three years and certified organic. No antibiotics or synthetic hormones are used on the cows (if antibiotics are necessary to save a cow, it cannot remain in the herd as organic).

The Pearsons select cows with traits that contribute to longevity, calving ease, and efficient production on a high forage diet. Monte believes the average age of cows in his herd is about twice that of a typical conventional herd. The dairy's cull rate — cows removed from the herd for reasons of health or low production — is about 12 percent, compared to a cull rate of 30 to 50 percent in conventional herds. Not included in the cull rate are cows sold to other producers for dairy purposes.

Trout Lake dairies have traditionally put their cows to pasture, unlike many dairies that confine cows to barns or feedlots. Organic dairies must provide pasture for their cows, so in Trout Lake we will continue to see cows grazing in the fields, a pastoral scene that for many symbolizes our organic valley.

TROUT LAKE FESTIVAL OF THE ARTS

Bonnie Reynolds

In 1996 a group of six people, presided over by Laurie Sherburne, Trout Lake School teacher, worked to develop a plan for Trout Lake's first art festival. The group's goals were to provide: a local venue for the work of regional artists; an opportunity for artists to increase their professionalism; and an opportunity for art patrons to learn about area artists. At that time there were few venues available for juried fine art — the Columbia Art Gallery and The Dalles Art Center were the primary regional galleries. With a non-profit 501(c)3 status, ten artists, and music by the White Salmon Jazz Band, that first year's event was held at the Trout Lake School. It was a promising success.

After two years, the event had grown to need a larger, more versatile site. Dean and Rosie Hostetter offered the use of their property, A Farm B&B, for use by the Festival. The third weekend in July has become the designated weekend for the event. The Hostetters' hospitality and location afforded an exciting opportunity for the growth of the project.

The committee's volunteers, knowledge, and skills have grown as has the area's fine art and music community. There are many venues today for fine and performing arts. Trout Lake's Festival now has 40 participating artists, music scheduled all day Saturday and Sunday, and a Saturday evening benefit dinner and professional performance.

The Trout Lake Festival for the Arts is credited with

raising the standard of service to, and expectations from, the artists. The committee has researched and implemented advertising plans that draw crowds from Portland and other areas within a day's drive of Klickitat County — 2,000 visitors are expected annually. A web site is maintained, containing current schedules and contact information: www.troutlake.org/arts.

Profits from the Art Festival are used to support projects for increasing the diversity of art and cultural opportunities in the region.

TURKEY RANCH

Rita J. Liska

Turkey Ranch is gone now, the last remains disintegrated into history, pushed over and burned a few years ago. But, this is its story, as told to me by Fred Weaver, who worked at Turkey Ranch while it was in operation.

Turkey Ranch was built west of Mill Creek by Loren Barrett in 1955 and was operated until about 1960. The ranch included a house that burned down and was rebuilt in a different location, along with several large sheds, a large brood house, and pens to contain the birds, whose wings were clipped so they couldn't fly. There were about 4,000 turkeys, both brown and white.

Once the young birds were large enough, they were turned out to forage in the woods with the rest of the turkeys. When ready for market, the turkeys were loaded into large semi-trucks and hauled away, supposedly to Portland.

Now the ranch has disappeared and been replaced by an ever-enlarging community referred to as Turkey Ranch, reached by the one-and-only Turkey Ranch Road.

VAGABOND PEACOCKS

Douglas L. Taylor

As dusk fell one day on our High Prairie farm, I caught a glimpse of bright blue and green motion. Then it was gone. Again the next day, and the next, these flashes occurred. The appearances became longer, and resolved into two male peacocks. They came just at dusk, flew into the oak, and roosted in the pine by the former Baptist church located on our place. My family named them Fred and Earl.

No one knows for sure where Fred and Earl came from. Peacocks are great wanderers, especially if they have been moved from their home territory and not penned for a while. Fred had full plumage with a long beautiful tail, while Earl had full plumage minus the long beautiful tail, perhaps having lost it in his travels. I also noticed that Earl was missing a toenail on his left foot.

They made this their home, accepting Julia (the Border collie) and Toby (the red rooster) as family. They even decided that the deck next to our dining area was just fine for preening feathers and making big messes. Of course, this was done without malice or forethought, but it didn't go over well with my wife, Dona. When they stayed in the barn or roosted over the metal roof of the church, I wondered whether they had a vendetta against humans.

When I was feeding Toby, Fred and Earl would often socialize with him through the fence, peacocks on the outside and rooster on the inside. They would put their heads close to the wire and just look. As soon as the grain was put in Toby's pen, he had visitors; it was up and over the top of the pen for the two peacocks to see what Toby was getting that was special. After checking this out and visiting with Toby a bit more, it was up and out again for Fred and Earl.

If something was happening over in the cattle corral, it wouldn't be long before you could see Fred and Earl flying up on the corral fence to see what they might be missing. They are very inquisitive, social birds.

The story that the peacock is a beautiful bird with a terrible voice is certainly true. The peacock also is a tremendous flyer. It can stand flat-footed at the base of the house and fly directly to the roof, particularly if a neighbor stops by and has his dog with him. At a safe distance on the rooftop, the birds can survey, scold, and not waste energy running. Other times they may be on the roof just to scout what's going on in the yard. They spend their nights roosting high up in the trees, but if it is raining, early in the morning you will find them in the peak of the barn atop the hay bales.

They stayed with us all winter. They would challenge Julia at her dog dish when we filled it with goodies, and she never challenged back.

After much strutting and displaying of their beautiful plumage this spring, by the first of May they had left our barnyard. They came mysteriously, and they have left the same way.

The Value of a Quince Bush

Kathleen Goode

Last summer my husband and I had to have a large cherry tree cut down in our yard because of serious decay and one large limb that threatened to damage our elderly neighbor's roof. I went over to let her know what all the noise was about, and she told me that was fine, just so long as I didn't cut down the quince bush nearby. She had had a quince everywhere she had ever lived and was enjoying ours. I promised not to do anything but a light pruning. Not far away, we have another quince bush that has run completely amuck and grown right up in front of our kitchen window.

This morning was one of the first warm spring days. I looked out the kitchen window as I poured a cup of coffee and was surprised to see a hummingbird feeding on the quince blossoms. We seldom see hummingbirds here in town and never three inches from a window. Usually we find that the "hummingbird" is really a moth. I watched closely as it fed and then rested on a branch It was very small — even for a hummingbird — with green back feathers and a cream and buff colored chest. The bird guide indicated it was a Calliope Hummingbird, *Stellula calliope*, but there had only been one other sighted in our county; perhaps I was mistaken.

Later that morning, my daughter saw a hummingbird at the window; this one was unmistakably a Rufous Hummingbird, *Selasphorus rufus*. It was a little larger, mainly the color of cinnamon, with a white neck band and fluorescent red chin. We watched until it flew off toward the blossoming pear tree across the yard. Half an hour later, my daughter again called my attention to the window, and there was a male Calliope Hummingbird. This time there could be no mistake; its signature red neck stripes were very clearly displayed as it sat on a quince branch. This was amazing; not just one, but three hummingbirds in one day!

Both the Rufous and Calliope Hummingbirds are on the National Audubon Society's Watch List. A recent report in our state lists them as an "early warning" species, meaning that there is concern about their diminishing numbers.

There is now an effort to band birds in that area so that more can be learned about their migration habits. The Rufous Hummingbird has the longest known avian migration relative to its size. The northern limit of their migration is in Alaska, the southern is in southern

Mexico. The Calliope Hummingbird is the smallest breeding bird in North America and the smallest in the world to undertake an annual migration.

Sitting quietly on a bench near my quince, I could see several more hummingbirds, each staking out its own territory. One Calliope male had chosen the quince for its afternoon hangout and would yell at interlopers with a staccato "chip" that sounded almost like a telegraph machine. Being no match for the larger Rufous that challenged it, it fled to the top of a flowering Hawthorn until the Rufous had its fill. These hummingbirds are likely just stopping to refuel, on their way to breeding grounds at a higher elevation. I will watch for them winging their way South for the winter again in July or August.

If you see any of these birds on the watch list, please report it at www.ebird.org so that more can be learned about their current numbers and habits. Meanwhile, I will only give our quince bushes a light trim and plenty of care. The fruit is not very exciting, but the visitors certainly are!

Personal experience
"About eBird: North America's destination for birding on the Web" http://www.ebird.org "Audubon Watch List"
Stokes, Donald and Lillian.1996. Stokes Field Guide to Birds; Western Region. New York: Little, Brown and Company.
"The San Pedro River Valley" http://www.sabo.org/birding/huacspv.htm

One of the strongest human bonds is that forged among men who have served together under enemy fire. Harold Hill and Bob Imrie, Goldendale, were not only lifelong friends, they both fought in the notoriously bloody Battle of the Bulge at the end of World War II. They often lamented the fact that while Klickitat County had Stonehenge, built by the Quaker Sam Hill, to commemorate the men who died in World War I, the county had nothing similar to honor veterans of other wars.

Harold and Bob met regularly with John Miller and other veterans for kaffeeklatsch in a Goldendale restaurant. One morning, after the subject had come up

VETERANS REMEMBERED

Mary Jean Lord

once again, they decided it was time to take some action. They formed a committee and began to solicit support from veterans and community organizations throughout the county. The response was encouraging.

The group decided that the memorial should honor Klickitat County veterans of World War II, the Korean War, Vietnam, and all wars since World War I. They agreed on a simple, but impressive, design of granite walls and pillars set on a platform. The memorial would have space to record the names of the dead, and benches on which the living could rest.

The next question was where the memorial should be placed. The Board of Directors for Maryhill Museum of Art, which owns Stonehenge, offered a site near Stonehenge and agreed to take care of it. This site met all the requirements of the veterans' group — it was near a well-traveled highway where people could see it and in a protected area, but it was off the road where it wouldn't cause problems.

The original group raised money among themselves to pay for the memorial, but they couldn't do it alone. As word of the project spread, donations poured in from the community, from all over the state, and from across the nation.

On the afternoon of August 22, 1995, thousands of people began gathering at Stonehenge for the dedication. Flags flew, and a bagpipe band from Fort Lewis played. At six o'clock the speeches began, and the audience turned solemn. After Navy Admiral Jack Barrett of White Salmon formally dedicated the memorial, a unit of F-16s delighted the crowd with a thrilling fly-over. Afterwards, people greeted old friends and reminisced over barbecue.

Thanks to the efforts of Harold, Bob, John and friends, future generations can remember the sacrifices of Klickitat County war veterans.

Ruralite, August 1995;
Personal experience.

VISIT FROM THE SHERIFF

Anonymous

People complain about the fact that in small towns everybody knows everybody's business — sometimes before you know it yourself! This can turn out to be very helpful at times.

A few years ago I was in the depths of reading a good mystery novel. It was nearly midnight, and the neighborhood was very quiet. Suddenly, there was a loud knock on the door which gave me quite a start. No one knocks on the door at midnight unless there's been an accident or emergency.

The sheriff was at the door. "Ma'am, I just wanted to let you know what we're doing so that you would not be startled." I had it fixed in my head that this was an emergency. The sheriff continued, "We're going to be moving some people out of the house down the street." Having spent nearly all my life in small towns, my response was automatic: "Well, officer, we don't have much room but they are welcome to stay with us."

The sheriff tried to stifle a smile; he had heard the same offer from many neighbors. "Thank you, Ma'am, but they'll be our guests this evening." Turned out the "move" was an arrest for running a meth lab, right here on Main Street! It seems the crooks did not know much about small towns. The neighbors had noticed the strange traffic pattern right away and called in the cops. Then, in true neighborly fashion, they offered their home as an observation point where the police could gather evidence.

The sheriff later said that small towns are a bad place for drug dealers to set up because all the neighbors have nothing better to do than check on just what they're up to. Thank goodness for nosy neighbors.

FROM WAGON TRAINS TO AIRPLANES

Frank Wesselius

Thomas O. Jenkins, born 1838 in Tennessee, came across the plains in a covered wagon with his parents Willis and Elizabeth Jenkins in 1844. The Jenkins family first settled in the Willamette Valley, then moved to Klickitat County in April 1859.

Thomas, "Uncle Tommy," was well known in the Klickitat area as he owned one the first ferries across the Columbia River at Columbus that he operated for over 30 years. He also owned a saw mill in Wahkiakus and farmed near Rush Soda Springs. He was a staunch Methodist, attending the same church in Goldendale for over 60 years.

When a biplane came to the Klickitat County Fair in the early 1920s, the pilot offered to take folks for a ride in his wonderful new flying machine. Uncle Tommie wanted desperately to try one of the funny looking machines. Friends and neighbors took up a purse to give Jenkins a ride in the airplane. The pilot took Tom all over the Simcoe Mountains clear to Mt. Adams and back, so he was able to see all the back country, mountains, and valleys that he had hunted and trapped in for 60 years. When he arrived back at the fairgrounds, he got out of the airplane, strode across the grounds with his head held high, shoulders squared, and his long white beard parted by the wind. He exclaimed, "Now I have seen it all, and I am ready to die."

Thomas died on January 11, 1924 in Goldendale after a short illness. A neighbor eulogized his passing with the following:

"One of the county's oldest settlers passed away with the death of Tommy Jenkins, known to many and liked by everyone who knew him. Righteousness, humility, honest, good will toward man personified — this was 'Uncle Tommy' not in words only, but in thought and deed; true religion, the reflection of good as far as it can be lived by man, was lived by him. This is sure the feeling of many, if not all of his acquaintances, and being convinced that Uncle Tommy is receiving his heavenly reward will console his many friends."

Thomas Jenkins had traveled by wagon train and oxen, horse, foot, boat, automobile, and airplane during his lifetime.

Family lore
Writing on back of a photo at
Klickitat County Historical Society

WAKEMAP MOUND

Mary Jean Lord

"The nativs of this village re[ce]ived] me verry kindly, one of whome invited me into his house, which I found to be large and comodious, and the first wooden houses in which Indians have lived Since we left those in the vicinity of Illinois, they are scattered permiscuisly on a elivated Situation near a mound of about 30 feet above the Common leavel, which mound has ...every appearance of being artificial." (Journal of William Clark, from Seeking Western Waters, by Emory and Ruth Strong.)

The natives who welcomed Clark were WishXam people, and they called their village Nixluidix. It is one of the oldest continuously inhabited villages in the world. Native Americans have lived and fished here for 10,000 to 11,000 years.

Nixluidix was located on the present site of Columbia Hills State Park, below Celilo Falls, at the head of the Long Narrows, where the half-mile wide Columbia River suddenly turned sideways and forced its way through a 240-foot wide channel in the basalt. Fishing stations, placed at different heights to take advantage of fluctuating water levels, lined the rocks along both sides of the Narrows.

The artificial mound was Wakemap Mound. It contained the accumulated refuse of thousands of years. Between 1953 and 1958, researchers raced to excavate it against the rising flood waters behind The Dalles Dam, but were only able to uncover part of the mound. They found trade goods in the top layers, and objects thousands of years old in the lowest layers. The precise age of Wakemap Mound is a controversy that may never be resolved.

Nixluidix was a great trade mart where thousands of natives gathered to exchange goods and ideas. The WishXam, together with their relatives the Wasco, who lived on the other side of the river, were the most important people on the Columbia River. They were the gatekeepers of the Columbia, the middle men. They were shrewd traders who commanded the respect of everyone.

The WishXam-Wasco were Chinookan. They were the translators between the Chinookan-speaking Coastal Indians and the Plateau Indians upriver, who spoke Sahaptin dialects. The Klickitats and other local Sahaptin people brought meat, roots, and berries to trade. Distant Sahaptins, especially the Nez Perces, who traded with Plains Indians, brought skin clothing, horses, and buffalo meat.

The main trade item of the Wasco/WishXam was salmon, which they caught, dried, pounded into flour and preserved in baskets lined with salmon skin. Lewis and Clark reported seeing tons of dried salmon "stacked like cordwood" near Celilo Falls and the Narrows. They also had shells and *dentalium* and prized European goods, such as copper pots, glass beads, and cloth uniforms obtained from coastal Indians, who had traded with the crews of passing ships. (*Dentalium* is the shell of a tiny creature that lives on rocks in deep water off the western coast of Vancouver Island. Extremely difficult to harvest, it was highly valued and used as money.)

The people came from far away, speaking many languages. Even traditional enemies of the Wasco/WishXam, like the Nez Perce, came to trade, and warfare was rare. The result was a fertile exchange of culture, ideas, art, and artifacts.

Native Americans in the Northwest were among the most prosperous on the continent, and the WishXam-Wasco were the wealthiest of all. Their culture was highly evolved. Archeologists recovered ground stone implements, beads, finely carved antler and bone animal figures, from the mounds and nearby cremation and grave sites. Petroglyphs decorated the basalt cliffs surrounding Nixluidix like paintings in an art gallery.

Tragically, only a few of the masterpieces in this "Petroglyph Canyon" could be removed in time. Wakemap and other mounds were covered over by the water. Sites that remained above water level have long since been robbed of their treasures and historical meaning by highway and railroad fills and by amateur collectors. Today, though Wakemap has vanished, Tsagaglalal, "She-Who-Watches," the stone guardian of the WishXam people, still looks out sadly from her perch above the drowned village.

Emory and Ruth Strong, *Seeking Western Waters*, Oregon Historical Society Press, 1995;

Emory Strong, Editor, *"Wakemap Mound: A Stratified Site on the Columbia River"*;

"Indians in Washington," published by office of Secretary of Washington State (no date)

WANT A CIGAR?

Frank Wesselius

Uncle Tommy Jenkins was a member of the 1859ers that were the first white settlers to come to the Klickitat area and stay. While he was operating a ferryboat across the Columbia River at Columbus, he owned a small farm on the stage road between Columbus and Goldendale, just above Fruit Flat. On this "plantation" he grew amongst his fruits and vegetables the only crop of tobacco raised in early Klickitat County. His farm is now part of the Sam Hill estate. Some said he learned to grow tobacco in Kentucky before moving to the Northwest, but there is no known history of the Jenkins family growing tobacco, and Tom left that part of the country when he was six years old.

He processed his tobacco into large chocolate-brown stogies and smoked them incessantly. The cigars were also used for barter and for his own amusement. When stage drivers and drummers came along, Tom would trade a stogie for goods, services, or freight charges. His amusement was when he gave them to the unaware, who did not realize the exceptional fortitude it took to smoke one of his homemade cigars. He would laugh and slap his sides with great amusement as the recipients would cough and wheeze while trying to finish these potent cigars.

Family lore

Ballou, Robert. 1938. *Early Klickitat Valley Days*. The Goldendale Sentinel.

Ballou, Robert. 1934. Early Experiments in Klickitat County with Tobacco Raising and Manufacture. *The Goldendale Sentinel*. Nov 22.

Wash Day Blues

Rachel Gunkel

While the hard life of local pioneers is well documented, many people do not realize that the drudgery of daily life continued nearly unchanged for decades. Not until rural electrification reached the small communities and farms of Klickitat County in the 1940s did the labor of running a household ease. The lack of a dependable domestic water supply was one factor that made home life difficult. Many families had wells, but obtaining water from them was a tricky business. Water was brought to the surface by hand pump, gas-powered pump, or windmill. In Maryhill, the most common method of pumping water was by windmill. On those days "without a particle of wind," the homeowner could dip a bucket into the well and haul up enough water for household use, but outdoor irrigation just had to wait.

Worse than a windless day was a dry well. This occurred fairly regularly in Maryhill, as wells tended to be shallow and the water table fluctuated with the seasons. Wells were often dry in winter, when the level of the Columbia River was low. "Dry!" moaned a column in *The Goldendale Sentinel* in February 1915. "Yes, all the wells at Columbus are dry as can be and the river is at the lowest it has been for years ...". When a well went dry, a family either had to trust that some precipitation would fall or carry water from the closest spring.

Doing the family laundry was the most dreaded of household chores, particularly when the weather was bad. Standing outside in winter weather while stirring the clothes in a tub of water over an outdoor fire was a backbreaking job. After being washed, clothes had to be rinsed free of soap, wrung out by hand, and hung up to dry. Clothes were usually hung out on porches, where they would be protected from becoming still wetter by rain or snowfall.

Rosa Gunkel summarized the situation in a letter written in January 1928: "The well is dry and the river frozen out quite a way, with six or eight inches of snow on the ground. I melted snow all morning, so I can have some water to wash with tomorrow. We will have to melt snow for drinking too, for we cannot go to the spring through all this snow."

Not until the arrival of electric power could the residents of rural Klickitat County do more than dream about the advantages already enjoyed by town folk: kitchen sinks and bathtubs with hot and cold running water, and that most coveted of modern conveniences—the electric wringer washing machine.

"From Maryhill" column, *The Goldendale Sentinel*, February 4, 1915 p.1; Letters of Rosa S. Gunkel, 1925-1928

WASHOUT RAPIDS

Carol Basse and Mary Jean Lord

Saturday morning, July 8, 1995, Carol Basse, Klickitat County PUD meter reader, and five other women put their rafts in the water at Mack's Canyon on the Deschutes River, Oregon. The sky was overcast, but the weather didn't look too bad, and they thought it would clear up. They knew every inch of the Lower Deschutes, having rafted it many times before. The rapids in this part of the river were gentle, and they were looking forward to a pleasant weekend together.

The first day they floated to the campground at Harris Canyon. They had just set up their tents when it started to rain, hard. The weather cleared just long enough for them to eat dinner. They went to bed early.

All that night it rained and the wind blew. The next morning when Carol crawled out of her tent, "Our four rafts were still tied and in the same place as the evening before. Only one thing was different. The river had changed to a dark chocolate brown …dark chocolate pudding brown."

The women were camped in a roadless section of the Deschutes. Their only way out was floating down the river. With hindsight, Carol says their wisest course would have been to stay put, miserable as it was. Instead, they decided to get out as fast as possible. They packed their wet gear and rowed out into the river. They didn't realize that this was no ordinary storm.

The river was running high, fast and muddy, the rain so hard they could hardly see. They floated quickly through stretches they normally had to row. Suddenly, above Free Bridge, they came upon a large, brand-new rapid. Carol found herself looking down into a five-foot hole separating the two parts of the rapid and pushed river right as hard as she could. Somehow all four rafts made it through safely. The new rapids, dubbed Washout Rapids, had formed when a huge slide of rain-loosened rocks and earth washed down to dam the Deschutes.

Adrenaline flowing, the rafters pulled over into an eddy to calm down and wait for the rain to slacken. In twenty minutes the water in the eddy rose six inches. The railroad trestle had washed out and rocks and debris covered the tracks. As soon as visibility improved enough to proceed, they hurried on down the river, anxious to report the track damage and stop any trains from starting up the river.

The wind and rains of the July 1995 storm did millions of dollars of damage in Klickitat County and Oregon. Carol and her friends would never forget the day they discovered Washout Rapids.

Ruralite Sept 95 p 33
Carol Basse's personal experience

WATER WITCHING

Mary Anne Enyeart

Wells are an important part of every rural home. Where to dig for water has always been a good question, and sometimes residents consult a water witcher to seek an answer. Not everyone has the gift of water witching. According to local lore, the water witcher takes a recently cut fork of a willow tree or bush, bends it like a wishbone, and walks around the property holding it firmly with the willow stick parallel to the ground. When the willow branch tips towards the ground with a strong tug, a vein of water is assumed to be underfoot. As the water witcher walks past the water vein, the branch rises again to its normal position. Some witchers today use copper wires instead of a willow branch.

Alvin Randall of Centerville tells the following story. A High Prairie landowner in the early 1940s contacted Joe Diver, a local water witcher, to come and locate a well site for them. Joe was known for having witched many local wells. He took his willow stick, walked across the property, and found a promising site, although it was down a draw and some distance from the house. The well was dug, and it did yield some water. Time passed and the property was sold more than once. The small amount of water and the distance it had to be pumped concerned the landowners. Each new owner wanted more water and had another well dug. However, these expensive new wells usually came up with less water or none at all. The most recent owners decided they would go back to the first well and have it tested. Putting a pump into the well to test it and pumping all night, they were amazed at the amount of water the original well gave. The water witcher had known best after all.

Interview with Alvin Randall

THE WELDON WAGON TRAIL

Keith McCoy

In 1908 two Husum orchardists, Elwin Weldon and Henry Hyndman, bought four sections of land on the Snowden plateau. The proposed orchard expansion was clearly visible from Husum, but distant by existing roads. To reach it, they had to go to White Salmon, then out Snowden Road, a distance of more than twelve miles.

They petitioned Klickitat County for a new road of approximately three miles to reach the new property.

The county had no money for more roads but did agree to assist with surveys and right-of-way arrangements.

Road construction depended on the money, labor, and sweat of those who would use the road. It served well until 1923 when the present Sanborn Road was pushed northward from the Snowden Road, and then it was abandoned.

The extremely scenic route afforded grand views of Mount Adams, Mount Hood, and the White Salmon Valley backed by the Cascades. This route was accepted for development as part of the Klickitat County trails system. The project was carried out by Dan Jagelski of the County Engineer's department.

I was asked to give a dedicatory talk about the new trail. We expected only a few to show up for the ceremony, but more than 130 people were there, including two hiking clubs from Portland that had come to be among the first to enjoy the Weldon Wagon Trail.

THE WESTERN MEADOWLARK

Kathleen Goode

One of my favorite birds is the Western Meadowlark. It is a popular bird, having been named the state bird of Kansas, Montana, Nebraska, North Dakota, Oregon and Wyoming. My own infatuation with it started at sunrise one fall morning. I was returning home after an all-night quilt-in at a friend's house. My windows were rolled down to enjoy the crisp cold air — all the better to keep me from getting drowsy on the trip. My pace was slower than usual because it was one of those magical mornings when everything is covered with frost; after a long, dusty summer, it was a sight to be savored.

I heard it before seeing it — flutelike notes that were as clear and beautiful as the surroundings. The little whistler was sitting on a fence post and didn't seem at all disturbed when I stopped my car for a moment. Maybe it wasn't quite awake yet, because I've never been able to get that close to one since then. I was completely smitten.

The western meadowlark is related to blackbirds but is much more musical and colorful. The bird is 6 to 10 inches long and has a yellow throat, chest, and belly. There is a distinct V pattern on the chest, if you can get close enough to see it. The rest of the bird is black and brown. Meadowlarks nest on the ground, living on a diet of insects and seeds. They build their nests by weaving bits of dried grasses into living vegetation. The nest is cup shaped and often includes a partial cover or even an entrance tunnel. The male western meadowlark normally has two mates; the females do all the incubation and brooding. The best way to find a meadowlark is to stop near any open grassland and just sit still and listen.

Personal observations

Western Meadowlark All About Birds by the Cornell Lab of Ornithology.

http://www.birds.cornell.edu/programs/AllAboutBirds/BirdGuide/Western-Meadowlark_d... , Western Meadowlark

http://www.gpnc.org/western.htm

WHEAT FARMING HISTORY

Beverly and Dick Wheelhouse

Wheat farming has been an important industry in Klickitat County since 1870, when John Burgen raised the first successful crop south of Goldendale. In the early years, grain was hauled by horses and ferry to The Dalles to be ground into flour by the gristmill there. In the 1880s, steam-powered threshing machines arrived in the county. A gristmill was built in Goldendale in 1878.

The first wheat shipped from the county was hauled by horse-drawn wagons to the Columbia River, where steamboats took it to Portland. Later, the Oregon Railroad and Navigation Co. built a spur line at Grants, Oregon, so wheat could be ferried across the river and then hauled on the railroad. In 1903 the railroad came to Goldendale through Lyle, Klickitat, and Centerville, which eliminated the long haul by wagon to the river.

By the 1930s, the days of threshing machines and steam engine had almost passed. A combine pulled by many teams of horses moved over the fields, making the job of harvest easier. The next improvement was the invention of the tractor to pull the combine. The horse days of farming drew to a close rapidly. In the 1950s, self propelled combines were made. The threshing principle remained much the same, but with a different power source.

In recent years some farmers, especially those in the eastern part of the county, have experimented with no-till farming. "No-till" is a system for planting crops without plowing, using herbicides to control weeds and resulting in reduced soil erosion.

Today, Klickitat County grain is shipped to Portland terminals by truck, railroad, and barge from elevators in Roosevelt, Goldendale, and Biggs, Oregon. In 2004, a total of 42,830 acres of wheat land was in production in Klickitat County, despite the land enrolled in government programs such as the Conservation Reserve Program (CRP).

Legal descriptions of land in the west are based on ranges, townships and sections — and often they are easier to understand if you read them from back to front. Meridians and base lines set the ranges and townships.

Klickitat County is northeast of its Principle Meridian, Willamette Meridian, which is in Portland, Oregon. From that point, township lines are located every six miles going north, and range lines are located every six miles going east. These lines form a grid of six-mile-square sections called townships. Each township requires two numbers to describe it: the township number (the number of squares north of the meridian) and the range number (the number of squares east of the meridian). Klickitat County contains townships 2 to 6 north (T2N - T6N) and ranges 10 to 23 east (R10E - R23E). For example, the Goldendale Library is in Township 4N and Range 16E. This means that it is located in the township that is 4 sections north of the east/west meridian and 16 sections east of the north/south base line.

The townships are divided into 36 one-square-mile sections of approximately 640 acres. These are numbered starting with 1 in the northeast corner, moving along the north boundary to 6, then dropping south for 7 and running east to 12. This snaking numbering continues to the southern boundary with 36 in the southeast corner. The Goldendale Library is in Section 20.

Sections are divided into quarters: NW, NE, SW, SE. For a land description, these quarters are further divided by quarters and halves down to five-acre

WHERE'S THAT? RANGES, TOWNSHIPS AND SECTIONS

Mary Anne Enyeart and Sara Wu

6	5	4	3	2	1
7	8	9	10	11	12
18	17	16	15	14	13
19	20	21	22	23	24
30	29	28	27	26	25
31	32	33	34	35	36

Township divided into sections

NW 1/4 of NW 1/4	NE 1/4 of NW 1/4	NE 1/4 = 160 acres	
SW 1/4 of NW 1/4	SE 1/4 of NW 1/4		
N 1/2 of SW 1/4		W 1/2 of SE 1/4	E 1/2 of SE 1/4
S 1/2 of SW 1/4			

Subdivision of a Section

parcels. In sub-divisions such as towns, Additions, Blocks, and Lots are designated. The Goldendale Library, being in a town, is described as Lots 10,11,12, Block 33, Central Addition.

Outside of a town, for example, the Stonehenge Memorial Park is in the northeast quarter of Section 4, Township 2 North, Range 16 East, and the southeast quarter of Section 33, Township 3 North, Range 16 East. This reduces to: T2N R16E (4)NE4 and T3N R16E (33)SE4.

Many of these divisions are imperfect, since they are based on perfectly flat land. Hills make the lines longer. Some of this slack, especially along rivers, is taken up by government lots, which are irregular to allow for a more regular layout around it.

The 1785 Continental Congress adopted this rectangular system that is used by surveyors today. The federal government designated that sections 16 and 36 of townships were to be used for schools. Proceeds from either the sale of the land or a commodity produced, such as timber, would be used for designated schools. Railroads were financed with other parcels. Both these institutions have traded some of their land for other parcels or sold them, sometimes retaining mineral rights, so the pattern is becoming less regular.

Ron Nelson of Klickitat County Title Company
Manual of Surveying Instruction, 1947
Standard Atlas of Klickitat County Washington, 1913, 1994.

WHITE CREEK GRANGE

Marlene Nygaard as told to
Mary Anne Enyeart

Around Bickleton during most of the 1900s, the Granges were vital, busy social and community organizations. Many good times were shared by Grangers and their families.

Sometime between 1935 and 1940, Sybil Kelly, Emma Schrantz, Marlene Schrantz Nygaard, Maude Binns, and Flora Kelly were cleaning the White Creek Grange hall. Emma opened the piano, and a whole family of mice leaped out and scattered around the hall. Emma yelled, "Mice!" and everyone chased after them, yelling at the top of their lungs — except Flora Kelly, who did her yelling perched on a chair.

Can't say Grangers don't have fun!

After serving in World War II and while pursuing an engineering degree, Hulan Whitson realized education was the field he actually preferred. Almost immediately after graduation in 1949 from Southeastern State Teachers College, Hulan and his wife, Berneice, headed West from Oklahoma in a brand new car that was not fully paid for!

They investigated jobs all over the Northwest without success until they stopped in Goldendale, where they met with the County Superintendent of Schools. There was an opening in the small community of Trout Lake, at the base of Mt Adams. They immediately went to meet with the superintendent and school board. Both Whitsons were asked to apply the next day, which they did.

They were in the classroom for the opening of school in Trout Lake just a few days later. Hulan taught seventh and eighth grade, and Berneice taught fourth and fifth. They both loved living and working in the Trout Lake Valley where they made many lifelong friends. They taught for two years in Trout Lake, then Hulan was offered a position as part-time teacher and principal at the junior high in the White Salmon School District — an opportunity too good to pass up. The Whitsons moved to White Salmon in the summer of 1951.

Hulan's career in administration and Berneice's in motherhood blossomed. After five years, Hulan moved to the high school as principal, and in 1959 he became the elementary school principal, where he remained until his death in 1970. During his last two years, he had a dual role as Elementary Principal and Assistant Superintendent of Schools for White Salmon.

At home, Hulan loved to maintain a large vegetable garden. It was quite common to see him working in the garden, cajoling neighborhood youngsters to help. He was also proud of raising and training German Shorthair bird hunting dogs.

Hulan's untimely death occurred on October 17th, 1970, while hunting turkeys east of Bingen on Burdoin Mountain. He was an avid hunter and fisherman, so he was doing what he most enjoyed till the very end.

In the spring of 1971, the School Board honored Hulan and his family by naming the White Salmon elementary school the Hulan L. Whitson Elementary School. Hulan had positively touched many lives

HULAN L. WHITSON, EDUCATOR

Hugh and Michael Whitson

through in his career in education. He was a warm, compassionate human being not afraid to make the hard decisions his positions called for. Everyone who knew Hulan had nothing but the utmost respect for him and his ways of dealing with both students and adults.

Family knowledge

WILD TURKEYS

Jerry Wilson

They stand around looking confused, muttering incoherently. They might have the odor of intoxicants on their breath. They are dressed in camouflage. They bow their heads in shame. They utter foul words. They are turkey hunters.

Efforts to introduce wild turkeys into Washington began in the early 1900s. Since 1960, when the first wild-trapped turkeys were introduced from New Mexico, Arizona, and Wyoming, turkeys have maintained naturally reproducing populations in Washington. Klickitat County has one of the largest turkey populations in the state.

Recreational interest in the wild turkey has increased along with the populations. The number of turkey hunters in Washington has increased from 689 in 1984 to over 15,000 in 2004, according to the Washington Department of Fish and Wildlife.

Those turkey hunters spend a lot of money statewide and in Klickitat County. Their money is not just for guns, shells and clothing, but to make sure the turkey population growth continues. A lot of turkey hunters belong to the National Wild Turkey Federation. This group has spent money and volunteered countless hours working with the Washington Department of Fish and Wildlife to insure that this majestic bird is here to stay.

I was hunting in the area of the upper Klickitat about two years ago, during the spring hunt. It was overcast and threatened to rain. I had walked into an area that I knew held birds. I had on full camouflage to blend in. I selected a large pine tree and sat down beside it.

As soon as I made a yelp on my box call, I got an immediate response. It sounded like a mature bird and was headed my way. I called again, and again the tom answered. But then I heard a yelping sound behind me. My first thought was that I had wandered into some other hunter's setup. The yelping continued, so I slowly turned my head to see what was up, and I discovered a small hen turkey coming down the hill behind me. My intent was to harvest this tom; hers was, well, not the same as mine.

I decided to let the expert do the calling, and she did a fantastic job. He would gobble every time she yelped. Then he started booming with his wings. (This is when a tom expands his wings downward toward and into the dirt. It has a "vroom" sound.) He was coming in very fast. He was in heavy brush, so I really never saw him until he was under a large overhanging fir tree. There he was, but in heavy shade. I could not see a beard even though he was only 25 yards away. I could not see the color of his head. On a tom turkey, the colors can change from red to white to blue. It depends on how much love or hate he has in his heart. He did not strut; he did not gobble.

I knew this was the tom the hen had called in, but I could not pull the trigger until I knew for certain. I had the shotgun right on him, just waiting to confirm what I was sure of. The little hen was doing her part to help with the triangle. He and I were eye to eye for a good three minutes. Then he made his move. He turned around and walked back into the brush. As he got into the brush, he fanned his tail. I think he had just given me the bird, but not the way I wanted. I laughed, and the little hen took off, leaving me all alone.

I picked up my gear and headed home. I did not get a turkey, but was left with great memory.

Personal frustrations
Washington Dept. of Wildlife

WILDFLOWER SWATCHES

Sara Wu

The hills on the north side of the Columbia River are bare and brown for much of the year. Spring sun and rain transform these open spaces with a myriad of wildflowers, bringing swatches of stunning color to Klickitat County.

The progression of blooming begins in late February or early March. Especially at Catherine Creek State Park, the grass widows (*Sisyrinchium douglasii var. douglasii*) make a purple blanket over the fields. Soon many varieties of desert parsley (*Lomatium sp.*) bloom along the roads and up onto the hills, producing a yellow sheen over vast expanses. The Columbia desert parsley (Lomatium *columbianum*), found only in this area, punctuates the yellow mass with its mauve-purple flowers and silvery green foliage. Low to the ground, gold stars (*Crocidium multicaule*) make a brilliant yellow mat. Western buttercups (*Ranunculu occidentalis*) appear under the oaks and in the meadows. Especially near the edges of the forest, great patches of yellow glacier lilies (*Erythronium grandiflorum*) nod their heads.

By mid April, flowers bloom in impressive profusion. The most striking display is the northwest balsamroot (*Balsamorhiza deltoidea*). It adds an orange-yellow glow to the desert parsley, punctuated by white-to-pink phlox of various species. Just as you think it cannot get any more dramatic, the purple lupines (primarily *Lupinus latifolius* and later *Lupinus leucopsis*) appear. The latter blooms into May and June, giving many hillsides a purple hue after the yellow has faded.

Another grand show is the camas. The white death camas (*Zigadenus sp.*) blooms first, with many showy spikes dotting dry rocky soil. In April and May, populations of the edible blue camas (*Camassia quamash* and *leichtlinii*) fill damp depressions, fooling you into thinking that you are seeing ponds.

The California poppy (*Eschscholzia californica*) is often viewed as a weed, but it is a native plant. Since it only grows at low elevations here, it has not covered the hills as it does in California. The gravel put along the roadsides has spread the poppies along Highway 14 to delight motorists with a riot of orange from late April through May.

Many other flowers bloom profusely, adding their spots of color — the pinks of qua(*Lithophragma sp.*) and the reds of Indian paintbrush (*Castlillja sp.*). The penstemons (*Penstemon sp.*) grow in great pink-to-purple clumps. From March through May, these and many other flowers make it hard to be anyplace else **but** Klickitat County!

Haskin, Leslie. 1970. Wild Flowers of the Pacific Coast. Portland, OR: Binfords & Most.

Personal communication with Jerry Igo (2005).

Jolly, Russ. 1988. *Wildflowers of the Columbia Gorge*. Oregon Historical Society Press.

WINDWARD

Kathleen Goode

Windward is an intentional community with 131 acres of pasture and forest lands high above the Klickitat River. The members are self-reliant individuals dedicated to establishing and demonstrating sustainable systems. They have created a large garden and raise goats and sheep. Windward fleeces have won numerous awards at the Klickitat County Fair. The community has also solved water problems and experimented with geothermal heating and cooling systems, earth-sheltered design, solar refrigeration, and grid-tied electrical generation. They are currently working on converting forest waste into automobile fuel, and aquaponics — the simultaneous production of fish and vegetables in a self-contained system.

A wealth of information about the Windward community, their activities, and bylaws is available at their web site: www.windward.org. Their newsletters, which include an archive, are a wealth of information on sustainable living. Issue 64 includes information on how they set up Vermadise (a 20-by-40-foot structure optimized for growing earthworms), and details about their new solar woodshed. Past issues have dealt with water resources, fire danger, flooding, sheep, goats, a building collapse, and what to do before you take down a damaged building. The community has created a treasure for those who do not want to learn such things the hard way.

Windward web site

WINERIES IN KLICKITAT COUNTY

Teddy Cole

Signs pointing to wineries have sprung up along County roadsides. Neat rows of grapevines now flourish on land once dedicated to pasture or orchard. Klickitat County has added vineyards to its long agricultural history.

Unique combinations of climate and terrain determine the character of wine grapes. Klickitat

County spans two different American Viticultural Areas (AVA); the western and central sections are part of the Columbia Gorge AVA, a tiny area compared to the much larger Columbia Valley AVA that includes the eastern part of the county.

Listed below are the wineries in business at the end of 2004. Most are open daily, some have seasonal openings, and a few are by appointment only. New vineyards are being planted, and new wineries being built. More information is available on-line at Wines Northwest, www.winesnw.com

From West to East:

Wind River Cellars
196 Spring Creek Road
Husum

Syncline Wine Cellars
307 West Humboldt Street
Bingen

Columbia Gorge Winery, and
Klickitat Canyon Wines
6 Lyle-Snowden Road
Lyle

Marshal's Winery and Vineyard
150 Oak Creek Road
East of Dallesport, north side of Highway 14

Cascade Cliffs Winery and Vineyard
8866 Highway 14
East of Horsethief Lake

Maryhill Winery
Highway 14, four miles west of the Highway 97 Junction

Waving Tree Vineyard and Winery
2 Maryhill Highway.
Off Highway 97 at the north end of the
Sam Hill Bridge

Chateau Champoux (soon to be part of the Horse Heaven AVA)
524 Alderdale Road
Turn north from Highway 14

Tourists enjoying Klickitat County's spectacular scenery may now enhance their trip by sampling wines from end to end.

Wines Northwest, www.winesnw.com
Klickitat Wine Country, klickitatcounty.org/Tourism
Visitor's Guide to Klickitat County, Washington, Spring/
    Summer 2005. Great grape magic in a glass.

WISHRAM CHAPEL CAR

Mary Jean Lord

Early in the 20th Century, the railroad owned a beautiful chapel car that was sent all over the United States, stopping for a few days or weeks at small, isolated places where there was no church. Wishram folks liked the car so much, they conspired to keep it permanently.

Ed Hayes, the car department foreman, slapped a "Bad Order" on the car, which meant the equipment needed repairs and couldn't be moved until it was safe. Whenever Ed or Tim Moriarty, the road master, received an inquiry about the car, they explained the Bad Order and offered assurances it would be fixed as soon as possible.

People had to cross many busy tracks to get to church, which was dangerous and inconvenient. Ed, Tim and businessman George Bunn got together to resolve the problem. "I'll donate the lot to put it on if you two can figure a way to get it there," George said. Soon, a track was laid to the lot, the chapel car was moved to it, and the track was dismantled, leaving no evidence it had ever been.

One day a letter came asking help in locating a lost car. It was important that it be found because it was the chapel car, and the railroad had decided to retire it and place it in a memorial park in Chicago.

The men had to confess. When officials arrived they were astounded to find the car settled far from the tracks and in constant use. After much discussion they decided to leave it in Wishram where it was needed.

When a new church was built, the altar, communion rail and pews from the old car were set up in it. New members wanted to install new furnishings, but the old-timers wouldn't hear of it.

Florence Bartholomew, *"The Early Days of Wishram,"*
    Ruralite, April 1963

WISHRAM ROAD

Mary Jean Lord

At first, the only road to Wishram was the railroad. The town was built close to the railroad at the junction where trains on the north-south trunk line along the Deschutes River connected with the main east-west tracks along the Columbia. Until the S.P.&S. Railroad bridge was finished in 1908, trains running "the Trunk" from Bend were ferried across the Columbia to a spot east of Wishram. The ferry, *Normal*, had tracks laid on its deck and could carry one engine and four cars.

The railroad didn't go to points north. Folks wanted to be able to get to Maryhill and Goldendale, and a narrow wagon road was built up the hill. The Model Ts everyone drove couldn't make it up the steepest pitches without help, so it was standard procedure for passengers to pile out and push.

Florence Bartholomew, *"The Early Days of Wishram,"*
Ruralite, Ap. 1963

WOMAN'S ASSOCIATION OF GOLDENDALE

Teddy Cole

The Woman's Association of Goldendale organized at a meeting June 10, 1912, held at the Methodist Church. Following passage of a motion "that a permanent organization for the uplift of Goldendale be formed," they voted to invite presidents of all women's societies in town to become vice-presidents of the new association.

After the organizational details, the women moved on to the next items of business: to establish a library and appoint a library committee to supervise its operation. By May 2, 1913, the Association had raised enough money to buy the lots where the library now stands. When the library building was completed, the Association met in one of its rooms until 1939, when they were able to buy the clubhouse located on the corner of Columbus and Broadway. In addition to their meetings, they held community receptions and dinners in the clubhouse and earned income by renting it to other organizations.

In 1928, the Woman's Association sponsored the formation of the Torch Honor Society, which later became affiliated with the National Honor Society, in Goldendale High School. They served an annual Honor Society banquet and presented pins to graduating members. The Association also gave at least one scholarship each year.

October 14, 1958 the Woman's Association, together with the federated clubs in the Mid-Columbia District, sponsored the organization of the Klickitat County Historical Society. In 1962, under the leadership of President Bessie Hornibrook, the Association helped to secure the Presby Mansion for the Historical Society's headquarters and museum. The many other entries in the Woman's Association's yearbooks show that virtually no aspect of civic life was untouched by their activities.

As membership declined, the women could no longer afford to maintain their clubhouse, and it was sold. In 1997, after eighty-five years of service to the community, the Woman's Association disbanded.

Cultural institutions don't "just happen." Far-sighted individuals build them, usually volunteering their expertise and talents, in order to create a hometown they can be proud of. The work of the Goldendale Woman's Association — their vision to see a need and their will to create a solution — is a testimony to the way livable communities are created.

Association records, on file at Klickitat County Historical Society

---

Woodland School #21

Joan Wilkins Stone

Nellie Jackson Schuster began first grade in 1922. She walked a short distance up Woodland Road and crossed Highway 97 to attend the one-room school house. She had plenty of company; brothers Leo and Otis and sister Vera.

Nellie's teacher was Gladys Jensen Beeks, who was only a few years older than some of the students. Mrs. Beeks taught all the grades, 1 through 8. She carried out all the janitorial duties, pumped and carried water to the schoolhouse, and split the wood to heat the pot-bellied stove. If she was lucky, a parent would stop by and split and carry some wood into the school.

Students were tended to one grade at a time. They might be asked to come to the front of the room and recite a poem, read aloud, or spell their assigned words. Math class always included work at the blackboard.

Students from the other grades worked quietly at their desks. Nellie remembers few discipline problems. The older students were asked to tutor the younger ones when needed.

Recess was outdoors in all types of weather. All ages played together. No one had a bat, so they used a board when playing baseball. A favorite activity was walking on top of the 1-inch wide board fence that enclosed the schoolhouse. "I guess we thought we were tightrope walkers."

Excitement abounded when the snow came. The hillside next to the school was steep enough to give quite a thrill on the way down, whether it was on a wooden sled, an inner tube, or an old tire.

The children packed their lunches to school, except for the Jacksons. They lived too close to the schoolhouse. "I was deprived because I had to go home for lunch; I would tell my Mom 'no, not beans again!'" said Nellie.

Nellie, as well as other Woodland School students Nellie Tallman Foster and Wilma Tallman Bane, still lives in Goldendale. Gladys Jensen Beeks continued teaching in the Goldendale Public Schools and taught many of the children and grandchildren of the Woodland School students.

Interview with Nellie Jackson Schuster

YELLOW BELLS

Kathleen Goode

The yellow bell, *Fritillaria pudica*, is a petite wild flower that grows in sagebrush and ponderosa pine ecosystems. In Klickitat County it can be found near Rowland Lake in the Columbia Gorge, in Wakiacum Canyon, along Mill Creek Ridge, the southern foothills of the Simcoe Mountains, and in upper elevations of the Columbia Hills. Sometimes referred to as Mission bell, it is one of the flowers cataloged by Lewis and Clark.

Each stem stands 2 to 6 inches tall, usually with just a single bell shaped flower gracefully inclining its head. These blossoms are bright sunshine yellow with a deep red basal band that spreads as the flowers age. Each flower is 1/2 to 3/4 inch long. The species name, pudica, means "modest." A close relative is the Checker lily, *Fritillaria affinis*. Bulbs of both these plants were used as a food source by Native Americans.

Yellow bells can sometimes be purchased at native plant nurseries, such as Milestones in Lyle. They are fairly difficult to propagate and transplant, so it may be best to visit them in their natural habitat.

Lyons, C.P. *Wildflowers of Washington, 2nd edition.* Renton, WA: Lone Pine Publishing, 1999.
Idaho Mountain Wildflowers http://wwwllarkspurbooks.com/Lily3.html

On a Sighting Near Murdock

ZEBRA

Numerous beasts make this place their abode.
Grazing along by the side of the road,
Bison and emus and zebras we've seen —
Even, sometimes, along Highway 14!

Teddy Cole

SELECTED BIBLIOGRAPHY

Alt, David. *Glacial Lake Missoula and its Humongous Floods*. Missoula MT: Mountain Press, 2001.

Ballou, Robert. *Early Klickitat Valley Days*. Evansville IN: Windmill Publications, 1997.

Bartholomew, Florence. "Pucker Huddle and why." *Ruralite magazine*, Dec. 1964.

Bleakney, Darlene Highsmith. *Dalles Mountain Ranch, museum of natural and cultural heritage of the east Columbia River Gorge*. Dalles Mountain Press, c1992. Reprinted by Salem OR: Lynx Communication Group, Inc., [2000].

Bunnell, Clarence Orvel. *Legends of the Klickitats, a Klickitat version of the story of the bridge of the gods*. Shaumburg IL: Metropolitan Press, 1933.

Collier, Penny. *Along the Mt. Adams Trail*. Maranatha Press, c1979.

Donaldson, Ivan J. *Fishwheels of the Columbia*. Portland OR: Binfords & Mort, [c1971].

Elmer, Jeffrey. *Trout Lake, Washington, historical & biographical information: newspaper articles, family stories, biographies*. Compiled and published by Jeffrey L. Elmer, Portland OR, [1998].

Fleming, Nelia Binford. *Sketches of Early High Prairie*. Portland OR: Binfords & Mort, [1949].

Guthrie, Woody, *Columbia River Collection*. Cambridge MS: Rounder Records Corporation, CD 1036, 1987.

Hill, D. Herman. *Finn Ridge chronicles*. Finn Ridge Arts, c2002.

Hill, Edwin G. *In the Shadow of the Mountain*. Pullman WA: Washington State University Press, 1990.

Hines, Donald. *Where the River Roared: The Wishom Tales*. Issaquah WA: Great Eagle Pub., c1998.

Hunn, Eugene S. Nch'i-wana, *"The Big River": Mid-Columbia Indians and Their Land*. Seattle WA: University of Washington Press, c1990.

An Illustrated History of Klickitat, Yakima and Kittitas Counties; with an outline of the early history of the state of Washington. Crete IL: Interstate Pub. Co., 1904.

Jolley, Russ. *Wildflowers of the Columbia Gorge: a comprehensive field guide*. Portland OR: Oregon Historical Society Press, 1988.

Klickitat PUD Ruralite magazine. http://www.klickpud.com.

Klickitat County 1999 street guide. Goldendale WA: Klickitat County, [1999].

Klickitat County Historical Society, *Klickitat heritage*. (Serial). Goldendale WA.

Ladiges, Jerry. *Glenwood: formerly Camas Prairie.* Glenwood WA: Ladiges, c1978.

Larson, Wanda. Biography of a Library. *Ruralite magazine.* August 1963.

Lyons, C.P. *Wildflowers of Washington: a Lone Pine Field Guide,* 2nd edition revised. Renton WA: Lone Pine Publishing, 1999.

Lyons, C. P. and Bill Merilees. *Trees, Shrubs & Flowers to Know in Washington & British Columbia.* Redmond WA, Vancouver BC and Edmonton AB: Lone Pine Publishing, 1995.

Mattson, Louise. *Centerville Finns, Klickitat County, Washington.* Finnish Lutheran Church, Portland OR: Finnish American Historical Society of the West, 1977.

May, Pete, Ed. *History of Klickitat County.* Goldendale WA: Klickitat County Historical Society, 1982.

May, Pete. *100 golden years, 1872-1972; a 1972 look at the history of Goldendale, Washington, at the end of its first century.* Goldendale WA: Goldendale Centennial Corp., [1972].

McCoy, Keith. *The Mount Adams country: Forgotten Corner of the Columbia River Gorge.* White Salmon WA: Pahto Publications, c1987.

McCoy, Keith. *Rowdy river: the wild and scenic White Salmon.* Victoria BC: Trafford, c2002.

McWhorter, Lucullus Virgil. *"Tragedy of the Wahk-shum: Death of Andrew J. Bolon Yakima Indian Agent."* Donald M. Hines, Ed., Issaquah WA: Great Eagle Publishing, Inc., 1994.

Metsker, Charles Frederick. *Metsker's atlas of Klickitat County Washington.* Seattle WA: Metsker Maps.

Neils, Selma M. *So this is Klickitat.* Published for the Klickitat Woman's Club by Shaumburg IL: Metropolitan Press for the Klickitat Woman's Club, 1967.

Oregon Archaeology Society. *Wakemap mound: and nearby sites on the Long Narrows of the Columbia River.* Edited by Emory Strong. Portland OR: Binford & Mort, 1976.

Ramsey, Guy Reed. *Postmarked Washington, Klickitat, Benton & Franklin counties.* Goldendale WA: Klickitat County Historical Society, 1977.

Roberts, Wilma. *Celilo Falls: Remembering thunder.* The Dalles OR: Wasco County Historical Museum, 1997.

"Roll On, Columbia." Eugene OR: University of Oregon, 2000. Documentary video.

Ruby, Robert H. *Ferryboats on the Columbia River, including the bridges and dams.* Superior NE: Superior Pub. Co., [1974].

Ruby, Robert H. and John A. Brown. *A Guide to the Indian Tribes of the Pacific Northwest, revised edition.* Norman OK: University of Oklahoma Press, 1992.

Schlick, Mary Dodds. *Columbia River basketry : gift of the ancestors, gift of the earth.* Seattle WA: University of Washington Press, c2002.

Standard atlas of Klickitat County, Washington: including a plat book of the villages, cities and townships of the county, map of the state, United States and world, patrons directory, reference business directory and departments devoted to general information, analysis of U.S. land surveys, digest of the system of civil government, etc., etc. Geo. A. Ogle & Co., 1913.

Strong, Emory M. *Stone Age on the Columbia River.* Portland OR: Binfords & Mort, 1967, c1959.

Tuhy, John E. *Sam Hill: the prince of Castle Nowhere.* Portland OR: Timber Press, 1983.

Ulrich, Roberta. *Empty nets: Indians, dams, and the Columbia River.* Corvallis OR: Oregon State University Press, 1999.

Vincent, Hubert C. *Bigger pastures.* W. Vincent, c1992.

For more books about Klickitat County, check the on-line catalog of the Fort Vancouver Regional Library, at http://www.fvrl.org/.

Also see Jeffrey Elmer's website,
http://homepages.rootsweb.com/~westklic/
and choose "Printed Reference Material."

LIST OF CONTRIBUTORS

Nancy Allen	Ray Gosney	Bob Rising
James Allyn	Rachel Gunkel	Marie Ritter
Bev Anderson	D. Herman Hill	Don Ritzchke
Pat Arnold	Harold Hill	George Rohrbacher
Judy Bane	Roberta Hoctor	Alexander Rush-Hallak
Nancy Barron	Gladys Hodges	Clay Schuster
Carol Basse	Patricia Horn	Barbara Sexton
Tom Beck	Bruce Howard	M.L."Charlie" Shattuck
Becky Migaki Beeks	Marty Hudson	Icey Sheeran
Bonnie Beeks	Michelle Krause-Cooper	Patricia Smith
June Boardman	Marjorie LaFond	Michael W. Steinbock
Joy Bradley	Meg Letterman	Toni Stencil
Ruth Miles Bruns	Rita J. Liska	Joan Wilkins Stone
Robert Bush	Mary Jean Lord	Judi Strait
Bruce Cameron	Sam Lowry	Douglas L. Taylor
Jon L. Carlson	Joy Markgraf	Joan Telford
Darla Carratt-Hoff	Keith McCoy	Judy Thomas
Teddy Cole	Geneva M. Meyers	Jim Tindall
Robin Dobson	Jo N. Miles	Bob Van Alstine
Lozetta Doll	John Miller	Barbara Purser Voreis
Tom Doll	Mary Ann Miller	Wendy Warren
Eleanor Dooley	Lee Musgrave	Frank Wesselius
David C. Duncombe	Talia Norman	Beverly Wheelhouse
Bev Edwards	Marlene Nygaard	Dick Wheelhouse
Mary Anne Enyeart	Barbara Patterson	Hugh Whitson
Wayne Eshelman	Monte Pearson	Michael Whitson
Naomi Fisher	Alanna Powell	Jerry Wilson
Mark Gibson	Buzz Ramsey	Sara Wu
Kathleen Goode	Phil Reid	Tim Young
Sissy Gorgus	Bonnie Reynolds	

ILLUSTRATION CREDITS

page	picture	Artist / Source
5	Ballou photo	Klickitat County Historical Society
6	Balsamroot	Ann Parker
8	Bighorn Sheep	Joan Crice
11	Bitterroot	Arlene Larison
12	Blockhouse	Klickitat County Historical Society
13	Blockhouse pool	Darla Carratt-Hoff
16	Bolon Monument	Ann Parker
18	Elk	Joan Crice
18	Burgen House	Rick Stitt
21	Camas	Arlene Larison
26	Canoeing photo	Sara Wu
35	Queen Marie/Sam Hill	Maryhill Museum
43	Conboy Lake, Mt Adams	Ken Scarola
48	Irving Couse house	Klickitat County Historical Society
51	Coyote	Joan Crice
53	Dalles Mtn. Buttercup	Arlene Larison
59	William O. Douglas	Klickitat County Historical Society
71	Biggs Ferry	Klickitat County Historical Society
77	Sam Hill Ferry	Klickitat County Historical Society
79	Clay and Art Schuster	Charl Schuster
82	Hanging Rock	Klickitat County Historical Society
86	Klickitat Canyon	Arlene Larison
89	Flying L	Ilse Lloyd
98	Goldendale Library	Klickitat County Historical Society
103	Goldendale Observatory	Ken Scarola
106	Gray Digger	Joan Crice
109, 110	1964 Flood photos	Klickitat County Historical Society
117	Hall Hotel	Klickitat County Historical Society
119	Hill's Barn	Rick Stitt
125	High Prairie Newsletter	High Prairian Newsletter
129	Horn glass	Harry Horn
131	Huckleberries	Ken Scarola
142	Klickitat Baskets	Ann Parker
147	Klickitat River Canals	Ann Parker
151	Lewis' Woodpecker	Dorothy Walter
155	Cougar	Dorothy Walter
156	Lipizzan horses	June Boardman
158	Rita Liska Territory map	Ann Parker

page	picture	Artist / Source
281	Rock Creek Loop map	Ann Parker
291	Wolf	Joan Crice
292	Timmerman Hanging	Klickitat County Historical Society
294	Gerald and Maria Timmer	Timmer family
298	Columbia River barge	Klickitat County Historical Society
301	Cattle drive	M.L. "Charlie" Shattuck
306	Treehouse lookout	Rick Stitt
309	Trout Lake Art Festival	Sally Bailey
312	Hummingbird, quince	Arlene Larison
332	Mountain, vineyard	Ann Parker
335	Woodland School #21	Nellie Schuster
336	Yellow Bells	Arlene Larison

INDEX

4-H 34, 48, 100, 173, 203

A

airplane 166, 315, 316
Alder Creek 37, 82, 183
Alderdale 77, 178, 236, 332
alfalfa 1, 50, 121, 280, 281
aluminum plant 189, 289
andesite 60, 89
apples 134, 177, 237
Appleton 126, 236, 263, 279
Army Corps of Engineers 85, 118, 131, 200, 288
art, artists 48, 54, 58, 90, 309
astronomy 103, 104, 270

B

B.Z. Corners 20, 176
Balch Lake 277
Robert Ballou 5, 83, 145
barges 278, 298, 299, 300, 301
barns 27, 33, 62, 70, 81, 118, 120, 121, 155, 187, 225, 238, 240, 280, 281, 301, 309, 311
basalt 44, 53, 95, 96, 160, 213, 218, 246, 273, 284, 317, 318
baskets 143, 151
bears 87, 122, 134, 155, 160
beavers 299
Bickleton 14, 15, 47, 52, 69, 82, 130, 147, 183, 210, 223, 244, 284, 326
bicycling 7, 8, 240
William Biesanz 20, 232
Bingen 8, 38, 57, 68, 153, 154, 234, 237, 244, 275, 301, 327, 332
blackberries 203
Blockhouse 2, 12, 83, 140, 182, 222
Blockhouse Hot Springs Resort 12
bluebirds 14
Bluelight 14
boa constrictor 258
boats 27, 33, 61, 70, 77, 78, 82, 86, 87, 94, 122, 131, 161, 168, 182, 188, 189, 298, 299, 301, 316, 318, 324

Andrew J. Bolon 16, 17, 182, 184
Bonneville Dam 58, 85, 236
Bonneville Power Administration (BPA) 39, 111, 115, 116, 282
bookmobile 153, 202
brides 167, 168
Bridge of the Gods 7, 163
Brooks Memorial Park 103
Paul Bunyan 215
John Burgen 324
William Burgen 18, 214
butte 28, 29, 36, 95, 107, 137, 147, 148, 215, 259, 306
butterflies 55, 205, 233

C

Camas 248, 301
Camas Lakes 20
Camp Goldendale 21, 22
camping 65, 66, 73, 86, 93, 103, 128, 131, 150, 202, 223, 269, 272, 284, 303, 321
Camp Mysterious 23
canal 23, 24, 53, 147
cannon 2, 184, 185
canoe 26, 90, 198
Carp Lake 2, 27, 28, 29, 215
Cascade Mountains 16, 17, 27, 45, 59, 96, 201, 213, 236, 323
Catherine Creek 11, 276, 277, 330
cattle 1, 9, 29, 30, 31, 46, 48, 66, 73, 75, 121, 127, 134, 140, 177, 179, 226, 227, 238, 259, 260, 263, 276, 281, 285, 296, 297, 301, 305, 307, 308, 311
Celilo 71
Celilo Falls 73, 115, 200, 218, 305, 317
cemeteries 32, 39, 55, 122, 141, 163, 164, 175, 223, 277, 280, 293
centennial 80
Centerville 32, 33, 34, 44, 76, 122, 172, 183, 214, 234, 235, 324
Chamberlain Lake 278
cherries 181, 230, 312
Chinese 117, 127, 128, 194
Chinook 144, 159, 175, 199, 317

Monument Road 2, 16, 184
Mopar 186
Motorsports 187
mountain lion 184
movie theatre 79, 271
Mt. Adams 9, 23, 30, 43, 59, 60, 76, 86, 90, 96,
      108, 123, 131, 144, 146, 158, 166, 168,
      190, 203, 208, 213, 248, 275, 279, 316,
      323, 327
Mt. Adams Orchard 56, 134, 176
Mt. Hood 108, 190, 277, 278, 280, 282
Mt. Hood Brew Pub 7
Mt. Jefferson 282
Mt. Rainier 108, 166, 190
Mt. Saint Helens 206, 208
mud 23, 64, 74, 83, 86, 88, 96, 109, 191, 227,
      250, 321
murder 12, 127, 182, 183, 184
mushrooms 192, 307
music 90, 137, 170, 176, 193, 194, 203, 207,
      219, 230, 231, 286, 294, 295, 309, 323
Music Teacher's Association 193

N

National Registry of Historic Places 44, 126
Native American 11, 43, 46, 47, 50, 51, 131,
      132, 151, 158, 170, 175, 194, 195, 198,
      218, 241, 281, 317, 318, 336
Arthur C. Newby 200
newcomers 46, 85, 201, 258, 295
Nixluidix 199
Northwestern Lake 302

O

oak 53, 121, 133, 150, 164, 192, 205, 270, 277,
      280, 282, 310, 330
Goldendale Observatory 65, 103, 203
Lick Observatory 273
James Ogden 186, 206, 208, 239
Old Lockups 208
Old Red House 126, 240, 241, 242, 294
orchards 41, 91, 92, 134, 181, 214, 230, 237,
      282, 322, 331
Oregon Territory 303, 305
Oregon Trail 139, 222, 303

P

partridge 122
party line 149, 211
peach-leaf willow 133
peacocks 170, 215, 216, 217, 310, 311
pears 56, 134, 146, 177, 237, 312
petroglyphs 4, 8, 198, 200, 218, 287, 318
Phoenix Festival 219
pigs 76, 120, 237, 238, 263, 296
pine 44, 53, 60, 81, 102, 108, 112, 121, 136,
      139, 151
Pine Marten 221
Pioneer Picnic 223
pioneers 5, 6, 9, 16, 18, 30, 33, 40, 41, 47, 55,
      128, 141, 180, 195, 202, 203, 213, 222,
      224, 231, 239, 266, 277, 280, 293, 319
Plateau Indians 3, 317
Pleasant Valley 62, 80, 82, 224
Ponderosa Park 106, 226, 227
Ponderosa pine 43, 102
porcupines 48, 156
Post-Clovis culture 3
post office 15, 42, 64, 72, 122, 133, 134, 140,
      211, 214, 240, 283
Pothole Lake 215
W.B. Presby 128, 129, 165, 231, 232
Presby Mansion 335
Presby Museum 203, 230, 231
Presby Ranch 165, 229, 231, 232
prohibition 229
Pucker Huddle 232
Klickitat County PUD 14, 15, 38, 39, 65, 67,
      68, 69, 70, 111, 112, 119, 130, 167, 188,
      189, 205, 227, 247, 255, 286, 287, 320

Q

quail 122
Queen Marie 35, 112, 170, 258
quilting 178, 267
quince 312

R

raccoons 205, 233
rafting 60, 78, 150, 160, 190, 202, 279, 320,
      321

Wishram 4, 38, 69, 71, 73, 94, 109, 118, 126,
    159, 195, 199, 286, 333, 334
Wishrams 195
wolves 9, 291, 292
Woman's Association of Goldendale 98, 99,
    152, 334, 335
Woodland 335
woodpecker 151, 152, 205
World War I 24, 150, 157, 211, 235, 258, 273,
    283, 313, 314
World War II 38, 57, 69, 157, 176, 177, 235,
    313, 327
WSU Extension Service 2, 100, 253

Y

Yakama Cultural Center 178
Yakama Indians 16, 239
Yakama Nation 8, 133, 182, 183, 184, 267,
    284, 288, 305
Yakama Reservation 8, 24, 60, 96, 139, 147,
    182, 190, 198, 260, 288, 305
Yakima 12, 15, 16, 58, 82, 93, 103

Z

zebra 337